THE LIFE AND WORKS

OF

BENJAMIN MARCUS BOGARD

Printed on the Bogard Memorial Press

The
Life And Works Of
Benjamin Marcus Bogard

VOLUME I

By
L. D. Foreman
and
Alta Payne

Published by Foreman and Payne, Little Rock, Arkansas
Printed by Seminary Press, Little Rock, Arkansas, U.S.A.

Copyright, 1965
By L. D. Foreman and Ernest Payne
Little Rock, Arkansas

Benjamin Marcus Bogard

DEDICATION

*In memory of the soldiers of the cross who
have in each succeeding generation handed
down this great heritage to those who
carry the torch of Christianity today*

and

*Dedicated to the host of
young preachers whose lives
have been touched by this man of God.*

CONTENTS

BOGARD THE WRITER

BOGARD THE EDUCATOR

SERMONS, SERMON OUTLINES AND POEMS

LIST OF PICTURES

PROLOGUE

"I have changed my mind about the book." This statement came as a disappointing surprise.

"Why?" I asked. Only a day or two previously we had discussed the matter of publishing a book of his life and works. At that time, we were in perfect agreement about it. In fact, we had gone so far to follow his instructions that my colleague, Ernest Payne and his wife, came to the home with me where the old gentleman lying on his death bed was to dictate the introduction to this book.

"Well," said this venerable soul. "I have given some thought to it and it seems like it might be vain." The tone of his voice and the expression on his face was such that I knew he was never more sincere.

"Uncle Ben," as we affectionately called him, was going to meet his Master in a few weeks. The doctors knew it. His friends knew it and he knew it. All his life he had sought to put Christ first. Now, at sundown, he was not going to permit a book to be written of his life and works that might glorify Bogard instead of Christ. I reasoned with him that the young men in the Seminary, the people of the churches, the religious world as a whole, but Missionary Baptists in particular, needed the benefit of his experiences, his sermons and his editorials. To write the book of his life would not result in his being placed above Christ.

"Very well," he then said. "Do as you think best."

Thus, he left the matter to our discretion.

If any person at any time should form the opinion that Dr. Ben M. Bogard had any thought of projecting himself in life or in death in such a manner as to even partially eclipse the light of Christ, he would be most unfair, for the subject of this work had no intention except to glorify the Christ and His work.

Mr. Bogard kept a record of his work for whatever value it might be to his ministry—not for vain glory.

A "prologue" is a classic way of saying "introduction." Its purpose is to tell you what the book is about. This book is about a man—not just an ordinary man—rather an extra-ordinary man. A preacher but not an ordinary preacher—an extra-ordinary preacher. In fact, he was such a giant of a character that a book just couldn't help being written about him. It was one of those things that had to happen.

This prologue is supposed to set forward three things: first, that he did not ask the book to be written; second, that a tremendous amount of Baptist history is woven in the fabric of his life and, third, that the man's life was so many sided, this fact alone necessitates a story.

There is more Baptist history wrapped up in the life of this man than perhaps any other. More people have said about him, "He was the greatest Baptist since the Apostle Paul" than of, perhaps, any other man living or dead. He lived almost eighty four years—sixty three of this time was devoted to the Baptist ministry. He connected an era of American pioneer saints of God to this modern age. He lived and ministered with such men as J. R. Graves, J. N. Hall, J. M. Pendleton, James P. Boyce and other great "pillars," yet lived to see and preach to a generation who enjoys the privileges of airplanes, radio, television.

Dr. Bogard lived through, participated in, the contro-versy arising in Baptist ranks as to the propriety of the churches using a tool or agency such as the Southern Baptist Convention and helped to form the American Baptist Associ-ation and the great series of literature published by it. He defended the faith from the polemic platform more than any man of any faith. He was despised by his enemies and loved by his friends because he "contended earnestly for the faith once delivered unto the saints."

Most ministers—or for that matter, most people—specialize in one field of endeavor; however, the variety in the life and work of this man is astounding. He was a missionary, an evangelist, a pastor, an educator, an editor and a writer of books. He was a debater. He had a great radio ministry. He was a counselor, traveler, a scholar, a philanthropist and a friend.

What did he consider the crowning achievements of his long and useful life? Let the reader judge for himself. When he came to die, he made no mention of his debates or of Antioch Missionary Baptist Church in Little Rock, Arkansas, where he had been pastor for twenty seven years, resigning and living out the remaining years as pastor emeritus, nothing of the books he had written nor of the churches he had organized, but of "two great monuments"—the publishing business in Texarkana, Arkansas-Texas and the Missionary Baptist Seminary—then above these great monuments, the tremendous number of souls who had professed Christ under his ministry.

L. D. Foreman

FOREWORD

A "foreword" is supposed to tell *why* a book is written. Well, believe you me there is a reason.

There have been times both good and bad in the history of Baptists. There may have been worse periods and conditions in "the Way" than the present—that's debatable—but sound thinking Baptists know our theological backs are up against an ecumenical wall—right now. The religious world has gone mad. There is more church going, more preaching, larger Sunday School enrollment, more schools of theology, more and better church buildings, but percentage wise, less "born again" salvation, less Bible truth taught than in any other period in the history of Christendom. Many nominal Baptist churches have moved so far from the Bible fundamentals that they are no more than the rest of the religious world, even insisting they are Protestant.

The "one world church movement" (ecumenism) is making itself felt. Day by day, with alarming speed, the lines of demarcation are being drawn. The times, therefore, demand this book be written; truth must be disseminated. Materials contained in this publication will fill the need of those seeking history of Baptists in the last one hundred years. It will provide Bible truth, inspiration and many hours of study and nostalgia.

WHY THIS JOINT UNDERTAKING?

Mrs. Payne, my partner in the undertaking, grew up in Antioch Baptist Church. Bogard was her pastor. He baptized her. He was "Daddy Bogard" as he referred to himself when talking to her. She was personally acquainted with him for twenty six years. Only brief periods when her husband was pastor of a church in Oklahoma and one in north central Arkansas was she away from Antioch Church.

Dr. Bogard was still editor of the *Searchlight* when she began working in the publishing business with Ernest Payne. She attended all the associational meetings and others which put her in personal contact with the subject of this work. He very often traveled with them and on many occasions he was entertained in their home.

When Ernest Payne, Mrs. Payne and I went to the Bogard home on the day mentioned in the prologue, to receive the introduction, he gave us the journals, constituting his diary—a month by month record of his sixty three years in the ministry. No one else knew he even had them, except Mrs. Bogard and even she was requested by her husband not to get them for us but to have Alta go into the study and bring them out. Thus, the records which will be read by the public for the first time in this publication were given to the Ernest Paynes and L. D. Foremans as our own property. Therefore, it is easily seen why both of us are honored and delighted to share in this enterprise.

It fell my lot by agreement with "Uncle Ben" to "see after" Mrs. Bogard following her husband's death. The church continued his retirement salary of $150.00 per month. This was put into a fund out of which I paid all bills—grocery, utilites, her newspaper—anything she wanted. At the time of her death, I made arrangement for burial. A lady in the church, Mrs. J. R. Dowell, Sr., selected the burial garments, hair style, and other personal things according to previous arrangements with her.

These things are entered into this record for the following reasons:

The first, being the fact we have every right to publish this work, for the materials, other than editorials and sermons appearing in various books and papers belong exclusively to us. These materials, consisting of journals (diaries) pictures, scrapbooks, sermon outline books, relics, documents were given to us before he died and were not included in his will.

L. D. Foreman

FOREWORD BY BEN M. BOGARD

———

I am living in the happiest period of my life—in a beautiful flower garden. This garden is made up of the good deeds I have tried to do through my life. It is marred somewhat by weeds, for I have not always sown good seeds, but the flowers predominate.

This flower garden is located in a great fruit bearing orchard of men and women whom I have helped to train for their life's work. In this great fruit bearing orchard are located two great monuments. These were not built for the purpose of becoming monuments, but they are just the same. One is the great publishing business in Texarkana, Arkansas-Texas that I have established almost altogether by my own efforts. I did all the work of establishing that institution until it became self-supporting, then I gave it to the American Baptist Association. Another great monument is the Missionary Baptist Seminary and while it was not built for the purpose of being a monument, it has become one just the same.

Above this great orchard and these two great monuments are a canopy of stars. These consist of the souls of men and women who profess to have been saved under my preaching. They shine as the stars in glory.

Ben M. Bogard

(*Note:* Dictated a few days before his death.)

BOGARD — THE BOY

The Bogard Family

PROLOGUE

Three sisters, Eliza, Laura and Sue, discussed in low voices the arrival of a new baby brother. It was a happy occasion for them. Somehow, the necessary tasks and responsibilities Mother could no longer do did not seem such drugery as they thought of a little boy in the home. Cheerfully they went about the cleaning, nursing and cooking.

For the mother, the birth of her first son, who was to be an only son, was bittersweet. What should have been a joyous occasion was marred by the hopelessness which threatened to engulf her as she glanced about the small log cabin which so vividly spoke of the deep poverty her family knew as they somehow eked out an existence on a rented tobacco farm, managing by long, ceaseless days of backbreaking toil to keep spirit and body together. Another mouth to feed— she had brought another child into the world to know the distress of privation and the aching weariness of long hours at work on a small plot of ground.

A scarcely audible sign escaped her lips as she thought of the time wasted lying abed. She needed to be at her loom making the clothing for the household and the extra clothes she could sell to buy a few of their needs. Though Nancy Bogard had been married at thirteen, she could not imagine thirteen year old Eliza at the helm of the home, keeping all of the responsibilities of the household going smoothly even with the help of Laura and Sue, however willing they were. Father could not help for his daylight hours were completely spent in the fields.

Nancy Bogard thought of her daughter Laura and her dreams to make her life more than that of a farm laborer. She breathed a prayer that Laura would have the chance she longed for and that this little son might make a place in the

23

world for himself. She resolved firmly that somehow they should have their opportunity.

She heard the girls tiptoeing into the room. She smiled as they came again to look at their new brother. "What are we going to name him, mother?" asked Laura.

"We'll name him Ben."

I

HIS EARLY LIFE

Linking two eras in the history of our country, Bogard was born during the reconstruction days following the Civil War and lived to see this continent a solid mass of sovereign states from the Atlantic to the Pacific. He was a human bridge spanning three generations and a part of the fourth. In 1868, the year of his birth, Minnesota was just ten years old, Texas twenty three and California only eighteen. Oregon and Washington were nine and twenty one respectively. Nevada was four years old and Nebraska only one.

What was the country like then? Well, vast regions of our country were still frontier lands. Colorado was made a state eight years later. Montana, North and South Dakota attained statehood twenty one years after his birth. He was twenty two years old when Idaho entered the Union, twenty eight when Utah came in. New Mexico and Arizona did not become a part of our Union until Bogard was forty four years old.

He witnessed every major invention and development that brought our civilization to the scientific age. He saw the telephone, radio and television come into use. When he was born, the mode of transportation was horse back, ox cart, the wagon, the riverboat and at the best, the ''iron horse''—the steam locomotive. He saw the development of the modern automobile and air travel.

When he was a boy, the women prepared their families' meals on the open fireplace and did the family wash in a stream or at the spring. He lived to see the modern laundry and push button electric cooking. When he was a youth most illness was treated with home remedies; when he died, he had the best medical care that science and skill could offer.

Ben was about nine years old when this picture of him and his sister was taken.

His was a glorious experience, but his contribution to the present generation of ministers who knew him personally is more wonderful for he was the living link that brought us into direct connection with the great stalwarts of a century ago. He knew personally such men as J. R. Graves, J. N. Hall, T. T. Eaton and dozens of others. About these great giants of the faith he told us and so we feel a vital connection with these people. Indeed he linked this generation with men and churches of an important epoch in the history of Baptists.

Ben M. Bogard was born near Elizabethtown, Kentucky, in Hardin County on March 9, 1868, in a small log cabin, similar to one not many miles away where another great man, Abraham Lincoln, was born.

Ben's early life was spent in Kentucky—called that "dark and bloody ground" commemorating the conflicts between various tribes of Indians—the slave state that did not secede—which had been explored by Dr. Thomas Walker in 1750, John Finley in 1767 and Daniel Boone in 1769. When Ben was only nine, the Bogard family moved to Union County in Kentucky.

Living on a rented farm was not an easy life. Ben's father toiled from dawn's breaking until dark as he coaxed a living from his small share of Kentucky. M. L. Bogard, like all of the Confederate soldiers, had returned penniless from the terrible War between the States. This "Great Cause" so bravely fought by a dedicated South meant ruin to its people, for everything had been swept away as the armies marched through the land burning and killing and leaving the countryside in devastation. There was no money for the returning soldiers and hardly any way to make any. Food and clothing were scarce. Many times bare feet made tracks in the frost for, at the most, one pair of shoes a year was the allotment for each child. However, Bogard was a hard working man with unbounded energy and had a good reputation in the community for honesty.

"The Old Kentucky Home"

Tobacco was the "money crop." This brought in enough cash to buy the barest necessities for the family. Corn provided coarse bread for the table and fed the hogs which afforded meat for the long winter months. No food or money was ever wasted in the Bogard home. Even the salt was reclaimed from the dirt in the smokehouse where the grease had dripped from the meat as it hung for curing.

As soon as Nancy Bogard could leave the bed after the birth of her fourth child, she was back at her work, spinning the thread which would be woven into clothing for her family. As the clothes wore out, they became carpets for the bare floors of the cabin or for the floors in neighbors' homes, for she braided the worn out colored bits of cloth into attractive rugs. The money from the sale of these rugs augmented the meager income from the tobacco.

With the help of her daughters, Mrs. Bogard managed all of the household tasks, as well as helping her husband with some of the farming chores when it became necessary. This was the unrelenting routine of the day for the Bogard family, hard work with little time for relaxation or play. But, as Nancy Bogard worked, she dreamed dreams for her family. She was not an educated woman as schooling goes. The daughter of Schoolmaster William English of Hardin County, she knew the value of an education though she had sacrificed it for marriage before she was fourteen years old. Though not trained in schools, she was highly learned in a very true sense, having disciplined her mental powers by management of the small income and her good common sense. Her industry and devotion to family set her apart as a woman of unusual ability. Devotion to God and dependence on Him gave her the courage and strength to go on day after day, hoping, dreaming, working and praying for something better for her children than she had known for herself.

Two other sisters, Arabella and Ollie, were born. These two shared in the daily work for there was no room for idle-

Mrs. Nancy Bogard

ness in any member of the family. The father was a hard
worker and he taught his children to work. He truly believed
the adage that an idle mind makes the devil's workshop. He
encouraged and taught them how to work by telling them
they were the best workers in the country and making them
believe it.

Ben's father was of German descent, a well informed
man, whom the boy believed to know everything. He was
widely read and Ben's infancy and boyhood was wrapped up
in newspapers and books. He took great interest in public
affairs and delighted to talk about men of the times. Ben's
boyish notion was that all he had to do was to ask his father
a question on any subject and the information would be immediately forthcoming.

When Ben was very young, he helped his mother at the
loom doing such things as very little boys can do. He learned
to weave, an accomplishment he never forgot. Since he knew
nothing of any kind of luxury, his early poverty was not so
hard to bear. Only the absolute necessities were bought and
not all of these, for sometimes months would pass when
there would not be one cent in the house. Young Ben still enjoyed life since he had no conception of anything better.

Ben was introduced to farming when he was scarcely old
enough to remember. His father taught him to drop tobacco
plants, then later to pull off the "worms and suckers." In one
of his later recollections, he said, "I was not much larger than
some of the worms, but I pulled many a head off and the suckers I pulled would load a train, I believe." A sucker is a shoot
from the roots or lower part of the stem of a plant. These were
pulled to keep them from robbing the plant of its strength.

IN CASEYVILLE ON THE OHIO

Ben was old enough to remember incidents just before
he moved to Caseyville, a little town on the Ohio River. He

said, concerning his recollections, "I only recollect two things
distinctly before moving to Caseyville. One was a fight, regular fist fight, my father had with a man named Farthing. I
have no idea what they were fighting about. But I did remember that my little dog 'Bob' took up for my father and
ran up and bit savagely at the unfortunate Farthing, tearing
his trousers and drawing blood and that too after my father
had him badly whipped. I had no particular interest in the
fight, being too small to understand what it was about and
feeling perfectly confident that my father could take care of
himself as he showed himself abundantly able to do. Just
why something bad will impress a child and something good
will not, is cause for study and at the same time should cause
us to be careful what we do in the presence of children, for
do not forget they absorb their surroundings. The other thing
I distinctly remember was the day my sister Arabella was
born for it was my birthday and I was that day four years
old. Always after that she and I had a big pound cake for
our birthday. That thing continued so long as we both were
together. Such wonderful pound cake our mother could make
—may be it was my child appetite that made it appear better
but it seems to me no cake has ever been so good as that
annual birthday pound cake. These two earliest recollections
bring me to Caseyville."

The Bogard family moved to Caseyville when Ben was
five years old. Here he watched with intent the big steamboats that trafficked the river. He saw the big fish that were
such "good eating" caught from these waters. Often, he
stood and watched the village blacksmith as he hammered
the iron. Mr. Sipes' blacksmith shop made an indelible impression on him. He met his first love in Caseyville. He
never forgot the neighbor's little girl who played with him
when he was a five year old boy. They spent many happy
hours together. Of this episode in his life he wrote: "We
were about the same size and if you do not think a little five-

year-old has ideas about the future when he plays with a little girl about his size you need to think again. I would give a ten dollar bill to know where little Annie Griffin is, if indeed she is living. Very likely she is some grandmother somewhere in this cold world, possibly doing well and yet may be she is suffering abuse from somebody. I wonder. But I have not seen her in over fifty years. We were little innocent children with no thought of what evil might come our way. These childish impressions show that the Catholics have the right idea about impressing children while they are very young. They declare that if you give them the child until it is seven years old they are not uneasy about the future. Alas! how careless we are with the little ones.''

SCHOOL DAYS

Ben's first day at school when he was six years old was a day to be remembered. He was dismayed when he saw the ugly spinster who was to be his teacher. He thought she was the homeliest woman he had ever seen, but he found her to be a kindly lady who took genuine interest in the children she taught.

Blakeley's school house was a little log building. A huge fire place provided the little warmth absolutely necessary. A desk ran all around the wall of the room and afforded a place where the children could be taught to write. No conveniences made the old schoolhouse comfortable, but children were carefully taught to read and write there. It was a sacred place to Ben as he applied himself, for he had a deep desire to learn all he could. His old ''blue back spelling book'' was an education within itself. When a boy or girl really knew that book, he could read anything that was not technical.

Beginning with the alphabet, the children learned to repeat both ways, ''up and down'' and learned to spell by beginning with "a-b," "ab," keeping on with one syllable at a time until these were finished, then began two syllables. When they reached "baker" they thought they were fairly well educated. This method of teaching continued until they came to such words as "incomprehensibility." They spelled by syllables pronouncing all of those just spelled until the long word ended. When a boy was drilled in that "old blue back speller" he could spell! The reading texts were moral stories that taught many valuable lessons other than how to read.

As Ben walked to school each day, he watched a new building go up. It was the Woodland Church, the first Baptist Church house he ever saw and one that was to play a very important part in his life. Here, he became acquainted with one of the workmen, Mr. Cute Quinn, whom he always remembered, not because he was a good man, but his outstanding accomplishment was the drinking of so much whiskey. Ben watched in amazement as the quantities of whiskey were consumed under the builder's mistaken impression that it would kill the lead poison he took into his system as he painted.

Whiskey was the remedy for everything in those days. Nearly everyone drank. Liquor was sold in the grocery stores just as molasses and other groceries were sold. One of Ben's earliest memories was of the Hall and Owens' Store, Spring Grove, Kentucky. The proprietor, though a good Presbyterian, sold whiskey in his store. He had what was known as a "quart license" which meant he could sell it by the quart. But then, as in all days, the liquor laws could be "winked at" and he sold it as he pleased, his pleasure being to keep a whiskey barrel in the store and a cup on top of the barrel. The men who came in took the cup and, holding it under the faucet, they drew a big drink for themselves and left a dime on the barrel top. The storekeeper was not selling whiskey. The men were taking it, but the cup was always conveniently there on top of the barrel so that the taking was easy. Liquor is and was essentially an outlaw and could not be controlled.

ON THE FARM

By the time he was nine years old, young Ben was plowing. The plow was equipped with a low handle that a short boy could reach and the horse was old and slow so that he was perfectly safe. It was an old field with no stumps or roots to bother him. That summer he plowed sixteen acres of corn four times.

The day he was old enough to be trusted to take a "turn of corn" to the mill to be ground was a "red-letter" day in his young life. How very gratified he was that day when his father placed a bag of corn on the mule, then sat Ben on top of the corn. Proudly, he set out with his load, but soon, quite literally, pride went before a fall. As he jogged along, he found himself and the corn quite suddenly in the middle of the road. The corn had slid from the mule taking him with it. He slowly got up and found himself uninjured except for his self-esteem, but how was he to get the corn back up on the mule? He tugged at the bag for awhile, but had to give up. It was a big problem for a little boy.

He sat down on the corn to wait. It seemed to be the only thing to do. Surely, someone would come along who would help him. Hours dragged by and his anxiety grew. Suppose no one came along. Finally, when he had almost lost hope, a kindly man came along and helped him back on the mule. This time he rode the rest of the eight miles to the mill without mishap. He was to find that this incident would be repeated often. Many hours were spent on that road as he waited for someone to come along and help him back on his mule.

When Ben reached Morganfield, many were waiting their "turn" at the mill. The miller helped him from the back of the mule and lifted the bag inside the mill to wait its turn for grinding. While waiting, Ben wandered up and down the street. He looked with suspicion and envy at a group of youths. Until this time, he had been satisfied with his lot, knowing nothing better, but now he saw young people laughing and gay in their beautiful "store bought" clothes. He imagined they felt superior to him and this aroused in him a distrust which was a part of him for many years. Had he but known it, the truth was he had a deep desire to be one of them, to enjoy the fun and friendship they had together.

As he wandered aimlessly about the community, he passed the Methodist Church house. He heard singing and started to go in. Hesitantly, he walked to the door and looked inside. He saw a congregation of well dressed people. He glanced down at his own shabby clothing. The thought entered his mind that these fashionable people would not want him and his homespun clothing in their fine church house. Half ashamed and half angry with emotions he could not understand, he did not go in. If he had gone in, he would have found a kindly people who would have welcomed him into their services.

He walked slowly away from the church house kicking the rocks ahead of him bitterly. Then he saw the same group of youths coming toward him. They were boisterous with the sheer joy of being alive. All of the emotions so suddenly built up within him in the last few minutes threw the boy into an unaccountable rage and he wanted to "lick" one of these "town boys." What a pleasure it would have been to brag to his country friends that he had whipped a town boy. No thought of his own embarrassment had he been "licked" ever crossed his mind. As the happy group passed him and went their way, loneliness overwhelmed him. Though the emotions were childish, the loneliness was just as real as that of an adult; however, even this experience was to help him in the future when he would meet those who felt as he had and needed his understanding.

As Ben grew toward manhood, the quietness of the farm developed in him the tendency to dream. Many years later he remembered these times and he wrote: "The country is the best place to think. Things are quiet and the rush and hurry of the towns are absent. The boy who follows the plow has time for meditation. There he can build air castles. He can dream of what he intends to do and to be in the future. After I had made a start toward being a preacher I would plow and think and my sermons would be turned over and over in my mind as I THOUGHT over passages of scripture and prayed for God to guide and bless." Away from the noise and hurry of city life, he built air castles and resolved to make them come true. His mother encouraged his dreams. She prayed daily that her only son would be called into the ministry. Her influence on him was so great that even his "castles in the air" were built with the resolve that he would never betray her confidence. In later years, he gave her the credit for much of his success, for many times he refrained from taking steps that might have caused failure and even ruin to his career because he did not want to hurt her. Even in the most discouraging circumstances and disappointments, Nancy Bogard prayed on in the darkness. Over and over she let him know that she was expecting mighty things from this only son and in trying to live up to these hopes, Ben was to build a great future for himself, for, as he wrote many years later, "Most of my dreams have come true. I have become in actual fact just about what I dreamed I wanted to be. My life has been a success if accomplishing what I set out to accomplish is success."

HAPPY TIMES

Christmas time was a happy time even in a poverty stricken home like the Bogard house. Though no money could be spent for a big celebration, Ben believed in Santa Claus.

He did not expect too much from that old friend of children.
A nickel's worth of candy and a box of firecrackers brought
unbelievable happiness to the little boy. He never dreamed
Santa was a myth until he was eight years old and gave that
pleasant, bearded old man the credit for these simple luxuries. When he learned there was no Santa, though he felt a
deep loss and a distinct pain, he understood, as most children do, that his parents had invented the fictitious old gentleman for his own pleasure. He never felt they had betrayed
him. Fancies must fade and realities take their place, so
when Ben lost his old childhood friend, the knowledge and
realization of his parent's unselfishness to provide these
simple pleasures came to him. Though only a boy, he recognized the sacrifices they made to make even this little dream
come true.

Sometimes, molasses candy supplemented the Christmas
bounty. Ben's mother made candy from sorghum molasses.
It tasted very, very good to a child who knew so little about
the material pleasures of the world. One of his very few real
boyhood luxuries given him came one Christmas. He had already enjoyed the annual nickel's worth of candy and the box
of firecrackers when a neighbor lady called him to her front
gate and gave him an orange. It was the first orange he had
ever seen. He lived in the country and there was no railroad.
All freight came by boat down the Ohio River, a very slow
process of shipping. Steamboats traveled at the rate of ten
miles an hour, so it took a very long time to ship oranges
from Florida to Kentucky. They were very expensive, twenty
five cents each or three dollars a dozen, so only the wealthy
could enjoy them. Few were seen in this part of the country
and Ben, so proud of his gift, selfishly ate it right then and
there instead of taking it home to share with his sisters.
Though this was a very small kindness to a boy, Ben always
loved the woman for it. The incident taught him that one
should be kind to children, for such graciousness is always

remembered with pleasure by the child. This lesson was to help him many years later, for many times goodness to a child wins the heart of a parent. When he became a minister, Ben Bogard remembered this.

One of the other great days during the year was Ben's birthday. On this occasion, his mother always made an old fashioned pound cake. This was the most expensive "sweet" the family ever enjoyed. It was a real cake and actually sweet, something not often enjoyed. He looked forward to March 9th each year and to this annual dessert with more anticipation than one can imagine, for this day was different than all others because of the pound cake. From the lack of luxury, he learned another great lesson. Ben Bogard was a man who learned a lesson from each experience in his life, and from these incidents in childhood he learned: "Children are now surfeited with good things until they do not appreciate their luxury. But the very fact that we had so few of the comforts and so little that was really good to eat made these small pleasures wonderful to us. As I look back now and realize that my mother did without the comforts of life, even the little comforts within her reach, to make us children happy, I begin to appreciate my mother as I never did when I was a child. I now know that if she had only been able to do so she would have given us every comfort. She did the best she could and how she managed to get by with it all is now a wonder to me."

II

HIS FIRST SUNDAY SCHOOL CLASS

Perhaps Ben Bogard would never have become a great Baptist preacher had it not been for a Presbyterian woman, Mrs. Robert Owen of Spring Grove, Kentucky. When he was about nine years old, one morning she came and asked his mother if she could "have Ben for her Sunday School." It was a school with only one class. Mrs. Owen was the superintendent, the teacher, the secretary and anything else a Sunday School needed. She had no literature except a New Testament. She did have small picture cards which she gave to those who would memorize ten Bible verses. When the student earned ten picture cards, he received a big picture. In order to get these prizes, young Bogard zealously memorized Scripture until he could quote all of the third chapter of Matthew. He learned exactly how Jesus was baptized when he learned the first gospel of the New Testament. He memorized the words, "Jesus, when he was baptized, came up straightway out of the water." He never forgot the Scripture. Later, when his older sister went through a ceremony she called baptism and an elderly Methodist preacher poured water on her head, the little boy knew that this ritual was not like Jesus was baptized as recorded in the third chapter of Matthew which he had learned so well.

The Presbyterian lady who taught him the Scriptures and the Methodist preacher who failed to follow this teaching made such a deep impression on him that he resolved if he ever joined a church, he would be put under the water as Jesus was. Though his baptism came many years later, he learned the lesson at this early age and determined there in the Presbyterian Sunday School class to be a Baptist. He gave the credit to Mrs. Owens though she never knew she had influenced him to be a Baptist.

TRAGEDY

Tragedy came into his life when Ben was only nine years old. His oldest sister, Eliza, only twenty two years old, died. The boy watched her die. For days, the Methodist preacher, Mr. Wall, made visits to the home. Ben saw Eliza make a happy profession of faith.

"Do you want to be baptized, Eliza?" he heard Mr. Wall ask.

"Yes, Brother Wall, I do," his sister answered and Ben wondered at the time how in the world this would be managed for Eliza was dying. She could not go to the water. Ben knew that she had not been baptized as Jesus was when he saw Mr. Wall bring water and pour it on her head. He called this baptism. Since he had learned what baptism was really like, Ben felt so strongly that this procedure was all wrong he would have cried out had he not feared punishment for such an act.

As Eliza lay dying before the eyes of the boy who felt so deeply the terrible emotions that beset him, he thought of his own soul's welfare. He thought, "What if I should die?" He was so young but death suddenly became real and terrible to him. After her death, he stood beside the open grave. With horror he looked into the narrow, deep opening in the earth. Terror gripped him as he saw Eliza's body lowered into that pit. Agony filled his soul. He felt as if he, too, were dying. He wanted to scream. The emotions were too terrible for a child's mind to bear without great harm resulting.

The grim, terrifying experience nearly cost Ben Bogard his sanity and his life. That night he went to bed and saw that open grave before his eyes. He closed them tight, but still the yawning cavern haunted him. When he finally fell

asleep, he awoke screaming and fighting. He felt he was falling through space at a terrific speed. He did not know where
he was and he was petrified with terror. He screamed and
pleaded with his mother and sisters to hold him and keep
him from falling.

"Hold me! Hold me! Help me, please. Don't let me
fall!" he screamed over and over. They held him and tried
to quiet him, but his fear was beyond description. They had
no idea of what was the matter with him and tried to comfort
him but there was no deliverance for him from this awful
shock.

The family doctor was called. He had no knowledge of
the nervous system and its diseases. He decided that Ben
had "worms" and treated him for this malady. When no
relief came, he treated the child for an enlarged spleen. The
medication prescribed caused great blisters to break out on
his body. Surely, the doctor did his best but he simply did not
know what ailed the child.

Another doctor was brought in. He diagnosed the illness
as an ailment in the spine. Medicine was rubbed on his back.
Again, blisters covered him. Still there was no relief.

Finally, after a long and painful illness, Ben was slowly
restored to health from the terrible nervous shock his mind
and body had endured at his sister's death. He was never to
completely recover from the horrible experience and from
that time on, he never looked upon a person in death if he
could avoid it. In thousands of funerals he conducted he did
not look, with but few exceptions, at the deceased. He
learned by terrible experience that a child should never be allowed to see a person die or to look into a grave. He realized
that this kind of emotional shock is too much for a child to endure until he is old enough to understand the meaning of
death. Even after fifty years, he could still feel the agonizing
sensations he had endured as a child. This contact with death
also made a very deep spiritual impression on him.

Tragedy was to strike his heart again in the death of another sister, beloved Laura, dearest of all sisters, whose life was snuffed out by the brutality of another. Her memory stayed with him always as he strove to be what she wanted him to be. Filled with ambition, she worked and studied until she was able to teach school. Then, earning a little money, as she taught she continued in school until she had provided a good education for herself. Ben went to school to her. She put new ideas into his mind. She fired him with ambition and gave him the instructions he needed as a child, implanting a desire in him to "amount to something." Ever after, he credited his mother and sister most with his own success in life, though he did not fully appreciate their efforts and sacrifices until much later.

III

REVIVALS IN THE COUNTRY

Not long after his oldest sister's death, J. L. Perryman came to Woodland Church to hold a revival meeting. Though Ben was only ten years old, he understood the evangelist's sermons. As he listened to the messages, conviction seized the heart of the child. He realized he was a sinner and he secretly prayed earnestly. No one seemed to think a little boy worth notice. They showed deep interest in other sinners present, but no one, apparently, cared for him. He always felt that, with a little encouragement and proper instruction, he would have been saved at this early age. The meeting went by but it was not forgotten. Though he tried to wipe out the knowledge of his lost condition, he could not erase the deep impressions made on his heart.

Another of the early revival meetings to make an impression on the boy, Ben, was conducted by a Mr. S. P. Brooks, a young preacher. The old fashioned ''mourner's bench'' was used, and, along with it, a procedure that was a very bad practice. Being only a small boy, Ben thought it all right since the preacher used it. Many years later, he was to see the terrible evil of such an ''altar call.''

In such meeting, the ''mourner'' or ''seeker'' came forward and took a front seat. Many times, two or three rows would be filled with the weeping penitents. They sobbed as though their hearts were breaking. While they were in the throes of such deep emotion, the members of the congregation were invited to pass by and speak to them, ''say whatever was in their hearts.'' A song was sung and the entire congregation, or so it seemed to a small boy, filed by. Each would shake hands and speak with the mourners. Perhaps

44

this would have been good except that what one person said was contradicted by the advice of another as Ben found out one night when he went to the "bench." One helper advised him to "Pray on!" Another instructed him to "Stop praying and claim the blessing." Others paused and asked him what he had been doing, if he had been praying, then told him to keep on for he was doing the right thing. Still others asked him the same question but said that this way was all wrong. Another asked, "How do you feel?" and told him he would feel "all right by and by." The next one said that feelings should not be relied on but he should trust the Lord and settle it right there. Ben was in the same predicament as the rest of the "seekers." He did not know what to do.

The purpose was good but the method was abominable—well nigh wicked—for it caused so much confusion. The preaching was safe and sound as the evangelist told the sinner the way of salvation. Many were saved by trusting in the Lord as he taught them to do, but the false instruction of the helpers caused many others to go away without Christ. This was another lesson that was to help Bogard, for he learned "first hand" that this type of emotionalism and false instruction should never be allowed in a meeting. Many years later he was to come to the conclusion that a preacher should preach the gospel, pray for sinners, give them true private instruction and stop at that, leaving their salvation between themselves and the Lord. This old abuse of the "mourner's bench" was so confusing and misleading that the boy was hopelessly lost in the maize of false instruction and the hypnotic emotional effect created by the workers. For four years at every opportunity, he sought the Lord at the "mourner's bench."

An exception to the practice was Major Penn, possibly the greatest evangelist this church ever had. He asked sinners forward for prayer but would allow no one except himself to instruct them in the all important eternity binding question.

After clear teaching and a prayer for them, he left their salvation in the hands of the Lord.

Revival meetings were common in the boyhood days of Ben Bogard. The Methodists, Presbyterians, Campbellites and Baptists all held their meetings every year. Everyone went to every meeting. While Bogard had learned the correct way of baptism, he knew nothing of the differences in the doctrines of the various denominations, so he went to all of the meetings and most of the people seemed to think one church was "just as good as another and that they were all trying to get to the same place anyway" and that "the church won't take you to heaven anyway." These and other erroneous ideas were held by the community's citizens.

Ben listened with interest to every preacher. In one of their meetings he nearly joined the Campbellite group. He attended a revival meeting at Shiloh Campbellite Church, several miles from his home. A Mr. Powell preached a sermon that seemed to him a very wonderful message. He told the congregation in glowing terms that all they needed to do was to come to him, give him their hands and say they "believed Jesus Christ was the Son of God," then he would dip them in water and that would give them "present salvation, bringing them within the covenant, and they could go right on and live good lives and finally get to heaven." This sounded very good to him and Ben found himself on the verge of going "down to the front." For some unaccountable reason, he did not go. This was the last Campbellite meeting he attended. Later, he thanked God that something kept him from responding to the invitation, for he would have been lost and perhaps would never have known the joy of personal contact with the Lord Jesus Christ.

Ben Bogard's parents were Methodists and as he said, "Nearly all my kinfolks were and are everything else instead of being Baptists." His father, however, became a Baptist when he was about twenty four years old and for nearly sixty years was true to this faith and took a great interest in the work.

As a little boy, Ben came in contact with many great preachers. These "elders," as they were called, influenced him very much. He made this observation about the titles of ministers: "When I was a little boy I never heard anybody use the title of 'Reverend' when speaking of preachers. They always said 'Elder' or 'Brother.' I do not remember to have ever heard a preacher addressed as 'Mister.' Always 'Elder' or 'Brother.' The word 'reverend' is used only one time in the Bible and it applies to God in that place. Romanism is behind the 'reverend' every time you see it or hear it. The Catholic Church wants the people to revere the priests and hence they put the title 'reverend' to all their priests. They go still further and append the title 'very reverend' and 'most reverend.' Baptists should not imitate Rome in any manner. Yet, we frequently hear Baptists say 'reverend' and they actually write it in their communications to the press and on envelopes addressed to preachers. I was not 'raised' that way and do not like it and it almost gives me the shivers to be addressed as 'reverend.' I know that nobody means any harm by it, in fact, they think they are using a title of respect and are just trying to be polite. But none the less we should all try to get out of such Romanist practice. 'Brother,' 'Elder,' 'Pastor,' 'Bishop' (which means the same thing as pastor) and 'doctor' are scriptural titles for preachers. The word 'doctor' means teacher and, certainly, teachers are mentioned as a scriptural designation of some of the Lord's workers. But 'reverend' is not a title to apply to any man. It belongs to God only."

One of the ministers who helped to mould the life of this youth was Elder J. B. Haynes. He was pastor of the Woodland Church many years before Ben Bogard was baptized by this congregation and for a long time afterwards. This great preacher served four good country churches as pastor for a long time. He lived on a little twenty acre farm in reach of his churches. He was loved and respected by the Bogard family who honored him as if he were, indeed, a father in the flesh. He came many times to their home where he would give "fireside sermons" and sit talking with them until late in the night. The family never tired of hearing him. This good soldier of the cross preached until his health failed. He was too feeble to work any longer and his last years were spent in suffering for want of food, clothing and other ordinary comforts of life. He gave himself to the ministry, partially supporting himself as he preached, so that he had no livelihood for his later life when he could no longer support himself. When this day came, the old servant of the churches was left to suffer alone. The people did not support the ministry. They erroneously reasoned that the preacher could farm and make his own living, then preach without pay since it was no more trouble for the preacher to come to church and preach than it was for the member to come to hear him. The damaging thing about this was they did not simply think these errors, but loudly proclaimed such ideas and so their practices continued to be "loose" and support for the ministry grew no better. Dr. Bogard later wrote concerning the work of old ministers of the gospel: "One good thing about it was that the churches used him as long as he was able to go. They did not have the 'young-man-mania' that some of the churches have now. *We need young men for war but don't forget we need old men for counsel.* The two should work together in harmony and there should never be a clash between old and young preachers. Old preachers should encourage the young and the young preachers should respect and honor the old."

Another of the preachers vividly remembered from his boyhood was Elder N. Short. He was a great, scholarly preacher, but he was also a dentist. As he traveled about the country preaching the gospel, he also practiced his "trade."

He was a good dentist. Several times he came into their community where he did dental work by day and evangelism by night. He was an old fashioned dentist who made the teeth for his patients. On several occasions, young Bogard watched wide eyed in awe and fascination as the preacher "vulcanized" the artificial teeth at the kitchen stove. The home where he was guest became a laboratory and Ben never tired of watching him at his work. On one of these visits, Elder Short made a set of teeth for Ben's mother. She used this set for twenty five years. The people never thought the preacher comical as he rode over the countryside on an old worn out horse, jogging along with a tooth drill, materials for making teeth, forceps and other necessary equipment loaded on the animal and his Bible in his hand. Preacher Short rode up to the house, unloaded his gear and walked in, making himself at home. He was always welcome and Ben Bogard thought him the best fireside preacher he ever knew. As he wrote: "We thought he knew everything that was worth knowing and when it came to the Bible and related subjects, he very nearly did come up to our conception."

Ben Bogard learned many lessons from great preachers. In his recollections he wrote: "My recollections of great preachers is both pleasant and unpleasant. They were so different. My biggest surprise was that upon close inspection every one of them was imperfect. When I was a little boy I thought all preachers were without fault. Don't know where I got the idea but I had it. It was a great shock when I first discovered imperfection in a preacher. The Bible shows up the faults of the New Testament preachers and the Old Testament prophets and I had read that but still the superstition clung to me that preachers always did right. Anything I heard bad about a preacher made me angry because I thought I just knew it could not be true. But I have lived to fully understand that all of them are at best but men and they would all be in hell if it were not for the grace of God. The fact is preachers should not be any better than anybody else. There is not a double standard, one for preachers and another for the rest of the people. However, a preacher should remember that his influence reaches further than most others and he should be exceedingly careful of his conduct because of the great amount of harm he may do among those he has under his influence.

"I heard a great evangelist, one who had the best reputation of any evangelist in America at the time I heard him. He was holding a big union meeting in Memphis. I was called there to assist in a protracted meeting at the Seventh Street Baptist Church, Elder I. N. Strother, pastor, at the very time this big union meeting was going on. Brother Strother and I went out at some of the day services as they were not held at the same hour we held our services. I listened and watched to see just what it was that gave this great evangelist his success. I made a discovery. It was pure psychology, mesmerism, emotion, pretense! Hard words do you say? Well, that was my decision. I was perfectly conscious of the fact that I preached more gospel in one sermon than he preached in a week and I know I was a better speaker than he, and I was further conscious that I knew more about the Bible than he did for he mixed it up shamefully and seemed not to know a thing about rightly dividing the Word. Yet he drew several thousand to each service and had thousands to confess Christ during his big meetings while I drew two or three hundred to hear me preach and had only fourteen public professions of faith in my Memphis meeting that went on at the same time his meeting went on. Why the difference? Brother Strother and I had several earnest heart to heart talks about this matter and he and I had the same opinion about the reason why.

"This big evangelist asked the people to please not invite him to their homes for meals or to stay all night. He said that if he accepted such invitations he would not be able to hold the meetings because if there happened to be a single person on the place, even a servant, who was unsaved he could not eat a bite until that one was saved and if he went to stay all night and he thought there was a soul in the house unsaved he could not sleep a wink and therefore please do not ask him to come because that sort of thing would kill him. I wondered why he could sleep in the big hotel where he faired sumptuously every day when the hotel was filled with sinners every night. I wondered how he could eat in the wonderful dining room of the same hotel when sinners were all around him and I wondered how he could sleep on Pulman cars when he traveled when a great crowd of sinners are riding on that train and the train might go into the ditch at any time and send them all to hell. Indeed I wondered and yet from the way the most of the people wept when he told such impossible stories showed me that they never thought of the absurdity of such talk. I mentioned this to Brother Strother and he said, 'Yes, I think as you do about it, but don't say anything in the presence of my children about it for they might lose confidence and possibly, even with all this imperfection, Brother . . . may lead them to Christ.' I had the pleasure of assisting in leading some of these same children to Christ and thank the good Lord I did not use such hypocritical pretense to get them saved. That same day when he said the things mentioned here he called the Evangelistic Committee together and informed them that the collections were short and he had to have one hundred dollars a day or the meeting would stop. That fool committee got exceedingly busy and rustled around the men who had money and secured the hundred dollars a day for him so that the soul saving could go on! The idea of a man being so in earnest about the salvation of souls that he could not sleep nor eat in a house where an unsaved man is, threatening to stop the meeting unless they dig up the one hundred dollars a day! Well, he did. Would the Lord bless the preaching of such a man? Yes. The Lord did bless the truth that was preached. It is the GOSPEL that saves and not the man who preaches it. The Gospel preached with a wrong motive, as for instance the one hundred dollars a day motive, will be blessed to the salvation of souls. Paul thanked God that the Gospel was preached even when it was done through envy and strife (Philippians 1:1-18). So do I and that is why I can work with preachers who show such imperfection and ask God to bless their preaching.

"Another great preacher whom I admired above almost all others was pastor of a great church in Kentucky. He had the ambition to be pastor of the largest church in the south. He therefore steadfastly refused to administer any sort of discipline and steadfastly refused to allow any names to be dropped from the church roll unless practically forced to do so in order to be able to publish the large number of members who belonged to the church. I visited his great church one day (it was a great church and he was certainly a great preacher) and by counting the seats it could be plainly seen that not over five hundred could be seated in the house without crowding. Yet the membership roll mounted up to about two thousand—the largest in the South at that time. Pride, ambition, desire to outshine his brethren, were plainly seen. Yet I must say he was a wonderful man. I loved him as I have loved few men in this world. He was an inspiration to me and helped me as a father would help a son. When he went home to glory the grace of God covered his imperfction and I expect to meet him up there.

"I have mentioned a great evangelist and also a great pastor to illustrate what I have found in varying degrees among my brethren in the ministry. When I see so many faults in myself and am conscious that it takes God's mercy to get me by it gives me a strange sort of comfort to know that I have plenty of company. Jesus said that there are 'none good but one, that is God.' If all the others were perfect and I imperfect it would be very discouraging. One preacher, who was found guilty of a great sin, was asked how he could stand up and preach when he knew he was so bad and he answered, 'When I preach I do not preach my own merits. I preach the merits of Jesus Christ. I do not hold myself up as an example but I hold up Christ as the perfect example.' "

IV

SLEEPING WITH JESSE JAMES

Some time after Ben's experience in Woodland Church when he had been convicted of sin but made no profession, he had a strange experience which nearly changed the course of his life.

There were no railroads through his part of the country then. No hotels or inns accommodated travelers in the wilderness territory. Strangers were entertained in the homes of hospitable people. As a rule, homes welcomed such guests for they could get news from other parts of the world.

Late one evening, an intelligent, personable man came to the Bogard house and asked to stay overnight. Ben especially enjoyed this break in the monotony of farm life so far away from civilization. He listened with wonder, entranced with the exciting tales of the talkative stranger as he vividly described the places he had been and the things he had seen. As most little boys would have done, Ben noticed that his little finger had been cut off. When he asked the visitor how this happened, the guest changed the subject, seemingly annoyed with the youngster.

There was no guest room in the Bogard house. Mr. Bogard explained that there was no spare room but he was welcome to share Ben's bed. The man said he must sleep somewhere and would "be glad to sleep with the boy." This was a real treat to Ben as there were very few visitors and, certainly, seldom any so entertaining. Ben reluctantly watched him leave the next morning. Later, he saw a picture of the famous outlaw, Jesse James. The picture looked familiar and Ben remembered the guest. It was him! It must have been—it looked just like him! He learned that at the very time the stranger had been in

54

their home, the outlaw was escaping after a bank robbery at Russellville, Kentucky, and had made his getaway through that part of Kentucky. It was safe for him for there were no railroads, telegraph or telephone lines. This was only a short time before the outlaw was killed April 3, 1882, murdered by one of his own men, Ford, who betrayed him for the price on his head.

Ben concluded that the man with whom he had slept and talked was Jesse James, the famous outlaw. He knew then that the reason for his sensitivity when the "stub finger" was mentioned was because it was one of the identification marks the wanted posters had used in describing him. When he found that he had slept with the bank robber, or so he believed, he somehow managed to get the book, "James and the Younger Brothers." He read it through many times, thrilling to the terrible tales as he lived through them in his imagination. He decided he wanted to be an outlaw like Jesse James. He began to practice shooting. He wanted to become a good shot, so kept on working at it until he seldom missed the mark he set for himself. Many nights he went to bed with wild dreams of running away and going West to become an outlaw. He saw all the romance his imagination wove into this kind of life, never realizing the heartbreak carried by ruthless killers. These dreams were not inspired by any ill treatment at home, for his family dearly loved him and he loved them. But, as he later said, "The devil was using Jesse James and that vicious book to ruin me. But the grace of God prevented it."

Bogard retained a strange admiration for the "wonderful bandit." He knew that James had come from a Christian home, but was ruined by the attrocities he encountered in the Civil War. He did not have the grace of God to help him and so allowed his bitterness to lead him into an outlaw world. Bogard later reminiscenced, "This should cause all parents to diligently seek the salvation of their children before they are thrust out into the world ... yet, there lingers in me a strange admiration for that wonderful bandit I slept with that night. He had many natural qualities to be admired. What a pity the devil captured this wonderful man. What a power he could have been in the army of the Lord! He missed his calling and was ruined. God had something for him that was good but he refused to answer God's call and, no doubt, made his bed in hell. Alas! His mother loved him to the end. When his limp body was delivered to her door, disgraced, crushed, humiliated as she was, she gave her wayward son a decent burial and erected a tombstone at his grave which had on it the sad words, 'IN LOVING REMEMBRANCE OF MY BELOVED SON, JESSE W. JAMES, WHO DIED APRIL 3, 1882, AGED 34 YEARS, 6 MONTHS, 28 DAYS; MURDERED BY A TRAITOR AND COWARD WHOSE NAME IS NOT WORTHY TO APPEAR HERE.' ''

SATAN AT WORK

Although the country provided none of the city-type "dens of iniquity" the devil still furnished just as many ways to tempt boys and girls to sin. Times change but the devil does not. He always uses whatever is at hand in the particular age in which one lives. Ben felt that town people were "stuck up" so had no special desire to "go to town." He lived eight miles from the nearest one which was Morgan-field, the county seat. He had no transportation except horse-back or a wagon so he was not much of a "city-goer." The roads were often bad, and the long, unpleasant trip took two hours if one drove very fast, but a boy did not have to go to town to find enough to "get into" for the country afforded many of Satan's allurements to provide entertainment.

Prohibition had never been thought of in those days. Almost every grocery store was a liquor store and the people drank. Though saloons were in the towns, the grocery stores also sold liquor and no one thought anything wrong of the people who drank except the poor mothers whose children were kept in rags because the money was spent for whiskey. These feeble protests were scarcely heard.

Liquor flowed like water and was nearly as cheap. It was in nearly every home. As a rule, all of the family drank and in nearly every family, there was a drunkard. Fathers placed whiskey before their sons and told them to, "Drink, but don't make a dog of yourself!" It was up to the boy either to drink in moderation or "make a dog of himself" because the alcohol that could ruin him was put there in his reach.

Almost everyone drank liquor and very few thought it wrong. Church members gave dances in the homes with free consciences. Stills and bootleg "joints" were plentiful notwithstanding the fact that liquor was made and sold by law. The practice was to evade the liquor tax. "Liquor has always been lawless and legal restrictions have not made an outlaw of the liquor business," was Bogard's opinion in later life.

Often Ben and his young friends slipped off to the dances where they would steal the whiskey brought there by the young men. The men hid their bottles out by a stump or under a fence corner or even in the corner of the house. The little boys watched them hide it, then when they came back for their drinks between dances, the liquor was gone. The boys drank it, some of them becoming so drunk they could hardly walk, then they slipped home and into bed so that their parents knew nothing about it. By morning, they had "slept it off" and the parents were none the wiser.

These experiences in the life of a boy later caused the man to go into the temperance movement, for he learned early that when whiskey is so easily available, young people will drink. When it is more difficult to obtain, there is less drinking. His early observations caused him to want prohibition because he firmly believed, as a result of this actual first hand knowledge, that legalized liquor causes more drinking than when it is prohibited by law.

Then there were the "Punch and Judy Shows" that took the place of present day movies. Many times they were cheap and vulgar, not the type of entertainment children should see. They did not "shoot craps" in the alleys, there were no alleys, but they did everything foolish and sinful they could think of as other people did.

"How often we hear old people say that churches and everything were better in the older time than now. They do tell us that everybody went to church and everybody was honest and all women were as good as they looked. It hurt to be disillusioned. The fact is that church members were not better in the olden time than now. The fact is morals were not as good in many respects as now.

"Women were imposed on more when I was a boy than they are now. They pinched themselves almost to death with tight corsets and ruined their health trying to look slender in the waist and wore their dresses down to the ground so as to sweep up all the filth on the ground when they walked. They were not supposed to have ankles and their feet were even hidden under their long skirts. Talk about short skirts. It may be they wear them too short now but I had rather see them wear trousers than to go back to those filthy long skirts.

"Horse racing, dog fighting and cock fighting were common. Nobody seemed to think anything wrong about such as that. Yes, church members and all. As for people being better then than now it is all a mistake. Then the ignorance of all of us was so dense that it is a wonder how we ever lived through it. We did not know that flies were disease carriers, notwithstanding the Bible says that "the flies corrupted the land" (Ex. 8:24). We did not know that mosquitoes caused malaria and that was why we shook with chills and fever. We did not know anything about infection and such a thing as a disinfect-

ant was unknown and surgery was so crude that to take a
man's leg off was considered a wonderful thing for a doctor to
do. About all the doctor knew was how to keep the patient
from bleeding to death. Blood poisoning was common because
the doctors did not know a thing about preventing it. As I
think of conditions back there the illusion I had for many
years that the olden time was better leaves me like the mist of
morning before the rising sun.

"The people lived on a smaller scale then and that is another reason why they were thought to be better. Transactions
between men were seldom big enough to attract much attention and hence little rascalities were not noticed. Then very
few read newspapers and a daily paper was almost unknown
and for that reason crime was not broadcast as it now is. We
lived in ignorance of the rest of the world and hence did not
know of the bad conduct of every man but now we have the
whole story of today's crime dished out to us for breakfast in
the morning. So this comparison of today with the days of
old is misleading because we did not know what was going on
then as now. It may hurt you to be disillusioned but you had
as well face the facts. We have robbers now but the robbers
soon come to their bad end. Back yonder the James and
Younger brothers went on with their criminal work for
TWENTY YEARS. Such as that is impossible now. Moonshiners ply their evil trade now but soon get caught but back
in the olden time nobody cared much about it and men went on
for many years before some envious liquor dealer got mad at
them and turned them in to Uncle Sam and then they were not
prosecuted very hard when caught. Men are dishonest now.
Yes. But well do I remember that my father paid a debt three
times before he had business judgment enough to take a receipt and stop the rascal from collecting again. These cases
illustrate the facts in the case. You are suffering from an illusion if you think everything was better back there than
now."

THE HANGING OF BOB FOWLER

When only twelve years old, Ben watched a hanging. Bob Fowler had been convicted of murder and rape. People gathered in from miles to see the legal execution of a man who, according to their standards, so richly deserved to die. Ben Bogard left early and rode ten miles to get there early to find a good position to see this terrible thing called a legal execution.

Bob Fowler was hanged in the yard of the Union County Jail in Kentucky. He was a large man, standing over six feet tall. He weighed about two hundred and seventy pounds.

Many years later, when Ben Bogard remembered this terrible scene, "the details made my heart come up into my throat." He stood about forty feet from the gallows—one of about ten thousand witnesses, the largest crowd he had ever seen up to that time. As the court house bell tolled the death march, the sheriff led the prisoner out of the jail, and with an officer on either side, they marched him to the scaffold beside which his coffin was placed. As the prisoner walked past, he paused and looked into this narrow box which was in a few minutes to be his last bed. He was pale as death, but nevertheless, walked steadily up the steps of the scaffold, looking out over the great crowd. He arrogantly announced in a clear, loud voice that he was guilty of the crime, but that he would have never been convicted if certain men had not sworn lies in order to convict him. He then named the men he had denounced as liars. As Ben later said, "I rather think they did for a man in the paws of death will not be very likely to voluntarily tell a lie like that." After this public denunciation, the condemned man knelt for prayer. "A Catholic priest prayed to all of the saints and to the Virgin Mary and a little bit to Jesus Christ for the salvation of the poor criminal. He then put an evergreen sprig into his bosom and gave him 'Extreme Unction' as they call it by anointing his head with oil. I shall never forget that abominable prayer and that silly ceremony. Poor Fowler was depending on that for salvation,'' Bogard wrote in some of his recollections.

After the religious ceremony, the prisoner's hands and feet were tied. The black cap was pulled over his head and face. The rope was slipped over his head and adjusted to his neck. The trap was sprung and he fell through the door with such force that the rope broke as if it had been a string. The victim lay on the ground writhing and twisting. Once again the rope was tied. He was jerked up, but not hard enough to break his neck. He hanged there and slowly died from strangulation.

Many emotions could be read in the faces of the "sight-seers." Some had come like vultures to a prey. Others had come because of morbid curiosity and some, like the pagans of old, with no more feeling than they would have in a present day football game—to be entertained. But to the child, Ben, who had come to his first hanging, the incident was one of horror. Years later he witnessed another. He turned away, sick at heart, as he saw for the first time the terrible results of sin. ''I wondered why such a fate should overtake him and not others,'' he later said. ''I had not at that time learned the Scripture 'by the grace of God I am what I am.' That poor man had spurned the grace of God. He knew nothing of the new birth. He was a poor lost sinner trying to save himself by the empty ceremonials of Romanism. I am not slurring Romanism. The same thing applies to anybody who spurns the grace of God and tries by any other means to obtain salvation. Poor Bob Fowler did not have the love of God in his heart. The fear of hell was the nearest approach to salvation he had ever made. Now his life was snuffed out at the end of a rope and his poor soul sank into hell unless all that the Bible teaches is false.''

EXPERIENCES ON THE RIVER

Surely there must be guardian angels who watch over children.

The Bogards lived about a mile and a half from the Ohio River. This beautiful river was sometimes called "La Belle Riviere" which implied it was a sheen of water as good to look at as a beautiful woman. It was a mile wide from bank to bank and as a very young lad, Ben often slipped off to go swimming. The river current was swift and deep enough to float a steamboat. Large freight and passenger boats plied the river all of the time. Many boys, good swimmers, were drowned as they used this river for a swimming pool. Somehow Ben escaped drowning and became a good swimmer.

For four years in succession at one time, the river overflowed the banks to a distance of eighteen miles wide. The waters rose till they reached the Bogard home. On these occasions Ben loaded a skiff with corn and hay and paddled it a half mile to a ridge where the horses, cows and hogs were kept for safety during the flood. Nearly freezing, he fed the animals, then with cold, numb hands paddled back to the house to enjoy a good, hot supper. How they enjoyed the warmth of a hot, log fire even though flood waters lapped menacingly at the floor with every movement of the wind.

On one of these days, Ben found his mother in distress. The wind had blown a big log under the house where it churned and whipped against the hearth of the fireplace until the hearthstone and the fire fell through the floor into the water. His mother had nearly frozen in the cold, damp room and there was no way to make a fire. When his father came home, a small stove was improvised in another room and the family managed to keep from freezing to death. Although the house was completely surrounded by water on these occasions, it was never destroyed, being on a ridge. Many neighbors were not so fortunate and their homes were swept away. These families were warmly welcomed into the Bogard home during their exiles. During these perilous times of high water, Ben became a fairly good oarsman which accomplishment was to be of great help to him at least one time in his later life.

AT THE MINES

Near the Bogard home was a coal mine which was of deep interest to Ben as it would have been to any young boy. He became very familiar with the mine, knowing every "room" in it. He was allowed to come and go as he pleased. One day when he wanted to go in, there was no light and no one to accompany him. The miners were a half mile under the ground. He wanted to go in and he did not want to wait. Going in alone, he felt his way about until he came to a room which turned off to the right. Thinking this the place he had planned to go to, he started to enter the room, but had not gone far when he fell headlong over a mound of dirt into the dense darkness. When he reached for the ceiling, he could not touch it and he realized he was in a room that might cave in at any moment burying him alive. For an instant, panic threatened to seize him, but he knew he must keep his head. Calmly, he began to feel his way out. It seemed an eternity before he saw the welcome sight of the daylight. Fearing punishment, he did not mention this trip into the mine. Years later, remembering the incident, he believed his guardian angel had protected him because of the work God had for him to do.

Another incident happened at the mines which almost caused him to commit a terrible crime. He was only ten when he became acquainted with a coal miner who was a great practical joker. Life is often taken quite seriously by a small boy and he did not know the miner was simply joking and having fun at his expense. He "picked at" the lad and said many things the boy considered mean and ugly. Ben thought he meant the jokes and often became so angry that he had a deep desire to kill the miner. After enduring such treatment a number of times, he secretly resolved to do so. As a boy he had a terrible temper and only the strict discipline of his father restrained him from doing things in anger that would have resulted in great grief to him. This was one of the times, for when he became the object of the practical jokes, he decided to watch for the opportunity to kill the miner.

One day this opportunity presented itself for the hated enemy was sitting on the ground at the mine with his feet doubled under him. As soon as he saw the boy, as usual he began taunting him. Lying on the ground was a sharp pick, just sharpened by the mine's blacksmith. Such an instrument straight from the blacksmith's shop was very sharp—sharp enough to go through a man's body when hurled at him. Ben grabbed the pick with every intention of plunging it through his tormentor's body. The miner had no idea that his life was in any danger for he was only joking. Ben decided he would take such abuse no longer and raised the pick. Suddenly, his child's mind remembered his father. He reasoned that if he did such a thing, he was sure to get a hard whipping for his father was a strict disciplinarian. Ben dropped the pick. Only the thought of a severe whipping saved him from at least attempting an act that would have ruined his life had it been accomplished. He had no idea of the magnitude of such a crime, for the moral aspect of the deed did not enter his mind. He scarcely knew right from wrong, but the fear of physical punishment caused him to desist from his purpose. This incident taught him that children should be chastened to help them grow through these years of irresponsibility into mature adults. He also learned from the experience that adults should not torment or tease children and gain their ill will, but if one must joke, it should be in a good natured manner and instill friendship rather than enmity.

When he had reached manhood, Ben M. Bogard came to this conclusion concerning the treatment of children:

"I find another thing to be true. The pleasant and kindly things of childhood are remembered better than the unpleasant and evil things. If we want to have a flower garden we must plant flowers, and if we want our children to have pleasant memories we should make life worthwhile to them. If we could impress on children the fact that they are to a large extent right now creating the memories that they must have through life, they can make it a flower garden or a field of weeds—according to what they put into their lives. What a responsibility there is on parents right here because the future recollections of their children is determined largely by the parents. Parents should endeavor to make it so that their children can sing in old age,

'How dear to my heart are the scenes of my childhood
When fond recollection presents them to view,
The orchard, the meadow, the deep tangled wildwood
And every loved spot that my infancy knew.' "

BOGARD — THE PREACHER

Ben M. Bogard at nineteen

Those who knew him will note a spark of familiarity in his right hand—even at eighty this was a familiar position (Reproduced from a tintype).

I

SAVED BY GRACE

Years had passed since the revival at Woodland Church when Ben Bogard was first convicted of sin at the tender age of ten years. Another evangelistic campaign was held. J. B. Haynes of Morganfield, Kentucky, preached, assisted by N. Short of Broadly, Kentucky. During this meeting, Ben Bogard trusted the Lord Jesus Christ and was saved. He made this surrender about half way home from the meeting as he rode his horse. "I wept on a bench for four years," he said, "but surrendered to the Lord riding home from meeting. I surrendered to the Lord—came to the end of my own strength and the Lord saved my soul and made me happy under the blood."

This meeting was considered a failure by a deacon in the church who complained, "It looks like we never can have another good meeting here. This meeting has been a failure. Only two have been baptized." The two were Ben Bogard and a middle aged man who died a few years after that and whose funeral was the first one the young preacher, Bogard, conducted. Bogard wrote, "My soul was saved and a prospective bandit was turned into a preacher by that 'failure.' Several thousand souls have been saved under my preaching and it has all come from that 'failure.' We cannot judge by appearances. Our failures are God's successes."

The young convert wanted to be baptized immediately, even though it was February and the ice at least six inches thick on the pond. He knew his salvation was sure whether he was baptized or not, but being saved he wanted to be an obedient Christian, therefore, the cold, wintry weather did not alter his determination to follow the Lord in baptism immediately, and it gets cold in Kentucky. It has been said that cows have frozen to death in open fields.

Woodland Church. Ben watched this house built. Later he was baptized and ordained by its authority.

History of Woodland Church.

Elder J. B. Haynes, as a Missionary of the Henderson County Association, visited our vicinity in company with Deacon James Threlkeld, in the spring of 1871. and found a number of Baptists who said they wanted to organize a Church; and Elder J. B. Haynes continued to preach for them at what was then known as Blacksley's School House. a destitute point, until in May, 1872, when a Church was organized, the Presbytery consisting of Elders J. C. Hopewell, F. J. Jessup and J. B. Haynes, which was organized by appointing J. B. Haynes Moderator, and F. J. Jessup Clerk. The constituent members were Thomas Conway, Nannie E. Conway, S. E. Lindsey, Mary A. Lindsey, Hantippe Thomas, Charles H. Hamner, Bettie Hamner, James Rice, Thomas Dillon, Sarah A. Garr and Thomas J. Garr. Since the organization of the Church James Rice, Thomas Dillon, Mary A. Lindsey and Thomas Conway have been called away by death. Two have been granted letters of dismission, but are still under the watch-care of the Church. One has cast his lot with a different faith and order; but the small and limited number of four, viz: Nannie E. Conway, S. E. Lindsey, Sarah A. Garr and Hantippe Thomas, who by the grace of God have been spared and stripped of all pride and vanities of life, are still buoyant in the faith once delivered unto the saints. The first meeting for business after the organization convened Saturday preceding the first Sunday in June, 1872. The Church proceeded to elect its officers, as follows: Elder J. B. Haynes was unanimously called as Pastor and Moderator, and he being present accepted the call. Thomas Conway was chosen Clerk and Treasurer, Brethren James Rice and Charles H. Hamner were chosen Deacons. The Church agreed to hold her meeting for business on Saturday preceding the first Sunday in each month, and still holds to the same day. Woodland was selected as the name by which the Church should be known. In August, 1872, delegates were appointed to meet with the Henderson County Association, and apply for membership, and it was received into that body October following, and remained with that body until dismissed by request in October, 1878, for the purpose of assisting in the organization of the Union County Association, and remained in that body until the consolidation of the above named Associations in November, 1888, now known as The Ohio Valley Association. In 1874 the Church agreed to accept the land donated by S. L. Veatch as the site to build our house of worship, where the house now stands. The building was completed in 1877, at a cost of about twelve hundred dollars. In September, 1876, Brethren J. W. Conway and J. H. Terrill were ordained Deacons. In the spring of 1880, Brother Thomas Conway, on account of declining health, resigned as Church Clerk, after a faithful discharge of duty for about eight years. In June, 1880, Brother S. E. Lindsey was elected Clerk and served faithfully in that capacity until the year 1885, when he resigned, on account of his own and his family's ill health. In March, 1885, Brother J. A. Givens was elected Clerk and is still performing this duty. In 1883 Brethren John W. Hammack and John G. Gore were ordained Deacons. Through the zeal and courage of the untiring and time-tried Pastor, Elder J. B. Haynes, true fellowship and kind brotherly love were perpetuated, and many glorious revivals and conversions were the fruits of his labor, at Woodland Church. During his Pastorship he baptized about eighty-five converts and about one hundred and twenty were added to the Church. May the God of all grace bless and reward him for his labors. In 1885 he resigned the care of the Church, on account of impaired health. In September, 1885, Elders C. H. Gregston and N. Short held a meeting at Woodland, which resulted in ten additions to the Church, and in October, 1885, Elder C. H. Gregston was called to the care of the Church, and served faithfully three years. Under his Pastorship thirty-five were added to the Church. He won for himself a reputation as a true and efficient expounder of the word of God. He resigned October, 1888, to the regret of many friends. In August, 1888, Brother B. M. Bogard was licensed to preach the Gospel, and in August, 1888, Brother T. A. Conway was licensed to preach. In January, 1889, Brother B. M. Bogard was ordained to the full work of the Ministry, the Presbytery consisting of Elders J. M. Phillips, D. D., G. H. Simmons, C. H. Gregston and S. B. Withers. In December, 1888, Rev. U. J. Fox was called to the care of the Church, whose labors we are still enjoying. He is proving himself to be a very zealous Minister. Statistics show 191 names enrolled on Church book. Present membership 106. The Church has for the greater part of her existence supported and maintained a live Sunday School; also not neglecting the assembling of themselves together in the capacity of prayer meeting. Woodland Church to-day, although she has met with a few troubles and reverses, is still alive to the good work of the Master, in warning sinners to flee the wrath to come, and pointing them to the Lamb of God that taketh away the sins of the world.

> This History of Woodland Church,
> Sweet vision of the past,
> Will linger on our hearts to cheer,
> Where'er our lots be cast;
> But soon we all must pass away,
> We know not when nor how,
> So others may read these cherished thoughts,
> A hundred years from now.
>
> S. E. LINDSEY, *Chairman.*

Miscellaneous.

ORDAINED MINISTERS IN OHIO VALLEY ASSOCIATION.

[We have gathered this information from the letters and other sources. If we omit any names it is for a want of information.—*Clerk.*]

J. B. Haynes, Sturgis; S. W. Martin, Bordley; S. B. Withers, Sturgis; D. J. Logsdon, Seven Gums; C. H. Gregston, Morganfield; T. N. Compton, now at Bethel College, Russellville; Jerry Engle, Clay; B. M. Bogard, at Bethel College, Russellville; J. R. Kennerly, Zion; I. M. Wise, Corydon; A. A. Niles, Cairo; W. W. Schwerdtfeger, Spottsville; G. H. Simmons, Henderson; A. Hatchett, Hebbardsville.

Licentiates.—C. J. Gouch, Clay; James Engle, Clay; T. A. Conway, Spring Grove; Henry Hale, Uniontown.

(Note: Bogard's name in list of ordained ministers)

71

In this pond in severe cold, Bogard was baptized by the authority of Woodland Baptist Church.

A hole was cut in the ice. It looked very much like the grave that baptism is designed to represent. Pastor D. J. Logston of Seven Gums, Kentucky, led the boy down into this icy grave and buried him with Christ in baptism that cold first Sunday in February, 1885. As he came up out of the water, Ben heard a woman say, "That boy must be sincere to be baptized in that ice water." She was right. He was never more sincere in his life for he believed baptism shows forth in a "figure" the salvation of the soul (I Peter 3:21). In one of his writings, Dr. Bogard said, "Since I have been in the ministry, I have baptized several times when ice was on the water. I never knew anybody to be injured by it and I never heard of anybody taking cold by being baptized in ice water. Protracted meetings are held in cold weather in the northern and semi-northern states because that is a leisure time with them. Their summer season is short and they need to lose no time during the summer months from their farms. Hence they chose the cold weather for protracted meetings. For that reason there are frequent ice water baptizings."

There were no training classes such as Baptist Young People's Unions or Training Course work in those days. Seeing the need of a teaching program of some kind, the preacher recommended that the church organize a "young people's prayer meeting." It was especially for the youth and for new converts such as young Ben Bogard was. The meeting began and was kept up for several months. The class was called "The Workers." They took turns leading the meetings. Their order of service included the reading of a passage of Scripture, then each one gave a talk and led in public prayer "turn about." In this manner Ben Bogard received his first training in public exercises and it was of great benefit to him.

From the very moment of his salvation, Bogard wanted to be a preacher. He read his Bible and looked forward with joy to the time when he would be preaching. It was easy for him to go to church, prayer meeting and Sunday School. The minister helped him by letting him know in advance that he would be called on to lead in prayer. He thought the time would never come when the church would "liberate" him to preach. "I never 'Jonahed' a day in my life!" he said. But it was three years before the Woodland Church finally licensed him to preach the gospel. This happy day came during the regular monthly business meeting on Saturday before the first Sunday in August, 1887 when he was eighteen years old. C. H. Gregston was then the pastor and became his father in the ministry. He took a great interest in the young preacher and taught him more of his early lessons in preaching than any other minister. He nourished Ben, first as a young Christian, and later as a young preacher.

"I felt the call of God to preach as soon as I joined the church and was anxious for the time to come when I should be preaching," he said. "I never shrank from the work a minute." I can't understand the feeling of so many preachers who seem to think it meritorious in them when they relate how they 'Jonahed' for years, ran away from their work until forced into it by severe providences of God. I love to preach and always did love to preach from the day I first got the chance till this day. I did not ask the Lord to allow me to go 'first and bury my father,' as it were, before getting into the work. I do not believe in a man rushing into the work and pushing himself on the churches or crowding the call of God but I do believe that when God calls a man to preach he should go right into the work. I got joy out of it and think others will."

Bogard was only a few months past nineteen when he preached his first sermon. His text was Matthew 28:18-20 and his subject "The Great Commission." He preached three times that year. He said of that occasion, "When I was a few months past nineteen years old I was licensed to preach. Elder C. H. Gregston was the pastor and he had me preach at the Saturday business meeting of the church because I had talked

with him about my call to the ministry and he told me to get
ready to preach and I chose a text that called for a big sermon
(Matthew 28:18-20). I spent twenty minutes discussing the
Great Commission. All I knew to say was that it is our duty to
preach the gospel to the whole world and I bore down on that
as hard as I could. But if anybody had asked me to whom the
Lord was speaking and to whom He gave the commission, and
what was implied in it, I could not have told him to save my
life. But ignorance being no crime in the estimation of that
church, they 'liberated' me to preach the gospel. That was
Saturday before the first Sunday in August and I was anxious
to get my license to preach so I could enter college that fall as
a ministerial student. There was no opposition and I began
preparing to go to college in September.''

Bogard spent his first year after being licensed to preach
as a student in Georgetown College. During this period of
school, he had ''charge of a mission'' and preached a number
of times. ''I received training in that work that will last me
through life,'' he said. ''It taught me to do *little things.*''

EARLY COLLEGE DAYS

Off to college at last! How happy the eager young preacher was as, with thirty three dollars and a few cents, he left
home for his great adventure. This money had to buy a railroad ticket to Georgetown, Kentucky, three hundred miles
away, purchase books and pay his board. After that, ten
months of school must somehow be financed. ''As I look back
at it now,'' he wrote in his *Recollections,* ''I wonder how I had
the bravery to start out with so little. But how glad I am that I
did!''

His First Trip

Nearly ten of his precious dollars paid for a ticket to

August 6, 1887

License

This is to certify that Bro, Benjamin Bogard is a worthy and commendable young man and we do heartily recommend him to the public, as an earnest and zealous christian.

This is to certify further, that after satisfactory evidence, that he is impressed with the duty of preaching the gospel: that he has been regularly licensed to preach the gospel by the Woodland Baptist church, at her regular monthly meeting Saturday before the first sunday in August 1887.

Done and signed by order of the church on the above date.

Rev, B. H. Cregston pastor/moderator,

J. R. Givens church clerk

Post office

Spring Grove Ky.

Bogard's License to preach

Red Studio's in Little Rock made this copy from the original on sensitive film and under glass. Note the dark edges indicating the fold of this document dated from year 1887.

76

Georgetown. This was his first real trip. He had never been away from home before and he knew nothing about people except those he had known in his local neighborhood. Out in the country where he lived, even the mail came only once a week and this was a big day. His contact with the "outside" world consisted of the small villages and towns close by. His confidence in people had never been shaken and so he trusted those he met completely. He naively thought everyone wanted to do right, therefore, he had no misgivings at all about his future. It looked bright and optimistic to a young man, even though he began his journey wearing homespun trousers made by his mother. To these "town people" he must have been, as he said, "a comical sight" but, "I did not know what to do and would have done almost anything any respectable man or woman might have told me to do. I felt like everybody wanted to do right. I did not know how to travel and it is a wonder I got to Georgetown at all. I did not know enough to go to a hotel and wash up when I had several hours between trains at Guthrie, Kentucky, did not know, as I do now, that all there is to do is to walk in like the hotel belonged to me and go to the bathroom and clean up whether I was a paid guest at the hotel or not. I thought that if I went to the hotel for such a purpose I would have been held up by someone and made to pay for it. So I was dirty as a pig because the dust had settled on me and the sweat had run out of me and the mixture made mud and a plenty! I know I must have been a sight to behold. So I took out up the railroad track until I came to a puddle of water by the side of the road. There I washed up and dried on my handkerchief and walked back to the station and waited for my train."

The route to Georgetown was through Louisville. Later he wondered how he got through the "big city without being robbed, unless it is that no robber would have thought that I had any money—I did not look like money." How strange and bewildering this place was. He had never dreamed of such a city in the world, limited as his knowledge of the vastness of

the country was. As he waited between trains, he walked aimlessly through the streets, gazing in undisguised, wide-eyed
curiosity. He went "into all sorts of places for it was all
strange and wonderful to me." He roamed about, looking into
doors and windows, until it was time for his train.

After riding all night, he arrived in Georgetown early in
the morning. "My! That beautiful blue grass country," he recalled. "The fine cattle and horses such as are seen nowhere
else in the world took my eye." The serene beauty of the countryside completely captivated him. He was always apprecia-
tive of nature's grandeur.

Ten more of the carefully guarded thirty dollars paid for
a month's board and then supplies must be purchased. When
he had bought only the absolutely essential books, he had only
three dollars and a few cents left. This did not discourage him
in the least. He was young. He was determined to learn. He
had the strength and hope of youth and knew without a moment's doubt that someway, somehow he would get the education he so earnestly sought. He would do any kind of odd job
to stay in school. No work was too menial for him if it would
bring in a few cents to keep him in college. At one time, he
taught an elderly Negro man to read for the compensation of
twenty five cents a lesson!

To an awed country boy's inexperienced eye, the college
was "so large and fine! The teachers seemed so learned that I
felt awed in their presence. I was happy for now was my
chance to get an education! I actually was in college! When
Dr. Dudley asked me what course I wanted to take I told him
I did not know but I wanted to get a good education and would
leave it with him as to just what my studies would be. Believe
in him and the rest of them? I should say I did. They knew and
I was there to learn. I suspected no danger. They were Baptists and I wanted to learn how to be successful in the Baptist
work. I was called of God to preach and wanted the best possible preparation. If I had gone there thinking I knew more

than my teachers, I should have been a failure. I wanted to learn and I kept both eyes and both ears open that I might learn. Except what I had seen and heard at the Union County Association, and I remembered very little of that, I knew nothing of conventionism. I had never heard of alien immersion and such like. I was clay and soft clay at that and the teachers were the potters.''

Bogard studied English, Greek, Latin, Mathematics and Science in the one year in Georgetown, where, as he said, ''Aristocratic people of the old sort predominated. I was a poor boy but they were kind to me and not once was I mistreated by any of them. The impressions made on me have lasted. Some friendships became permanent.'' In spite of being a ''country bumpkin'' with no money, the young student's memories of that year were only pleasant ones, unmarred by any bitterness, strife or troubles, or any ill-treatment from anyone.

Like every other phase of his life, the good predominated. Even the memories of college fell into the same pattern. He cherished these wonderful memories. Only once in a while did he recall the instance where some of the college students made fun of his homemade jeans when he first arrived at school. His mother had spun the yarn and woven the pants. ''Where did you get them britches?'' some of the boys teased. The only thing that seemed to really hurt him about this was that his dear old mother had made those pants for him and he took it more of a thrust at her than at himself. As we say, only once in a while he would think of these unpleasant things. Most of the time his memories were of the good things.

One of those constant friends was Professor S. C. Mitchell, a student teacher who taught him his first lessons in Greek. He was the pride of the college and later became the son-in-law of Professor A. T. Robertson who taught Greek in the Southern Baptist Theological Seminary.

Mr. Mitchell was an enthusiast on the subject of missions.

He sought to instill his zeal into the hearts and lives of his students. He wanted to exact from everyone of them the promise to be foreign missionaries. "He was a very good speaker and some of us looked forward to the time when he would be pastor or missionary in a very prominent way. But he settled down to teaching in Richmond College, Virginia, and while no doubt he accomplished much as a teacher, it seems a pity that such a brilliant man should not devote himself entirely to the ministry. But maybe God had not called him to preach. Anyway, he has done very little of it."

T. P. Dudley, the college president's nephew, became his close friend as did Francis W. Taylor, the first student preacher Bogard met upon his arrival in Georgetown. Though Mr. Taylor was a third year student, he did not assume the condescending attitude toward the young preacher that many "upper classmen" take toward the freshmen, but rather "graciously received me and made me feel like staying instead of being discontented. I have been thrown with him more since that time than with any other of the students. I assisted him in a protracted meeting with the Third Avenue Baptist Church, Louisville, Kentucky, and he assisted me in the First Baptist Church, Charleston, Missouri."

W. J. Puckett, Cave City, Kentucky, remained a close friend through the years. He and Bogard corresponded frequently. "We think very much alike on the great questions that disturb our Baptist people today," Bogard said of him. "While all the others were kind and friendly, no others made any deep impressions on me. An idea I want to get over is that a student absorbs his surroundings. What a student absorbs is of as much importance as what he learns from books. I was very much like a sponge at Georgetown. I came very nearly absorbing all that was there. This shows the importance of putting our youth in the right sort of school for he cannot come out as he went in no matter how he might try."

In June 1888, young Bogard returned home. He plunged

into the work of his calling. Though not yet ordained, he was not idle. He preached seventy sermons and witnessed thirty six conversions that first year after his first year in college.

FIRST EVANGELISTIC CAMPAIGNS

The first invitation to help in a meeting came from Bogard's pastor and friend who had helped him with his first sermon. C. H. Gregston had taken great interest in him and was his father in the ministry. "He taught me more of my early lessons in preaching than any other preacher. It was he who nourished me as a young Christian and then later as a young preacher," Bogard wrote of this faithful friend and pastor.

Mr. Gregston sent word to young Bogard that he needed help in a "protracted meeting" at Little West School House, about ten miles from his home. Bogard was dismayed. He felt completely inadequate for so great a task. He did not have enough material. He replied that he could not possibly help. "I only had three sermons to my name and that would not be enough sermons for a protracted meeting. I just could not go I thought." Mr. Gregston was insistent and advised him to come and preach the three sermons he had, then if he could do no more than that, he would "at least do what I could. I went. Thank God I did. I told Brother Gregston frankly that I had only three sermons and did not know where anymore would come from as I had exhausted my store of Bible knowledge in making those three. That may sound funny to you but it was serious business with me! Brother Greston told me to get up and preach one of the three and he would pick it up if I made a failure. I must have done well for he did not pick it up but let it go as I preached it and there was good interest."

The next morning Mr. Gregston said to Ben, "Let's go out in the yard under the shade tree and make a sermon." The two men sat down together. The older preacher read a passage of

Bogard at Twenty-one

Reproduced from a tintype, the first picture showing a mustache.
Intelligence is expressed here by his sharp features.

83

Scripture, then asked the young one what he thought of that passage. Ben gave his opinion. Gregston said, ''That is good! Now, write it down as your first point.'' This continued until the young man had another sermon. ''He pushed me into making enough sermons that I preached every night for two weeks. When that meeting closed I had enough sermons to hold a meeting all by myself. It was C. H. Gregston who gave me that wonderful help. The meeting resulted in several professions of faith and baptism. I was encouraged and much of what I have been since that time is due to Elder Gregston's helping me. He showed me how to help young preachers and I have been trying to help and to encourage young preachers ever since!''

From the time of that first meeting, young Bogard was kept busy in ''protracted'' meetings. He learned a great deal from these meetings, as he wrote:

''My experience in protracted meetings may be of interest, at least the memory of them interest me. I held a protracted meeting in a place called Walnut Bottoms, Henderson County, Kentucky, and the experiences there made a lasting impression on me. It was a rough country. A bootleg joint was in a hundred feet of the school house where the meeting was held. It was run by a poor unfortunate man named Baker. He had seen better days. We are told by some that there were no bootleggers and moonshiners when the liquor traffic was legal but I know better. That man Baker was a bootlegger. He had a grocery store and along with it he sold whiskey without any legal authority to do so.

''The bootlegger was delighted to have the protracted meeting. He thought it would bring a crowd of people to the place and he felt he would sell a lot of liquor as a result. I did not know he was selling whiskey until after the meeting started. The way I got acquainted with him was very interesting. Here is how it was. I had been engaged by the local Baptist Association to go there to hold the protracted meeting and it was new and raw territory. I drove a little horse hitched to a road cart and went boldly into that God-forsaken country and as I went I inquired for Baptists. Nobody had heard whether there were any Baptists in that country or not. I drove on and finally came to Baker's store and went in and told him who I was and what my business was. He was delighted to have me and insisted that I eat dinner with him. He said his wife was a good woman and would be glad to have me. The dear woman was very kind and showed she, too, had seen better days. She was reared a Methodist but was no church member. They offered me a room with a good bed and said that I could stay right there and they would feed me and furnish a room for me until the meeting was over. He even went so far as to get an old steamboat headlight and fill it with oil and put it in the school house to make a light to read by in the dingy building. He told everybody who came to the store that a 'boy preacher' was there and introduced me to everybody and a good congregation came to the preaching. He made a fine 'advance' man, so to speak, and almost everybody in all that part of the country soon came to the meetings. The school house overflowed.

"On the first night after service Mr. Baker came to my room with a glass of liquor and asked me to take a drink with him. Said it was no harm and that I had exerted myself in preaching and needed a stimulant. If I had been a drinking man I never would have accepted liquor under such conditions. So I declined as politely as I could and told him I did not drink. He said he admired that in me because in fact it did not really do any good to drink. His motive evidently was to compromise me and thus get the advantage of me. The meeting increased in interest until souls were saved and the interest ran so high that Mr. Baker began to show that he would rather I would change boarding houses. A kind friend told me that it would be best for me to get out of his house and I could come and stay with him. The meeting kept increasing in interest until the men who had been buying liquor from Baker quit it and they professed faith in Jesus Christ and offered themselves for baptism. An arm of a church at Smith Mills, Ky., came down and received the candidates for baptism and it was decided to organize a church there. God was showering His blessings on the 'boy preacher' and it was real success. My bootlegger friend became my enemy. Rough times began. He put bad boys up to disturbing the meetings, and one morning I found a note under my door which said that I would be given just twenty-four hours to get out of that community or the mob would attend to me. What was I to do? They were outlaws and might hurt me, even kill me.

"With a prospective mob before me I did a rash and foolish thing. I do not pretend to excuse myself for so doing. I did wrong but it worked. The wicked idea came into my mind that I knew how to shoot, having slept with Jesse James, as I have related in a former article, and because of that had practiced shooting until I became an expert shot, and the wicked idea came into my mind that in all probability they would pay well for their trouble if the mob came to get me. Remember I was still a boy, a twenty-year-old boy, and I had not developed the bump of caution that I now have. So I went to a young man friend and asked him for a pistol and he soon had one for me. I walked deliberately over to Baker's store and threw down a piece of money and said: 'Mr. Baker, let me have some cartridges, No. 44.' He handed out a box and I took the pistol and loaded it before him and then put the pistol and the rest of the cartridges in my pocket and said: 'I received a note this morning that ordered me out of this community. I just came over to tell you to say to the boys that when they come they had better bring a wagon along with them for they will have to be hauled away.'

"I knew that Baker was at the bottom of the mischief and that he was the one who wanted to get rid of me because it was breaking up his wicked business. Instead of the meetings helping him sell liquor it was taking his customers away from him. The bluff worked for I heard no more about the mob. What I ought to have done was to get a number of the better people together and asked for protection. But I did not for I felt fully able to protect myself and it is providential that no mob came because I know I would have shot into them and no telling how many would have been killed and possibly I, too, would have been killed and if not killed the stain of human blood would have been on my hands and my whole life would have been brought under that cloud. Thank God for the guardian angel that stopped them from coming.

"The church was organized and I count that as one of the most successful meetings I ever held. God was with the 'boy preacher' and He protected and led, and real missionary experience was enjoyed. What became of Baker and his poor wife? She professed faith in Jesus Christ and was a happy convert but he refused to allow her to be baptized. She soon died and I have no doubt she went to that sweet rest that remains for the people of God. Poor, miserable Baker went from bad to worse until he died with delirium tremens, a most horrible death. Alas! 'He that being often reproved and hardeneth his neck shall suddenly be destroyed and that without remedy.' I wonder if I tried hard enough to reach him and lead him to Christ. The good Lord forgive me if I failed to do my part. But I know I preached Christ to him and I know it failed to reach him.

"As I look back at several protracted meetings I held while a 'boy preacher' I am made to wonder why I succeeded. My preaching was immature. My theology was crude. My education was very limited. My inexperience was dangerous. My youth was an asset because it attracted the people who are always looking for something different and the 'boy preacher' was certainly different. My enthusiasm was great, I truly expected to live to see the world taken for Christ, little dreaming how bad my theology on that point was. I was zeal-

ous and never tired in the work. My whole life was before me
and I looked forward to great things. Scriptures that applied
to children of God I sometimes applied to sinners and passages that applied to sinners I frequently used on the Lord's
people and my innocent ignorance was great. As I look back at
it now I wonder how in the world I ever got through. But there
is a passage in God's Word that says the 'weak things of this
world are used to confound the mighty.' The success was
from God for the Lord knows it was not from my experience,
equipment or knowledge. I shall never cease to thank God that
so many were saved under my poor preaching and when I
reach the other side I expect to meet a goodly number who
were saved under my preaching at Walnut Bottoms and other
places where I held meetings during my youth. I sometimes
wish I could get back some of the things I had then but no
doubt if I had them they would not work with a man of mature
years.''

In another of his recollections, he wrote:

''My recollection of ridiculous things happening in protracted meetings might be interesting. There are all sorts of
fools who come to church and sometimes intelligent people do
silly things.

''When I was only twenty years old, just a boy, I was holding a protracted meeting in Henderson county, Kentucky. I
had preached a very enthusiastic sermon and everything
seemed favorable for good results and I worked up to the point
where the invitation was to be given and while everybody was
animated by the sermon and everything seemed set for a favorable response, I called for a song and the song leader pitched
the song so high it could not be sung more than half way
through the first line. We had no organ or other instrument to
assist and depended on the leader getting the song started
right. Of course the singers broke down and had to stop. I saw
their predicament and well knowing that it is very difficult to
get right after once starting wrong I asked him to select an-

other song and while he was hunting for it I started to fill in
the time exhorting but was stopped by a man who had been
misbehaving all through the services. He had talked and talked
and talked until I asked him to stop and he did not stop talking
when I asked him to. I then rebuked him severely and it looked
as if he had come to disturb and if possible break up the meeting. Now this same man arose while the singer was hunting for
another song and asked permission to speak. I do not know
why I permitted him to speak but I did. He began by offering
profuse apologies for having disturbed my meeting. He then
began to exhort the young people to not do as he had done for
he had wasted his life and ignored God. He told them he hoped
they never would be guilty of doing as he had done that night
and said they should all do as the 'boy preacher' had told
them to do and they never would regret it. 'But,' said he, 'I
did not arise to preach a sermon nor to deliver an exhortation.
That is out of my line. I am representing the Henderson
Gleanor, a newspaper of high grade and I came here tonight to
get subscribers for that paper and I thought while they were
looking for a song it would be a good time to speak of the
merits of that paper,' and he tried to rattle on. But I stopped
him and told him that he was in gross disorder and had vio-
lated the law by disturbing religious worship. Of course, about
all I could do then was to dismiss the congregation. All interest had evaporated.

"The next morning before I got out of bed he was on the
front porch of the house where I spent the night. He had come
over to ask forgiveness. He said he was drunk the night before
and never would have done such a thing if he had been sober.
He begged me not to have him arrested for his bad conduct. I
told him I did not want to do him any harm and so far as I was
concerned I would not have him suffer for his crime and that I
hoped he would not do a thing like that again. He thanked me
profusely. The next issue of the Henderson Gleanor gave me
the biggest boost I think I ever received. Certainly it was the

greatest up to that time. To read it you would have thought
that a young Spurgeon was holding that protracted meeting. I
was a real wonder in the pulpit and so on. He was trying to
make amends for his bad conduct. To say the least of it that
man had an eye to business and believed in using every opportunity.

"Another protracted meeting when I was still a boy, this
time about twenty-one years old, was in Christian County,
Ky. The meeting was a success. Large crowds attended. A
young lady lived near the meeting house and her parents were
good church members but she was not saved. They kindly gave
me a room in their good country home. Of course she and I
were thrown together over and over again during that series
of meetings. We walked together to and from church and the
people began to talk. They just knew that this would be 'a
match.' They discussed how well suited to each other we were.
Some even mentioned it to me and I heard that they teased the
girl about it. I cared no more for her than for any other nice
girl. She was good company and I did not discover a thing
wrong with her except she was not saved. She came forward
for prayer and was perfectly sincere about it. She sought the
Lord and found Him. But the way it came about upset me as
nothing ever did before nor since. She, with a dozen or more
other boys and girls, came forward for prayer the night she
was converted. There had been several professions. She was
sitting on the front seat. The song was just about coming to an
end. I was standing right in front of her waiting for the song
to close and I was intending to give some sort of invitation so
soon as the song closed. Just as the singing stopped she was
saved. She sprang to her feet and threw her arms about my
neck and gave me such a hug as would never be forgotten. She
hung on and it seemed an age before I pried loose from her
and then she ran over to her mother and began to hug her. She
had the hugging kind of religion and made her start on me.
The people lost all idea of the solemnity of the occasion and

began to laugh. It was 'enough to make a dog laugh,' so they said, but it was at my expense. The next day the people came to church laughing and they laughed every time they saw me or the girl. They teased the poor girl until she was well nigh distracted. I went through that community over a year after that and the first man I met came at me laughing. I believe that if I were to go back there even at this late day some one would remember it and laugh. Thank the good Lord the girl was saved and here is wishing that she married some good man who has given her all the hugging she wanted for I have not seen her since but I certainly did not like the public spectacle she made of both of us the night she was saved. She meant no harm for she was so happy in her Saviour's love she really did not know what she was doing.

"I held a fine meeting in Union County, Ky., when I was twenty-two years old. There were four baptized at the close of the meeting, only four, but the church was greatly revived and these converts seemed to be first class. I did the baptizing. On coming up out of the water, after baptizing a man, he said: 'Come up to my house after we dress for I have a dollar for you.' I went and he looked and looked and looked and could not find the dollar. He said, 'I wonder if I had that dollar in my trousers pocket I was baptized in.' He looked in the wet pocket and sure enough there was the dollar. It had been baptized too. He gave me the baptized dollar. I have often thought that it would be well for others to have their pocket books baptized. Do you get the idea?"

The young preacher performed his first marriage ceremony December 8, 1888, when he united Mr. Frank Baurer and Miss Ann Bruce in marriage. In his *Recollections* Bogard wrote: "In my second protracted meeting on the first day of the meeting a young couple came to be married. It was my first marriage ceremony. I shall never, never forget Frank Baurer and Annie Bruce, in Walnut Bottom, Kentucky, the ones who were married. They were a fine young couple away out in the country, at least twenty miles from the nearest rail-road. They were unspoiled by what we call modern society. These young people, after being made happy in marriage, came on to the services and both of them were saved. They joined the church and I baptized them. It was also my first baptizing. I put them under the water at one time by having them put their arms around each other and with one ceremony, I laid them beneath the water, symbolizing their death to sin and raised them up together, symbolical of their resurrection to a new life. If there is another preacher in the world who married his first couple and baptized that same couple the same week, it being also his first baptizing, I should like to hear from him.''

That year Bogard helped in evangelistic meetings at Little West School, Woodland Church (with pastor C. H. Gregston), two at Walnut Bottoms School House and started one at Anderson School, but had to discontinue it because of the rain. Of the meeting in his home church he wrote, "This being the church of which I am a member, I received nothing for my services.'' He also preached to Highland Church, Seven Gums, Mt. Olive, New Harmony, Henderson City and Clayville Churches. At Woodland Church that year he made his first attempt to preach on the subject of communion, "My ground was restricted church communion.''

Bogard experienced his first assignment as a delegate to an association in 1888. It was not his first time to attend messenger meetings of associations, for he wrote in his *Recollections:* "I shall never forget the first association I ever attended. I was a small boy and the association was known as the Union County Association of United Baptists. The messengers met at Woodland Church where I afterwards became a member and where several years after I was ordained to preach, but I did not know what it was all about. I distinctly remember how Dr. J. W. Warder, Secretary of the State Mission Board, was there and how he tried to get the association to endorse conventionism. His effort was a failure and the proposition to become a part of the convention system was turned down by an almost unanimous vote. I remember some of the speeches that were made and I especially remember how Doctor Warder tried to convince them that they could go into the Convention and still be free and independent Baptists. But the messengers could not be convinced and he left the association disappointed. I knew nothing of what the Bible said on the subject and I did not understand much of the arguments but I did know that the association refused to go into conventionism.''

At this time the ''Baptists in that part of Kentucky were called United Baptists. Some in Kentucky and Tennessee are still called by that name and I have heard of still others in several of the states. But some of the so-called 'United Baptists' in Missouri and in the northern part of Arkansas and possibly other places are in fact not sound Baptists. One bunch is in reality Freewill Baptists and still another is in substance, plain 'Hardshell.' But the United Baptists in Kentucky were just Missionary Baptists and such men as John A. Broadus, J. R. Graves, J. M. Pendleton and J. N. Hall were United Baptists. The way the designation 'United Baptists' came to be was two factions in Virginia and the Carolinas united and to emphasize their unity called themselves United Baptists.''

WHO WERE THE UNITED BAPTISTS?

Since Bogard was a United Missionary Baptist, that is, he belonged to one of their churches and preached for them, we should understand who they are. They were just what the name implies—united.

The first fellowship of Baptist Churches in America was known as the Philadelphia Association. This association of Baptist Churches came into being in 1707. It was simply a cooperation of Baptist Churches and as all associations of Baptist Churches, was a means whereby the churches enjoyed fellowship and assisted each other to enlarge their work in missions and establish other churches. In those days the churches were located far apart, as was nearly everything else in this new land. These were well established, doctrinally sound churches and were regular in "faith and practice, therefore, were called "regular Baptists."

In 1742, they drew up and declared to the world their "Confession of Faith" and, while they had one statement which advocated the "laying on of hands on baptized believers," the Philadelphia Confession is still a statement which is and can be endorsed by "regular Baptist Churches" today. It is noteworthy that the doctrinal statement of the American Baptist Association says, "this association is made up of regular Missionary Baptist Churches." The term does not connotate a particular brand of Baptists but simply reccgnizes that they are regular in doctrine and practice to the New Testament pattern.

Now we turn our attention to a situation arising in 1740, 41 and 42. An Episcopal minister was born in England in 1714 and came to America to begin his evangelistic work in 1737. He was only twenty three years old and had been associated with John Wesley. These brethren had forsaken their Armenian theology for Calvinism and, undoubtedly, were born again. To say they were enthusiastic in their work would be a gross understatement, for it was reported that "shrieking, crying, weeping and wailing" was witnessed among Whitfield's hearers.

Whitfield declared "all men by nature under sin" and that the "righteousness of Christ alone is the ground of justification of sinners to be received by faith." These Bible doctrines were his preachments along with "the absolute necessity of the new birth which is solely the work of God's blessed Spirit." One must remember that he was not a Baptist minister though he was certainly preaching Baptist doctrine as far as salvation from sin is concerned. History teaches that all

classes, sects and denominations turned out in swelling crowds
to hear him. His disciples were called "NEW LIGHTS" and
his work the "NEW LIGHT'S STIR." Many of the Episcopal
(established order) preachers were converted to his movement
and their evangelistic meetings were very successful. The par-
ish clergymen were divided, some endorsing, others condemning the "New Lights." The opposition was successful in getting a law passed to confine all ministers to their own parish-
es; however, the great revival fire was burning and there was
no way to stop it at that time.

Naturally, since these people had "tasted the heavenly
gift" and had fallen in love with the Lord Jesus Christ, they
were never satisfied to go back to the dry religious services of
the established church, therefore, they formed religious societies called Separates because they had been separated from
the established church. The "Separates" first took their name
about the year 1744. There were many rags and tags of the
established church in these Separate Societies, such as infant
baptism; however, the new converts in these societies were
taught to "throw aside tradition and take the word of God
only as the guide in all matters of religious faith and practice."
This was in perfect coincident with all Baptist teaching and
"... ultimately led thousands, among whom were many ministers to embrace" the Baptist faith and become Baptists. These
new Baptists still held the appellation "Separate" and so
were referred to as "Separate Baptists." They held the same
doctrines of the Regular Baptists. In time, the Regular and the
Separates were united and, therefore, called United Missionary Baptists. So, when we refer to the United Baptists, we do
not speak of a strange and foreign group but the very fore-
fathers of the faith of those who are now the Missionary Baptists of the American Baptist Association. There is, at least,
one local association in Kentucky well over a hundred and
fifty years old. It is the Cumberland United Baptist Association. This group of churches affiliate in the American Baptist

Association on a national scale and perpetuate the name "United" on the local level.

"It is a pity," Bogard said, "that all Baptists are not united and could be, in fact if not in name, really UNITED. But alas! We are still working on the unification problem. Very well do I remember hearing Mr. S. E. Lindsey, clerk of Woodland Church, read the minutes and church letters before the business meetings and those minutes and letters always said, 'We, the United Baptist Church of Christ,' etc. The meaning of that is the United Baptized Congregation of Christ. What a fine name! Wish it were true of all congregations and that they were in unity as the name indicates."

The Union County Associational meeting was at Bethany Church near Sturgis, Kentucky, in October. Bogard represented Woodland Church and served on these committees: corresponding letters to sister associations, foreign mission and religious literature. By this time he had become an "avid convention man" having accepted without question his professor's ideas on the subject. He wrote, "I attended the Baptist Church (Georgetown) of course. The second time I went to church a Methodist lady joined the church on her Methodist baptism. Dr. R. M. Dudley, president of the college, moved that she be accepted on her baptism. Professor Ricker, teacher of Mathematics, seconded the motion. Elder W. J. E. Cox was pastor of the church. He later was pastor in Pine Bluff, Arkansas. On her Methodist baptism she was received into full fellowship. I knew that was not the way it was done in my home country. But I reasoned like this—that I was a green country boy and my people lived way out in the country. They were not educated and while our preachers down there were honest they just did not know any better and now since I was in college and attending a college town church where the teachers were all members of it surely they knew and who was I to question their practice? So I became an alien immersionist, and by the time the year was out I had become a convention

man and went home a convention preacher and an alien immersionist. I felt that it was my duty to teach our dear people
the way of the Lord more perfectly. I attended that same association which I had seen go against conventionism and the
association for the first time in its history lined up with conventionism. I was to blame for it. They have been lined up ever
since. As I go back to that wonderful country and look over
my 'old stomping ground' my conscience hurts me when I
think I was the cause of that whole country going into conventionism.''

He preached one sermon at a circle meeting at New Har-
many Church in Webster County, Kentucky. He also visited a
circle meeting at Mt. Pleasant Church, Henderson City, Kentucky.

His ministerial work that year netted him exactly $108.30.

III

EARLY PREACHING DAYS

Ordained

Two years after he was licensed to preach, Ben M. Bogard was ordained to the "full work of the gospel ministry." On January 15, 1889, the year he was twenty, a presbytery consisting of J. M. Phillips, C. H. Gregston, S. B. Withers and George H. Simmons, after an examination that lasted over two hours recommended his ordination.

On January 21, 1889, Bogard organized the Ohio Valley Church at Walnut Bottoms, assisted by Deacon R. W. Abel. He was elected as pastor. This was his first pastorate and he only served until August 11th when he resigned in order to attend college.

BETHEL COLLEGE, RUSSELLVILLE, KENTUCKY

Ben Bogard enrolled in Bethel College on September 16, 1889 and stayed until June 12, 1890. He re-entered September 11, 1890 and stayed till June 12, 1891.

These college years were very "lean years" for the young preacher as he struggled to get an education. Philosophically, he accepted his poverty and later wrote, "I thank God for being poor. I distinctly remember hearing Professor A. F. Williams, who was one of my teachers in Bethel College say that a poor rich boy should be pitied. 'Poor rich boy' sounded like a contradiction but I have lived to understand what the old teacher meant. Very few men amount to much who are born in the lap of luxury. The poor boy from the country is the one who may be depended on to amount to much in this world. The

Henderson Ky Feb 18th 1889

"This is to certify that at the request of the Woodlawn Baptist Church Union Co Ky. we whose names appear below Baptist Ministers in good standing in our respective churches and regularly ordained to the work of the Gospel ministry having organized ourselves into a presbytery, did after a full and careful examination of Bro B. M. Bogard and being fully satisfied as to his fitness for the work, with the full consent and approval of the church, ordain him to the full work of the Gospel Ministry in the Baptist churches. Done Jan. 15, 1889.

We most cordially commend him to the confidence of the

99

very hardships he is compelled to endure make a man of him, develop his muscles and preserve his morals and put ambition in him to go to the top. The rich boy feels he is in need of nothing and hence he makes little effort. This is true almost without exception. As I now look back over the years and can remember how I thought that if the day ever came when I could have good 'store' clothes and a gold watch I would have all the happiness I wished. I thought everybody was rich who had as much as two or three thousand dollars in property, and ten thousand seemed to me like an immense fortune. I had no money to go to college—no money for anything. I struggled through and now I am glad of it. The struggle was the best part of my education.''

At Bethel, he received most of his ''training for the work I have spent my life in.'' There he came in contact with such men as gentle, yet great, Dr. W. S. Ryland who taught science. The great scholar, Professor C. P. Shields, taught him Latin and Greek. A German, John Henry Damm, taught him to read and speak the German language. Professor John P. Fruit, later of William Jewel College in Missouri, was his English teacher.

''I thank God for college associates and fellow students,'' he wrote. His friends were T. N. Compton, H. A. Copass, Dexter G. Whittingill and others who, though good friends, did not impress him so much. T. N. Compton became a mighty preacher, though he lived to be an old bachelor. ''I little thought he would live a bachelor when we used to go to see the girls together. While he has missed the pleasure of a home of his own, some woman has missed a wonderful husband for he was one of the truest men I ever knew.'' ''Deck'' Whittingill became the president of the Theological Seminary in Rome, ''right under the Pope's nose, so to speak . . . in the shadow of the Vatican . . . His life has been endangered by Rome's emissaries. He is under constant surveillance and must be exceedingly careful about what he says or writes. He wrote a let-

ter to me a year or two ago and did not sign his name, but went
off to another post office to mail it so that it could not 'leak
through' as to his writing it. What he said was about the persecutions by Romanists. They talk about toleration here but
they do not practice it where they have power to coerce others.
He is under constant surveillance of Mussolini's spies. Such
great men as they are to be proud of and I count them all my
personal friends. With some of them I have not always been in
exact agreement but no differences between us have ever
marred our personal friendships and admiration of each other
. . . All of them are scholars but Whittingill and Copass are
eminent. It was part of my ambition to excel Copass and Whittingill in making good grades in our college work, but I never
succeeded. One hundred was the highest grade anyone could
make. I made it in Greek, German and Science a great deal of
the time but Copass and Whittingill made one hundred in
everything, examinations and all, for two whole years. They
broke the record of college work.'' Though Bogard did not
succeed in his ambition, he was no mean scholar. His report
cards show his least grade was 93. Most of his grades were
above 95 and some 100's.

Much of what Bogard was to become could be determined
by the men with whom he associated and admired. He learned
as much as possible from the lives of these great men. Of
Boyce Taylor, Murray, Kentucky, he wrote: ''He is a wonderful man. He keeps me half angry with him much of the time
because of his inconsistent way of doing, but he is a most remarkable man. He was never a real student but was jolly and
full of fun all of the time—nobody ever caught him seriously
studying his books—but he has a great mind and he absorbed
enough to graduate and his career as a preacher has been mar-
velous. He has never had but one pastorate, Murray, Kentucky, and there he has stayed for about forty years and has
built up a great church that is independent of all bosses except
Boyce. But when we consider the large number of souls who

BETHEL COLLEGE.

RUSSELLVILLE, KY., _Nov 3rd_ 18 _89_

Report of Mr. _B. M. Osgard_

for month ending _Nov 9_ 1889

English	100
Natural Sciences	
Arithmetic	
Mathematics	100
Latin	
Greek	
German	
French	
Mental and Moral Science	100
Deportment	100
Absent from Recitat'n (times)	
Tardy (times)	

The maximum in standing and deportment is 100.
Perfection in deportment and an average standing of
90 in studies, entitles one to be on the Honor Roll.

W. S. RYLAND, President

BETHEL COLLEGE.

RUSSELLVILLE, KY., _Oct 5th_ 18 _89_

Report of Mr. _B. M. Osgard_

for month ending _Oct 4th_ 1889

English	100
Natural Sciences	
Arithmetic	
Mathematics	96
Latin	
Greek	
German	
French	
Mental and Moral Science	99.5
Deportment	100
Absent from Recitat'n (times)	
Tardy (times)	

The maximum in standing and deportment is 100.
Perfection in deportment and an average standing of
90 in studies, entitles one to be on the Honor Roll.

W. S. RYLAND, President

BETHEL COLLEGE.

Russellville, Ky. 11/27 189 0

Report of Mr. B. Mc. Bogard

for month ending 11/28 189 0

English	
Natural Sciences	
Arithmetic	
Mathematics	96
Latin	100
Greek	99.5
German	
French	
Mental and Moral Science	
Deportment	100
Absent from Recitation (Times)	8 84
Tardy (Times)	

The maximum in Standing and Deportment is 100. A perfect deportment and an average standing 90 to studies, entitle one to be on the Honor Roll.

W. S. RYLAND
President.

BETHEL COLLEGE.

Russellville, Ky. 189 0

Report of Mr. B. Mc. Bogard

for month ending 10/31 189 0

English	
Natural Sciences	
Arithmetic	
Mathematics	94
Latin	99
Greek	99
German	99.9
French	
Mental and Moral Science	
Deportment	100
Absent from Recitation (Times)	
Tardy (Times)	

The maximum in Standing and Deportment is 100. A perfect deportment and an average standing 90 to studies, entitle one to be on the Honor Roll.

W. S. RYLAND
President.

BETHEL COLLEGE.

B. M. Bogard

W. S. RYLAND

UNITED STATES
POSTAL CARD
ONE CENT

RUSSELL...

NOTHING BUT THE ADDRESS TO BE ON THIS SIDE.

Mr M. L. Bogard
Spring Grove
Ky

104

have been saved under his ministry and the immense amount of mission work that great church has done under his leadership, the fact that he makes it hot for the machine which seeks to enmesh and enslave the churches, we can thank God for Boyce Taylor. I cherish the memory of the days when we sat together in classes and read Greek and Latin, studied logic and figured on the blackboard together. In spite of the strong divergence of ways and methods he and I employ I am glad I can say that I thank God for him along with the others who have been mentioned.''

Ben Bogard had the insight and wisdom which enabled him to learn and profit from the good characteristics he found in those he chanced to encounter in this early, moulding period of his life. He said of other great men he was privileged to know:

'' 'We become a part of all we meet,' some one said. Whether this is true or not, it is a fact that we are influenced by all we meet. Hence, the importance of a good environment. The man who has mixed and mingled with all kinds of people enough to really know the conditions under which they live and to be able to appreciate their view point has had in that very experience an education that is much needed. As I look back I count myself fortunate in that I have come in contact with all kinds of people, having been in the homes of the poorest, even in western dug-outs, and from that on up through the homes of the middle class and last, more than once, in the homes of millionaires. I have seen and felt the life of all classes. I have been in the homes of the most worldly and also among those who are whole hearted children of God. Experience is a good school and fools will learn in no other. But happy is the man who can learn by experience and also learn in other schools.

"I may not amount to much but what I am I can be accounted for largely by what I have absorbed from great men. It has been my happy lot to meet the greatest on earth. The first really great man to become apart of my life was Elder H.

M. Wharton, of Baltimore, Md. He came to Georgetown, Ky., when I was there in college and held a protracted meeting and in my youthful eyes he was the greatest preacher in the world. I now know better but I then thought that all that was necessary was to be like Wharton and all else would fade into insignificance. I REMEMBERED his sermons. They burned into my soul and when I preached I could not help but imitate him in manner, method, and even tone of voice. I do not know how many precious souls were saved under my cheap imitation of H. M. Wharton. He was a typical evangelist, emotional, full of pathetic stories, and withal sound in the doctrine of grace. I shall always be glad that I met Wharton in my youth. He filled me with a desire for the salvation of souls and to this day I am using much of the material I ABSORBED from hearing Wharton preach, but I became enough master of myself to quit imitating him. There was only H. M. Wharton and when God made him he broke the mold and I do not think there shall ever be another like him.

"About that time I came under the influence of the stalwart T. T. Eaton, pastor of the Walnut Street Church, Louisville, Ky. If two men could be exact opposites Eaton was the exact opposite of Wharton. Wharton was soft, winsome, pathetic, a wooing sort of preacher. He was not an orator but he held his audience spellbound by his beautiful, winsome, earnest manner and O, THE MUSIC IN HIS VOICE. Eaton was rugged, strong, logical, stern, and at times very caustic. He presented ideas and he depended on his IDEAS going over. He did not move one so much as he provoked him. To hear him preach you would feel that he was so far superior to you that it humiliated. You were not DRAWN TO HIM but he DROVE YOU TO THE TRUTH. He could tell a story in a most wonderful way and his stories were not told to stir the emotions but to drive home an idea. Believe me he did drive ideas. He could say more in thirty minutes than most preachers could in two hours. To say the least of it I found myself imitating Eaton—a poor imitation to be sure, yet it was done. I imagined if I could combine Wharton's winsome ways with Eaton's stern, strong force it would be an ideal combination. Whether I succeeded or not does not matter, but I am conscious that I was greatly influenced by both men. Good for me that I was, for a young man, in the plastic state, is too apt to adopt some extreme and neglect the opposite virtue. Eaton was a good opposite to Wharton and the influence of the one counterbalanced the other. Eaton was another preacher who was unlike all others. God only made one of him and then broke the mold.

"I heard Geo. C. Lorimer, of Boston, and P. S. Henson, of Chicago, and John A. Broadus of the Louisville, Ky., Seminary, and my estimate of them is that they were just a little better than thousands of other great men of the same sort. They were each the very best in their classes but the classes were large. But *Eaton* was in a class to himself and so was Wharton. I heard J. B. Hawthorne, the best orator of them all, and he kept me thrilled with his beautiful periods and flights of fancy and eloquent gestures. He impressed me as being a wonderfully great man but did not make me think so much of what he was saying and, forgive me for saying it, Christ seemed to come in as an incident rather than the center of the sermon. But his eloquence was hopelessly beyond me and I did not try one time to imitate him.

S. H. Ford was a combination all his own and in some ways the best preacher in his day. He took great pleasure in encouraging me as a young preacher and I revered him as a father. He combined pathos, wit, logic, winsomeness like unto Wharton, with the oratory of Hawthorne, and the stern caustic elements of Eaton. Such a combination I never saw in any other man. He prepared most of his sermons in bed. His daughter, whom I knew quite well, said that when she found her father lying abed in the morning and did not get up when called that the best thing to do was to let him alone as there he would lie until his great mind had evolved a sermon. I saw him thus evolving a sermon one morning and at eleven o'clock that day he preached it and it moves me yet. I came in to see him that morning and his daughter pointed to a bed room with the door partially opened and I could see him lying on the bed and she said that he must not be disturbed as he was preparing his sermon. When I heard him preach it I was glad that I did not disturb him. Great men have their peculiarities and that was one of his. My intimate correspondence and association with Doctor Ford put valuable stuff into my life. Nobody ever tried to imitate him for there was no way to go about it. But one could absorb much of his personality and certainly he could express his ideas so that all could understand.

"I heard J. N. Hall and J. R. Graves a number of times. I never heard either of them debate. The fact is the only man I ever heard debate before I went to debating myself was Elder A. S. Pettie, and while I am at it let me say that he was a great preacher and a good debater. Pettie made things so plain, so easy, so clear that one could hardly keep from imitating him. But only a fool would try to imitate Hall and Graves. Could you imitate a cyclone or tornado? Could you imitate the swelling of the ocean? Even so, it was futile to try to do as they did. They could not be imitated. But BOTH OF THEM influenced me as I absorbed from them by hearing them preach and watching their wonderful examples. Both of them were real debaters and real evangelists. Both won wonderful victories in debate and yet from the debates they would go into revivals that would sweep whole communities. I do not hope to reach their power but the combination of debater and evangelist is my ambition."

While a student in Bethel College, the young minister preached each Saturday and Sunday. Every week end found him on his way to a church somewhere. It did not become too wet or cold, too hot or stormy or muddy for him to fill an appointment to preach. Sometimes, when he reached his preaching place, services might be "rained out" and his congregation fail to appear, but he allowed nothing to keep him from his preaching engagements. "Several country churches allowed me to practice on them," he wrote. "And they paid me a little money along, enough to about pay my railroad fare and have left over to pay my board and buy my books. Anyway I preached regularly all through my life in Bethel College. This is a fine thing for a boy preacher to do. He puts into practice what he learns as he goes along. The churches were kind to me and put up with my inexperience and imprudence and my going out to preach resulted in my meeting the young lady who afterwards became my wife."

This outstanding characteristic was almost an obsession with him for he would not miss an appointment if it were humanly possible to fill it. He had little patience with preachers who were careless about forgetting or failing to meet engagements. This is illustrated by this incident of which he wrote:

"The people at Morse Mill, Missouri, remember how I crossed Big River at Cedar Mills when the high water was raging in order to get on the Morse Mill side of the river so as not to miss an appointment there in a protracted meeting. I crossed that river in a skiff when nobody believed it could be done because of the swift current and there are several living witnesses to it living up there in Missouri right now. A great crowd came out to see me drown when they saw I was determined to cross. But they missed their guess. My experience while a boy in Kentucky enabled me to go safely over. I have always made it a rule not to miss an appointment and such a thing as an overflowing river did not stand in my way."

In October, 1889, Bogard accepted the West Mt. Zoar Church and the Mt. Zoar Church. Besides these pastorates, he preached to churches at Uniontown, Little Bethel, Smith Mills, Cedar Hall in Logan County, New Barren Springs and Concord in Christian County. He went over into Southern Indiana, seven miles from Mt. Vernon to hold a meeting. The

weather was too severe for services but he "found destitu-
tion" there. He held meetings in Little West Church, New
Hope in Henderson County, Smith Mills and New Pleasant
Hill in Christian County.

The Henderson County Association convened with Zion
Church in October of 1889 and he attended the meeting where
he was "appointed to take charge of the Walnut Bottoms mission and allowed $5.00 a trip to said mission." That same year
in July and August the state board of missions, cooperating
with Ohio Valley Association "appointed him to work as a
missionary and colporteur in the Ohio Valley Association."
He was also appointed by the District Mission Board of Ohio
Valley Association.

In September of 1889, he visited the Green River Holiness
Association in Corydon, Kentucky. He stayed for five days
and "learned much about the holiness brethren. The meeting
was filled with intense excitement."

During this year he moved his membership from his home
church, Woodland, for the first time. He received a letter of
dismission to join the Russellville Church the third Sunday in
September.

His journal shows for 1889, 144 sermons preached, 78 conversions, 75 additions, 20 baptized by himself, four revival
meetings held, three pastorates of a few months each, the organization of one church, 115 Bibles and religious books sold
and received for services the sum of $155.70.

He continued to serve West Mt. Zoar and Mt. Zoar in
Kelly as pastor through 1890 and until September, 1891, when
he resigned to accept other work. In February, he preached to
Whipporwill Church in Logan City for J. B. Shelton, pastor.
"I administered the Lord's Supper Sunday morning, February 23rd, but did not partake of it myself as I was not a member of that local church." He also preached at Crofton, Kentucky, in Woodburn, Lewisburg, Marion and at his home
church, Woodland. He held revivals in Kelly, Earlington and

Oak Grove in Logan County. At the Oak Grove Dedication he took an offering of $75.00 to pay off the debt of the church.

April 3, 1890, the Bethel Association Mission Board employed him to labor as evangelist in North Christian County during the summer. He began this work on May 24th at Mannington, Kentucky with a nine day meeting. Beginning June 20th, he held a twelve day meeting at Empire, Kentucky, followed by one at Johnson's School House near Bainbridge, Kentucky. His last mission meeting was at Macedonia, Kentucky. He was paid $1.50 a day by the board.

Other meetings he attended that year was the "Ministers and Members Meeting" of Clear Fork Association at Lewisburg, Kentucky and the Ohio Valley Association in Henderson on October 16th. At the "Ministers and Members Meeting" he discussed the subject of *Sanctification* at the request of the congregation.

He attended circle meetings numbers six and seven of Bethel Association at Crofton, Kentucky, on the Fifth Saturday in November and discussed "Foreign Missions."

In May, 1890, Bogard delivered his first "prohibition" lecture in Lewisburg, Kentucky. He wrote of his first interest in the temperance movement: "A few years after that the temperance movement came along. People were asked to sign the pledge to abstain from drink but nobody thought of such a thing as prohibiting the sale of liquor by law . . . I joined the first temperance society I ever heard of. It was the 'Independent Order of Good Templars.' That was a great educator. In that good templar lodge I learned wonderful lessons on the evils of drink. We enjoyed programs and it was in a Good Templar Lodge that I made my first speech. Got along fine until I got about half way through and there I forgot everything I ever knew and had to stop short off. I was trying my wings and fell but the effort showed me that I could use them and so I tried again. I am not the only boy who failed when he tried to make his first speech. But I am getting too fast for my nar-

Bogard with his "Temperance Ribbon"

rative.

"A short time after that I remember the first effort that was made to get any sort of prohibition. At Raleigh down in the Ohio River, was a regular doggery, a whiskey hole, and there was disorder, fights and everything else bad. A gentleman got up a petition and tried to get the people to sign it to close up that hell hole. But he was not successful. The people (most of them) said that the grog shop man 'made his living' selling liquor and they thought he had 'as much right as anybody to make a living.' So there now. The hell hole continued doing business at the same old stand. Talk about drunkenness, I saw as high as fifty Negroes and a few white men mixed in with them all in a fight at the same time. No police, no sheriff, no constable any ways near. If I did not know that such was true it would be hard to make me believe such as that ever existed.''

This third year of his ministry Bogard preached 179 sermons and enjoyed the reward of 36 conversions and 43 additions to churches. He preached in eight meetings, held two pastorates, organized four Sunday Schools, married two couples and received $236.61 for his services.

In 1891, he served the Crofton Church through November, having changed the meeting date from the second Sunday to the third Sunday of each month. He, evidently, pastored this church as a part of his work for the Bethel Mission Board, for on June 11th, he received $12.50 for the second quarter of work at Crofton, also $12.50 for the ''fourth quarter of pastoral work at Crofton,'' December 22nd and from the same board in October.

Bogard accepted the call of the Rocky Ridge Church, Trigg City, Kentucky for the second Saturday and Sunday in March, indefinitely. In September, he attended a ''fiftieth anniversary of the organization of the church, had the assistance of A. M. Meacham and John S. Cheek.'' He accepted the position as pastor of the Battle Creek Church in Coopertown, Tennessee, ''conditionally'' preaching there in September and October. He then ''closed the work'' to accept the pastorate of the church in Princeton. He preached for pastors in Earlington, Princeton and Guthrie, Kentucky, during 1891. He held a meeting in Battle Creek Church with J. W. Boyd assisting for three days, others in West Mt. Zoar, Concord Church and Minton's School House in Trigg County. J. S. Cheek assisted him in a meeting in Crofton. He preached four sermons in a Presbyterian meeting house during October at Pleasant View, Tennessee.

On the fourth Sunday in June, he ''met a large congregation of old friends and companions'' and during the third week

Lynn Onida (Owen) Bogard

of September, "a large congregation and I met many old friends" when on these two occasions he went back to preach to his home church, Woodland, in Union County.

The Little River Association met at Blue Springs Church in Caldwell County, Kentucky in August and he preached two times and took part in discussions on missions, literature and Sunday Schools. He received wages a part of the year from the Bethel Association Board of Missions for work in the Crofton Church.

He attended a circle meeting at Kelly, Kentucky, on the fifth Saturday in March and discussed "Brazil" then on Sunday, "Missions" was the topic of his sermon to them. He attended the 7th and 8th Circle Meetings of the Bethel Association the fifth Saturday and Sunday in May and discussed "Religious Literature." He visited this same circle meeting at Concord Church on the fifth Saturday in August and discussed "Foreign Missions."

MARRIED AT HIGH NOON

Somehow, in August between preaching a revival meeting, attending an association, a circle meeting and a fifth Sunday meeting, preaching every Saturday and Sunday night and some afternoons and beginning another revival meeting, the young preacher managed to find time to be married.

"I united in marriage with Linnie O. Owen on the 18th day of August, 1891, at high noon. Rev. J. W. Boyd, Kelly, Ky. officiating," he noted in his journal.

In his *Recollections,* he wrote, "I found her in Christian County, Kentucky, near Hopkinsville and I just knew she was to be my wife the first time I saw her. Lucky for me, or rather providential that I met the one I did. A man's wife, and especially a preacher's wife, can make or break him and many a wreck is found along life's way caused by a bad match called marriage."

Ben Bogard met Lynn Onida (Meacham) Owen when he went to Kelly, Kentucky, to hold a revival meeting. She was a young widow with a baby daughter. John F. Meacham and Mildred Jane (Boyd) Meacham, her parents, had two other children, a daughter, Alma, and a son, George. Lynn's husband had been Frazier Wesley Owen, Jr., a businessman who was a partner with his father in the General Mercantile business where they "sold everything from hairpins to wagon wheels."

The young, attractive widow was a serious, quiet petite girl. She had the reputation of being the most beautiful girl in Christian County. When her daughter, Lela, had grown to be a young lady of seventeen, she went back to Kentucky for a visit. A typhoid fever epidemic broke out and Lela had to get a permit after an examination so she could visit her friend. She sought the sevices of one Dr. Brown who turned out to be an old friend of the Bogard family. After asking about the health of her mother, he asked Lela, "Did you know your mother was considered the most beautiful girl in Christian County?"

"No!" cried Lela. She had never thought of her little, serious mother in such a role, remembering that Lynn's only comment on beauty was, "Just do as well as you look!"

She was, evidently, a lovely, well bred young lady, for years later when Ben Bogard was an older preacher and a successful one, he wrote: "What I am has been largely what my wife has encouraged me to be. She came of a good family and several great preachers are her blood kin. She is a real Baptist, a true child of God, an industrious worker in the church and a real keeper of the home. I count myself happy and fortunate to have such a wonderful mother, who along with a wonderful sister started me off right and then to so soon find such a true wife who has always encouraged me and in addition to that has prevented many mistakes that I would have made. I think that if it had not been for mother and wife I should never have succeeded. Jars, discords, fusses and quarrels are strangers in our home."

Mrs. Ben M. Bogard

117

IV

"SETTLED" PASTORATES

Princeton—1892-1894

Bogard served as pastor of the First Baptist Church in Princeton, Kentucky, during 1892 through June of 1894, ministering to them on the first and third Sundays of the month. He noted in his journal, "congregation increasing."

The First Baptist Church of Princeton was organized March 39, 1850. Its first meetings were held in homes and in the court house. In April of 1850 a committee was appointed to select a building site. The lot was selected and a wooden building erected which served as a home for the church until 1878. During the war between the states the Union forces took possession of the building and used it for a hospital and stable, turning the pews together to provide feeding troughs. The house was greatly damaged and in May 1876 a committee was appointed to bring the matter to the attention of the Federal government. At this same time a committee was appointed to sell the church building and secure a more convenient site for a new house. A lot was purchased and a beautiful brick building erected at a cost of about $4,000.00, then dedicated free of all indebtedness in December, 1879.

The church elected a committee to secure a parsonage "immediately" and it was secured February 10, 1892. Brother T. S. McCall, president of Bethel Female College preached for him on the third Sunday in October.

The church building was struck by lightning July 30, 1893, and remained in ruins for nearly two years. When Bogard resigned his work in Princeton in 1894, the records showed a membership of 120 and an average attendance in the Sunday

Bogard's first parsonage

School of about 60.

Of his pastorate in Princeton, he wrote, "My first settled pastorate, after leaving college was at Princeton, Kentucky, where I served the church half time and gave the other half to country churches."

The young couple moved into the new parsonage as soon as it was built, where they "made their start in a settled pastorate and where our son, Douglas, was born."

The country churches Bogard served at this same time were Rocky Ridge Church on the second Saturday nights and Sunday mornings, the congregation at Minton's School House on the second Sunday nights, and the Harmony Church on the fourth Saturday nights and Sundays. He continued work as pastor to these churches until 1894.

In addition to this work as pastor of so many churches, he preached to the church at Cerulean Springs, to a congregation in Harris School House, Willonia in Trigg County, Cedar Hill

School House, Mt. Olivet and West Union congregations in 1892 and two churches in Union City, Tennessee and Dawson, Kentucky, in 1893.

On the fifth Sunday in December 1893, Bogard preached two sermons in the church in Fulton, Kentucky, and accepted the church for "full time work." This was his first full time pastorate.

During this same period from 1892 until 1894, Bogard held meetings in these churches: Olivet (which "seemed a failure"), LaFayette, Whipporwill Church, Rocky Ridge ("two conversions from Methodists") in 1892. In 1893, he engaged in meetings with Mt. Carmel, Locust Grove, the church in Kuttawa, South Union, Whipporwill, Pinkneyville, LaFayette and in 1894, Harmony, Wingo, Arlington, Cloverport, Wingo, Oran, Missouri, Morley, Missouri, Bleda, Missouri, Diehlstadt, Missouri, Providence in Ogden, and West Union. During this period A. C. Darius preached in a meeting for him at Princeton and J. J. Porter of Jerseyville in the Fulton Church. He attended the Sinking Fork Church and spoke on "Centennial of Missions."

Other than his meetings and full time pastorate in Fulton, Bogard preached to Olivet, the church in Moscow, Union, church at Kelly, Highland, Woodland and the church in Morganfield.

Fulton, Kentucky, 1894

Bogard began his work at Fulton on the second Sunday in January and moved on the field February 14th. In the change of fields, T. E. Richey of Princeton and C. E. Perryman supplied for him in his pastorates. He resigned the Fulton Church in October. The resignation at first was protested but finally accepted to take effect at the close of the year.

About the pastorate in Fulton, Dr. Bogard wrote in his *Recollections:*

"I have made one failure in pastoral work—one only. Some of my work has not been as successful as I wanted it to be but there has only been one failure. I accepted the pastorate at Fulton, Kentucky. Wrong motives led me there. I was running away from a hard job in which it would have been glorious to succeed but I was afraid to take the risk and I saw in Fulton, Ky., a pastorate where I would be associated with J. N. Hall, one of the greatest preachers who ever lived, and he was editor of the *Baptist Gleaner,* and the fact that I would be at Fulton would put me in a place of prominence that I coveted. Remember I was young, only twenty-six years old. I offer that as my apology for this unholy ambition. It was not the right motive. A preacher should look for a place where he can be most useful and bring the greatest glory to God. But that motive was not what caused me to go to Fulton. It was worldly ambition. The result was I failed miserably. God would not give me success under such conditions.

"Several things contributed to my failure. One was J. N. Hall. He was my friend and he remained my friend until the day of his death and I cherish his memory as I do the memory of no other man who ever came into my life. But he was a GREAT MAN and in the glory of his greatness at that very time, he overshadowed me. I was measured, in the estimation of the people, by him and I could not measure up to his size. The people expected a twenty-six year old boy to preach and behave like J. N. Hall. The fact is they wanted Hall for pastor and he would not accept. He wanted to be out in the field holding meetings and debates and working for his people. But since the people could not have him for pastor they wanted the one they did have to measure up to Hall. It could not be done. So there I was. The result was I quit just in time to miss being asked to quit. I have always been able to discern what is in the minds of men and to avert calamities.

"I quit with nowhere to go. I did not have twenty-five dollars to my name. There were four of us in the family, the two children being small. My wife and children, confident as they were, never knew the fix I was in. I have made it a rule to never tell any discouraging thing at home.

"Just then, I shall never know why, I received an invitation to come to Cloverport, Ky., and conduct a protracted meeting. I just did have money enough to buy my railroad ticket and leave a little change with my wife to pay the small bills that must be met. When I arrived in Cloverport I had exactly fifteen cents in my pocket. I stayed there two weeks and the Lord gave us a great revival and between thirty and forty were saved and about as many baptized. They paid me well for my services and I went home not knowing what next. In about a week there came a call to come over into Missouri and hold some meetings at Oran and Morley, Mo. I went and the Lord showered His blessings and a great revival came to both churches, then I went to Deihlstadt, Mo., and held a protracted meeting. Some of the brethren at Charleston, Mo. heard about a young preacher holding a meeting at Deihlstadt and they came up there to hear me preach and they told me they were looking for a pastor and wanted to know if I would come and preach a sample sermon for them. I told them I was not put up in sample packages and I could not do it. I never have believed in preaching sample sermons and I have never done such a thing in my life. The brethren went back and reported that a very independent young preacher was at Deihlstadt and that if they wanted to sample me they would have to go there and fall into the meeting and see for themselves. Some of them did so and the result was I was called to Charleston, Mo., for full time and they gave me a preacher's home, that they called a 'parsonage,' to live in and the salary was sufficient to live on in comfort. I stayed there four years and formed life time friendships and the Lord blessed my labors there.

"Just then came a mysterious call to Searcy, Ark., for a protracted meeting. Why on earth did they call for me in Arkansas? I came to find out that Joe G. Hall, a brother of J. N. Hall, had moved to Searcy and he it was who called their attention to me. The result was that my failure at Fulton, Ky., resulted in forming the friendship of Joe Hall and through that human instrumentality I was brought to Arkansas. God was in it and He overruled my Fulton failure for good and as I see it now I never would have come to Arkansas if I had not gone to Fulton. Very nearly all that I have ever accomplished in life came out of that failure." But we are getting ahead of our story.

In 1895, Bogard accepted the care of the church in Wingo, Kentucky, preaching to them every third Sunday. In June he resigned this work to assume the full time pastorate of the church in Charleston, Missouri. He began his work there in April, noting, "the work started off well," and served as their pastor until the first Wednesday evening in January, 1899, when he resigned to accept the care of the church in Searcy, Arkansas. During this tenure of duty, he assisted in the ordination of W. T. Atwood at New Bethel Church near Charleston where "I conducted the examination," evidently the first time he had acted in this capacity in an ordination service.

While pastor at Charleston, he had to witness the sentencing of a criminal. This was his story of the incident:

"While I was pastor of the First Baptist Church, Charleston, Missouri, two brothers, Joe and Jim Albright, had committed murder. When the officers went to arrest them they resisted the officers. When the sheriff had failed to take them, the Prosecuting Attorney, who had been a friend of the criminals, went out to their house where they had barricaded themselves and sought to persuade them to surrender. Jim Albright shot the Prosecuting Attorney and he died soon after he was shot. Thus the crime became a double and an aggravated one.

Later they were surrounded and captured and Joe died of pneumonia before he could be brought to trial. Poor Jim was tried and convicted and condemned to die by hanging. I heard all of the trial. He was guilty. He stood up for sentence and I never shall forget the words of the judge as he gave the sentence. He told him what a terrible crime he had committed and that the jury had found him guilty and now it was his sad duty to pronounce sentence. He set the time for the execution and said that upon that date, 'You shall be hanged by the neck until you are dead, dead, dead, and may the Lord have mercy on your soul.''

"Again my heart came up into my throat. I thought of the final great day when final judgment will be pronounced on poor lost sinners. It was just too bad. He deserved to die but how very bad it all was. The grace of God had been spurned and the terrible end came. On the date set he was hanged. I did not see it. I did not want to see it for one scene was enough for me. But I saw the throng that came to see it and saw the funeral procession of his very few friends who followed him to his disgraceful grave. And his old mother was there! It was not so bad to be hanged as it was for the poor mother who must suffer like that.

"About six months after that Jim Albright's sister got married and they sent for me to come out to that country home and perform the ceremony. When I got there I was met at the door by the heartbroken mother. She gave me a seat in the front room and on the wall was the picture of J. R. Graves. She pointed to the picture and said: 'Do you know who that is?' I assured her that I did and that I was a great admirer of Graves. Then she said: 'I am a Baptist of the J. R. Graves sort. I lived for a long time in Tennessee and tried to be faithful to my church. But my husband was such a sinner that I dropped out. Then came the terrible crime of my sons which broke my heart. I have seen better days.'

She broke down and wept and I wept with her. Poor woman! Sin had ruined her life and yet she was not guilty. Her husband had been killed in a fight and her boy, Joe, had died and thus escaped the gallows and Jim had been hanged. Her daughter only was left, now she was leaving home. Tragedy! Sin did it. I tried to comfort her but what could comfort a woman when her husband and two sons died as criminals and had gone to hell? Brother preacher, you will have to experience the like of this to understand what I had on my hands in this case.

"But for the grace of God I might have been a Bob Fowler or a Jim Albright. God knows the poor mother mentioned needed the grace of God to sustain her while going through all this."

First Baptist Church, Searcy, Arkansas, 1899 — 1903

He began his duties in Searcy on February 1, 1899, noting in his journal, "My pastorate in Searcy is, all things considered, the most satisfying I ever held."

Churches to whom he preached other than his pastorate in Charleston during these years were: the church in Fulton, Kentucky (1895), the churches in Oran, Audubon, Missouri, and Smith Mills, Kentucky ("Here I met old friends of other years"), 1898.

In 1895 he held meetings in Oran, Morley, Bleda, Diehlstadt, Missouri, the Providence Church in Ogden, Kentucky, West Union Church and had the assistance of T. N. Compton to help him in a meeting in Charleston. In 1896 C. F. J. Gate assisted him at Charleston and he helped A. J. Edmonson in Sikeston, Missouri, E. L. Craig, in Cairo, Missouri, W. K. Rudolph at Vienna, Illinois and F. W. Taylor at Louisville, Kentucky. In 1897 he assisted H. J. LaTour at Oak Ridge, Missouri, J. A. Hamlin at DeSota, Missouri, and held a meeting

in Caruthersville. F. W. Taylor and Harry A. Belton helped
in a revival meeting at Charleston. In 1898 he worked with W.
G. Reeves in Bloomfield, Missouri and A. L. Powell in Searcy,
Arkansas, and in 1899, assisted W. M. Barker at El Dorado
Springs, G. C. Harris at Mt. Home, Arkansas, M. T. Webb at
Beebe, T. C. Mahan, Walnut Ridge and New Hope Church in
Lonoke County, Arkansas. At Searcy, he had the assistance of
Harry A. Belton for three weeks during which time, he
"trained the choir and congregation singing and preached a
few sermons."

Of his pastorate in Searcy, Arkansas, from February,
1899 through 1903, he wrote in his *Recollections:*

"When I came to Searcy as pastor they were worshiping
in an old dilapidated meeting house. Efforts had been made
to get money enough to repair the building and they could not
raise four hundred dollars, the amount necessary to make the
repairs that were absolutely necessary to make the decency
and comfort of the building. I held a protracted meeting in
which about thirty were received for baptism. I suggested to
the church that we build a new ten thousand dollar house.
They said it could not be done, that they were not strong
enough, and besides that they had even failed to raise the four
hundred necessary to repair the old house. So I met with dis-
couragement from the start. I kept pressing and pressing until I got them to agree to build sometime in the future and that
we would work toward that end.

"The next move was to secure a suitable location for the
new building. I selected a fine location and learned that the
three lots could be bought for six hundred dollars. I then insisted that we raise the money and buy the ground. It took
heroic effort to get the money. They had cold feet but when I
finally showed them that the ground would not run away and
we could buy it and let it wait our time to build they permitted
me to go on and secure the money and buy the lots. They would
constantly remind me of the fact that they had failed to raise

the four hundred dollars to repair the old house. I tried to show them that we could raise ten thousand dollars as easily as we could raise the four hundred. When you come at a man with a four hundred dollar proposition he cuts his contribution to fit. He will give you possibly five dollars and may be less for it is not much and thinks 'if all will do as well as I have done it can be easily raised.' But when you go at him with a ten thousand dollar proposition he sees the need of liberality and will bring himself up to that point. Our people have done business on the peanut and pop corn idea too long. That is one chief reason why we do so little. We do not attempt great things for God and do not expect great things from God.

"The old house was badly located—away out to one side of town as is usually the case with our people. It seems that Baptists formed the habit of hiding out during the days of papal persecution and they seem unable to get out of the bad habit. How many times do we see a Baptist church house stuck off to one side as if we were ashamed to come to the front? So I told the Searcy people that we should put the new church down in town where a stranger would not have to get a blood hound to hunt the church. We bought the lot. That was at least a start.

"The next move that nearly caused some of them to fall over was to suggest that we secure a good architect to draw plans for a ten thousand dollar house. Some fought it. That never fails. *You can count on somebody fighting anything that looks like a forward move.* But we overcame that opposition and paid two hundred and fifty dollars for the picture of the proposed new house. That picture, with the specifications, was brought to the meetings of the church and the people saw what was proposed. Then I said, 'Let us raise the money and build the foundation' and some said it could not be done. But they ALLOWED me to go on and try. I tried and secured six hundred and thirty dollars, the amount necessary to pay for the foundation. The foundation looked good but right there we had to stop. Money was all gone and no more in sight. The foundation was covered up and the work stopped.

"Just at this point I visited Miss Mary Gentry, who has since then married Mr. Walter Welch and is now a widow, and was talking with her about making a nice contribution toward building the church. I went to her hoping to get five hundred dollars. When I had related to her the situation and that if some one would lead off with a nice contribution it would start an interest that might put us over the top, so to speak, she said: "I have been thinking about this matter and have decided to make a contribution. I have some surplus money and would like to give it to the new building and I wonder if three thousand dollars would be enough for me to give?""

"I was astonished. My prayer had been more than answered. I told her to give her check for twenty-five hundred dollars and hold back the five hundred for a time of future need. She did so and the two thousand and five hundred was in the bank to the credit of the building committee in less than an hour.

"Next Sunday I related to the church what Miss Gentry had done and it certainly set things astir. One brother got up and said he saw now that he had been foolish in holding back and wanted to contribute two hundred and fifty dollars. Another said he was ashamed of himself for having held back, not believing he could give five hundred dollars and so it ran on until nearly the whole amount needed was subscribed and the building went right on up. At the time it was completed it was the finest Baptist Church house in the state of Arkansas and it is not far behind even now for, notwithstanding it has been standing there for more than a quarter of a century, it is still a very nice church house. I stayed on and preached the Gospel in that meeting house for three years after the new house was built and resigned to accept the pastorate of the First Baptist Church in North Little Rock. My work in Searcy was a glorious success. I suppose I baptized not less than one

hundred during the five years I was there, and NO DEBT
WAS LEFT ON THE CHURCH. I hate debt. In all my work
I have fought the idea of debt and so far have managed to
keep the churches where I have preached out of debt except in
a small way.

"The Searcy work was the envy of the convention people.
It was a strong church and had a fine church house and they
wanted it. I did not think of rascality and church stealing and
so did not have the deed to the property fixed so they could
not steal it and no sooner than I left they began to set their
plans to steal the church. There were a few convention men in
the church and they objected to every preacher that was suggested—something wrong with every one of them. Their real
reason was they did not want an association Baptist preacher
but wanted to hire work till they could get a convention
preacher. They got a bunch of exactly nine convention men
and one lady who was not a conventionite together on a very
rainy day and called J. S. Rogers. The lady protested but they
went on any way. When the membership learned what had
been done, they made a mistake in not meeting at once and declaring the action of that faction void and calling a preacher
in harmony with the church. But they reasoned that one year
will soon be out and we can get rid of Rogers and call another
preacher then.

"But they reasoned incorrectly. They had not had any experience with convention schemers. Rogers came and began
work when he knew that the situation was as I have related it.
The brethren refused to help support him and they thought
they would freeze him out. But the STATE BOARD came to
his rescue and put up enough to tide him over. Meantime four
of our leading brethren died. Some moved away. Rogers held
a protracted meeting and got in near seventy young members
who of course were largely subject to his will, naturally so for
they had joined the church under his preaching. Thus by death
and removals and the new members who had come in he se-

cured a majority by the end of the year and he continued until
he landed the church in the convention. That was the first big
church steal we experienced.

"I built that church. Those who know, will tell you and
some are still living to testify, that it would not have been
built if I had not done what I have related in this article. My
name and my picture are in the cornerstone. But I would not
be welcome to even preach in the house that I built and as I
go along the streets of Searcy, as I have done several times
since leaving there, my recollections are sad indeed concerning how we lost the great work and how my five years there
as pastor was largely nullified by this convention scheme. But
the large number who were saved under my preaching there
will not call the work I did a failure. It was indeed a success.
But the experience of that church should teach us to have
deeds to church property fixed so that conventionites can't
steal the houses after we build them."

Even though Bogard's time was well filled pastoring
churches and preaching to others, he managed to attend many
of the associational meetings. In 1896, he was elected clerk
and preached one sermon in the meeting of the Charleston Association at Harmony Church, four miles from Birds Point,
Missouri, where he attended as a messenger from First Baptist Church, Charleston, Missouri.

In 1897, he "attended a meeting at Mexico, Missouri,
called the Brothers Union. The meeting was in session from
June 24th to 28th. The object of the meeting was to discuss
Gospel Missions and to see if those who are called Regular
Baptists and those known as Gospel Mission Baptists are
agreed as to doctrine and practice. The meeting was perfectly
harmonious and all differences were laid aside and both sides
agreed to henceforth work along the same lines. Reverend G.
P. Bortick, a missionary returned on vacation from China,
and myself were invited to be present and address the meeting which we did. These Regular Baptists have been known

as 'hardshells.' While on this trip I preached at Mt. Gilead Church in Howard County, Missouri, where the Regular Baptists and Missionary Baptists were worshipping in what they called a 'union house.' "

That year he attended the Cape Girardeau Association at Oak Ridge, Missouri, and engaged in some of the discussions and was messenger to the Charleston Association at New Bethel Church near Charleston where he was elected clerk and preached the introductory message, also engaging in some of the discussions.

In 1898, Bogard attended the Ministers and Members Meeting, Charleston Association at Oran where he discussed missions and the Franklin Association, Farmington, Missouri where he preached one sermon and took part in discussions and "while there many new acquaintances were made." He went to the twenty second annual session of the Charleston Association at Vanduser, Missouri, where he was elected clerk for the third time and made reports on Education and Charleston Baptist College, as well as one from the Advisory Board.

Bogard went to the Caroline Association at Beebe, Arkansas in 1899 as a messenger from the Searcy Church. Here he made a report on Foreign Missions and "preached at the Baptist Church by appointment of the body." He went as a messenger from the Searcy Church to the Baptist State Convention in Jonesboro and said of this meeting: "It was a splendid gathering and harmony prevailed. I served on the Committee on Negro Education and spoke once in the Sunday afternoon missionary mass meeting. I preached by appointment on Sunday night at the Second Baptist Church."

During the first twelve years of his ministry, up to the turn of the century, he summarized his work in his journal: 67 meetings held, 27 denominational meetings attended, 74 funerals conducted, 3250 pastoral visits made, 56 marriage ceremonies performed, 2100 sermons preached, 106 other speeches and addresses, 260 prayer meetings held, two churches organized, assisted in ordaining 3 deacons and one preacher, two church houses dedicated, and 647 conversions witnessed under his preaching. He baptized 178 of these and had 724 additions to the churches in his work. For his services during these years, he was paid $7,132.97. During this time, he served as pastor of eleven churches, though some of these were three and four at a time.

In these twelve fruitful years the young preacher had learned many things. Note some of these experiences during that time which taught him such valuable lessons:

"Hard knocks are good for anybody as it toughens and strengthens. We are told to endure hardships and to even rejoice in tribulations and persecutions. My disposition, my nervous constitution, is such that I do not suffer under opposition as some men do. I am not excitable, perfectly cool under all circumstances and in all situations, yet there were some things that came my way when a boy preacher that tried me to the limit. Some of these things come into every young preacher's life but I think I had a few that others have been graciously permitted to miss.

"I will mention a few of the ordinary trials of a young preacher first. One is flattery. The people are gushy over a boy peacher. They tell him he is a wonder and that he has the older preachers bested by a wide margin. If the young preacher will only live a few years he will become a Spurgeon. Such is the impression made by the gushy friends. You need much of the grace of God to overcome such as that. I think I was told a hundred times that such a wonderful preacher as I was did not need to go on in school for I could beat those who had gone to school already and I have never ceased to thank God that I had sense enough to know that this was bad advice.

"The fact that he is a young 'boy preacher' will draw the crowd. They come through curiosity. Then his youth attracts the young people especially. And the girls—Nuf said. They act the fool over any young preacher. There are two reasons why the girls act the fool over young preachers. One is the good girl wants a clean young man for a husband and if not for a husband she likes to be with a young man who is of good character and she concludes that surely the young preacher is that sort of man. Sometimes they are sadly disillusioned. I have known some young preachers who were very bad. They soon come to the end of their row. They wind up with a scandal and get out of the ministry. The mystery is that more of them do not go to the bad.

"Then come the bad girls. One would not think that bad girls would care for preachers. But they do. The bad girl thinks it is great to get a preacher boy going her way. Every boy preacher has this trial. It is playing with fire and, alas, some get burnt. The marvel is that there are so few young preachers who go wrong. They have the opportunity but the grace of God prevails in the great majority of cases.

"My opinion is that very few young preachers ever go wrong. The few who do are, in nine cases out of ten, caught and exposed. They soon run their course and the result is that nearly all preachers who go on with the work for any length of time, by that very fact, prove that they are clean men. My experience along that line greatly increases my confidence in preachers.

"Another trial a boy preacher is compelled to pass through I experienced in full measure. There are those who flatter, as I have just said, but there is the very opposite to be endured. There are many who seem to think that a boy preacher should be fully settled on all parts of the ground and that he should be practically infallible and there is no allowance made for age. If he goes with the girls he is called a flirt and if he does not go with them they say he thinks himself too good to associate with 'OUR GIRLS.' He no doubt 'goes with the rich girls' over yonder somewhere but thinks himself above our people. If he wears good clothes he is 'stuck up' and 'has more money than we have and hence we will not pay him anything. If he dresses shabbily he 'ought to go to work' and make some money and buy decent clothes. If they ask him a question he cannot answer he is a very poor excuse of a preacher and, believe me, they pour the questions in.

"Two actual experiences I had, I will relate. One was over in the hill country in Kentucky. I was preaching during vacation (school vacation) and I knew the sort of place I was to hold the meeting in and I selected what was once a good suit of clothes but was worn threadbare. I was actually ashamed to wear it where I was known. I preached through the meeting and we had a good revival and I remember distinctly that there were seven baptisms as a result of the meeting. They paid me the sum of one dollar and fifty-five cents. When the good brother who raised the money gave it to me he said: 'I am sorry that I could not raise more for you but the people say that since you dress so fine they think you have more money than they have and would not give anything.' He was not making sport of me. They actually thought I was dressed up like a rich man. Right then I did not have five dollars to my name and wanted so much to get a little money ahead so I could go back to school the next fall. But I forgave them and meekly took my medicine. It was ignorance on their part.

"Another experience that is common to young preachers was that I became obsessed with the idea I should be an evangelist. They all get that way. The excitement, the glamour, the activity it calls for attracts a young preacher. I was saved from that foolishness by a habit of mine that has stayed with me all through the years. I watch successful men and note the things that make for their success and try to copy them as closely as possible. Doctor T. T. Eaton, and Doctor J. M. Pendleton were my ideals for preachers. I read an editorial by Eaton in the *Western Recorder* that said that this notion all young preachers seem to get should be resisted at least until after the young preachers have some experience as pastor so he would know what a pastor has to contend with. I saw his point. Then came Doctor Pendleton, who was active at the time, and as pastor held a wonderful meeting in the church where he was pastor and in reporting it gave a note of warning about certain evangelistic methods that are harmful to the churches. I changed my mind and decided that I would be a pastor and along with my pastoral work do as much evangelistic work as possible and I never cease to thank God for the decision I made. It has made my ministry a success. It caused me to be in direct touch with both evangelisic work and pastoral work and a preacher is not what he ought to be unless he knows both sides of the work. If this experience shall help any of our preacher boys I shall be glad.

"Soon after I had a most trying experience. It came near driving me out of the ministry. I was seated in church. Spring Grove, Ky., and a man fell down with a terrible epileptic fit. It did not do my nerves any good. But I shook it off. Then I went to Crofton, Ky., and as I preached, a man fell over in a terrible fit. Of course it ruined the service and coming so soon after the other experience it weighed on me. I then went on down to West Mt. Zoar Church, near Kelley, Ky., and preached and while I preached another man fell with epilepsy, a most nerve racking thing. It was getting on my nerves, one coming right behind the other and all of them in church service. I went from there to Battle Creek, Tennessee, and while I was preaching a man fell with the most terrible fit I ever saw. It broke up the service. A dear brother invited me home with him and I was almost afraid to go to sleep lest I have a fit myself. If you have never had such a series of things like that you can't appreciate my feelings. Next morning at the breakfast table a lady sitting right by my side eating fell with a hard epileptic fit. I was nearly crazy. It looked as if an evil spirit was pursuing me. Then I went to the Blue River Association in Kentucky. An arbor was built near the church where they had preaching for the overflow crowds. The messengers

would stay in the house and transact business and preachers
would take it turn about preaching to the overflow crowd under the arbor. They sent 'the boy preacher' out to the arbor.
While I was preaching the best I could a lady on the front seat
fell with a terrible fit.

"I made up my mind to quit. God pity me. It was the most
trying thing I have ever had. I did not quit. Nobody has had
any more fits in my services from that day to this. But one
more would have ruined me.

"My confidence in humanity led me into several dangerous places. At Spottsville, Ky., to illustrate, the bad boys
actually staked out a bad girl to ensnare me. She failed to get
my attention in all other ways and as a last resort came to the
mourners bench pretending to be seeking the Lord and thus
compelled me to give her some attention. I talked with her
about her soul and she invited me to her home to talk some
more. I went. I soon found she was seeking me and not the
Lord. Talk about boys leading girls astray all you please, but
that girl did her level best to ensnare me and failing she went
back to her pals, who had staked her out for me, and told them
that she had made a failure and one of the dear boys, who was
saved along with 44 others during the meetings, came and told
me what had been done. HE WAS WAITING TO SEE IF
SHE SUCCEEDED BEFORE HE SOUGHT THE LORD!
If I had yielded to that siren's song that boy might never have
been saved! I had no idea that there was so much at stake! I
had no idea that so many were watching to see what would
happen! It makes me think of the wonderful song:

'Through many dangers, toils and snares
    I have already come,
'Tis grace has led me safe thus far
    And grace will lead me home.' "

V

THE TURN OF THE CENTURY

At the beginning of the new century, Ben Bogard was still pastor of First Baptist Church in Searcy, Arkansas. During this year, J. N. Hall, of Fulton, Kentucky, editor of the *American Baptist Flag*, assisted him in a series of evangelistic services. Though there were no "visible results" this meeting was a high point in the young minister's life for he greatly admired Hall.

A new church building was constructed at a cost of $10,000. It was made of pressed brick trimmed with stone and had a slate roof. The inside finish was of hardwood. Construction went on during 1901 and in March 1902, the church moved into a new home. The pastor felt the congregation was progressing with great strides, for he wrote: "The church was never more prosperous than now," and toward the end of the year, "On Sunday morning November 30, the church, having been given a week's previous notice, by private, secret ballot, reelected me as pastor, only two voting in the negative. This I esteemed very complimentary as I had been pastor in Searcy about four years and had gone through the struggle of building a new church house and had spent so much of my time away from the field engaged in newspaper work. The church was never before so thoroughly a unit on all propositions. The call, as was the first, was for an indefinite period and not for a year as is so often the custom with churches. This practically ends four years service as pastor in Searcy and a new year will begin with uncertainty as to the future. The relations between pastor and church is pleasant."

He stayed with the church until the close of 1903 when he resigned to accept a call from the First Baptist Church of

An early photograph. Bogard was immaculate in dress and clean of body.

Another early photo. Bogard beginning to show age, but before he wore
glasses. This picture reflects the high forehead and sharp eyes
of keen intellect.

North Little Rock, then known as Argenta, his services to begin December first.

During these first three years of the century, Bogard preached to a number of churches other than his pastorate and held many evangelistic campaigns. The churches were: 1900, Dripping Springs Church, White County, Arkansas, and in 1903, he preached one sermon at Fulton, Kentucky, where ''I met many old friends but there had been many changes since I was pastor there ten yars ago. While in Fulton, I conducted funeral services for Harold, son of Joe G. Hall.'' He preached to Liberty Church at Walkers, Arkansas, Woodlawn Church at Wilmar and made a tour of the Bartholomew Association preaching in Hamburg to the Promise Land Church, Berea, Enon, Shilo, Flat Creek and Monticello, where he ''did good business for the paper, preached ten sermons, took two collections for missions . . . sold some books and made many friends.''

He preached to the Bethlehem Church in Little Rock a number of times. Although never pastor of this church, he was nevertheless, vitally connected with it. In his *Recollections* he wrote of it:

''Recollections of Bethlehem Church, Little Rock, Ark., are filling my mind today. This is a church I saw when it was born and then I watched it die. Jesus said: ''Upon this rock I will build my church and the gates of hell shall not prevail against it'' (Matt. 16:18), and the church institution has lived on according to that promise until now and shall live on to the end of the world. But individual congregations have come and gone, served the Lord for a number of years then died. Bethlehem Church was one that served God for some twenty-five years and then passed away. It is a case of the Lord removing the ''candlestick'' (Rev. 2:5), as He threatened to do with a church in Asia and such things have been experienced all through the ages.

''When I was pastor at Searcy, Ark., I was asked to come

to Little Rock and help organize a church and when I came I
met Elder W. A. Clark and a few of his friends and we gathered in a little three-room house at 26th and Bishop Streets,
away out in the suburbs of Little Rock. Possibly fifteen or
twenty were there. It was in the center of a growing section of
Little Rock that has since built up until a large population
surrounds the place where the church started. The prospect
pleased and it seemed to be the Lord's will that the church be
established. It was done.

"Several preachers labored in the early years of the
church and it grew and prospered. It ran up in numbers until
possibly seventy or eighty members belonged there. For several years it was a full time church and Elder Frank Davis
preached every Sunday there. Then came Eld. G. S. Anderson
and he preached every Sunday for at least two years. Then
came a church fuss and a number of the members went out and
joined Central Church further down in town, a church that
was established on the DEMERITS of other churches and
was made up of disgruntled members from other congregations and that church soon became involved in discord and
church fusses until it broke up in confusion and the members
scattered. The disgruntled members who went out from Bethlehem were samples of the other and Central Church died. It
ought never to have lived and its living had much to do with
the beginning of the downfall of Bethlehem Church. Some
mighty fine people were involved in the trouble. but they were
led into it by others and were made to suffer because of it.
Some of them went to the convention, some "went to the
dogs,' figuratively speaking, and a few still tried to serve God
in a Scriptural way.

"Bethlehem Church never fully rallied after this church
trouble and it was the beginning of a series of troubles that
finally led to its death as a church. As I think back I am filled
with emotion because of the recollection of some of the finest
people who ever lived who held their membership in Bethle-

hem Church.

There was Brother Elijah Sears, a real friend and brother of this writer. He was for some time the business manager of the Baptist Sunday School Committee which had its beginning in Little Rock. His good wife did most of the work but he held the official position. He held that position until Elder M. P. Matheny became manager and Matheny was also a member of Bethlehem.

Brother Elijah Sears' daughter, Mrs. Kathryn (Sears) Heard, was Brother Bogard's nurse at the time of his death.

"Matheny was one of the noblest men who ever lived, a great man, a great preacher, and a true friend. I saw him tried fully in more than one time of trial.

"Then came Eld. W. M. Barker, one time business manager of the *Baptist Publishing Company* and later editor of the *Baptist Flag*. He was a great preacher, one of the best I ever heard. He was that sort of men who would die rather than surrender a principle. Elder W. A. Clark, one of the real noblemen, with whom I labored for four years in the old *Arkanansas Baptist,* was another worthy who was in Bethlehem Church. It was my privilege to hold membership with all these worthies for I held membership in Bethlehem until I moved to Texas.

"The church continued to exist, but barely more than to exist, for several years until the trouble came into Antioch Church and the pastor of Bethlehem seemed to think he saw an opportunity to capitalize on the trouble in Antioch by siding in with those who were making the trouble, hoping to get them into Bethlehem Church by that means. Antioch excluded thirteen members who sided with the trouble maker and since that time has gone on in peace and harmony and has grown from a small church of one hundred members to over three hundred members. These thirteen excluded members were invited to join Bethlehem, which they did. Because of that fact (receiving excluded members into its fellowship), Bethlehem was refused a seat in the Baptist State Association. One of Bethlehem's true souls told me that she prayed as ferverently as she ever did in her life that the church might not be received into the association because she knew it was not of God. She was a member there but had no power to prevent the ungodly work that was done, but she could pray. Her prayer was answered and while she knew it meant the downfall of the Bethlehem Church she rejoiced because right had triumphed over wrong. This good sister attends Antioch Church regularly now and has always stood true to the cause. Those were troublous times and hearts ached but right triumphed and it meant the death of Bethlehem.

"Here is how it went: Four of the thirteen excluded ones left Bethlehem and went into a convention church. Two moved away into the northern part of Arkansas; one weak woman ran away with another man and left a heart broken husband and a little child about four years old and has not been heard of since. Three others moved into a Negro section of Little Rock and never go to church except once in a while they go to the nearby Negro church—down and out so far as religious life is concerned. One poor man of the thirteen hanged himself to a rafter in his garrett and his cold dead body was found by his wife some hours after the terrible deed. What became of the other two I do not know. The pastor who invited them to join, when he knew they were excluded from what he ought to have regarded as a sister church, left the Baptists and went to the Presbyterians, the fact being that he never was a real Baptist, and the few who were left were discouraged and overwhelmed with opposition and they gave up. The remnant, seeing the injury that had been done, and recognizing that God's blessing had been withdrawn, got together and made amends for the evil that had been done so far as they could by selling the church property and giving the money to our Missionary Baptist College at Sheridan and then gave each other letters and disbanded. The church did a great deal of good. Souls

were saved within its meeting house and they gave assistance
to the mission cause but because of disorder and sin the "candlestick' was removed. The church is no more. Its memory is
pathetic. May we all learn the sad lesson."

Revivals held the first three years of the century were:
El Dorado Springs, Missouri where he assisted W. M. Barker
(who later assisted him at Searcy) ; Carlisle, Arkansas, where
he assisted C. A. Ownes; Melbourne, Arkansas with William
L. Smith; El Paso, Arkansas, with M. T. Webb; Little Union
Church near Morganfield, Kentucky, with C. H. Gregston;
these were in 1900. In 1901: assisted S. S. Sims in Benton,
Arkansas; with B. J. Matthews at Zion Hill about seven miles
from Little Rock; helped J. A. Smith in Haynes, Arkansas
and T. A. Conway in Rock Springs Church in Webster County, Kentucky. Each of these meetings lasted from five to
twenty days. In 1902: Second Baptist Church, Ft. Smith; M.
S. Kelly at Prattsville; Plumerville, Arkansas; Haynes, Ark.
In 1903: Bradley (Indian Territory) ; Antioch Baptist Church
in Little Rock, Arkansas with L. Guinn. This totaled seventeen evangelistic campaigns (684 sermons) these three years
in addition to his full time pastoral work, his travels in interest of the paper and missions and the various churches he
preached for.

He recalled many experiences of these meetings. In his
Recollections, he wrote:

"Some little things that have come into my life make me
think of the Savior's statement that a "cup of cold water giv-
en to a disciple" shall not lose its reward.

"Nearly thirty years ago while in a protracted meeting at
Prattsville, Arkansas I was in the humble home of Elder Miles
Kelly, at that time, I think, pastor at Prattsville. But of that I
am not sure for possibly Elder Joshua Halbert was pastor or
it might have been that Elder Wm. Tucker was the pastor.
But that is beside the purpose of this narrative. All three of
these dear brethren were in that meeting with me, but I did

the preaching. Being a visitor in the Kelly home I asked where I could find the water and Brother Kelly said, 'I will get the water for you,' and he went and brought me a big gourd full of water. I told him that he should have allowed me to get the water for myself and he replied, 'I want the reward the Savior promised when He said that if we give a cup of cold water to a disciple we shall not lose our rewad.' That remark impressed me and I have told it many times where I have preached. I have been the happy recipient of such a 'cup of cold water,' as it were, many times in my life.

"Twenty years ago I was at Hartford, Arkansas, tired and weary and my head was aching. I had been out in the country and had gone through a strenuous day and was what we call 'all in.' A good brother came by the railroad station where I waited for a train and saw me and invited me over to his house to eat supper. I told him I feared that we did not have time for that and I did not want the train to leave me. He went off and in a few minutes came back with a big cup of hot coffee and said that he wanted me to drink it as it might help my head. I drank it and sure enough it eased my aching head. I cannot tell how much I appreciated that cup of coffee. It was such a kindly act. I shall never forget it and I believe that he did exactly what the Lord meant when He spoke of the cup of cold water. 'Inasmuch as ye have done it unto one of the least of these my brethren, ye have done it unto me.' When he meets the Lord and the Lord reminds him of the cup of coffee he gave through Him at Hartford, Arkansas, the dear brother may not remember it, but the Lord remembers.

Back in the old Indian Territory days, before there was any such state as Oklahoma, I was out in that territory holding a protracted meeting. When the meeting closed and I was asleep on the train that was taking me out of the red man's land, our train was wrecked. I was awakened by the shock and looking out of my car window I saw the cars were turned over on their sides and the one I was in was almost turned over.

The track was torn up for a long stretch and there we were. It was about six o'clock in the morning and there was no dining car on the train for they did not have them at that time and there was no eating house anywhere near. I was hungry. I asked the conductor how long we would be there and he said it would be in the afternoon when we could get away. I pulled out over the hill looking for somebody who might have something to eat. I saw a tent and went to it and in the tent I found an Indian squaw with three Indian babies. I asked her if I could get breakfast and she said I could. While I was eating that Indian breakfast, her husband, a big buck Indian, came riding up. I ate on and enjoyed my corn bread, boiled beef and coffee. The Indian man never spoke to me until I had finished eating and then I offered them pay for my breakfast and he said, 'No pay for eat. Indian glad to feed white man.' I thanked them both for their kindness and gave the little fellows a nickel each and beat it back to the train. I did wrong in leaving as I did. I should have tarried long enough to have read a portion of God's Word and preached them a sermon and offered prayer for them but I did not. How bad it is that we miss such opportunities. I suppose all of us failed to use opportunities to speak for our Lord and I regret that I missed this one. That Indian family did not know they were entertaining a Baptist preacher but the Lord knows they fed a representative of His and I wonder if that Indian and his squaw will be reminded in the judgment that they fed a Baptist preacher that morning and in doing so they fed the Lord Jesus since what is done to one of the Lord's servants—brethren—is counted as done to Him. 'A cup of cold water given to a disciple shall not lose its reward.'

"All this reminds me. If you are to enjoy a flower garden you must first plant the flowers and cultivate them. Our lives when looked back on after the lapse of years, will be like a flower garden or a field of weeds. Which? If we fill our lives full of good things and kindly deeds and pleasant experiences we can in our memory look back on a beautiful flower garden. If we misspend our life and fill it with evil deeds and unhappy experiences we shall have a patch of weeds to view from memory's hill top of recollections.''

Of his resignation to the First Baptist Church in Searcy, he wrote: ''Having received a call to the care of the First Baptist Church of North Little Rock (Argenta) Arkansas, I resigned at Searcy and accepted the work to begin December 1, 1903.'' He had finished nearly five years of pastoral work in Searcy.

First Baptist Church, North Little Rock, Arkansas

Ben M. Bogard was pastor of First Baptist Church of Argenta (now North Little Rock), Arkansas, from December 1903 until the end of 1904 when he resigned, saying, ''It is my purpose to spend some time in general field and evangelisitc work.''

During the year 1904, in addition to pastoral duties, Bogard preached to churches in Augusta, Trenton, Russellville, Spring Creek near Elm Springs, Springdale, Clarksville and gave the address at the cornerstone laying of Landmark Baptist Church, England.

On the field in 1905, during the month of January, he preached five sermons in Wynne, Arkansas which ''resulted in the better element of the church withdrawing from a large body of irregular, disorderly members and forming an independent, separate church.'' Other churches to whom he preached that year were in Deleware, Bald Knob, New Hope in Grant County, Bethlehem and Pilgrim Rest near Little Rock, Arkansas, in Fulton, Kentucky, South McAlester in Indian Territory and the dedication sermon of the Bethlehem Baptist Church in Little Rock on the first Sunday in May when the church was dedicated free of debt.

In June he made a tour of Kentucky in the interest of the Baptist Publishing Company and preached to churches in Morganfield, Woodland, Mt. Olive, Henshaw, Sturgis, Cerulean Springs, Harmony in Caldwell County, Marion and Princeton, preaching sixteen sermons. On this trip he "did some business for the company and had a very pleasant visit among my friends and former pastorates."

Evangelistic meetings were held with G. W. James in Strawberry, S. P. Davis in Austin and J. W. Avery in Redfield, all in Arkansas. Others were held in Bethlehem Church in Little Rock, in Bald Knob, Prattsville, the Philadelphia Church near Jonesboro and Zion Church near Lowell where "I preached 24 sermons and the church which had been seriously divided was brought into harmony and brotherly love." He helped W. Tucker in the Mt. Olive Church in Saline County and preached seven doctrinal sermons at Sheridan.

At the close of the year 1905, he wrote in his journal: "I was extended a unanimous call to the care of Argenta Church on November 1, my work to begin December 1, 1905. I accepted the work. Having previously served the church as pastor, the call was hardly to be expected." Again in 1906 he wrote, "A call for another year as pastor was extended to me by the unanimous vote of the Argenta Church at the regular annual business meeting November 11 and I accepted the work." He closed his work with the First Baptist Church of Argenta, 1907, and W. R. Crutchfield, at his recommendation, was called as successor. Once again on November 15, 1908, he "accepted a call to become pastor of the First Baptist Church. This makes the third term as pastor of this church." This time he stayed until September, 1909, then closed his work there.

During his pastorate in Argenta, C. R. Powell from Jacksonville, Texas, assisted him in meetings in 1906 and 1907. In addition to pastoral duties, he preached to churches in Magnolia, Ozark, Liberty, Stamps, Bethlehem in Little Rock, Mt.

Zion near Williford, Traskwood, all in Arkansas, and made a tour of Calhoun County. In 1908 he worked as missionary until November and also preached in Woodland Church, Kentucky, while he was visiting his parents.

During 1910, 1911 and 1912, he preached to these churches, many of them several times: Bethlehem and Antioch Churches in Little Rock, churches in Atkins, Argenta, Damascus, Sheridan, Beebe, Nashville, County Line near Nashville, Social Hill at Benton, Buford, Whitman, all in Arkansas. He also preached in Josephine, Avery, Denison, Blue Ridge, Frankston, Rockwell near Itasca and Coopers Chapel in Hill County, all in Texas. He preached to Parrish Chapel near Dyersburg, Tennessee, and in Marlow and Stratford, Oklahoma, as well as in Alton, Missouri. He preached for a Negro Baptist Church near Itasca, Texas.

Revivals held during the period from 1906 until 1914 were with these churches: In Arkansas, East Union Church in Saline County, with E. L. Page in Bryant, a meeting in Waldo, Center Grove Church near Bearden, one in Buford, Pilgrim's Rest Church in Baxter County, Whiteville Church near Gasville, one at Maynard, Balch, Atkins, New Edinburg, County Avenue in Texarkana, Nashville, Tupelo, Haynes with J. W. Sims, Naylor, Leola and Stamps; in Tennessee, Selmer, Seventh Street in Memphis; in Texas, Josephine, Nienda Church near Hamlin, Johnstown Church near Rosalie, Kerr's Chapel near Sherman, Garrison, Big Sandy, Reese, Bloomfield, Clebourne, Pontotoc, Bethany near Sherman, Maydelle; in Louisiana, Cotton Valley and Loring; in Missouri, Cooter, Morse Hill, Naylor and Alton; in Oklahoma, Marlow, Porum, Comanche, Mt. Towson and Adamson; at Sixty Avenue Baptist Church in Tampa, Florida, and Wingo, Kentucky, also a tour of South Mississippi which included Louin, Union, Union Seminary, Sharon, Shady Grove, Hickory Grove, Spring Hill, Springer and Big Springs.

His meetings for 1908 are not included here but will ap-

pear in his association work in the next volume as will those
held while he was doing missionary work for the association in
1915.

Pastorate in Itasca, Texas

In June, 1912, Bogard accepted the pastorate of the church
in Itasca, Texas, which position he held until he closed his
work there in 1914 and moved to Texarkana at the end of the
year. During this period, he also gave part time service as
pastor to the church in Bloomfield, as well as holding speaking engagements to the churches in Kelty, Avery, Enloe, Josephine, Rockwell near Itasca, Hedley and Willow Springs near
Pottsboro, all in Texas, and to the churches in Bradford, England and Pecan Grove near Keo, all in Arkansas. In addition
to these duties, he held meetings in Naylor and Leola, Arkansas, Morse Hill and Ware, Missouri. Others were in Garrison,
Big Sandy, Reese, Clebourne, Pontotoc, Bethany Church near
Sherman, Maydelle and one for his pastorate in Bloomfield,
Texas. He also preached a series of meetings in Adamson,
Oklahoma.

In 1915, he worked as a missionary and in 1916 accepted
the work as supply pastor for the church in Blue Ridge, Texas,
preaching there on the third Saturdays and Sundays each
month until December. During this same period, he served as
fourth time pastor to the Farmington Church near Howe, Tex.
In 1917, he accepted the call as pastor of the church at Waldo
for half time and the work of Friendship Church in Arkansas
one Sunday a month. During 1916, 1917, 1918, 1919, he served
as part time pastor in Waldo, to the Friendship Church, the
Farmington Church and from September 1919, churches in
Chidester and Taylor, Arkansas, as well as those in Kerr
Chapel and White Rock, Texas. In addition to the work of
guiding these churches in pastoral work, he held revival meetings in the following churches: in Arkansas, Holly Grove,

Trenton, Colt, Strawberry, Carthage, his pastorates at Waldo and Friendship, Rehobeth Church near Marvell, Trenton, Cypert, Colt, Poughkeepsie; in Texas, Oakwood, Pritchell, Corine, Cushing, Kerr Chapel Church near Sherman, in Naylor, Missouri, and Leedy, Oklahoma. He held more than one meeting in some of these churches during the years of 1917 through 1919. He also held speaking engagements of one day or night each to these churches: in Texas, Farmington, White Rock in Grayson County, Pleasant Grove near Denison, Minden, Mt. Enterprise, Jacksonville, Corinth near Crat, Sulpher Springs near Cushing, also at Cushing, Mt. Zion near Whitesboro where he organized a Sunday School, Avery and Dialville; in Arkansas, County Avenue, Carthage, Hopewell near Carthage (4 sermons), Friendship Church (ten sermons), Rondo (seven sermons) Fulton, Marvell, Cypert, Grange, Bethel near Waldo, Patmos (four sermons and assisted in dedication of new church house, third Sunday in May, 1918) Caldwell, Malvern, and Gurdon. In some of these places, he preached a number of times at different periods.

Bogard at approximately forty years of age

VII

ANTIOCH BAPTIST CHURCH
Little Rock, Arkansas

On May 1, 1920, Bogard began his work as pastor of Antioch Missionary Baptist Church in Little Rock, Arkansas, which was to be his last pastorate for it continued the next twenty seven years of his life. He had conducted a revival meeting there which began the 4th Sunday night in March and continued for eleven days. Previous to this, he had held two revival meetings. He was 52 years old.

Antioch Missionary Baptist Church was organized in 1889 by Elder Jasper Breeden. The twelve charter members who went into this new church were Mr. and Mrs. S. R. Skeen, Mr. and Mrs. E. Breeden, Mr. and Mrs. J. W. Snow, Mr. and Mrs. C. Breeden, Mr. and Mrs. Mami, Grandma Skeen and Miss Viola Sessions. The organizational meeting was held in a little country school house, then the new church moved to Lone Pine School Building in 1891. In 1892, a church house was built on what is now 2102 Brown Street. This log building was ''out in the country'' then, but now it is well inside the city.

The first pastor to serve in the new house was Frank Davis. The name Antioch was given the church by Grandma Skeen. Pastors who preceded Ben Bogard were: Jasper Breeden, Frank Davis, Preston McCarty, L. Quinn, J. C. Vaughn, S. L. Pine, A. L. Brumbelow, J. T. Moore, W. A. Dodd, R. S. Taylor, Stewart Davis, R. L. Richardson and John W. Avery. Bogard had this to say of some of the former pastors, ''Two of the pastors were traitors and tried to ruin the church. They were S. L. Pine and Elder Dodd. But for the brethren, Skeen and Tom Hayes, they would have wrecked the church. By the grace of God, they succeeded in holding the work together.

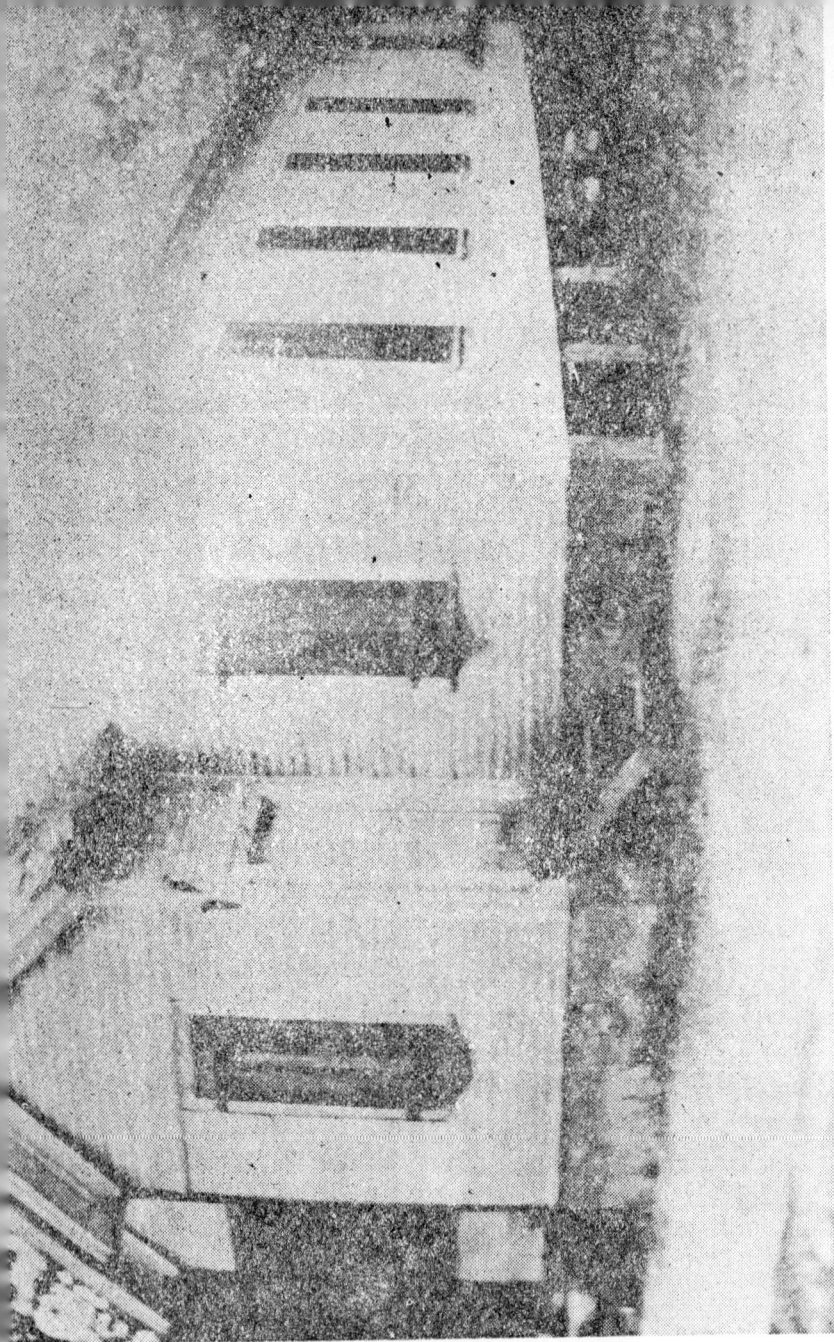

The original church house of Antioch Baptist Church, later bought by the Bogards, remodeled and used for the pastor's home. Dr. Bogard provided in his will that the home was to be used by his widow until the time of her death, then become the property of the Baptist Seminary. The home still stands.

In 1925 the foundation was laid for the second building used by Antioch Church on the northwest corner of Twenty Second and Brown Streets.

Then came Brother and Sister Fred Colon who kept the fires burning for many years. The church would have died if it had not been for the persistent work of Brother and Sister Colon. (Mrs. Colon is now the widow of John Donham and though unable to be very active, is still a member of the church—L. D. F.) . . . Possibly the most outstanding pastor of the list is Elder L. Quinn. His work endures to this day, and two of his grandchildren, Mrs. Billie Keeton and Mrs. Cleora Spain are active members of Antioch Church at this time.''

The brethren who began this work little dreamed of the great future the church was to enjoy. Mr. and Mrs. Skeen were buried in St. Augustine, Florida beneath monuments of stone, but Dr. Bogard felt that Antioch, too, was a monument, for he said, ''To them more than any others is due the credit for the life and success of the church.''

When Bogard began his pastorate in Antioch Church, being editor of the *Baptist and Commoner,* he immediately began a column in this paper called *The Antioch Pulpit* under which caption was printed in outline form the sermons he used in his pulpit. Under this caption was this explanation: ''Under this head will be published the sermon outlines preached by Pastor Ben M. Bogard at Antioch Church, 21st and Brown Streets, Little Rock, Arkansas. If you are in the city, take South Highland street car and get off at Brown Street, and you will be in one-half block of the church.'' One of the very first sermons preached in the Antioch pulpit reflects his leadership of this people:

ACCEPTABLE SERVICE

''So likewise, ye, when ye shall have done all those things which are commanded you, say, We are unprofitable servants: we have done that which was our duty to do.'' —Luke 17:10.

I. There is no such thing as a work of supererogation. The Catholic idea that we can do more than is our duty and thus get indulgences is contrary to this text. When we have done all that we possibly can we have still done only our duty. One should never do less than his duty.

1. God does not balance accounts with us. Some think that we may do good and it will set our credit, and when we do evil it will be charged against us, and if the evil overbalances the good we shall be lost and if the good overbalances the evil we shall be saved. But such an idea is contrary to the scriptures. We are expected to do right in our every act and the smallest deviation from the right is sin. The soul that sins shall die is plainly taught in the Bible (Ezek. 18:4). The sinner has only one way to escape and that is by the mercy and grace of God. We can't merit heaven, since, when we have done all possible, we must consider ourselves unprofitable servants as we shall have only done our duty.

II. All our service should be reasonable service. "I beseech you, brethren, by the mercies of God, that ye present your bodies a living sacrifice, holy acceptable unto God, which is your reasonable service." —Romans 12:1. All service of the Lord is reasonable. The command to be baptized is reasonable for it is a symbol of the doctrine of the resurrection. The observance of the Lord's Supper is reasonable for it is a symbol of the suffering of the Lord. Christian giving is reasonable for it expresses our devotion to Christ. So with all the duties enjoined by the Lord. No unreasonable thing is commanded.

1. Too many are controlled by impulse. Their feelings are their guide. A gentleman told a prominent preacher that he could not believe in close communion because his mother was a Presbyterian and was the best woman he ever knew and yet she had never been baptized, and why should she be shut away from the supper? The preacher simply answered: "How pious must one become to be justified in disobedience to the command of the Lord?" The man dropped his head and said "Good day," and went out. To be governed by impulse is dangerous or the devil may cause the impulse. An ignorant negro may, under the impulse of a good sermon, shout the praises of God. On his way home a sight of a fine roost of chickens may cause the impulse to steal chickens. Where nothing but impulse controls he may both shout and steal.

J. M. Newburn tells of addressing a crowd of negroes on prohibition and he worked them up by rising vote to declare themselves for prohibition and they all promised to vote for *prohibition at the approaching election,* but after he made his speech a liquor man came along and addressed them and they all promised to vote against prohibition. The man who is governed by impulse is controlled by the latest impulse, whether right or wrong.

2. Too many are controlled by convenience. Millions of people know their duty but are unwilling to overcome difficulties to do their duty and hence duty remains undone. If duty lies along an easy road they will do it but will not do it against odds. A king put a pot of gold under a big rock in the middle of the road. Many drove around the rock. But one man stopped and removed the rock and was rewarded by securing the pot of gold. There are great blessings in store for the one who does his duty in the face of difficulties. However difficult, we should let God's word control.

3. Too many are controlled by popularity. They never ask if a thing is right but they want to know if it is popular. Henry Clay was told that he could be president if he would not advocate certain principles. He made the famous answer: "I had rather be right than president." I wish some Baptists had that spirit. Even our parents should not be our guide except as they follow the Bible. It will be found to be expensive to be right but the reward is great. We must be willing to forsake parents to be worthy of Him." —*Baptist and Commoner,* December 29, 1920.

IN THE BEGINNING

When Dr. Bogard moved on the field in Little Rock and began his work with Antioch Church, the membership was 100. These one hundred were badly scattered in what was then almost a rural community in the edge of the city. The church began to grow under his ministry with eighteen additions to the congregation in May, his first month as pastor. This pastoral work, however, was only a part of his great ministry. He was a dynamo of energy putting into his life everything he could. It is almost impossible to imagine how he managed to crowd into the days all the varied activities that made up his work. He seemed never to tire and remained in excellent health. It is interesting to note the churches to whom he preached other than his own full time pastorate. They were:

In 1920: Gurdon, Chidester, Taylor, Friendship, Casa, Eaglette, Dover, Malvern, Beech Grove, Vimy Ridge, Fairview, Sheridan and Hooker in Arkansas, as well as three sermons preached in a school house in Shawnee, Oklahoma. He conducted revival meetings in Belmont, Mississippi and Benton, Arkansas. Besides these speaking engagements and revival meetings, he was busy conducting Bible Schools, doing mission work, debating, writing, doing editorial work and going to as many associational meetings as possible. These things, however, are dealt with in other chapters.

In 1921: churches preached to were Lowell, Sheridan, a school house in the W. A. West settlement six miles from Adona, all in Arkansas; to the Ebenezer Church near Henderson, Texas and the church in Winfield, Alabama. He preached four sermons to Mt. Zion Church on the Pettit Jean Mountain in Arkansas and held revivals for the church in Haworth, Oklahoma, and the Beulah Church near Oak Grove, Louisiana. He preached twenty three sermons in tent meetings held for his own pastorate in Little Rock. The tent was put up on 8th and Pulaski Streets.

In 1922: sermons were preached to the church near Newark, to churches in Magnolia, Danville, Newport, Wynne, England, Kingland, Russsellville, Rison, Mt. Ida, Blythville, Sheridan, Leola, Piggott, Bryant, Rector, Fordyce, Hickory Ridge, Carden Bottoms (following a debate), Magness, Emerson and Centerville near Texarkana, all in Arkansas. He held revival meetings in Haworth, Oklahoma, and at Yacana Church near Mena, Arkansas.

In 1923: churches in Carthage, Texarkana, Oak Grove Church in Cleveland County, Ben Leonard, Calico Rock in Arkansas; to churches in Burnsville, near Baldwyn, Mississippi, churches in Poteau and Newkirk, Oklahoma, and the church in Winfield, Alabama. He was evangelist in a meeting in Prattsville, Arkansas, which resulted in forty professions of faith. D. N. Jackson assisted him in an evangelistic effort in Antioch Church where there were thirteen additions

In 1924: churches to whom he preached were Broken Bow, Oklahoma, Danville, Barton, Jonesboro, Troy, Mineral Springs, Friendship, Fayetteville, and Dierks, Arkansas. He also held services in the County Hospital, the Florence Crittenden Home and the Arkansas Penitentiary a number of times. He preached in revival efforts in Prattsville, Arkansas, and Hodges, Alabama. He also gave the address for the Graduating Class of the Missionary Baptist College in Sheridan and was granted the honorary degree of Doctor of Laws (LL.-D.). He was messenger from Antioch Church to the final meeting of the General Association December 9-10 in Texarkana. The American Baptist Association was formed and "what was called the unification was effected." He made three addresses in this meeting.

This was the year Antioch Church purchasd two lots at Twenty Second and Brown Streets and built a pretty little stucco building for worship services. This house comfortably seated approximately two hundred. The church entered the new house of worship on the last Sunday in May, 1924. Dr.

Bogard bought the old church site and remodeled it into his home where he lived the rest of his life and where he died.

The Bogard Home, 2102 Brown Street in Little Rock, converted from the first Antioch Church building (see page 154) presently owned by the S. P. Wades, long time friends of the Bogards, and maintained in a remarkable state of preservation as their home.

For the next nine years of his pastorate in Little Rock, Bogard continued to increase his activities. He preached to these churches: Arkadelphia, Donaldson, Midway, Kentucky Church near Benton, Bearden, Kotter, Carthage, Lunenberg, Hickory Ridge, Strawberry, Binger, Nashville, Center Grove near Collins, Sheridan, England, Benton, Ft. Smith, Mabelvale and Searcy in Arkansas; Lake Charles, Louisiana; Winfield, Alabama; Cabin Hollow Church near Somerset and the church in Sturgis, both in Kentucky; the church in Wewoka, Oklahoma, Hatley, Mississippi, near Amory and Central Baptist Church in Memphis, Tennessee. To many of these churches he preached several times during the years.

Revival meetings in this period were with: Spring Creek at Benton, Prattsville (three meetings), Antioch near Zion, Center Point, Antioch near Hampton, Promise Land near Hamburg (two meetings), Beech Grove, Springfield, Poughkeepsie, Delight, Cedar Grove near Mobley, Ft. Smith, Mt. Pleasant near Cabot, Haynes, Providence near Judsonia, Imboden and County Avenue in Texarkana, all in Arkansas; Hodges, Alabama (four meetings); Naylor, Sullivan, Morse Hill (two meetings), Missouri; Gillespie, Illinois; Bogalusa, Louisiana. In connection with the meeting in Ft. Smith in 1931, he "assisted in organizing a church beginning with eighteen members and there were eight additions to the church after its organization."

Through the years 1926, 27 and 28, especially, many of his lectures were on the subject of evolution. It was his subject when he spoke to churches in Hickory Ridge, Tomberlin, Greenbrier, Mt. Vernon, Hamlin, Searcy, Harmony near McCrory, Armstrong Springs and Gravel Hill in White County, Lenasque, Pleasant Grove near Carlisle, Humphrey and Haynes. His address at the college banquet in the Sheridan College in 1926 was on the subject of evolution. In many of these churches he brought more than one lecture pointing out in no uncertain terms the terrible evils of this teaching. He gave much of his time fighting the practice of teaching evolution in the schools. Many of his editorials were on the subject. This is a typical one:

"DEGENERACY, NOT EVOLUTION, IS A NATURAL TENDENCY"

"We hear a lot about evolution but no one ever SAW ANYTHING that had evolved. NOTHING WAS EVER KNOWN TO EVOLVE FROM A LOWER TO A HIGHER UNLESS IT WAS DONE BY CULTURE—never by natural tendency. The rule is DEGENERACY. Everything runs

DOWN HILL if left to itself. Let us note the following:

"Left alone everything runs from good to evil. Note the tendency in children to go wrong. You must constantly correct them and hold them back to keep them from going to the bad.

"Left alone everything runs from health to disease. It is a constant fight against disease germs and decay.

"Left alone the human race runs from civilization to savagery. Instead of coming from a lower to a higher the people get worse unless there is special effort made to prevent the evil tendencies leading to ruin.

"Left along men degenerate in worship. They go from monotheism to polytheism—from the one God to many gods and to the worship of idols. It takes special effort all the time to hold humanity to the right course in anything.

"It takes culture; it takes religion; it takes divine power to hold the human race out of ruin. The tendency is downward all the time. Since we SEE all around us evidence against evolution why should anybody believe in it?

"Instead of believing that men descended from the ' anthropoid ape,' which is a high grade monkey; instead of believing that men descended from any sort of lower animal, the *facts* all point toward man degenerating into apes—the apes coming from man instead of men coming from the lower animals. There is ten times as much evidence in favor of that idea than can be imagined in favor of evolution.

"THERE IS NOT ONE SINGLE FACT THAT FAVORS THE IDEA OF EVOLUTION. It is all based on a WISH that it might be so and the wish is based on the dread of a God before whom we must all appear. In order to get rid of God evolutionists have guessed that evolution is true.

"Shall such a GOD-DISHONORING G U E S S BE TAUGHT IN OUR TAX SUPPORTED SCHOOLS? Help us circulate the petition to initiate a law to prohibit evolution being taught in our tax supported schools in Arkansas and then get people to the polls on the next election day and have the

law passed by the people to prohibit it. We will send you blanks
and you get your neighbors to sign it and thus help the good
work along. Just drop us a card and we will send the blanks.
ANYBODY can circulate the petitions. Address American
Anti-Evolution Association, 14 Arcade, Little Rock, Arkansas." —*Baptist and Commoner,* August 24, 1927

Upper left: A candid shot, a rare photo, of Bogard in motion. It was his habit to come to a complete halt and stand like a statue when he saw anyone with a camera.

Upper right: A baptismal service in the early days before Antioch had a baptistry, in the lake at Roselawn Cemetery. Other photos are of Bogard, his wife and preachers with whom he conducted meetings.

VIII

TO THE WEST

On May 22, 1927, Bogard began his first tour of the west. This trip captivated his mind and held him almost spellbound, so fascinated did he become with these things so foreign to his environment. He held three evangelistic meetings, beginning with one in Portland, Oregon, which lasted two weeks. On to Lynwood, California, he continued six days, then traveled to Denver, Colorado, where he began a meeting June 30th and preached a six day series of messages. He also spoke to churches in Caldwell, Idaho, Hillsboro, Oregon, and visited the Middle Oregon Association at Cloverdale, Oregon, where he made three addresses and preached four sermons. Visiting the Eastern Association of California and Oregon in Klamath Falls, Oregon, he made three speeches and preached four times.

Ben Bogard loved travel, and he was interested in the progress of the work of Missionary Baptist Churches in every section of the country. So, though he never traveled simply for a vacation as he pointed out in his writings, his vital concern for all of the work took him to many places and he never failed to appreciate the beauty of the countryside. His delight in new places and things and his naive assumption that no one else had seen them either was almost childlike as one may note in his editorials which reflect this characteristic. He wrote of this first trip to the west and his undisguised amazement at the sights he saw. His writings, more than anything else, give a clear picture of the man. Note this editorial describing the tour of the west:

"I recently attended the meeting of the Eastern Baptist Association of California and Oregon, at Klamath Falls, Oregon. It is very much the sort of association as the Middle Oregon Association, of which I have already written. The entertainment was superb. Preach, preach, preach! Never saw people so hungry for preaching. They have preaching three times a day and devotional services of thirty minutes three times a day. Four hours and a half of worship in every day. And they stayed four full days. Nobody seemed to get into a hurry to get away.

"But no wonder they love to have preaching and devotional exercises. They live so far apart. Lynwood, California, church belongs to this association and the messengers must travel seven hundred miles to get to the association. The average distance all the messengers have to travel is about three hundred miles. This association covers twice as much territory as the entire state of Arkansas. The great distance cannot be appreciated by people in the South and East.

"There was a distinctly hopeful note sounded in this association and a forward move was made in mission work. The American Baptist Association was endorsed by unanimous vote and peace and harmony prevailed. They seemed to think this editor came there to preach for they had him preach four times. This was certainly appreciated.

"From Klamath Falls, Oregon, the editor went seven hundred miles south to Lynwood, California, and preached some doctrinal sermons to try to stiffen the backbones of the saints there . . ." —*Baptist and Commoner,* July 13, 1927.

"Come travel with me as I make the long journey along the coast. Leaving Klamath Falls, Oregon where I attended the Eastern Association of California and Oregon, I went seven hundred miles south to Los Angeles, where I assisted the pastor, Elder Fred Reusser (pronounced Ryser), in a six days' protracted meeting. The trip was a very interesting one. I had heard of the difference in climate between the part of California east of the mountains and that west of the mountains. But I experienced it in a very impressive way. Coming through the

Joaquin (pronounced Waukeen) Valley, I was uncomfortably warm, really hot. The heat was oppressive. Before getting to Los Angeles the train runs through a tunnel under the mountain and it takes just six minutes for the train to run through the tunnel to the Los Angeles side. It was blazing hot when we went into the tunnel and when we came out on the other side I saw people reaching for their wraps and my coat felt comfortable and when I got off in Los Angeles I put my overcoat on and wore it in comfort. Only six minutes between the hot country and the cool western slope.

"Los Angeles is a wonder. There are more people living in Los Angeles and its suburbs than live in the entire state of Arkansas. There are about two millions of people living in that settlement and every sort of people you can think of are there. Religiously things are in a bad way. Lynwood is a suburb of that city and it is a town three miles through. I found a sound church doing business for the Lord. I preached doctrinal sermons all the time I was there as I felt that that sort of preaching would do more good than the other sort. The Lord blessed the church with a revival and there were five additions; two by letter and three by baptism. The church has a wonderful opportunity as it is the only church inside a population of two millions which stands for the true faith. There is a prospect of another church starting in another suburb and there could be a dozen such churches established within that territory if we only had the men to put on the field and the money to support them.

"On my way to southern California I passed Mount Shasta, the most glorious sight I ever saw. It was covered with snow and the sun shined just right for me to see it in all its glory. If the glorious throne of God has any more glory than Mount Shasta it will take the tongue of an angel to describe it, and hence I shall not undertake it. We have a church at Mount Shasta and while they have had their troubles and difficulties they seem to be in better shape now and Pastor Livingston seems to be a congenial brother and he said that his attendance at the association at Klamath Falls was worth much to him . . .

"From Los Angeles I went on the Daylight Limited to San Francisco, a distance of five hundred miles, without one single stop. That was the longest non-stop journey I ever made. The train is fitted up as fine as a first class hotel. It has a dining car where they serve a five course dinner and supper. They have a cafeteria car also where you can buy a short lunch any time of day you want it. The train runs along the sea coast for many miles, so near that many times you could throw a pebble from the car window into the water of the great ocean. A wonderful and restful, invigorating trip.

"From San Francisco I headed for Denver, Colorado, and on the way stopped a whole day in Salt Lake City, the headquarters of the Mormon Church and I studied Mormonism at headquarters all day. I went through their museum and saw the private belongings of Brigham Young, the second president of the church. Saw his private desk, his chair, his cradle where his numerous babies were rocked to sleep, for he had nineteen wives. I stood by his grave and along side of him were buried several of his numerous wives. He flew high and lived in licentious luxury for a few years—but here is his grave. He has gone to account to a God whose word he scorned while living. The picture is dark. Let us draw the curtain. I stood by the statue of Joseph Smith, the founder of the Mormon church. He died at the hands of a mob at Carthage, Illinois. It is all over with him too. But what evil he wrought while he lived! A woman in Vermont had him in her Sunday School class when Smith was a small boy. When she learned that her former pupil had turned out so bad and had established the Mormon Monster, it is said that she never smiled again. She was known as the 'sad woman.' No wonder she was sad. If she had only led that boy to Christ it would have prevented the establishment of the Mormon church and saved the world from its curse. But she failed! Alas! Sunday School teachers, you never know what will be the future of that child you have in your class. The destiny of many thousands were in the hands of that Vermont woman. She did not realize it until it was too late. May the Lord help our Sunday School teachers to magnify their office for they can never tell what good they may do and what evil they may prevent!

"In another day I was in Denver where I met the smiling face of Pastor Rice. He is a fine mountain guide, and while my primary purpose in going to Denver was to help the struggling church there yet Rice kept his auto hot showing me the wonderful mountains. We made three mountain trips and went to the top of the highest mountain in the United States, Mount Evans, and waded snow on the fourth day of July, and we went to the top of Lookout Mountain and visited the grave of Buffalo Bill (Col. Cody), and the last trip was into Indian Hills. Rice tried himself in showing me a good time while I preached the gospel to his struggling band of faithful people who call him pastor.

"No one can appreciate the long distances between places on that Western Coast unless he actually makes the trips from one place to another. Our brethren are scattered but a finer set of people never lived. Anyone stands true to principle in such unfavorable spiritual environment will stand true anywhere. Need not be uneasy about a man like Moore, for instance, who has stood through the years in that spiritual atmosphere and not wobbled on the gudgeon. I want to go back again. They need help and I enjoyed helping. It presents our greatest opportunity for future work. Churches can be established by the hundreds if we can only get the men to do the work . . ." —*Baptist and Commoner,* July 27, 1927. (What a prophecy!—L. D. F.)

These writings preserve the opinions and sentiments of this pastor, preacher, missionary—reflect keen concern for and interest in the present and future of Missionary Baptist

Churches. They indicate his feeling for the aesthetic, as well as practical things.

One can picture his wide-eyed appreciation of the sea-coasts and the mountains as he was to see them for the first time.

Picking oranges in Florida where he conducted many meetings and debates. Standing in the snow with Pastor Frank Ridgeway in Detroit, Michigan. Bogard traveled from east to west, north to south spreading the gospel.

IX

THE "LAND OF FLOWERS"

Again Bogard's amazement and interest in new experiences, such as traveling on a pullman, or eating on a diner is vividly revealed in his description of his first trip to Florida in December, 1928, to hold a debate and assist in a council to settle a church trouble.''

"Two things took me to Florida. One was a debate with C. B. Douthitt at Mulberry, Florida, and the other was to sit in a council at Pensacola to help settle some trouble there among the brethren. I did not go on a pleasure trip but because duty called, yet to say I got pleasure out of it is to put it mildly. It was a pleasure indeed.

"I went to bed in Little Rock on board a sleeper several hours before the train pulled out and did not know when the train left Little Rock because I was asleep. I was awakened at Memphis and had time to eat breakfast before the Florida train pulled out. Everything is so comfortable on board train now. It is like sitting in a nice parlor and entertaining company.

"On the Florida train I fell into conversation with two learned physicians, teachers in the Medical College in Memphis, and enjoyed their learned discussion of the things scientific that were mentioned. I asked them the direct question as to how they ran a medical college without teaching evolution and they both promptly said that they did not need evolution in a medical college. One of them especially said that he believed that the Creator made all things according to His wisdom and that while man was in some particulars similar to lower animals it was like a builder who makes houses, some of them huts, some are cottages, some mansions. But that does

173

not signify that the mansion developed from the hut but only that the builder chose to make different kinds of houses, yet all of them in some particulars resemble one another. Looks like any simpleton would have thought of that but strange to say there are some who think that because we see some points of similarity between man and the lower animals that man must have evolved from a lower animal.

"Went to bed again at Atlanta, Georgia, and was told that the train would reach Jacksonville, Florida, at seven in the morning and that I could stay on the sleeper until seven forty five. I awoke at daylight and looked at my watch and it was six o'clock. I turned over for another nap and here came the porter and shook my mattress and said we were in Jacksonville. I told him it was only six o'clock and he said that we were in Eastern Time now and it was an hour earlier there. That only illustrates how big our country is. The earth is round like a ball and as you travel east you go in that direction and when the traveling is west the watches must be moved back an hour each thousand miles or thereabout—not exactly but approximately that.

"There was a white frost in Jacksonville that morning and the folks explained that such as that was not very frequent there. But it was sure enough frost. But the train soon had me on the way to Plant City, Florida, and I forgot all about the frost. There was very little frost down in that Plant City country. Some of the very tender plants were bit a little but no great damage was done. Garden truck of every kind was seen everywhere and for beauty I have never seen that part of Florida excelled.

"Lakes are everywhere. These lakes are reminders of the great icebergs of the glacial period that once slipped down from the North Pole for that is what caused them. Plenty of proof for this statement. The great mountains of ice that slipped many, many years ago, made great depressions in the earth by the mountains of ice turning over and hitting the earth hard in certain places and the holes made are the lakes now. When that ice and snow melted, it of course, left the holes filled with water. There are the lakes, hundreds of them, to show for it. They are filled with wonderful fish and are fine for boating. No other state in the union has so many beautiful lakes.

"I enjoyed the orange and grape fruit groves. They are beautiful beyond description. Strawberries by the carload were being shipped to New York, Washington City, and other big cities and the farmers were getting one dollar and fifty cents a quart for these berries. I stood right there on the platform and saw them selling for that. That means that the retailer in the cities must get a great deal more than that to come out whole. Of course this enormous price will not hold up long. It was Christmas season and the berries were to supply that demand. After the Christmas season has passed no doubt the berries dropped down to possibly fifty cents a quart. But think what that means to the farmer.

"All about everywhere were truck farms with tomatoes, cabbage, lettuce, beans—just everything that we are accustomed to in other states in May and June. I went out in the tomato field of Brother Brewer of Auburndale, Florida, and saw twenty acres of fine tomatoes growing and putting on fruit right there in the latter part of December. A few plants had been frost bitten but only a few and the rest were pushing ahead and that one field of tomatoes was a little fortune because they will ripen in January and get on the market when there are none in any other state. That means enormous prices. Brother Brewer, who is an Arkansas man, took great pride in showing me his tomatoes and orange and grape fruit groves. I was entertained in his nice home in Auburndale one night. His wife, daughter and son tried to see how pleasant they could make it for me.

"Dr. M. M. Hamlin, the moderator of the Missouri Baptist Association and pastor of several churches in Missouri, is in Lakeland for the winter. He attended the debate at Mulberry and I went on to Lakeland to see him one day and found him out in his fine grapefruit grove about three miles out from Lakeland. He was as happy as a sixteen year old out there with his wife working among the trees. He was actually at work. It showed on him too because his health has not been good, but he is greatly benefitted by the climate, the eating of the grapefruit and the exercise he gets working in that orchard. Such wonderful fruit! Sister Hamlin found one cluster of grapefruit that had fifteen on it. Clusters of from three to seven are common but fifteen was unusual. They call it grapefruit because it grows in clusters like grapes only this fruit is of enormous size, one grapefruit being equal to size to several big oranges.

"I enjoyed being in the fine orange and grapefruit groves. Brother J. B. Simmons is a preacher near Plant City, who is held in the highest esteem. A box of oranges and grapefruit from his son's grove was sent to this editor's wife in Little Rock and still another to the editor's mother in Kentucky. I could not think of anything nicer for Christmas than a big box of about two hundred oranges and grapefruit to each of them.

"At Mulberry, where the debate was held, I met much kindness. The debate was held under the nice, comfortable tent used by Elder Ben Evers in his mission work. He is missionary of the Florida Baptist State Association. Although the debate lasted six days I only stayed one night in Mulberry. That night was spent in the good home of Brother and Sister Collins. They live by the side of a big lake full of fish and alligators. Yes, there are thousands of alligators down in Florida. They do not bother anybody unless somebody bothers them. They occasionally pick up a pig or a dog for breakfast but unless there is great imprudence they never bother a man. The reason I did not stay in Mulberry all the time was because the brethren would not let me. There was somebody with his auto every time to take me all the way from three miles to

twenty miles to stay all night and then to look at the wonderful fruits and flowers all day in a different community. It
suited me exactly. I did not want to be imprisoned in a hotel—
let me get out among the people, especially when they are such
people as I found down there. By that method I saw the country.

"Florida is a big flower garden. Unless you have been
there you never saw the like. Right in the middle of winter,
there were great banks of flowers. I never got tired of looking
at them. As a rule I do not look out of the car windows while
traveling because travel is an old song with me. But I kept
both eyes busy all the time I was in Florida . . ." —*Baptist
and Commoner*, January 9, 1929.

Again in 1930, Bogard made a four months tour of the
Pacific Coast, leaving May 26th. Antioch Church gave him
leave of absence, calling D. N. Jackson to fill the pulpit for the
time he was absent. He preached 122 sermons and made seven
speeches in these places: San Diego, Lake City, Mt. Shasta,
Roseville, Oroville, Lynwood, Ventura and Bellflower in
California; Fossil, Silver Lake, New Pine Creek, Lakeview,
Mitchell, Prineville, Gateway, Cloverdale and Portland, Oregon. He witnessed twenty one conversions and 25 additions to
churches in these meetings and received $376.04 for his serv-
ices. He attended two associations and preached over the
"Church of the Open Door" radio broadcast in Los Angeles.

SUCCESS AT HOME CHURCH

In April 1933, Bogard preached for the revival effort of
Antioch Church in which there were thirty professions of faith
and fifty additions during the two weeks period. Thirty two
were baptized.

At the end of 1933, Ben Bogard had conducted forty five
years of work in the ministry. His journal gives this statisti-
cal record of his labors:

Churches pastored	18
Revivals held	279
Debates held	193
Sermons preached, 8876 and lectures 3865	14,741
Weddings performed	302
Funerals	237
Conversions witnessed at his preaching	2164
Baptized at his hand	693
Additions to churches	3,904
Received for services	$53,676.23

He had enjoyed editorial connections with the *Arkansas Baptist, Baptist Flag, Baptist Magazine, Baptist and Commoner* and had written fifteen books and pamphlets. He had preached in sixteen of the United States.

On October 1, 1934, the enrollment of Antioch Church had reached 434. Approximately 668 had been added to the church since 1920 when Bogard became pastor. The 668 added to the membership of 100 shows that of the additions, 334 had been dismissed from the church, in one way or another, but there had been a net growth of 334 members.

X

ANOTHER ERA BEGINS

The year 1934 was to begin an important era in the life of this man whose time was filled with interests so varied. Vitally concerned about every phase of the work of Landmark Baptists, he tried to preach to all who called on him, traveling far and near to debate, lecture, preach, evangelize and conduct Bible Schools.

In addition to his full time schedule of duties as pastor of the rapidly growing Antioch Church, he managed to help other churches. He preached to the First Baptist Church of Itasca, the Ennis and Waxahachie, Texas churches in June and, in July, to the Gravel Hill Church, as well as the Rocky Springs and Bethel Churches in Mississippi, these last two while engaged in a series of evangelistic messages with Mt. Zion Church, eight miles from Amory. Other revivals held that year were with Center Hill Church in Searcy, Friendship Church in Arkansas, the First Baptist Church, Trinity Heights in Dallas, Texas and the Missionary Baptist Church at St. John, Kansas, where he "preached thirteen sermons and materially aided the church in settling serious trouble in this membership." He also gave an address before the Ladies Missionary Union in Italy, Texas, while he was holding services at Itasca. He held Bible Schools in Unity Church near Jonesboro and one in Corsicana.

This was the year when he "organized a Baptist Bible School in Antioch Baptist meeting house October 16. Have engaged the assistance of Eld. J. Louis Guthrie and Mrs. J. Louis Guthrie as teachers. I teach one hour a day. It is a training school for preachers and other Christian workers." This was to be the crowning achievement of his mighty ministry,

179

but more will be said of it in another chapter. He did note at the end of the year in his journal, "The Baptist Bible School which I began in Antioch Church house, October 16, has prospered and every prospect is hopeful. There is associated with me in the school, Elder J. Louis Guthrie, Ph. D. Fifty Six students enrolled the first year."

After the beginning of the "Baptist Bible School" in Antioch Church, the ministerial load became steadily heavier as he taught regularly in the school. He continued his full schedule of pastoral duties for Antioch Church, as well as answering calls made from all over the nation. He maintained his habit of attending as many of the various associational meetings as he could, keeping up with the growing work and helping to promote it.

During 1935, in the latter part of January and the first of February, he preached a series of two weeks' meetings for Antioch Church in Little Rock. Other revivals that year were in Bald Knob from June 10th till 22nd in Hodges, Alabama for nine days beginning July 23 in which "42 professions were made and the converts baptized." Near Amory, Mississippi, he preached a seven day meeting beginning August 5th at Mt. Zion Church. He held a meeting beginning August 12th for Bethel Church in Dorsey, Mississippi and one at Somerset, Kentucky beginning Tuesday after the first Sunday in September. He preached in the afternoons during this time for the church in Science Hill, Kentucky, and to three other churches nearby at odd times, preaching 35 sermons in all in this period of time in Kentucky. He attended a Baptist Fellowship meeting in Memphis during May where he preached once and gave sixteen Bible lectures in the ten days there. He also preached to the Friendship Church near Tupelo, Mississippi on August 17th while he was holding the meeting in Dorsey.

In April 1935, Dr. Bogard announced to the church that an addition to the building was needed. The congregation was growing larger. The Bible School needed more classrooms. He asked that the people "study about it, pray over it and be ready for it."

The deacons met Wednesday night, May 29th and discussed plans and specifications presented by a Brother C. A. Booher. On June 2nd, they recommended that the church be enlarged. The vote was postponed until June 5th when the church passed the motion to enlarge the church building with six opposing it. A committee to submit plans was composed of Brethren Booher, J. C. Whitley and Claud M. Pritchard. These were drawn up and the church adopted them on June 19th and the committee was discharged. Brethren Booher and Whitley were employed to take charge of the enlargement. The other six deacons were appointed to counsel with these two and on July 7th, Brother Booher was granted authority to purchase the materials.

This enlargement approximately doubled the size of the then existing church property. It extended the back of the church westward all the way to the alley. The new part had nine rooms—four upstairs and five down—in addition to two rest rooms. The overall measurement was approximately 40 x 40 feet square and the roofline continued without a break giving to the outside the appearance that it was a part of the original structure. It was built of stucco, the same material as in the building of which it became a part. There were two outside entrances. A double door into the hall came from the alley and one door on the Twenty Second Street side. An inside entrance from the pulpit area placed one on the second floor. From there a stairway in the middle of the building led to the ground floor.

This addition necessitated altering the church building, especially the auditorium and two small rooms on either side of the choir loft. These two class rooms were taken out, the platform which constituted the choir loft and pulpit area was moved back approximately twenty feet and a baptistry installed on a landing in the center and rear of the auditorium behind the pulpit. On either side of the baptistry and entrance, a stairway of some three steps led up to the second floor level of the new addition. The glass front was put in the baptistry which, at that time, was quite an innovation and caused considerable wonderment when the baptistry was filled with water the first few times and the candidates were seen as they were immersed in the water.

At first the addition had no floor in the basement area except the earth. This was later filled with sawdust which was little or no better than the earth itself as when it was dry, it created quite a dust. A year and a half later the floor was paved with concrete.

This was the house Antioch Church used for the rest of Dr. Bogard's life and from it, he was to be buried.

Antioch had 37 new members added under his ministry that year. Additions to all churches under his preaching totaled 92. He held five meetings, fourteen funerals, nine weddings and preached 178 sermons, gave 74 addresses and baptized 10, though he witnessed 62 conversions. For these services, he received $1470.28.

In the year 1936, Bogard preached a sermon to the newly organized White City Baptist Church in the suburbs of Little Rock in June and one in August. Out in the open air in the quietness of two cemeteries, he spoke to gatherings celebrating Memorial Day. One of the services was near Hatley, Mississippi. He preached to the Independence Baptist Church near Neelyville, Missouri, December 1st, while engaging in a debate at West Fork near Bunker, Missiouri. He held meetings in Hatley, Mississippi, beginning the Monday after the fourth Sunday in July, for the Mt. Gilead Baptist Church near Burnsville, Mississippi beginning Tuesday after the first Sunday in August and one in Strawberry, Arkansas, beginning Monday after the fourth Sunday in August. He taught four Bible Schools of three days each in Kentucky during the month of July. One of these was at Pitman Creek Church near

Somerset, Kentucky, one at Somerset, one at Nancy and one at Argyle. These schools were held during the time he was engaged in a debate at Windsor. During one of these long periods away from his pulpit, Dr. J. Louis Guthrie supplied and on another occasion, Hoyt Chastain filled his pulpit. Antioch Church enjoyed 36 additions under the ministry of Bogard that year.

A summary of his accomplishments of 1936 indicates that he held three meetings, three debates, five funerals, eight weddings, preached 157 sermons, gave 114 addresses, enjoyed 33 professed conversions, 56 additions to churches and baptized 12. He received $1,529.72 for his services.

Bogard continued to fill his time completely in the Lord's work. In 1937 he wrote in his journal, "Beginning July I left Antioch Church in the pastoral care of Elder J. Louis Guthrie for ten Sundays as I was away in protracted meeting work." During these summer months, he held meetings in Bay Springs, Mississippi, (eleven days, twelve additions), in Frankfort, Alabama near Russellville (thirteen days and fifteen additions), Hatley, Mississippi, near Amory (eleven days, two additions), Mt. Zion near Smithville, Mississippi (eleven days, twenty eight additions), Mt. Gilead near Burnsville, Mississippi (thirteen days, ten additions) and Strawberry, Arkansas (eleven days, four additions). Besides the revival meetings, preaching to Antioch that year and teaching, he found time to preach two sermons for a church near Kascinsko, Mississippi, one at Canalou, Missouri and exchange pulpits with H. S. Thomas at County Avenue Baptist Church in Texarkana. He preached to the Central Baptist Church in Ft. Smith in December. This sermon was broadcasted over the radio. He held a revival meeting for Pauline Baptist Church at Monticello in June. During the eleven days of this meeting, nine professions of faith were made.

ENTERTAINING THE AMERICAN BAPTIST ASSOCIATION

In March, 1937, Antioch Church entertained the American Baptist Association messenger body meeting, Bogard the host pastor. At the time the financial depression was being felt all over America. There were no modern motels in Little Rock, only a few "tourist camps" which were little more than rooms with beds in them. Hotels were not expensive by today's standdards, but no one had much money. The custom was to entertain out of town messengers and visitors in the homes of the membership and friends of the host church. Homes were opened by the membership and friends of the church who invited the guests in for beds and meals. The pastor made arrangements to rent a number of cots for men who would avail themselves of these makeshift beds to sleep in the basement of the church. This was a tremendous task for Antioch Church and the minutes reflect the necessary preparations which were started several months before time for it.

January 6, 1937: "The pastor asked to appoint a committee to solicit from business firms and other help on this entertainment. Chairman appointed E. L. Johnston and E. E. McMurry to see the Chamber of Commerce, inform them of the coming three day session of the American Baptist Association and ask their help . . ."

February 10, 1937: "The pastor discussed the entertainment of the association at great length and suggested appointing three ladies to have charge of cooking, the menu, and the serving of coffee. It was moved and seconded that Mrs. Russell be employed as cook, Mrs. Lipke to have charge of the menu and Mrs. Durham the coffee serving . . . C. M. Pritchard asked that a committee be appointed to do the purchasing of food . . ."

March 10, 1937: "Chairman Bogard reported that he had secured fifteen minutes a day time from each of the three radio stations. Nine broadcasts of fifteen minutes each during the meeting of the American Baptist Association . . .

These minutes also reflect a rumbling on the horizon.

"There had been a great deal of opposition and confusing articles printed in a 'would be leading paper' especially against our pastor and Vaughan Davis called for a standing vote of confidence in our pastor. The entire audience stood and was kindly thanked by the pastor.

"The chairman asked that all who could have their cars at the church Monday afternoon in order to meet trains, busses, also, to conduct visitors to homes assigned."

The business meeting of the church which followed the messenger meeting reflects this report: April 9, 1937: "The pastor submitted some items of expense which he had paid as follows: Army cots $22.50; printing badges . . .

"It was further ordered that Elder Filer Seal be paid $5.00 for his work and use of his car in taking speakers to radio stations, conducting visitors to home, etc., during the meeting of the American Baptist Association . . .

"Upon suggestion by the chairman, the Ladies Auxiliary was asked to write a letter of appreciation to all firms, and individuals not of the membership who helped in the entertainment, thanking them for their help. The ladies were paid $1.50 for postage expense . . .

"E. L. Johnston reported that his committee having seen the Chamber of Commerce and having their promise of help which did not materialize, nothing further had been done in the matter and asked that the committee be discharged. After discussion by the chairman and others the report was received and the committee discharged . . .

"C. M. Pritchard moved that a letter be written the Chamber of Commerce calling attention to their failure to take advantage of the opportunity to advertize Little Rock to the many visitors. Duly seconded and the clerk was instructed to write the letter."

At the meeting of the American Baptist Association, Antioch Church offered a resolution calling for an audit of the Sunday School Committee manager's books. When the audit was made and the manager was not fired, the church resolved to purchase no more Sunday School literature from them as long as the condition existed.

"A RESOLUTION

"WHEREAS, It has come to the attention of the messengers assembled in this the 1937 session of the American Baptist Association, meeting at Little Rock, Arkansas, through talks made on the floor and through a member of the Sunday School Committee that the need has arisen for a thorough investigation of the financial affairs of the Sunday School publications—the receipts and disbursements of the Sunday School Committee, managed by Elder C. A. Gilbert for the American Baptist Association.

"That all may be done in fairness and impartiality toward our brother, we recommend the following:

"1. That an audit be made of the business for the past three years.

"2. That the audit be made by an auditing firm such as is used by banks and trust companies.

"3. That this audit be begun at once.

"4. That all records, books used in this business be placed in the hands of responsible party or parties until the auditors have completed the task.

"5. That five brethen be selected to look into the matter of this audit, employ the auditing firm and have charge of it for the association.

"6. That pay for the auditing firm and cost of this procedure be taken from the receipts of the business.

"7. That copies of the audit be made available to all religious papers connected with the Association as soon as same is completed."

The church clerk, E. E. McMurry, noted on this resolution: "This resolution was opposed at the American Baptist Association meeting, March 16-17-18, 1937, Antioch Baptist Church, and was strenuously and persistently opposed by the 'clique' from Texarkana. Resolution carried and audit ordered as provide in the resolution.

Antioch voted to buy no more literature from Texarkana; this added another duty to the pastor's already crowded schedule. The church minutes of June 9, 1936, noted: "Because of the action of the majority of the Sunday School Committee in retaining as manager one who by his own admission is incompetent and untrustworthy and the business having been audited by nationally known auditors was completely ignored by a majority of the committee, said committee issuing a resolution commending the manager to the brotherhood, although the auditor's report showed $8,314.31 more literature mailed than the recorded receipts for the seven quarters checked, the Antioch Missionary Baptist Church resents this action of the committee in usurping the authority of the churches, therefore the following resolution was offered:

"WHEREAS, The majority of the Sunday School Committee, against all principles of good business usage and procedure have retained as manager one proven incompetent and unworthy of trust, we, the Antioch Missionary Baptist Church of Little Rock, Arkansas, withdraw our support of the Sunday School literature and agree to neither purchase nor use in our Sunday School any literature published by the Sunday School Committee of the American Baptist Association as long as this condition exists."

"The question of literature was raised by several and it was moved and seconded that the Sunday School Superintendent, Vaughan Davis, be authorized to investigate and select what he thought was suitable and to purchase same for use in the Sunday School. The motion was amended by adding that

Mrs. Dowell be named to select and purchase the B. Y. literature.''

September 15, 1937: ''The chairman stated that in view of the unsettled condition of the American Baptist Association Sunday School literature, he had prepared and was having printed lesson leaflets for use in Sunday Schools and asked that the church use same in their work. Upon motion and second the church voted unanimously to use the literature prepared by our pastor, Dr. Ben M. Bogard.''

This resolution made by Antioch Church under the leadership of Dr. Bogard was to have far reaching effects. However, the details of it are discussed in the part of this book captioned *LITERATURE.*

ANTIOCH BACK TO THE PINE BLUFF ASSOCIATION

This was also the year Antioch Church changed affiliation from the Lonoke Association to the Pine Bluff Association, the original "local" (district) association in which Antioch Baptist Church fellowshipped. When the Lonoke Association was organized, it needed numerical strength and whatever financial assistance it might receive, as well as fellowship of Missionary Baptist Churches, and while the Lonoke Association embraced churches north of the Arkansas River and east of Little Rock, Antioch Church decided to fellowship this young association for whatever benefit it could be.

In 1937, the Antioch Church decided to fellowship once again in the Pine Bluff Association. After all, it was geographically situated in that association and the young people and the ladies in the church had their activities on an associational level with the Pine Bluff Association.

Rumors were whispered that certain brethren were going to make an issue of Antioch Church and pastor returning and block their being fellowshipped in the the Pine Bluff Association. If this was successful, the very fact that the church was denied this fellowship would be a club in their hands with which they could do great damage over the American Baptist Association by amplifying this refusal of association. The issue was going to be that the pastor and the church had stopped using the Sunday School literature published by the A.B.A. in Texarkana. Actually, Antioch was boycotting the literature and encouraging other churches to do so to force attention to the irregularities in the Sunday School office.

Bogard did not avoid a fight and he had many tricks up his sleeve. He noted that the church formerly fellowshipped in the Pine Bluff Association and that the young people were presently fellowshipping with the other youth in the Pine Bluff Association, so he took the matter to the church and the church voted to discontinue representing in the Lonoke Association and to petition once again for fellowship in the Pine Bluff Association.

The ensuing fight at the messenger body meeting is related in the chapter on LITERATURE. This fight, led by Bogard against the mismanagement in the Publications Business in Texarkana, the business he had started many years ago, was becoming more and more explosive. The church was with him in the controversy and on March 10, 1937, the entire congregation gave him a standing vote of confidence.

Choir

Because the music department in the church was not developing as the pastor thought it should, he led Antioch to elect M. M. Hagood as the assistant to the pastor "to direct the music, train a choir and assist in the Sunday School and Young People's work." In order to make this work more effective, Bogard also asked the church to elect Miss Berneice Jamison (now Mrs. Sam T. Hester) to be the pianist. A combined motion was made that this request of the pastor be granted. Because Miss Jamison was not a member of Antioch (although she was a Baptist) her election was thoroughly discussed by the membership of the church. There was some opposition to her being pianist; however, the motion was carried. Mr. Hagood and Miss Jamison were elected. Because of the opposition and to show her good faith, she submitted a statement to the effect that she believed in and endorsed the doctrines and practices of the Antioch Church, that her not being a member was because of purely personal reasons and family consideration. She pledged to do all she could to help the church and never at any time to do anything contrary to the doctrines or practices held by the pastor and the church. (Later, when she married, both she and her husband became members and are still a part of Antioch Church.) Many people did not know the gentle nature of this great man but his admiration of Miss Jamison's talent revealed this often hidden esthetic turn to his character. Once after a service when he watched her as he always did, her hands moving so easily over the keyboard, he said, "I never saw anything so beautiful as Berneice's hands when she plays the piano."

The music department progressed under the leadership of these two and in December, 1937, Bogard wrote in the *Orthodox Baptist Searchlight,* which he then edited: "Under the direction of M. M. Hagood, assistant pastor, the Antioch choir has developed into a great choir . . . Brother Hagood gives instruction in vocal music, how to read music, at each rehearsal and on Friday afternoons he also gives free instructions in music to all who want the lessons."

XI

HALF A CENTURY A PREACHER

The year 1938 marked the beginning of Bogard's fiftieth year as a minister of the gospel. Consistently, energetically active, this man never wasted his time. He had, through the years, taken a keen interest in every phase of the work all over the United States. Unstintingly, he had given his time and energy, travling into Oregon, California, Florida, Louisiana, Mississippi, Georgia, Missouri, Kentucky, Texas and all over Arkansas in efforts to strengthen and build the churches. Though in his seventieth year, his activities did not diminish. He curtailed none of his varied speaking engagements, debates, writing or preaching. Rather, he seemed to increase them that year. He spent four months in evangelistic campaigns. He never seemed to be tired or ill but according to his own words, always felt "bully."

Down in Ashley County, in the southeast part of the state is Promise Land Baptist Church near Hamburg. Bogard taught a seven day Bible School here in which seven professed faith in Christ and were added to the church. Typical of him, his journal reads: "The pay I received went to the Missionary Baptist Institute." Then all the way across the state to the western border to preach in Van Buren for ten days in March but noted "not much interest." More than three hundred miles away to Corsicana, Texas, he went in May to hold a ten day meeting where he rejoiced in ten additions to the church.

In March, Bogard attended the messenger body meeting of the American Baptist Association in Knoxville, Tennessee, as a messenger. In this meeting he preached one sermon and gave two addresses.

In July, he "left Little Rock the middle of the month and

held revival meetings up until the last of September, leaving Elder J. Louis Guthrie to supply the Antioch pulpit in my absence . . .'' Meetings held during this period were: June 13-23, Grand Glaze, Arkansas, where he "baptized five in White River; Plainview Church near Weatherford, Oklahoma, July 12-21; July 21-August 8, Marlow, Oklahoma, where twenty three were added to the church; Frankfort, Alabama, near Russellville, August 10-21, ten professions of faith; Mt. Gilead near Burnsville, Mississippi, August 21-September 2, fifteen additions; Strawberry, Arkansas, September 4-18, ten professions and Poughkeepsie, Arkansas, September 18-29, twenty professions.

In November Antioch Church called C. N. Glover to help Bogard in a meeting. Thirteen were added to the church making a total of fifty additions to Antioch that year under the preaching of their pastor and the evangelist.

Though the church continued to grow under his leadership, the opposition kept up the reports that "Antioch had been torn up by her pastor," that it was a dead church, to which thrusts Bogard answered in his paper with articles showing her continued progress.

He spent all of the month of December in Georgia and Florida speaking to many churches. The Christmas holidays interrupted a large period of the school work so it was an opportune time to crowd in some extra work. On this tour he preached to these churches: in Georgia, two sermons at Waterloo Church in Tifton and seven sermons in El Dorado; in Florida, ten sermons at Greenville, seven sermons at Bell, twelve sermons to Pine Level Church near Sparks, six sermons to Glenwood Church in Jacksonville, three sermons to Pleasant Grove near Oxford, two sermons in Auburndale, one sermon at Mulberry, to Beulah Church near Plant City and also Lone Oak Church near Plant City, five sermons in Clearwater, two in St. Petersburg and two in Pensacola.

A summary of the work done by this tireless preacher in

his seventieth year is almost unbelievable. He held nine revival meetings, one debate, two funerals, four weddings, preached 290 sermons, gave 66 speeches and lectures, witnessed 141 professions of faith, rejoiced in 154 additions to churches and baptized 63. When in Little Rock, he also taught classes each day in the Baptist Institute for eight months. He received for his work that year $1,641.58. All of this was accomplished in addition to the responsibilities entailed as pastor of a growing church and dean of a theological school steadily increasing in the number of students and classes. Bogard raised the money to keep this work of training the ministry growing and going. He had always helped young ministers and so poured his energies into this work he loved so dearly and which he referred to as a monument and as his greatest achievement.

1939

In addition to pastoral duties during the year 1939, Bogard continued to travel and preach. He visited Itasca and Dallas, Texas, preaching to the churches in this area. He held meetings in Seminole, Oklahoma, as well as at Garden Grove Church near Shawnee and Plainview near Weatherford, Oklahoma. Meetings in Colorado were held in Pueblo, Fowler, Mt. View Church near Denver, Kirk and he preached a sermon at Montrose, Colorado, while engaged in a debate there. Other meetings were held in Frankfort and Hodges, Alabama, in Leola and Strawberry, Arkansas and one at Tot near Corinth, Mississippi. The revival in Hodges, Alabama, was his eighth and resulted in forty two additions to the church. Bogard suggested that the church authorize G. W. Holcomb, a visiting minister from Hamilton, to baptize. In the eight revivals and two debates, two hundred and forty five came into the church. He wrote of this last meeting with them: "In this last meeting heaven came down our souls to greet. At least a thousand people attended the meetings at night and from two to three hundred in the day meetings." —*Orthodox Baptist Searchlight, September 11, 1939.* He also attended a fellowship meeting in Ardmore, Orkahoma, where he preached. And, "During 1939 I have been editor and manager of the *Orthodox Baptist Searchlight* and have been dean of the Missionary Baptist Institute and have taught the Bible one hour a day during the eight months school. No change has been made in my work for the future," he wrote in his journal as a summary of the year's work.

During the month of April, J. E. Cobb, secretary-treasurer of missions for the American Baptist Association, visited Antioch and preached. Bogard wrote of this meeting, "From all indications peace and harmony will prevail in the ranks from this time on. Dr. Cobb stated that he greatly appreciated the fellowship and co-operation of Antioch Church . . . The fight is over and the victory has been won. Let there be peace and fellowship in the future." —April 25, 1939, *Orthodox Baptist Searchlight.*

In connection with the opening of the Missionary Baptist Institute, Antioch Church held a Fellowship meeting October 3-12, services beginning each day at 9:30 and continuing throughout the day with evangelistic messages by S. C. Hammock of Bogalusa, Louisiana. Each morning W. Lee Rector spoke and the rest of the time was taken up by R. Nelson Colyer, W. O. Patterson, C. N. Glover, J. Louis Guthrie, E. C. Gillentine, A. J. Kirkland, M. B. Hubbard, W. A. Reese, M. W. Overton, L. J. Crawford, J. W. Kesner, A. T. Powers, Vernon Barr and others.

Often there were questions as to how Bogard could pastor a full time growing church such as Antioch was and still be away so much of the time. He answered these with a short editorial in the *Orthodox Baptist Searchlight:*

"Being pastor of the Antioch Church for full time, how does he get away so much to hold meetings, teach short Bible schools and debate? The answer is that Elders L. D. Foreman Dayle Capell and J. Louis Guthrie, all connected with the Missionary Baptist Institute and all of them great preachers, supply for him while he is away and the church is well pleased with them and the church prospers under their ministry. Good arrangement." —September 11, 1939.

Antioch continued to prosper with additions to the church, as well as material gains. A new roof was put on the building. A beautiful oil painting was placed in back of the baptistry by Mr. and Mrs. Vernon Heard. This greatly added to the attractiveness of this important place in the church building.

Antioch kept up her progress in bringing new and interesting speakers to the church:

"Antioch Church, Little Rock, is still enjoying a revival . . .

"Then came Eld. Daniel Rosoff and his father Harriett Rosoff with Mrs. Charlotte Colburn, their pianist, and that evangelistic party stayed with the church eight days and notwithstanding almost continual rains and the further obstacle that many of our best people were out of town and the further fact that school commencements were coming on right at the same time, yet the Lord blessed and there were four public professions and additions for baptism besides others by letter. The result of all these efforts was we had a nice baptizing. Antioch Church does not depend on protracted meetings for conversions and baptisms as that good work goes on all through the year.

"Daniel Rosoff is a Jew and is a mighty preacher, sound in the faith, and successful in his work. He lectured to the students of the Missionary Baptist Institute every day and preached at night. On the last night he and his father exemplified the Feast of the Passover and notwithstanding it was the worst of stormy nights a great congregation heard and saw the Passover Feast just exactly as it is observed by the Jews all over the world to this day . . . Antioch Church now has a membership of five hundred and fifty members and is steadily growing. Praise be. Fellowship fine.''—B.M.B. *Search-light,* June 10, 1939.

The Texarkana controversy did not seem to be over though the publications business in Texarkana was in competent hands and Bogard stopped printing additional literature, for he wrote in September, ''The organized effort to smear the pastor and injure the church is answered by the Lord who keeps on adding new members to the church. Congregations fine and fellowship excellent.''

That year he gave full time leadership to Antioch, but also held ten meetings and one debate. He preached 216 sermons beside the 41 radio addresses and the 25 speeches and lectures. Conversions witnessed that year were eighty four and 134 additions to the church. He received $1,700.65 for his services.

TWENTY FIVE YEARS IN LITTLE ROCK

1940 marked Bogard's twenty fifth year as pastor in the Greater Little Rock area and his twentieth year as pastor of Antioch Church. In March of 1940 his church honored him with a surprise celebration—a Homecoming Day, Sunday March 31st, as this was the day he would complete his twentieth year. It was planned as a surprise for him and all preparations were made while he was in Florida in a meeting. The *Orthodox Baptist Searchlight* carried an article April 10, 1940, written by him about this service in Little Rock. A similar one was carried in the *Arkansas Gazette,* a Little Rock newspaper. This article, among other things, observed that ''Mr. Bogard holds the record of being the oldest preacher in point of service in Greater Little Rock.'' The church contributes every Sunday to some feature of mission work and maintains a Bible School and the Missionary Baptist Institute. . . Much of Dr. Bogard's time is spent away from Little Rock and he has preached and lectured in nineteen different states during the past twenty years. . . The church is in almost perfect harmony and fellowship.''

The church membership had reached 533 at that time and the goal for this special day of honor was to have that number present. In July 1940, Dr. Bogard led Antioch to set Dr. J. Louis Guthrie ''apart for this special work'' of assisting the Texas and Oklahoma brethren in doing such work as he finds to do since there was a need of someone to lead in the Lord's work in these fields; that the masses were asking for someone capable of teaching and leading.

At the business meeting October 9, 1940, the church unanimously voted to pay the pastor a stipulated salary of $150.00 a month. Up until this time, he received whatever came in the ''basket'' collections. At this meeting the church membership was 528 and the Sunday School 312, average of 150 in Prayer Meeting. ''The Bible Institute is conducting a Bible Study Class at 7 o'clock each Wednesday night led by Dr. J. Louis Guthrie for those who work and cannot attend the Institute to have an opportunity to attend at least one class offered by the school.

This year there were 11 regular teachers on the staff. $340.56 was contributed to the school that year by Antioch.

April 10, 1940, Dr. Bogard explained that due to Mrs. Berneice Hester's illness she would not be able to serve as pianist for some time and nominated Louise Heard for assistant pianist. She was elected unanimously. ''Beautiful oil painting presented by Mr. and Mrs. Vernon Heard for the baptisry.'' (Thanks expressed Nov. 15, 1939.)

In addition to his pastoral duties, he preached to First Emmanuel in Pine Bluff and Pine Ridge near Joaquin, Texas. He held meetings at Hephzibah in Emerson, Arkansas, in Russell, Arkansas and one in Emmanuel Baptist Church in Pensacola, Florida, with pastor E. E. Rice. While on tour in Florida in December he preached at Bell, while he was there in a debate, also at Greenville, Dade City, Brushwell, Clearwater, St. Petersburg, Auburndale, Beulah near Mulberry and Mulberry. He brought a message to the messenger body at the American Baptist Association in Laurel, Mississippi, as well as, making a speech to this group.

In 1940, he held three meetings, three debates and preached a total of 150 sermons, and gave 45 addresses and 46 radio addresses. He witnessed 41 conversions and 67 additions to churches, receiving $1743.78 for his work.

1941

In this, his fifty third year in the ministry, his work began to diminish some, though he still carried a heavy load for a man of his age. He helped to organize a church at Baseline, eight miles out of Little Rock, during the month of July where he preached the message for the service. He supplied for the pastor in Mineral Springs Church, Texas and attended Fellowship Meetings in Ennis, Texas and Fort Smith, Arkansas. He held only one meeting that year with Ernest Rippetoe at Stephensville and Pontotoc, Texas and one debate, but preached 105 sermons in addition to the 155 radio sermons and 2 addresses. He witnessed 18 conversions and 100 additions to churches, receiving for his work $1,850.00. He was privileged to preach at Woodlawn Church in Union County, Kentucky, where he had begun his ministry fifty three years ago. He said, ''A full house greeted me June 15th. At night I preached in Morganfield and at both places met many old time friends.''

Hoyt Chastain preached in a two weeks revival in Antioch Church that year and 26 were added to the church.

In September, 1941, Bogard formed a partnership with James MacKrell in the radio work ''known as the Bible Lovers Revival. This broadcasting is done twice every week day and once on Sunday. The work was done over KLRA, Little Rock, Arkansas.'' Mr. MacKrell had been, for some time, affiliated with the Convention people, but in Bogard's words, ''got filled up on their unscriptural irregularities and came out from them . . ." Bogard, with others, helped him to organize an independent Baptist Church which was named East Side Missionary Baptist Church.

His work with Antioch Church kept prospering. He wrote, "The Antioch Missionary Baptist Church, Little Rock, Arkansas, had a baptizing in January and also one in February and here is hoping the Lord may continue to save souls and that the baptizings will go on at least once a month all through the year. The congregations fill the house to the back corners at the regular Sunday services and harmony of a most unusual kind is experienced in the membership. The radio work is kept up and the *Orthodox Baptist Searchlight* is prospering beyond our fondest imagination—everybody is happy." —*Orthodox Baptist Searchlight,* March 10, 1941. Again in July he wrote of baptisms in the church and of the fellowship.

August 18th marked the golden wedding anniversary of the Bogards. The church did not forget their pastor and surprised him with a party to which two hundred and fifty members and friends came to offer congratulations and help them celebrate this happy occasion. A wedding cake with fifty golden candles was on an altar surrounded by golden tapers. After prayer, singing and speeches, dinner was served by the young people of the church. Of this occasion he wrote, "The wonderful expression of love bound the pastor and church closer together after having been together as pastor and church for twenty one and a half years. 'Blest be the tie that binds our hearts in Christian love' was sung heartily."

In September, he made a motion that Homer D. Myers be be "assistant *to* the pastor." His duties as a helper were to do visitation work since this had become too much for the pastor with all of his other responsibilities. The fact was stressed that he was not to be an "assistant pastor" but only an "assistant *to* the pastor. He was to fill the pulpit only when the pastor or the church asked him to. He seemed to understand this arrangement and accepted the position on these terms.

Golden Wedding Anniversary. Members of the church arranged the celebration.

The church elected his wife to be the clerk, thus separating the work of clerk-treasurer. Later, Mrs. Myers became Dr. Bogard's secretary for a time.

This was the year Bogard led the church to buy some opera chairs for the auditorium. They could be bought from a theatre for $1.50 each. Since the treasury had no money to buy them, J. Louis Guthrie loaned $300.00 interest free and J. C. Fuester, another member, loaned the other $150.00 on the same generous terms. J. R. Dowell and students from the Seminary placed the chairs in the church.

At the end of 1941, the annual report of the church showed great progress made in finances as well as in the membership.

Bogard published a story in his paper, saying, ". . . as cold facts which refute the story peddled around that Antioch Church is about dead. Wonder when the dear misguided brethren will quit peddling falsehoods about Antioch Church and pastor . . . the Sunday School under the superintendency of E. L. 'Ned' Johnston is the best we have ever had. Peace, harmony, unity almost perfect, prevail in the membership for all of which we thank God and take courage."

1942

Bogard held four meetings and only one debate in 1942. He preached for Pastor S. T. Francis and the First Baptist Church in Ennis, Texas, also at Trinity Heights Church in Dallas. He was the evangelist in two week's meeting in Texas the first of July. He first spent a half day with A. J. Kirkland in his home, then went on to Ebenezer Church where Z. E. Wolverton was pastor. He stayed a week there, witnessing the baptism which followed his meeting, then went with J. R. Welch, pastor, to Pleasant Hill Church for another campaign. These weeks were enjoyable to him as he recalled times in the distant past when he had preached there. He also held a meeting with Pastor Herbert Brown and the church in Paris, Ark.

Elk City, Oklahoma, was the place selected for a "Teaching Revival" in which he preached each night, then held two teaching services every day. Pete Thomas was the pastor of this church.

In August, Bogard in company with Dr. J. Louis Guthrie, took a "wonderful journey to cool Colorado." They visited churches there, though they went primarily to attend the Midwestern Association which was made up of churches in Colorado and Kansas. He preached to the Bible Missionary Baptist Church in Denver, Colorado, and for the Park Hill Church in Pueblo. Both he and Dr. Guthrie helped in a Bible School in Tabernacle Baptist Church, Pueblo, where M. B. Hubbard was pastor.

The work at the church continued to prosper under his leadership. There were numerous baptizings, though not many revival campaigns. "While protracted meetings are good it is better to keep the good work going all the time," he wrote when announcing another baptism at the church. In April, 1942, he wrote, "Antioch church is prospering as never before. Not only do we have frequent baptizings of new converts, but the finances of the church runs over the top. No special effort is made to raise money, but each Sunday the collection plates are passed and the people bring their money to church voluntarily without any collectors. Up to date the pastor is paid in full and there has accumulated a large surplus in the treasury and the church took that surplus and bought $1200 worth of Defense Bonds."

During this time when the United States was at war and there were shortages in many things, he wrote an editorial, typical of him:

"Shall the Tire Situation Keep People from Church?

"People went to church in large numbers before there was such a thing as a rubber tire of any sort. If they want to do so they can go to church after such things as automobiles are out of existence. Where there are street cars and busses the matter is easy. In the country where there are no public conveyances they can still hitch up 'Old Beck' and drive to the meeting house and walking is not all taken up. Selah! Surely n**o** saved person will stay away from the house of God to save tires. Save them some other way or let them wear out. Don't begin saving at the house of God. To save rubber that way will be to save rubber and lose the joy of salvation. The New Testament says, 'Forsake not the assembling of yourselves together . . . —unless there is a tire shortage? The Lord's meeting house should be the last place to stop driving to. Did you think of doing so?'' —*Orthodox Baptist Searchlight,* July 25, 1942.

1943

Bogard had accumulated such an amount of work by 1943 that his traveling was greatly curtailed. He wrote:

''Having twice as much to do in Little Rock as I can get done—preaching twice every Sunday and having charge of the mid-week prayer meetings and speaking over the radio every Sunday morning at 8 o'clock and frequently doing the radio work during week days, editing and managing the *Orthodox Baptist Searchlight,* the most widely circulated paper in its class in the world, and teaching in the Missionary Baptist Institute and being treasurer and financial manager of that great school and also treasurer and financial manager of the Bible Lovers' Revival, a radio work that reaches from the Atlantic to the Pacific oceans and requiring from three thousand to six thousand dollars a month to keep it going, all of that on my hands, I thought it best not to accept calls to hold protracted meetings but stay strictly on the job here in Little Rock. But I could not resist the temptation to go back to two places calling for me, one at Hodges, Alabama, where I have held three debates and eight protracted meetings and the other at old Antioch Church near Atoka, Tennessee, where I held a very successful meeting twenty-five years ago. What a joy to go back to such places and labor with them in the gospel again." —*Orthodox Baptist Searchlight,* June 25, 1943.

Of the work at Antioch, he wrote, "We are not doing any wonderful things, but the Lord has given us a continued revival for the last several years. We have not had protracted meetings but souls have been saved in our regular services. In the last two months the Lord has given us three middle-aged men, married men with families, and we rejoice to know that our labor has not been in vain. We have had two baptizings and we are hopeful of others being saved," then in the August 10, 1943, edition of the *Searchlight,* he wrote this interesting article:

"The Baptist Church 'Showcase' Revival at
Antioch Church (Little Rock) Continues

"When did the protracted meeting begin? There has been no protracted meeting—it is a continued revival at the regular services of the church—the pastor doing the preaching Sunday mornings and nights with a Wednesday night prayer meeting. That is all. Have not had a protracted meeting in several years in the sense generally understood by the expression, protracted meeting. But many are saved and they make public confession and are baptized in the regular Sunday services.

"Sunday, July 18, was a great day in Antioch Church. At the morning service a young man in the Flying Forces of the Army, visiting his parents, made public profession of faith in Christ. His wife, a Roman Catholic, came to church with him and it was her first time to hear a gospel sermon. She had not been inside a Baptist church house before and she asked a lady, 'What is the show-case back of the pulpit for? It was explained to her that what she thought was a 'show-case' was the baptistry. She heard the gospel for the first time and was deeply impressed when her husband made public profession of faith. We announced that he would be baptized that night in what his wife thought was a 'show-case.' At night she, too, made public profession of faith and was baptized with her husband. They put their arms around each other and the pastor baptized both of them with one dip. The young man's father came that night and he also made public profession of faith and he, too, was baptized, making four baptisms that night. The Lord has given us five married men and one married lady during the last two months and we thank God and take courage. Maybe we need a protracted meeting but we are getting better results at the regular services than some churches get by having protracted meetings. We are in favor of protracted meetings but why not keep the good work going all the time?

"That young married woman who thought the baptistry was a 'show-case' little dreamed that she would be in that 'show-case' that very night. But the grace of God brought her into that 'show-case' where she and her husband and the others mentioned really did show by being baptized that Jesus was buried and arose again. Thus we see 'show-case' is really a good name for the baptistry. Show cases are where a merchant shows his goods, displays his wares and the baptistry when used, shows—displays—those who believe that Jesus died for our sins and was buried and arose again according to the scriptures (I Corinthians 15:1-5).

"All through the year Antioch Church uses her 'show-case.' "

His revival in Hodges that year was Bogard's ninth one there and because the war had taken so many of the young men away and others had gone to work in defense plants, the people warned there might not be large crowds as there had always been before; however, he wrote, describing this meeting, "The people came in droves, the whole hill was covered with people and an average of seven hundred came every night, the large house overflowed and one hundred and fifty to three hundred pople could not get in the house but listened quietly throught the open windows and doors . . ." He also said, "Some of the richest experiences of my life have been at Hodges and if my life history is ever written in a book, one full chapter must be given to Hodges."

In the preparation of outlines, chapters and other information for this work, we had planned a special place for the Hodges, Alabama work in which Bogard figured so prominenly. We little realized nor remembered he had written this statement in 1943. So, the expression certainly has a note of prophecy in it. Though we did not know he said it, we had prepared a special section for the Alabama Church (in Bogard, the Debater).

By 1944, Dr. Bogard had been with Antioch Church for twenty five years and it continued to prosper. He was in his 76th year and seemed still to be in the prime of his life, though he did very little traveling because of the tremendous responsibilities at home. He wrote:

"The Editor Away From Home Very Little

"The work is so heavy in Little Rock, by the time he does the work as pastor of Antioch Church and edits and manages the *Orthodox Baptist Searchlight* and attends to the radio broadcasting and serves as manager of the Missionary Baptist Institute, that the editor can be away from home very little. He has refused to accept engagements that were offered to him this summer that would have taken three months to fulfill. He did manage to get away for a protracted meeting in Duncan, Oklahoma and another with Pastor Wayne Cox at Walnut Grove Church, Tennessee, and still another at Arbor Grove Church near Hoxie, Arkansas, with Pastor Paul Goodwin. The Lord blessed in each of these engagments. In Tennessee he was entertained in the home of the pastor and at Arbor Grove Church in the home of Brother Neice. Better entertainment could not have been given if a first class hotel had been engaged for the purpose.

"Antioch Church is interested in the whole field and does not selfishly demand that the pastor spend every day in their midst. The voice of Antioch Church goes out wherever the pastor goes and the members feel this responsibility and enjoy helping in the great work. The work in Antioch is well cared for by the assistant to the pastor, Homer D. Myers, when the pastor is away. The Missionary Baptist Institute has such a good faculty that some member of the faculty substitutes for the editor when he is gone. Altogether, it is a happy arrangement with which evidently the Lord is pleased." *(Orthodox Baptist Searchlight,* September 25, 1944).

This year Bogard gave the property at 3300 Asher Avenue to the Missionary Baptist Seminary. It consisted of an entire block on Asher. The plot was named Bogard Court in his honor.

At the closing of this year, he wrote:

"Closed 1944 And Opened 1945 With Baptizings

"Antioch Church, Little Rock, Arkansas, had the happy experience of two public professions of faith the last week in the year 1944. During the last week there were twelve additions to the church. One was awaiting baptism and the last night of 1944 the church administered baptism and the first Sunday night in 1945 there was another baptizing. Good ending of old year and good start for the new year. We are hoping to keep the baptistry wet all through the year . . ."

1945

Antioch voted to build a house on the back of the lots of the church property on Brown Street to house the printing equipment Dr. Bogard bought and gave to the Seminary. The first *Searchlight* was printed on this press March 10, 1945. The press was to be "A Strictly Religious Print Shop" as he noted in his editorial in this paper: "When we were getting the fine machinery installed in the Missionary Baptist Institute Print Shop, a good brother said: 'I will get out and secure a lot of printing for you,' meaning he would hunt up a lot of commercial printing for us. I thanked him for his interest and said, 'My brother, we do not need business, and we will not accept any commercial printing, for our printery will be strictly religious printing—the *Orthodox Baptist Searchlight* and books written by the faculty of the Bible School and if we have time will print religious books written by our brethren whoever they may be, not *no profit making work* . . .''

"We expect to keep the press hot printing this paper and the numerous books that are to be printed. It is not a commercial shop and *it is not a profit making shop*. It is the Lord's work and *nobody is making profit on the work turned out by this printery*. B. M. B.''

This was like a dream come true to the man of God who knew the value of the printed page and any other avenue that would keep the work of Christ before the people. Often, he would stand in the shop and listen to the noise with a smile on his face. "It's music to my ears," he often said.

During the entire year, the paper continued to carry reports of the numerous baptizings in Antioch Church. In May, Dan Gilbert held another series of meetings and was present for the Commencement exercises of the Seminary.

Bogard spent the month of August in California.

As is usual in most churches, at some time, someone will begin a campaign against his pastor. It seems no church can be completely free of people who simply begin such underhand whispers. Antioch's membership was no exception, though it is often someone outside the membership who starts the talk. Reports are exaggerated to make it sound as if many people are dissatisfied when in reality it is only a very few. That year it was whispered about that Antioch wanted a younger man for pastor. Because of the continual innuendoes afloat, Bogard gave the church an opportunity to vote as to whether he would continue as their pastor. This is his report of what happened:

"The Greatest Honor I Ever Received

"After having preached for Antioch Baptist Church, Little Rock, Arkansas, for twenty six years and in addition to that having held three protracted meetings in which I did all the preaching it was to be expected that some of the members would prefer to change preachers. Such is the case in nearly all churches and it would be surprising if it were not true in Antioch Church.

"There was a persistent rumor that the church wanted a younger man, and knowing the almost universal craze for youth that prevails in nearly all the churches, I talked with one of the deacons and suggested that the church might get a younger man for all that I cared—if the church wanted to swap off the old pastor for a young man I was willing to do it. I also told the deacons in a deacons meeting that if the church wanted a younger man it would be agreeable to me for I had as much as one man ought to do in looking after the interests of the Missionary Baptist Institute, as its president and editing and managing the most widely circulated paper that exists among our people, the *Orthodox Baptist Search-light*. So I told the deacons that I intended to ask the church to vote whether I should go or stay and that the vote would be a secret ballot so that nobody would be embarrassed by being compelled to stand up and vote against me. That would make it easy for anyone who might want me to go to vote for me to go.

"At the largest meeting that ever met in Antioch Church, the house being filled to the corners, with a membership of exactly seven hundred and four there was found only three votes for me to go. When the vote was announced the church

Only picture ever made with his hearing aid. He wore the hearing aid for about three years.

—a great house full—burst out in loud applause, a thing never seen in Antioch Church before.

"Did I appreciate it? Never such an honor came to me before. Those who have been passing it around that Antioch Church was tired of me as pastor and that the members wanted a younger man have their answer. The church by this wonderful vote decided that a pastor seventy eight years old was young enough for them. I announced, when the applause ceased, that since they had so enthusiastically voted for me to stay, that I never expected to ask them to vote on me again. The church does not have the unscriptural annual call, but the pastor asked them to say by vote whether he had stayed long enough and you have the answer. I have started in for a fresh ten years hard work in the church and the Missionary Baptist Institute. Please, brethren, work with me for the next decade. Ben M. Bogard."

1946

Bogard kept reporting the keen interest and spiritual atmosphere in Antioch Church which resulted in frequent baptisms. Interest became so intense that a revival in the regular services caused a meeting to start. It was a "Young Peoples' Revival," the preaching being done by the "boy preachers" in the Missionary Baptist Institute. This was an added blessing to the church since it followed a trying time when a number of members who had followed Mr. Myers, the assistant to the pastor, when he left the church after being relieved of his duties. Of this meeting, Bogard wrote, "A business meeting recently that some feared would bring trouble, really brought joy and a revival broke out right in business meeting—five fine people joined the church that very night and there was enjoyed the finest spiritual feeling the church ever experienced. Souls are being saved and a baptizing will have been enjoyed before the readers read this."

He wrote in March, 1946:

"Greatest Revival Ever Seen in Antioch Church

"Just as the rumor went out that Antioch Church (Little Rock) was torn all to pieces and ruined, a great revival came upon the church, the best revival any of the members recall seeing in that church. Praise be to God.

"Congregations are larger, the Sunday School decidedly better and the prayer meeting much larger—more than two hundred attending on an average; the ladies auxiliary is more than twice as large and the collections on an average twenty five per cent larger and the fellowship fine, the best seen in many years. Harmony, unity, brotherly love almost perfect, certainly very excellent. Thirty four joined the church in the last five weeks, thirteen of them by baptism. All of this at the regular services of the church. It is not a protracted meeting revival—just the results seen in the regular Sunday Services. This is not reported in the sense of boasting but in the sense of gratitude to God for giving us showers of blessings."

Dan Gilbert was with the church once again in April of this year, bringing two lectures in the day and one at night. These were more prophetical than teaching or evangelistic messages.

Bogard was invited to preach the morning and evening sermons on the occasion of the 15th year anniversary of Central Baptist Church in Fort Smith, Arkansas with their pastor, J. W. Kesner, which was May 19th. It was a homecoming day and Bogard enjoyed the occasion immensely.

Enemies of Dr. Bogard kept the rumor going that Antioch Church was steadily going down. Much of this whispering campaign was the result of anger when seventeen people went out of Antioch with Mr. and Mrs. Myers and joined the Temple Church in Little Rock. They had become involved in the "Myers case" and were dissatisfied in the church. He notes in his record of this occasion that sixty six others had gone out that year but at least half of these were preacher boys and their wives who took letters to join churches of which the young men became pastors. This was a normal situation, as it often occurred. Since the time the seventeen had left, seventy six others had joined, beginning the very night the faction left. Exactly the number was baptized as the number who had left, as well as, the best offerings. He said, "All along during these twenty six years there have been people in Little Rock who have told the members that they would 'join Antioch Church if they would get rid of Bogard.' One brother says right now that he is waiting for Bogard to die and then he will join Antioch. That brother has floated around among the churches, having joined at least four churches trying to find where he could be pleased and now he is waiting for Bogard to die so he can join Antioch. Several who read this will recognize who it is I speak of.

"What we need to do is to be constantly in prayer and live constantly within the will of God and greater prosperity lies out before us. We should be dissatisfied with the accomplishments of the past and press on to greater and better things.

"When I heard the rumor that the church was going down under my leadership I fully made up my mind to resign if the facts proved the rumor to be true, for I certainly do not want the church to go down on me. But when the facts disclosed the truth that the church has increased in every detail, I decided I would not resign."

During the month of August Bogard engaged in revival meetings and Albert Garner supplied the pulpit of Antioch Church. His meetings were in Hodges, Alabama, Corinth, Mississippi and Strawberry, Arkansas. He usually spent his vacations—Antioch allowed him four Sundays a year—in this way. He said, "It is real rest in the sense that change of work is rest and relief from responsibility is no small part of the resting."

As always, going to Hodges was almost like going home. He had already preached ten revivals here and had three debates. He especially enoyed working with Brother Wheeler

Overton in this meeting. He said, "I have held ten protracted meetings in Hodges and all of them resulted in baptizings and I think the last was the smallest, there being only twelve. At the close of one of these meetings I baptized fifty one and over half of the church in Hodges have come into the church under my preaching. It is like going home for me to go to that fine community." He gave special attention to the song director, D. W. Wright. This man was ninety one years old but his voice was still clear, and Bogard said, "The sight of a man 91 years old leading the songs is worth going a long ways to hear."

He received offerings for the Seminary, subscriptions for the *Searchlight* and an offering for himself in each meeting: "I came back to Little Rock feeling much better and stronger, in fact better than I have felt in two years. Preaching twice a day and some of the time three times a day for a month is rather active for a preacher in his seventy eighth year. But I never felt like traveling on more than I do as I write this account of a happy and fruitful month . . ."

In September, he had an urgent invitation from the brethren in Fayetteville Association to visit with them. He loved the trip through the beautiful Ozark mountains. He preached in this meeting and received a very nice offering for the Seminary. Leaving the association, he visited the church in Van Buren with Pastor Herbert Brown and was asked to preach.

The last picture ever made of Brother and Sister Bogard together by Dr. Hoyt Chastain.

XIII

PASTOR EMERITUS

On Wednesday night, January 8, 1947, Ben M. Bogard offered his resignation as pastor of Antioch Baptist Church. He had been preaching for fifty nine years, twenty seven of them as pastor of Antioch. His resignation was to take effect as soon as the church could secure another pastor.

"PASTOR'S RESIGNATION

"After several weeks of prayerful consideration I have decided that it will be better for me and for Antioch Church for me to resign. Therefore, I offer my resignation to take effect as soon as a new pastor can be secured and settled on the field to give full time to the work as pastor. No one has asked me to resign and not one has even suggested that I resign.

"I have no idea of retiring from active work as preacher but will really begin an enlarged and expanded work by accepting invitations of other churches to preach special sermons and by giving more time to the Missionary Baptist Institute teaching short Bible Schools wherever the opportunity presents such work.

"I shall remain in Little Rock and be subject to the call of Antioch Church for my service that I can give, such as supplying the pulpit at the request of the pastor and as counsellor when asked for counsel, but under no conditions will I offer my advice unless called upon to do so by the church or pastor. By this course I can do more for Antioch Church and more for the cause of Christ than if I remain as active pastor. I am not forsaking you but stand ready to help at any time if needed.

"I wish to express my appreciation for the co-operation

and fellowship that exists at present and that has existed almost all the time I have been pastor, and for the fine way the majority of the membership have stood firmly when confusion or any sort of trouble has come into our ranks. I have been confident of the fidelity of the members all along during the almost twenty seven years I have been pastor. I have never been the least uneasy when I have been away for even months at a time, for I felt sure that you would be found in good order when I returned and I have never been disappointed.

"To remain so long in a pastorate—twenty seven years—is a record breaker for our churches not only in Arkansas but all over the land. This fact is a compliment that is to be cherished by both the pastor and church, and the fact that almost perfect fellowship now exists in the church, and the fact that success in soul-saving, and success in all the work of the church continues to this day, makes my resigning a pleasure. This is much better than to resign when the church is running down and discouraged, and very frankly I will say I do not want to wait until that sort of thing might be.

"I have no intention of retiring, neither do I intend to take a furlough. I was called into the ministry for life and shall continue as an active preacher so long as I have strength for it, and this resignation only changes the character and scope of my work and I firmly believe that I shall be more useful in this new relation.

"Sincerely, by the grace of God, Ben M. Bogard."

The auditorium of Antioch Church was completely filled that night. It was the largest business meeting ever held in the church, as large an attendance as the Sunday morning services. Harmony, unity, fellowship—almost perfect—prevailed in the membership. When the resignation was accepted, E. L. "Ned" Johnston, deacon and Sunday School superintendent made a motion that Bogard be continued as pastor-emeritus of the church. This motion carried by unanimous vote—Bogard became pastor-emeritus for life with a salary from the church. The salary was set at $150.00 per month. This was continued even to his widow until the time of her death. The service closed as the congregation unanimously sang fervently "Blest be the tie that Binds" and then enjoyed a handshaking." Two new members received the hand of fellowship and at the same time the hand of appreciation was enthusiastically given to this grand old soldier of the cross for his long, unselfish years of service.

Bogard's plans were to help get a new pastor settled on the field, then he hoped to accept invitations from every part of the country. This work would include teaching short Bible Schools, preaching on any subject requested, lecturing or serving in whatever capacity he could and holding evangelistic campaigns. His health seemed to be in excellent condition when he left the church as pastor and took up the strenuous activities he had outlined for his future.

Antioch Church called L. D. Foreman, pastor of the First Baptist Church in Sheridan, to succeed Bogard as their leader. The evening service of the outgoing pastor's last service, March 30, 1947, was climaxed with a baptismal service, a fitting, finishing touch to a long, dedicated profitable ministry. The new pastor did the baptizing for the church at Bogard's suggestion.

Bogard was soon deep in the work of holding meetings. In May, he spent four days with the church in Holdenville, Oklahoma, and Carol Christian, pastor, then four days in Barling, Arkansas, with Pastor H. D. Moon, and four days in Pueblo, Colorado with Tabernacle Church and Isaac Smith, pastor. While there he also preached for the Macedonia Church and Pastor Raymond Lambuth.

In May, Bogard "had a pleasant visit with the churches in Van Buren and Ft. Smith, Arkansas." He also helped in a Bible Conference in Corsicana, Texas, with the Missionary Baptist Church and Pastor A. J. Kirkland who was a lecturer at that time in the Missionary Baptist Seminary making regular trips to Little Rock for this purpose. He spent four days with Vernon Barr and the South Harwood Church in Dallas, Texas, then several days in the Wanderer's Home Church a few miles from Piggott, Arkansas.

Bogard supplied in June for Pastor Walter Lovelady and the Main Street Baptist Church in Pine Bluff, Arkansas. He made a tour of Southern Mississippi where he had in the past held seven debates. J. E. Roberson was his "bishop" (overseer), taking him from church to church. He went to Union Church near Lucedale, to New Home Church across the line in Alabama and while there went over to Citronelle. From here he traveled to Wiggins, then Perkinston, Mississippi, where he enjoyed preaching to good congregations. The last church he visited in that state was Paramount Church where Mr. Toney was pastor. From Mississippi, J. E. Moore, pastor in Wiggins, drove him to Bogalusa, Louisiana where he was "turned over" to J. M. Stuart and preached in the three churches he served as pastor—in Bogalusa, Pine and Varnada, Louisiana. In July, the traveling preacher, returned to Louisiana to preach in an evangelistic campaign in Franklington with Pastor Carl Sullivan and the State Line Church. He enjoyed preaching in a meeting in Prattsville, Arkansas, too, where he had held seven meetings in the past and had baptized over a hundred converts. He went into Missouri to be with L. H. Owens in Sullivan, close to St. Louis, then made a trip into northern Mississippi where he held a meeting with Mount Zion Church, eight miles from Amory. This was his fifth meeting with them and he had held two debates there. In the meetings eighty one had been received for baptism. F. M. Holcomb was the pastor. At the close of this meeting, he went to Hatley to visit in the revival being held there by evangelist Alvan Rester.

September brought other meetings, one for the Promise Land Baptist Church near Hamburg, Arkansas, and while there he went over to Maplevale Church to preach to them,

REVEREND B. M. BOGARD
Little Rock, Ark.
PREACHED EVERY SUNDAY
FOR 61 YEARS!
WITHOUT MISSING A SINGLE SUNDAY

From Robert Ripley's "Believe It Or Not."

then in October, to the Pettitt Memorial Church in Bogalusa and assisted in the first week of the new school year in Bogalusa Bible School. He held his sixth "protracted" meeting with the church at Poughkeepsie, Arkansas and preached for one service in the church in Russellville, Arkansas.

County Avenue Baptist Church where he had once held membership called on Bogard to supply their pulpit for the month of October while their pastor, I. K. Cross, was away touring the west. He carried on the radio broadcast there and completely enjoyed this work for he was "back among many old time friends.

Bogard's picture appeared for the second time in Ripley's "Believe It Or Not" which was carried in the *Arkansas Gazette* October 5, 1497. Under it was the notice, "Reverend B. M. Bogard, Little Rock, Arkansas, preached every Sunday for 61 years without missing a single Sunday."

BACK IN FLORIDA

In November, Bogard made another tour of the beloved Florida work. By this time, being in constant demand and "on the road" he was fearful of being unable to carry on, but wrote:

"DOES ME GOOD TO TRAVEL

"I was afraid that the strenuous work of traveling from church to church and preaching every night and sometimes two or three times a day would be too hard on me, but I fatten on it. Been at it now for seven months and never felt better in my life. The Lord is blessing me in my ministry as never before and I am dated far ahead. Instead of stopping, the work has doubled up on me. Why should a preacher retire until he has worn his old tires out? A preacher who can stop preaching with a clear conscience should never have started preaching in the first place. In the good fight of faith, there is no furlough."

If the reader wonders what care his wife had during his long trips away from home, loving friends watched out for her. She lived in the Bogard home only three doors from the church. Neighbors (Jessie Files and Mrs. Brosious) on both sides were members of Antioch and looked out for her welfare as though she were a part of their own families. The grocery-man, C. V. Heard, was a member of the church. All she had to do was let her wants be known and he would bring the groceries to her door. The J. R. Dowells, a deacon and his wife, lived just back of them.

The pastor lived just one block away, and looked in on her nearly every day—other members were constantly checking. She was happy to be busy among her flowers and in her yard.

The Florida tour was arranged for him by S. J. Akers, his "bishop" on this trip, with whom he stayed in southern Georgia. The Big Creek Church near Fitzgerald was engaged in a meeting with Harris Crittenden assisting Pastor R. J. Eldredge and after Bogard preached twice here, he was driven to Greenville, Florida, where he preached that night. This was to be an eight weeks tour with a schedule to preach every day except one. He wondered if he could stand the strain of so much work for he would soon be eighty years old. He spent seven days with Pastor Harris Crittenden at Greenville, then spent a day with Bell Baptist Church and in the home of Ben M. Williams. As always, he rejoiced in the beauty of nature and especially was fascinated by the long moss hanging from the trees ("the trees wear long whiskers," he said) and the beautiful Suwannee River. He noted the "deep jungles through which tourists may drive, looking at the deer and once in awhile a bear and millions of ducks and wild geese, and hundreds of lazy alligators—a hunter's and fisherman's paradise."

Traveling on to Ocalla, Florida, he was met by J. E. Sinclair who acted as his "presiding elder" while he was in the "extreme southern" part of Florida. What he called extreme southern was really the middle part. He went to Pleasant Grove near Oxford to be with Pastor J. E. Altman, then to Pine Grove Church at Christmas and on to Temple Church in Kissimmee. He had once received a call to pastor this church when he was a very young preacher, but this was his first time to be in it. Carl Moss was the pastor.

For the first time, Bogard saw Brahman cattle and said of them, "They are hump-backed like buffalo and very large. They are wild and dangerous but very prolific and make wonderful beef. It was a new thing for me because I did not know such cattle were in the world. It was worth the trip to see those cattle. I first thought they were buffalo but I never saw white buffalo before. Anyway, if they were painted gray or brown, I would still believe them to be buffalo."

The old preacher was then taken to Auburndale to be with Pastor J. J. Johnson and "the Lord opened the windows of heaven" when four men and women made professions of faith and were received for baptism. He then traveled on to his "old battle-ground"—Mulberry where he had held a debate some years before, and Pastor Otho J. Owens. He preached in Lone Oak Church where W. W. Watson was pastor and visited with the widow of "Daddy" Simmons, a dear friend who for years sent him oranges and grapefruits from his citrus grove each winter. His next stop was with the church at Ardella and J. H. Dorman, pastor, then to Lacoochie with pastor, W. F. Connell. In Jacksonville were four churches and he preached to all of them making his home with E. E. Swearingen, pastor of South Riverside Church, then on for a week in Pensacola, and from there to Gull Point with Pastor Carl Stephens, then closing his tour in Pace with pastor, Ben Howse.

Always, Bogard wrote vivid descriptions of Florida's unsurpassed beauty and at the end of this trip he wrote,

"WHEN IS THE BEST TIME TO GO TO FLORIDA?

"Anytime is a good time, but in the summer and early fall is really best. In the winter time, it is wet, rainy and unpleasantly cool. In the summer the flowers and the fruit are in their glory. The weather is cooler in Florida during the summer than it is any where else in America. Come to Florida to escape the heat in the north. It seems strange but it is true—the breeze from the sea accounts for it. I may never be permitted to visit Florida again, but that will not keep me from wanting to."

Gradually, the old warrior was getting ready for the inevitable time that he knew must come before very many years. He had carried the load for so long and although he had been accused of building a work around himself, he knew this was not true. While on his trip to Florida, he wrote to L. D. Foreman who had succeeded him as pastor in Antioch Church,

"Dear L. D.:

"Here I am in this great hotel really resting a full day before going to Pensacola . . .

"I am feeling fine but am actually getting homesick. I shall have only a few days at home when I get there as Texas is calling loudly and I intend to answer the call . . .

"I am glad to note that you are gradually working into the *Searchlight* as a regular writer. I have not insisted on you doing this because you had a tremendous task when you became both pastor and president of the school. I don't think you realize that *the future of the Searchlight* depends largely on you. It is a difficult matter to settle. Not every man can carry the load of THREE MEN like I did for years, and how I did it without breaking down I do not understand. During the last year I have been unloading on *you and Payne,* especially. I hope you may develop your ability to write *one column* and *half-column* editorials. You are good on long stuff and a little practice will do the other for you. As I pass out of the work you will need to take it up, not a part *but ALL OF IT*.

"As ever, yours, Ben M. Bogard.

He always looked ahead and he did not plan for his life only but for the work after he had gone. He built always with this in mind, that the work keep on going even though the workers had to lay aside their tools for someone else to pick up. He taught and he trained many, many young men so that the work would be going, as he planned, until Jesus comes.

1948

March 9, 1948 was Ben M. Bogard's eightieth birthday. The octagenarian started this year off with a tour into "Red Man's Land" as he called Oklahoma. Earl Lewallen, pastor of Liberty Baptist Church in Shawnee, arranged his appointments. His first engagement was with Garden Grove Church and the pastor, R. T. Rorie, then Central Avenue Church in Oklahoma City with Pastor Gunn. The Indiana Avenue Church T. L. Duren, pastor, was his next stop then he lectured to a new Bible School started in Central Avenue Baptist Church in Oklahoma. In Wewoka, he preached for C. M. Lewallen and in Holdenville, for Carol Christian, pastor, then to Mission Home Church near Wewoka with Pastor Goodnight. He was for three days with Earl Lewallen and the Liberty Church in Shawnee, then concluded his tour with the church in Seminole and Gilbert Burch, pastor.

The latter part of the year he went to Ferndale, Michigan, to be in a meeting with Pastor Frank Ridgeway. Though his slight limp was increasing and his age beginning to be quite evident, his first childlike interest in the things about him was still keen and his delight in new experiences and sights was still as intense as when he was a youth. His mind was active and alert. He particularly enjoyed this trip north, especially to be able to go on into a "foreign" country when Mr. Ridgeway took him into Canada.

One of Bogard's characteristics was that he never missed an appointment or an engagement he had promised to fill. On

December 29, 1948 he missed his first prayer meeting when he had the responsibility of leadership.

He began his Mexican radio work in collaboration with Hoyt Chastain and Dan Gilbert in April. He made elaborate plans for a work which he hoped would be far reaching. However, it did not become the gigantic program he had hoped and dreamed of.

January 5, 1949, Bogard entered the Baptist Hospital in Little Rock. For over a year, he had suffered a heart condition and now it became very serious. For awhile, anxious friends were fearful for his life, but prayers from all over the country and the skill of modern medicine brought him home again and by February, he was again making plans for future work. He was scheduled to preach the annual sermon for the messenger body meeting which was to be held in Little Rock that year. He called it his "Farewell Address" for, he said, he had given the annual sermon four times and had preached at least twenty other times for this body at especially appointed hours.

He thanked the Antioch Church for their concern for him while he was hospitalized:

"I have believed that the members of Antioch Church love me but now I know it. You have covered me up with kindness while I was in the hospital. Cards of sympathy and encouragement poured in to me and you made my hospital look like a FLORIST SHOP—such wonderful flowers and to me the most beautiful flowers in the world because the natural beauty of the flowers was increased by the beautiful love shown by the givers.

"I believe the Lord has answered my prayer and will permit me to see the great educational building finished. This will be the most beautiful building in the world to me. What a picture it will be—three fine dormitories in front and the educational building in the background—a crescent shape. That is my ambition. I hope everyone will fall in and help bring this to completion. I hope to see you face to face in church service soon. Blessings on all of you.—Ben M. Bogard, Pastor Emeritus.''

His plans now were to give much time to editing the paper and to the writing of books. This he did with the writing of editorials, devoting himself to this last great "fight" for the national association he had watched develop and had such a great part in through the years.

Antioch had a Seminar in March in which each of the faculty members presented a lecture on one of the fundamental doctrines of Missionary Baptists. These were later published in a book called "Credenda." Dr. Bogard's lecture was on "God."

He was invited to visit California in 1949, but declined saying, "What a pleasure it would be to spend two or three months in that wonderful state. But it cannot be at this time."

When Pastor L. D. Foreman was away in Florida and in California Bogard filled the pulpit for him. The people still enjoyed his preaching and souls were saved as a result of his messages.

Dr. Bogard left in April for a tour of East Texas; however, while in Texarkana with Herbert and Mary Brown he suffered a heart attack. Mrs. Mary Brown wrote this account of the experience:

"It has been a long time since the event of Bro. Bogard's heart attack in our home in Texarkana. The dates are hard to recall but the things that happened are very vivid. As best we can remember it was in 1949, possibly in the spring.

"We came home and found him sitting in our living room; we were not really surprised because he had come many times unannounced. Our home was his home when he came to Texarkana. He was to conduct several days of meeting at Beverly Missionary Baptist Church. Seemingly he was feeling well. Every morning he made the remark of how many days he had gone without his heart medicine, not knowing it was hurting him.

"Then one morning (possibly Saturday) while listening to Herbert preach on the radio at 8 o'clock he took sick. He began walking the floor and gasping for breath. Jerry and I begged him to let us call the doctor but he kept saying he would be all right. But finally we disobeyed him and started to attempt to get the heart specialist we knew—at this time he was so bad he had fallen partly across the bed and we had to get him in the bed. We couldn't get the doctor we wanted but were able to get a young heart specialist, Dr. Eagles. He came immediately and began working with him and called the ambulance. He said Bro. Bogard would have been dead in a very few minutes. Then he worked with him all the way to the hospital. He was seriously ill several days. Herbert and the other preachers of Texarkana stayed with him in the hospital until he was able to return to Little Rock. His intention was to make a tour of East Texas after Texarkana. He did get to make the trip later.

"Bro. Bogard said many, many timess that I saved his life. I have a letter that he wrote to me while Herbert was ill saying that. It was a harrowing experience and I was always so grateful to Dr. Eagles for coming so quickly."

In August, 1949, the old minister preached for Vimy Ridge Church. That Sunday was a big day. His sermons were interpreted for the deaf in the congregation by Knox Shelton who "signed" as Bogard spoke to the group. In the afternoon, he preached the ordination sermon in this service. This interpreting in the sign language seemed to fascinate Dr. Bogard as he told of it once again being done in the ordination service. That night he went to the Olive Hill Church and preached to them. This sermon was recorded so that it could be used at later times. He also supplied in the pulpit for Bethel Baptist Church in Morrilton that month.

In October, Bogard was permitted to be with the churches of the Spring River Association in Arkansas. "I know almost every pig track in that beautiful mountain country and have

held protracted meetings and debates in every section of it,"
he said. He visited with Little Springs Church at Poughkeepsie
and preached three times. He then spent a day and night at
Strawberry, Arkansas, and then over to Mt. View Church
where a "good congregation greeted me." On to Cave City, he
spent five days preaching for the church there and attended
the Spring River Association which met with them during that
time. Once again his appreciation of the beauties of God's
handiwork was expressed in his editorial: "I was entertained
in a 'cabin' so they called it, but it was a palace to me. Cave
City is situated over a great cave, second only to Mammoth
Cave in Kentucky. How far under the ground the cave goes
nobody knows for it has never been fully surveyed, but it must
run for miles—a river runs underground with water clean and
cold and around the mouth of the cave is a beautiful park and
in that park are a number of fine stone buildings which they
call tourist cabins, but in fact they are palaces. Everything
modern in their fixtures and I lived in luxury while there. People from thousands of miles around come there to rest and
enjoy the luxurious 'cabins.' "

In December 1949, he made a "long triumphant tour in
Texas" in answer to urgent invitations from the brethren
there. He had preached in all parts of Texas and served as
pastor there in the past and so it was a joyous journey to visit
these "old time places" and meet so many good friends and
brethren of "yesteryears." So many came to him on this trip
and expressed their deep feeling, "I was saved under your
preaching," thus, as he put it "giving me a foretaste of heav-
en for I think one of the finest things in heaven will be to have
people come to us and tell us that they are in heaven because
of the gospel we preached that led them to Christ. I had several such experiences on this trip."

His first stop was at Longview with Pastor A. J. Wall. A
number of people had come in for Bible Conference and as he
put it, "they had me preaching in one hour after I got off the

train. I preached on the 'Leadership of the Holy Spirit' and such a responsive audience is seldom seen. He preached twice to the men connected with the LaTourneau establishment, speaking for thirty minutes, his message being broadcast. He spent Sunday with Albert Garner and Bethel Church and spent several days lecturing before the students of the Texas Baptist Institute. He preached twice for the Calvary Church and Pastor R. E. Rodgers. He was with Pastor Riley Dale and the church at Brownsboro, Texas, then with Bill Lee at Arp, Texas. Out from Henderson and Longview at the Brooks Chapel Church, a workers' meeting was scheduled. He visited the fellowship and said, ''They honored me by having me preach in twenty minutes after I got into the house . . . Preach, preach, preach and lecture every day since I have been in Texas. Somebody may say, 'I thought you had retired.' If you call such as this retiring, then I have retired. But I have another name for it. I have only changed my work and am really preaching oftener than I did before I resigned as active pastor at Antioch. I hope to preach until the last day of my life and, if the Lord will, I shall die in the pulpit.''

From the Mt. Zion Association fellowship he went to White Oak Church and Pastor O. H. Griffith. The oil wells interested him. ''Oil gushes out of the earth. The wells do not have pumps to pump it out,'' he said. ''All they have to do is to turn a faucet, as it were, and the oil gushes out. Fabulous wealth lies under their feet. What a pity that only a few who live there know that all this wealth belongs to God. Some are gradually learning this great truth. I had the pleasure to preach Wednesday and the next morning I addressed the students and faculty of the High School. I lectured on 'Science and the Bible.' ''

The next lap of his trip took him to Dallas and the South Harwood Baptist Church with Vernon Barr, pastor, where he also enjoyed a visit with his old friend, L. S. Ballard. That friendship had been strained due to differences of opinion, but on this trip, he wrote, "That is all in the past and L. S. Ballard and Ben M. Bogard are their old selves again and will work in harmony together until Jesus comes for His saints."

At the invitation of J. E. Hollingsworth, Bogard went to Ft. Worth and preached three nights. He visited Bible Baptist Seminary, the school operated by J. Frank Norris. He had a nice visit with Norris and also B. F. Dearmore whose church was an "independent church" that is, it had no fellowship with any association. It was one the churches branded "Gospel Mission" churches.

He met with a large group from various parts of Texas in Corsicana December 15-16 in a mass meeting to counsel together concerning the "un-Godly and un-Baptistic action of the 'Beem-Ay' (Baptist Missionary Association.)" From here he went to Hillsboro to be with Pastor Chester Guinn and preach to his church.

In this, the very evening of his life, Bogard still made plans for an active future. Concerning old age, he wrote:

"Real Life Should Begin at Sixty-Five

"The Bible average life is seventy years instead of being the limit as many believe. If it were not for wrong living, such as over eating, drinking strong drink and keeping late hours and various forms of dissipation, men and women would live much longer than the generations past.

"I am now at the age that I always thought was a very old age. The fact is I thought fifty was old when I was a boy. My personal experience has been that I was only getting ready to live when I was forty and hardly had a good start until I was fifty and at sixty I really began to do things. After passing sixty I had my famous debates with Warlick, published in book form and my debate with Amiee McPherson before six thousand people and published in book form, and then my debate with Hardeman, the greatest I ever had, after I had passed seventy, and published in book form and best of all at

At the 100th Year Observance, Princeton, Kentucky, Bogard was asked to bring the centennial message. He was the oldest preacher from the standpoint of age, service and former pastorate.

sixty-five, along with Dr. J. Louis Guthrie, established the Missionary Baptist Institute, which *I regard as the greatest achievement in my life.* And now since resigning as active pastor, I am preaching more sermons than I did when I was active pastor and then the Lord opened the Tampico, Mexico radio to me and I am preaching to many thousands practically every day. Thank God.''

Four days in Princeton, Kentucky, brought special joy to Ben Bogard as he went back to this church where he was once pastor to preach to them and help celebrate their one hundredth anniversary.

After returning from his trip into Kentucky, he made the journey to Lakeland to be in that historic meeting when the ''split'' came in the ranks of the American Baptist Association. He endured this trip well for a man of his years.

In June, 1950, Bogard preached to the Holland Chapel Church for Pastor J. A. Holland, the missionary who organized it and for whom it was named. Then, later he supplied for Pastor Lawrence Crawford in the church in Warren while the preacher was away in a revival meeting. He wrote of this appointment, ''If I were twins maybe I could go to all the places inviting me, but such a place as Warren makes me want to repeat . . .''

Because of his health, he had to miss the meeting of the messenger body of the American Baptist Association which met with Central Baptist Church in Ft. Smith, Arkansas, March 13-15, 1951. The messengers in the meeting voted unanimously to send him a telegram expressing appreciation for his great service to the American Baptist Association and to have a prayer for his recovery. His picture and an article appear in the front of the yearbook of that meeting. This, the first meeting after the ''split'' was a wonderful meeting with a large crowd and a great number of churches representing. These facts were sent in the telegram to the old preacher resting at home.

XIV

THE DEATH OF A SAINT

"Precious in the sight of the Lord is the death of his saints." —Psalm 116:15.

This great man was a "saint" that is, he had been saved and added to the great host of saints listed in the Book of Life. Though an outstanding figure, he was also so very human. He made mistakes as all men make, but he made them trying—he did not sit idly by while others worked. Because of his deep convictions and his defence of his faith, that faith once delivered to the saints, he made enemies. As one writer said of him, he had no hero-worshippers. His admirers respected him for his work's sake. He had many enemies and many friends. He was either loved or hated. His life touched the lives of many people and he will be remembered as Spurgeon, Graves, Pendleton and other heroes of the cross are remembered as a great leader of men.

Though his life was spent with relatively few illnesses, his last days were to be filled with suffering and his body wracked with pain. He did not die in his pulpit as he had so often said he wanted to do. He died in his home—a few close friends in the adjoining room and L. D. Foreman, Ernest Payne and Kathryn Heard, his nurse, at his bedside. These three did not leave him through the vigil of that last, long night and were with him when his youthful spirit left the tired worn out house it had occupied for so long a time.

A PUBLIC FIGURE

Bogard made his mark even on non-Baptists who recognized his greatness as he took a stand on political matters, in community affairs and on any issue where right should prevail. His picture and an entire column appeared on the front page of the *Arkansas Democrat:*

"BEN BOGARD, BAPTIST LEADER, DIES
"*Emeritus Pastor of Antioch Dies After Long Illness*

"The Rev. Ben M. Bogard, 83, nationally-known Baptist minister, died in his home at 2102 Brown early today of a heart attack. He had been ill for over a month.

"He has been pastor of churches in Kentucky, Missouri and Texas. His last pastorate was at Antioch Baptist Church in Little Rock, which he held for 27 years before resigning to become pastor emeritus four years ago.

"The Rev. Mr. Bogard was founder of the Missionary Baptist Seminary, now located at 3310 Asher.

Sponsored Anti-Evolution Law.

He was one of the sponsors of the initiated act in 1928 which prohibits the teaching of the theory of evolution in Arkansas public schools.

"Later he came to the defence of Charles (Atheist) Smith, New York City, president of the Association for the Advancement of Atheism, Inc., when the latter was arrested at his Main St. atheist headquarters. He was arrested under terms of an old ordinance prohibiting showing of obscene scenes in a play. The charge was based on a display saying that "Evolution's true; the Bible's a lie; God is a ghost."

Bogard championed Smith's constitutional right of free speech and offered to debate him on the existence of God.

Used Radio Early.

A pioneer radio minister in Arkansas, he is said to have started the first regular weekly religious radio program in

Little Rock. This program, now in its 20th year, is still going on. For the last three years he has had a regular transcribed radio program broadcast out in Tempico, Mexico.

Known throughout the religious world as a religious debater, he held undisputed title of having engaged in more religious discussions and debates than any other man. One of his most famous was a series with Amiee S. McPherson in a huge tent on E. Washington, North Little Rock, about 15 years ago.

"He was the founder of the 'Missionary Baptist Church Life,' a religious paper which he gave to the Missionary Baptist Seminary. He was also founder of the Sunday school literature of the American Baptist Society which is now used throughout the world.

"The Rev. Mr. Bogard was a member of the Magnolia Lodge, Union Chapter Royal Arch Mason, Occidental Council of Royal and Select Mason and the Hugh De Payens Commandery No. 1.

Survivors include his widow, Mrs. Lynn Omida Bogard; a daughter, Mrs. C. T. (Lela) Ryan, North Little Rock, and a son, Douglas, Phoenix, Ariz.

"Funeral Thursday.

"Funeral services will be conducted at 1:30 p. m. Thursday in Antioch Baptist Church. Burial will be in Roselawn by Drummond & Co.

"A native of Elizabethtown, Ky., he attended colleges in Georgetown, Ky., and was ordained a Baptist minister at 19 by Woodland Baptist Church in Union County, Ky.

"He was the first missionary of Ohio Valley Baptist Association.

"Active until his retirement, the Rev. Mr. Bogard was once featured for never having missed a Sunday service during his 60 years as a Baptist minister.

"He had traveled extensively throughout the United States with revival camps and Bible schools and was the author of several religious books. These included: "Baptist Waybook" which has been translated into Spanish and Japanese and used throughout the Baptist world; "Pillars of Orthodoxy' and the 'Bible Proved by Science.' "

Similar space was allotted to his death in the *Arkansas Gazette*. Both the *Gazette* and *Democrat* editorialized him.

"Rev. Ben M. Bogard.

"Rev. Ben M. Bogard was perhaps most noted in the ecclesiastical world as a guiding light of the Missionary Baptist Church, a tireless debater and a pioneer in the field of religious radio services. But Little Rock will remember him even more as the pastor of Antioch Baptist Church for more than a quarter of a century and for the fighting qualities with which he built his church and with which he was ready at all times to defend not only his own religious doctrines but the basic right of free speech.

"Two occasions on which he demonstrated these qualities won him national publicity. In one he debated Biblical prophecy with Amiee Semple McPherson, founder of the Four Square Gospel Church, when the famed woman evangelist visited North Little Rock. In the other he sprang to the defense of the constitutional rights of an atheist lecturer who was arrested in Little Rock for erecting what police deemed a sacrilegious sign.

"A prolific writer, Mr. Bogard established the Sunday School literature still used by American Baptist Association churches, wrote a number of books and articles, and was editor of the Missionary Baptist Searchlight. Twenty years ago, he established the program of Sunday radio services still being heard.

"These accomplishments stand out as the schievements of a man of boldness, irrepressible enthusiasm and unquenchable faith." —*Arkansas Gazette*

"Rev. Ben M. Bogard.

"A philosopher deplored that so little fire is mixed with our clay. Because of this, he said, we live in too low a key. We do not have enough lasting enthusiasms, enough headlong zeal to stay with our purposes till they are accomplished.

"But if that is true of many of us, it was not true of the Rev. Ben M. Bogard, who passed away Tuesday at the hale age of 83. There was fire in him which inspired decades of unflagging effort, and won recognition throughout the religious world of his abilities as a leader.

"The Reverend Bogard was pastor of Antioch Baptist Church in Little Rock for 27 years before he resigned, four years ago, to become its pastor emeritus. His vigorous spirit constantly sought wider activity. He is credited with having pioneered the first weekly radio religious service in this city. He dipped into the publishing field, and as a debater had far-reaching reputation.

"It was eloquent of the man that when Charles (Atheist) Smith came to Little Rock, and was arrested for putting up a sacrilegious sign, Reverend Bogard defended his constitutional right to free speech. Then, characteristically, he challenged Smith to a debate.

"There was a hearty cheerfulness in this fighting parson which won him a host of friends. Many who knew him less intimately admired him for his resolute convictions. He lived a fruitful life, and he leaves an emptiness where he so long stood as a man of enthusiastic faith." —*Arkansas Democrat*

Many religious papers of the nation carried editorials of the death of this man and his work. Though many disagreed with him, they admired him. The *Faith and Southern Baptists,* Editor I. W. Rogers and writer, E. P. Alldredge, said:

"Dr. Ben M. Bogard, outstanding leader of the American Baptist Association, and one of the most famous Baptist debaters that ever lived, died at his home in Little Rock, Arkansas, May 29th of a heart attack. He was 83 years old. While this writer was a college student, he heard a debate between Dr. Bogard and Dr. I. N. Penick on mission methods. While our sympathies were with Dr. Penick, yet we considered Dr. Bogard the better of the two debaters. He was a native Kentuckian and was, for awhile, pasor at Fulton and Wingo. His last work was as pastor of Antioch Baptist Church, Little Rock, where he founded and was president of a Baptist School."

His body laid in state until 4:30 P. M. in Antioch Baptist Church house on the day before the funeral where many, many came to pay their last respects. Services were conducted at the church house, May 31, 1951, at 1:30 by L. D. Foreman and Conrad Glover with the crowd overflowing into the yard and up the street.

"Except for the feeling of sympathy for dear Sister Bogard and the family, there was nothing sad about his funeral. It lasted for two hours, but no one was in a hurry, not even those who had to stand or who could not get into Antioch Church. It was more like the dedication exercise of a great religious monument. The main sermon by Dr. L. D. Foreman was a classic . . ." *(The Baptist Monitor,* A. J. Kirkland, editor.)

The sermon as reprinted from the *Missionary Baptist Searchlight:*

FUNERAL SERMON FOR DR. BEN M. BOGARD

L. D. Foreman

Perhaps no one has ever undertaken a greater task than I have. The occasion demands so much. Hours could be sepent in eulogizing this man, yet, for reason known to all of us, we cannot keep this good family here for such a long period of time.

Dr. Bogard, like every other person, has preached his own

funeral. What the minister says over your body, when you are gone, will depend on what you do while living here in that body.

About the time Ben Bogard was twelve years old, a man, riding a horse, stopped at the gate of the country home and ask the Bogard family to "put him up" for the night. This was not out of the ordinary for the early days, because towns and cities were scattered far apart and hotels and inns were few. Newspapers were hard to get, and since there were no telephones or radios in the country, the news traveled slowly. Most families were glad to receive a stranger and entertain him in their home. The man dismounted the horse, the father provided stall and feed for it while the mother prepared the evening meal. Later on, after that meal, the stranger sat and talked to the family, telling them many fascinating things about his travels. Young Bogard listened and was enthralled. He wished that he, too, might be a wayfaring man. Later that evening, when they retired, the boy and the man slept in the same bed. On the morrow the stranger left, but not without leaving an ideal in the boyish heart.

Later that day or early the next, a band of soldiers came riding up to the same house, their horses were lathered and panting; they were in persuit of the notorious gangster and outlaw, Jesse James, who had come that way a few hours before. Not until then did the family recognize the fact that they had housed a fugitive from the law. All this added to the young Bogard heart, and he determined to be another Jesse James. He learned to shoot a gun and to ride a horse and laid awake often at night planning to "run" away from home and become a highwayman.

Brother Bogard told me that he secretly harbored this idea in his mind until the night he was saved. In fact, he went to church where Brother J. B. Haynes, of Morganfield, Ky., was holding a meeting in February in 1885, and that night it seemed that the preacher directed the message of Christ straight at him. The preacher told of sinful man and how Christ loved them. He told them that Jesus had come from heaven to suffer and take the place of man who is doomed and damned. He told them that if they would trust the Lord, He would save them. Conviction gripped the heart of the sixteen year old boy and he trusted that Christ. There, that night, in the hills of Kentucky, the devil lost a highwayman and the Lord enlisted a soldier. During the month of February in 1885, Brother D. J. Logston, of Seven Gums, Ky., took the new convert into a watery grave, made by chopping the ice away, and there, administered the ordinance of baptism. This he did by authority of the Woodland Baptist Church in Union County, Ky.

I tell you all this that you may know something of the grace of God. Dr. Bogard has said over and over again: "But for the grace of God I would have been another Jesse James."

Ben Bogard told me that he wanted to preach from the time he was saved, and at nineteen, having been called of God into the ministry, the Woodland Baptist Church "licensed" him to preach. Like Abe Lincoln, who was a contemporary of Ben Bogard's father (and the two of them went with their father to the same mill), he studied every book and paper he could get his hands on.

He wanted to attend Georgetown College and his father told him he could have a certain plot of ground there on the farm, with the understanding that he was to plant a crop of tobacco (the chief money crop of the country), harvest it and use the money to go to college. He carefully prepared the soil, planted the crop and had wonderful prospects for a harvest. Tobacco puts on much weight in the latter part of the season with the heavy dews and the nineteen year old boy was waiting as long as he could to harvest the tobacco. He wanted every pound he could get, for the tobacco sold by the pound, and every cent counted. When the day came that he decided to harvest the crop of tobacco the next day, he looked over the field and saw the tobacco standing there, a wonderful heavy crop. He knew he had worked hard all the summer, but now he was going to reap the benefits of it. Now he could go to school, pay the tuition, buy the necessary clothes, books and pay all fees. He went to bed happy that night intending to get up early the next morning and start his work of harvesting. When he arose the next morning there was a heavy frost on the ground, the tobacco ruined—worthless. It seemed all hopes were blasted.

This boy sat down and reluctantly wrote a letter to the president of the school telling him his embarrassed and heart broken condition. The president of the school wrote back and said, "If you want to go to school, come on; a way will be provided." This is one of the reasons Dr. Bogard has gone so far in his benevolence toward young students.

He entered school with $33.00 to pay tuition, buy books and pay board for the year. He cut wood for people in the community. He dug gardens. He took care of horses for doctors. He did the chores about the homes, making a quarter of a dollar here, a dime there and a half dollar over there. He even taught an aged Negro man to read, getting fifty cents per lesson. The Negro met Bogard on the street and ask if he were not one of the boys at the college. Bogard told him he was, and the Negro asked if he could come to his home and teach him to read as he wanted to read his Bible. Bogard did go into the home of the Negro and taught him to read.

When he went to college, he went wearing homespun clothing that had been made by his mother. The wool was sheared from the sheep on the farm; his mother spun the wool then wove the cloth and made his "jeans." They were rough and loose fitting and Dr. Bogard has both laughed and cried while telling me how the boys at college, the ones who had better clothing—the "store bought" kind—made fun of his homemade clothes. How many of us would stay and study under such adverse circumstances? I have seen with my own eyes the report cards he got. Believe me, there was no laughing matter—100 in English—100 in German—100 in Psychology, and on and on.

Sixty-four—going on sixty-five years, he has been a faithful preacher of the Christ. He has always had two or three times as much to do as one man ought to do, but he did this work with enthusiasm and with a smile.

The Baptist ranks have lost one of their great generals. There have been many outstanding men among us; a few of these have, through their services, attained a position of true greatness, but only now and then has there been a Paul, a Graves, a Hall, a Guthrie and a Bogard, in our 1900 odd years history.

The stewardship of this man goes unquestioned, as far as I know, and I have been the same as in the family now for nearly eighteen years. Certainly, no person will doubt his fidelity to his convictions.

Dr. Bogard has traveled in many of these United States, Canada and Mexico. He has preached, taught Bible schools and held debates. He has pastored churches in Kentucky, Missouri, Texas and Arkansas. His last pastorate was this, the Antioch Missionary Baptist Church. He was here 27 years to the day when I was installed as pastor. We then made him pastor emeritus, placing him on a small salary and gave him the right to go and come as he wished. Many months of these four years have found him far away from home, trying to fill the hundreds of requests for a visit to this church and to that one. He was not *retired*—he hated the word "retired." He said when the Lord called a preacher He called him for service, and there was no end to that service until the Lord called him home. This, Dr. Bogard literally put into practice. He preached, wrote editorials for the paper, wrote books, etc., until he became bedfast.

His crowning work was when he and two others, Drs. J. Louis Guthrie (now deceased) and Conrad N. Glover founded in their minds the Missionary Baptist Seminary and Institute, and Antioch Baptist Church authorized its founding and adopted it as its theological school. That was over seventeen years ago. Today it is rapidly making its mark in the world and this past school year over two hundred and fifty training for the ministry and missionary work enrolled for study.

Dr. Bogard said there is only one place I had rather have my name written than in the Lamb's Book of Life, and that is on that cornerstone in the Seminary Building.

Dr. Bogard had convictions and he stood by these convictions He was called by some who did not understand him a "fighter." Dr. Bogard did fight sin and the Devil. He was willing for all men to have their constitutional right to believe and practice what they wanted, but he had no endorsement for stupidity. He thought men ought to have a reason, and a scriptural reason at that, to enjoy their constitutional rights for religious belief. When the champion of the *Association for the Advancement of Atheism in America* was here in Little Rock, a number of years ago, he set up a place on the main street—a place to give away tracts, literature, and disseminate Atheism. He was placed under arrest by the Little Rock Police Department. Dr. Bogard stood for the constitutional rights of the atheist and against the larger part of the religionists of this city. He contended that Smith should have the right to propagate his doctrines if he so wanted to under the protection of the United States Flag, but at the same time challenged Smith to a public discussion on the subject of the "Existence of God." This is a fair example of what the man believed. He thought that any one had a right to worship God or not to worship God and that according to the dictates of his own conscience, but whatever a man believed, he should have a reason for believing it. If he had no reason, or if his reason could be proved false he thought that person should change his opinion. He had no tolerance for stupidity.

This gives rise to the subject of debating. Dr. Bogard has

said over and over again that he has had more religious debates than any other person, living or dead. These numbered 237. His ability as a debater is known all over these United States. He has met most of the contenders from the many denominations in America along with the atheists.

His ability as a teacher is also widely known. He has taught preachers the Word of Life for many, many years. Many who have not had the privilege of sitting at his feet, listening to his lessons, have read his works. The books he has written are many. The papers he has published have been read both far and near. The last paper, the *Missionary Baptist Searchlight,* he gave to the Seminary.

A number of years ago, he started a series of Sunday School literature. Two others were with him in the project but chiefly the work was done by Dr. Bogard. Their office was here in Little Rock, and for sometime the office was in the building occupied by the Masonic Lodge on Fifth and Main. Later this work, which had become very profitable, was given to the churches of the General Association, now known as the American Baptist Association. When you people study your Sunday School lesson for next Sunday remember this.

The *Baptist Way Book* is a very popular book which is and has been used by Baptists all over the world.

There is no man living or dead who has contributed more time, energy, money and knowledge than Ben M. Bogard. He counted it a joy to give all this. He felt that his very best was what the Lord deserved.

There is not a preacher anywhere who has more friends and on the other hand there is not a preacher any where who has more enemies. People either loved or hated Ben M. Bogard. People loved him because he told them the truth and people hated him because he told he truth on them. When he found unhealthy and unchristian conditions going on in the office of our publications, the very publications he started and gave to the Baptist Churches of the A. B. A., he exposed that condition. This has caused many to heap contempt and calumny upon him. They have tried vainly to smear his character and ministry. Their efforts are comparable to the damage a tadpole might do while swimming under a battleship.

Some who did not understand said Bogard was meddling. But what would you have done if you had started the series of literature and found such a condition? Would you sit idly by?

Brother Bogard said, "When I die, I had rather have one thing written on my tombstone than any other thing in the world: "I have fought a good fight."

Brother Bogard was bedfast for a little over a month. This was a climax of about four years of retarding health. He suffered a slight stroke about four years ago. Many of his close friends did not know this; he kept working. Then came a slight heart attack and then a permanent heart condition that finally brought on other conditions which resulted in his homegoing. Brother Bogard had experienced most of the things that come in a full rounded out life except sickness. Just a few years ago he was hospitalized for the first time.

Even after he had preached for sixty years he was featured in "Believe It or Not" by Bob Ripley, as a man who had not missed a Sunday service during his ministry.

He had planned and hoped to preach a sermon and drop in the pulpit—from the pulpit to heaven. His lingering illness seemed providential—it gave him the experience of a full, well rounded life.

During the times of his sufferings, when he was in the valley, with the billowing pall of darkness over him, when the thunder of aches rolled, when the lightning of pain crashed against his body, when the poisonous winds lashed through his every fiber—there came, occasionally, a streak of light, piercing even all the darkness, a light that could readily be recognized as that sound, and above average, intelligence possessed by Brother Bogard.

Suffering? Yes, but at the same time not overcome. He

had moments of rationalism even minutes before his death. His last statement of faith was made to me and members of the family when he said slowly and with failing tongue, "If I am lost, I'm lost; if I am saved, I'm saved—I have turned the entire matter over to the Lord." My preacher brethren, that is faith.

We had been planning a book of his life, a biography; and he and I had selected and stored in the right place, many, many editorials, pictures, sermons, etc., looking forward to the day that he should write that book with the understanding that if he did not get to write it himself, I would see to it that it was done. One day, just before he went upstairs, he called me in and said that he had thought it over thoroughly and decided that the book was for "worldly glory" and that, as far as he was concerned, the book was out; that the editorials and sermons could be republished if we saw fit but that his part of the book was out; meaning, of course, that he was having nothing to do with publishing a book of his life for he felt that it was for "worldly glory." I assured him that the religious world needed the book and he finally said, "Well, whatever you think is best on that." I tried to get away as soon as possible after that as I had the key to give us permission to publish the story of his life.

He gave the preachers standing by many a topic for sermons. I remember a few now. Once he said "Out of what and into what?" Stop and think that over for awhile; it will grow on you, coming from a man who was passing over.

Again, after he had been still for over a minute, not a breath drawn during that period of time, his eyes set, he began breathing again, shook his head and finally cleared his eyes, looked at us and said with a thick tongue, "Happy!" and afraid we would not get it he forced a smile and said again, "happy," then four times—the first two very loudly—the other two faintly, "Hallelujah!" That is a Hebrew word meaning "Praise be unto Jehovah."

We could go on telling the many rich things he uttered, but suffice to say, that it appears the whole matter was providential. He had been a champion in defending the faith, he was a teacher, par excellent, of truth. He had witnessed of the saving faith of Christ in most of the states of the union. He had told people over and over again that the faith of Christ is good to live by and good to die by. Now it seemed that the devil had been allowed to torture his strong body and to lay upon him a trial of faith. There is no doubt in my mind but that the devil had challenged God concerning Ben M. Bogard. "The great defender of the faith has never really suffered bodily affliction, but now let me lay this strong body in the ash heap of sufferings and he will deny you," and the Lord, as he did Job, turned him to the devil to prove that even in the darkest hour he would be faithful.

I ask every one to read the fifteenth chapter of I Corinthians. This is the one funeral passage of Dr. Bogard. I have heard him preach funerals so many times from the 15th chapter, that I could repeat them nearly word for word. Some of you can too. That chapter tells us that we are planted in a body of corruption but raised in a glorious body. This body is now going to be planted in weakness but will be raised in power. We do not know when the change will come, but it is just as necessary to slip out of this body and go home to be with the Lord, as it is to be born in this world, if we enjoy heaven.

Dr. Bogard was a member of the Masonic Fraternity. He was a member of Magnolia Lodge No. 60. He held a life time card. He was proud of that card. He assured people that it was not presented to him because he was old and had no earning power—and that is true, for he received it a long time ago —but that it was presented to him by the lodge after he had made several addresses on Masonry. He was also a member of Union Chapter Royal Arch Masons Occidental Council No. 1, Royal and Select Masters and Hugh de Payens Commandery

No. 1. He was exceptionally proud that he was a Sir Knight in the Commandry, a Masonic body founded upon the principle of the Christian religion.

Let me here express my personal feelings to Sister Bogard and the family. I am glad that I live in a time in the world that I have. I am glad that I have come in contact with the family. I am glad that I knew Ben M. Bogard. He has meant as much to me as any other man; I cannot say more but as much. He was as a third father to me. My own lies sleeping yonder in Alamo Cemetery in California. Dr. Guthrie, who was as a second father, is not with us any more and I was very close to this, God's servant. I know how he felt toward me.

Mrs. Bogard has spent a lifetime being a perfect example of a true preacher's wife. She has been wonderful to him all of his life. Not long before Dr. Bogard became bedfast we were out in the car together, doing some business down town, and he talked to me about her. I think this is sufficient; we can extol the virtues of Dr. Bogard, we can praise his long years of ministry, but take Sister Bogard out of it and his ministry would not be what it has been. A preacher's wife can either make or break him. Thank God she has made him. Douglas, the son, thank God for him, and Mrs. Ryan, the daughter. Douglas came back here from Phoenix, Arizona. He left his own companion there to stay by the bedside of his fatther. He has, through the long weeks, spent few hours in sleep, most of the time to assist, and he did a wonderful work. I know that it is embarrassing to him to even mention it. His attitude is that "he was my father and I was glad to perform the duties of a son." Thank God, he felt that way.

To all of you, you have done what you could, you have nothing to regret. Mrs. Kathryn Heard, the nurse, whom Dr. Bogard depended upon so very, very much, I know it is also embarrassing to her to mention it. She spent hour after hour at the bedside, until hours ran into weeks and never complained. Dr. Bogard depended upon her more than he did the doctors themselves. "She has the magic touch," he told me.

Brother Bogard is not dead. He is alive, literally, in glory. I think he has already told Dr. Guthrie about the progress of the Seminary. Dr. Guthrie went home a few years ago and his life was in the Seminary, now he has learned the news of the progress that has been made. Moreover Dr. Bogard will not die as long as the Christian age shall last, for he has already planted enough seed in the field of Christian education to last from generation to generation of preachers. There is not a Baptist preacher in America who has not been influenced in one way or another by Ben M. Bogard. There are preachers who never heard of him, but they have read that which has been written or taught by him, or, on the other hand, they have come in contact with people who have been influenced by him.

"With a cheery smile and a wave of the hand
"I cannot say and I will not say

That he is dead—he is just away!
He has wandered into the unknown land,

"And left us dreaming how very fair
It needs must be since he lingers there."

Dr. Bogard was a scholar, he was well grounded in the field of literature. Language and public speaking were favorite studies. Perhaps the best example of what his opponents thought of him as a debater was when one said, "You may not agree with Bogard, but when he gets through speaking you will know what he said," and again, "It is easier to disagree with Bogard than to answer his arguments." He was a philosopher. On life, he said, "Life itself came from God and should be used for God. We owe our existence to God. Why were you not born a horse or a dog? Because God willed that you should be a human being and not a beast. Do you appreciate the fact that you are a human being and not a beast? If so, then you should use the life God has given you for God." He went on to say, "Life is not an end in itself but a means to an end that God may be glorified."

Brother Bogard was a philanthropist. Few, if any, were ever turned away from his door. Over and over again he said, "There are no pockets in a shroud." He wanted to use the money he had to benefit mankind. Many a time when he was warned that he was, perhaps, helping people who were not worthy—just grafters—he said, "Well, I had rather help a lot of people who don't need it than to risk not helping the man who does." He paid off mortgages on homes, he bought milk for babies, he bought medicine for the sick, he bought groceries for widows and orphans. He sold all his houses, he closed out all his stocks and bonds before he crossed over, so he could use what he had for the benefit of the church and the Seminary.

The radio was his delight. He realized the possibilities of radio preaching long before the common run of preachers. He was one of the first, if not the first, to have a regular weekly radio program. This program of the Antioch Church is about twenty five years old. It has been on various stations, and at different times but nevertheless a regular radio program. He helped to pay for the large 100,000 watt radio station in Tampico, Mexico, and maintained a twice a day program from that station until recently. He made the transcriptions here and mailed them to Mexico. That radio station covers the United States, parts of Canada and Alaska, all Mexico, parts of Central America and even goes out to Hawaii. We have had mail and hearing from all these parts of the world telling of the program. Some have been saved, many have been indoctrinated, and even preachers have entered the Seminary, hearing of the school from this broadcast.

Well, I have been telling you only a small part of what the man has meant for God in this life. It would take volumes and

days to do him justice. But when we put all his ministry together—the preaching, the pastoring, the teaching, the benevolence, the radio—we cannot outweigh the fact that one time,
in the secret of his heart, he went to the Lord in prayer and
asked Him to have mercy on his poor, lost condition and received the Lord Jesus Christ to be his personal Savior. This
fact outshadows them all. He was saved by the grace of God
and lived a life to prove it. His one aim was that souls be
saved, and if he should have his way today he would want me
to preach a gospel sermon and make an invitation to sinners.

What he was and is, he is by the grace of God. He will be
missed for years to come. In the American Baptist Association, the State Association of Missionary Baptist Churches
of Arkansas, the local association, the Seminary, the church, he
will be missed, but in the hearts of all of us, he is still alive.

I look forward now to the resurrection more than ever before. One by one, my friends are gathering over there; I am
anxious to meet them there.

The Scriptures teach us that "they shall come from the
east and the west and from the north and the south and shall
sit down with Abraham, Isaac and Jacob in the kingdom of
heaven." God hasten that day when we shall all clasp hands
again on that beautiful shore.

XV

A POET'S HEART

In dealing with human souls, Dr. Bogard often thought of death, not morbidly, but factually, knowing that every life must someday be spent. As any minister must do, he tried to make his hearers and readers conscious of the fact that they, too, must one day meet the "grim reaper." Though those who knew him would hardly take him for a poet, a few times, his poet's heart was evidence in his writings. Many years before his death, he composed this poem:

DEATH, THEN HEAVEN
By Ben M. Bogard

Death takes the beautiful and young,
And stops the sweetest song e'er sung;
It smites the old, the young, the brave,
It hastens all into the grave;
All move with steady certain tread,
Both thoughtless youth and hoary head;
    The hearse is always full.

All men in their turn shall die;
Our days are swiftly passing by;
The grave, the worm shall claim their own,
The poorest man, the king enthroned
But we shall triumphantly arise,
To claim our home above the skies,
    The triumph of the dust.

In heaven are no sighs and tears,

No wrinkled face, nor whiting hairs;
Forever young and undecayed,
There youth and beauty never fade,
There pleasure is without alloy,
As when the morning stars in joy,
    Their sweetest anthem sung.

In heaven are no toils and cares,
No stooping forms, no scalding tears;
Her mansions never crumble down,
No cruel wind has ever blown
In heaven where the good and brave
Have overcome both death and grave,
    And praise the Savior's name.

Our happy hearts shall thrill with joy,
Our pleasure be without alloy
When we have triumphed over death,
And heaving glory fills our breast,
There'll be no eyes all filled with tears;
Our aches and pains, and toils and fears
    Shall all be left behind.

What heavenly joy, O blessed thought!
That Jesus' blood our souls hath bought!
Our joy shall be without decay,
And sweeter, brighter, every day,
The presence of our Lord shall be
The greatest pleasure we shall see.
    O praise His holy name!

THE WORTH OF A SOUL

The Christian's life is measured by the work he does for
Christ. What is the worth of a soul? What would you give in

exchange for your soul? Because of the life of this man, millions of lives were touched. Thousands were won to the Lord.

No exact figure can be given as to the known number of saints added to the Lamb's Book of Life as a result of the well spent hours of this wonderful old warrior—leader in the army of the Lord. Up through 1942 he kept an itemized journal, a record of each convert, each baptism, money received and other information, but after that the days were too full—he neglected noting these items. From that time the numbers must be gleaned from his writings. By 1942, he had won 2,704 souls to Christ and 3,837 had been added to the church, 924 of whom had been baptized at his hand. After that time, in the numerous revivals, he reported members that would total into the hundreds—enough souls to populate a small town will help populate the eternal city of God.

SERMONS AND SERMON OUTLINES

BY THE PREACHER

VICTORIOUS OVER DEATH
(Radio Sermon)

We should rejoice when we are prepared to meet an enemy. The Bible says death is an enemy and we are assured that we may be triumphantly victorious over death.

"Death is swallowed up in victory. O death, where is thy sting? O grave where is thy victory? The sting of death is sin" (I Corinthians 15:54-56).

I. NOTHING OCCUPIES OUR THOUGHT MORE THAN DEATH. It is well to think of death, for when an ordeal must be endured it is well to be prepared for it. To be over-concerned about it would make us unhappy, but to lightly dismiss it would be foolish.

1. DEATH BRINGS US TO THE JUDGMENT. Hebrews 9:27, "It is appointed unto men once to die, but after this the judgment." There is no escape from this for God made the appointment. We can make and break appointments, but we did not make this appointment. God made it and He will see to it that it is met. Christian Scientists tell us there is no death. The Bible says there is and common sense and observation tell us there is, and thus, we see Christian Science is neither Christian nor scientific. It is "science falsely so-called."

2. THOSE WHO ARE LIVING WHEN CHRIST COMES WILL BE CHANGED, THE CHANGE BEING EQUIVALENT TO DEATH. I Corinthians 15:51-52, "Behold I show you a mystery; we shall not all sleep, but we shall all be changed, in a moment, in a twinkling of an eye, at the

last trump: for the trumpet shall sound, and the dead shall be raised incorruptible, and we shall be changed." The meaning of this is clearly that those who are alive on the earth when the Lord comes back to the earth, will not go through the ordinary process of death, but will not have any advantage over the people who have died, for we who are alive and remain "shall be changed"—the same change that would have taken place by the process of death. It shall be done in "the twinkling of an eye," and since the time will be so short there will be no time to prepare for it if we wait till the Lord comes. Better prepare for it now while you have time and the opportunity.

II. DEATH TO A CHILD OF GOD IS VICTORY. "Death is swallowed up in victory." A victorious death should be the ambition of all. Death is considered an enemy and we triumph over the great enemy. "The last enemy that shall be destroyed is death," I Corinthians 15:26. Since the contest must come it would be foolish not to prepare for victory.

1. DEATH WILL BE A SERVANT TO GOD'S CHILDREN. I Corinthians 3:21-22, "All things are your's; whether Paul, or Apollos, or Cephas, or the world, or life or death." When the enemy becomes our servant we shall indeed enjoy victory. Paul declared that "death is gain," Philippians 1:21. Paul did not look upon death as annihiliation or going into unconsciousness—going out of existence. He, being inspired, spoke the mind of God when he said, "For to live is Christ and to die is gain." It would be no gain for a man to become unconscious or go out of existence.

2. FOR A CHILD OF GOD TO DIE IS TO BE CROWNED. Paul looked forward to the "crown of righteousness, which the Lord, the righteous judge, shall give me that day," II Tim. 4:8. I have seen triumphant death. When J. C. Maxville died in Searcy, Arkansas, he told all his family goodbye, one at a time, and asked all of them to meet him in heaven. Then he said, "Let me rest, I am tired." He went to sleep

as sweetly as a babe on its mother's bosom. When J. J. Crow died at the same place, he told me that it was no trouble to die. He said he was happy in the grace of God and that had sustained him. Many cases could be cited. "Death is swallowed up in victory."

3. THOSE WHO ARE UNPREPARED WILL SUFFER DEFEAT IN DEATH. "The sting of death is sin." Unless sin is atoned for by the blood of Christ in your case you will be stung in death. Voltaire the blatent infidel, died in misery and drove his infidel supporters from his death-side, told them he was lost and that they were to blame. "Begone! It is you that have brought me to my present condition. Leave me, I say; begone! What a wretched glory is this which you have produced to me." When the infidel, Gibbon, died he said: "I must die—abandoned of God and men." He further said: "All is lost; finally, irrevocably lost. All is dark and doubtful."

You have the right to victory for the Lord has offered it to you. "Thanks be unto God that giveth us the victory through the Lord Jesus Christ."

Many people live in constant dread of death. Death itself is a painless experience and the dread of death as a physical experience is a delusion. Those who are ill suffer very little from such a dread, those who are in good health are apt to fear it most.

When the time comes, Mother Nature tenderly smooths the way, so that it seems as natural as to fall asleep.

We do not dread going to sleep when we are fatigued; we look upon it as a boon, but sleep is a twin brother of death, the absence of consciousness. We love sleep and the only dread we have after going to bed is that we may not be able to sleep. More people suffer from the attempt to sleep, than sick people from the thought of dying, or in dying itself.

Physicians who are often at death beds will tell you this same thing. The will of the patient yields to the mandates of the death angel. It is remarkable also, to see how easily and gently the affections unclasp their earthly hold. Those who have been at many death beds can testify to the wonderful sweetness and resignations of the departing one, when all the others at the bedside are in tears and agony. To the believer, the apostle's words are made true in Hebrews 2:15, "Delivering them who through fear of death were all their lifetime subject to bondage." Our hymnology needs to be revised where it refers to the transition. There are no "Jordan's Stormy Banks." There is no "Death's Dark Sullen Stream," and by the testimony of physicians, there is no place in a dying experience for "The Last Mortal Agony."

The vast majority of the race breathe out their life as gently as you would fall asleep, unconscious of suffering.

The angel of death hovers over the couch like a sympathetic friend, and in almost every instance David's words are sweetly realized, "He giveth sleep."

Let there be no worry about dying grace. That will be supplied when the time comes. What we need now, is living grace, and after all, life is more to be dreaded than death, for life is constantly shadowed by temptations which may mar our souls and harm our influence. We need not prepare to die, but rather prepare to live. For if we live right, we shall surely die right. Living is solemn. For the kind of life we live affects not only us, but all whom our lives touch.

What an inspiring joy the Christian view of death affords. A friend tells us how he was walking one summer afternoon in a forest, and found a bird's nest on the ground with four beautiful eggs in it. Stooping to examine them, he found the eggs all empty.

Had someone robbed the nest? No. The mysterious life within those eggs had matured. The birdlings were enjoying their freedom in a nearby tree. Better off with all the cerulean to soar in than residing in the confines of the shell.

Have you not thought the same way when at the graveside

you have said goodbye to a dear friend. The body lowered into the tomb was only the empty shell. The spirit had flown, and you rejoiced that there was one more in Heaven, one sceptre more, one star more in the firmament.

When doubt or distress of mind comes to us on this subject, let us remember Jesus' words as John records them, "Behold, I am alive forevermore; and I have the keys of death and the grave." Ask Jesus for the key when you want any problems solved touching the future life. He has lighted up the gloom of the grave and made its gate to turn on golden hinges. He made the cross His pillow that we might pillow our heads on the precious truth of immortality. *(Orthodox Baptist Searchlight,* July 26, 1943)

THE GREAT GOD ETERNAL

Text: "God is a spirit," John 4:24.

That there is a great self-existing, eternal God, the creator of all things, is the only reasonable solution of the mystery of existence. The evolution theory of existence denies the existence of any first great cause. They start with "protoplasm" but fail to account for the existence of "protoplasm," whatever that may be conceived to be, for bear in mind no man ever saw any protoplasm. It is at best a guess, or as the evolutionists themselves declare, only "a working hypothesis" which means a working guess or supposition. *So evolution starts with a guess and is based on a supposition.* A theory that has a guess for a start and a supposition for a foundation should at least be modest in its claims.

Evolution, as an explanation of the existence of all things material, is unreasonable. Nothing can be evolved that is not first involved. A thing can't be rolled out that is not first involved. Hence creation was a necessity. What is reason? It is judging that which we do not see and have not actually experienced by what we do see and have experienced. I reason that corn, if planted under certain conditions, will germinate and grow and come finally into maturity and that I shall enjoy a harvest. I reason that corn, if planted in winter time, will rot and I shall not enjoy a harvest. Why do I thus conclude? Because we have seen it done over and over again and also have the record of it having been done for generations in the past. What is may have been and may continue to be. That is reason. We also see that corn, under certain cultural conditions, will change in form and in quality. This cultivation and breeding may continue indefinitely, to what limit no one knows. But we also know that corn will not improve itself and the most highly improved corn if planted under ordinary conditions and the cultural methods continue to be neglected, will revert back to its old primitive condition. So with the breeding and developing of animals. They are subject to a very high development by cultural methods but that same fine stock, thus developed will, if let alone, revert back to the old scrub stock from whence it came. There is nothing in nature to show that anything, let alone by a higher power, will develop. But under the culture of a higher power, the development may be indefinite. Thus a man is a higher power than a hog and man may develop the hog to wonderful limits as has been done, but in all the development the hog remains a hog—just a developed hog, not developed into some other sort of animal. Let the hog alone for a few years and discontinue the cultural methods and the same breed of hogs will revert to the old scrub stock from whence it came. This is true of vegetables, fruits, and animals. It is true of mankind. The habits of life, climate and culture develop different types of people. Hence the different races and colors, sizes, morals and intellect. But if by some means the type found in one part of the earth can be transplanted to another environment the type will change, but in all the changes of types, the types one and all continue to be men and women, not some other sort of animal.

Thus we see that there is nothing in what we see or have

experienced or have any record of that will show that one sort of animal has developed until it changed to some other sort of animal. Since no one ever saw such a change, since no one ever experienced such a change, and we have no record of such a change ever having been made, it follows that it is contrary to reason that such a change ever has been made. It will therefore necessarily follow that evolution is unreasonable. We are reasonable beings and why should we throw to the winds our reason by adopting a notion that was created in an infidel brain?

The Bible tells us that God created of one blood all nations of men (Acts 17:26). The Bible tells us that everything reproduces after its kind (Gen. 1:24-25). We find in actual experience and observation that this is true. Then the Bible furnishes us the only reasonable statement of the existence of things. It therefore follows that it is reasonable to believe what the Bible says, for what the Bible says conforms to reason and evolution does not.

The Bible declares that God created the heavens and the earth and the order of creation mentioned in Genesis is the exact order discovered by geologists in their examinations of fossils found in the earth. The order mentioned in the Bible is (1) Mineral life, (2) then plant life, (3) then animal life (4) then human life (Genesis 1). So does science, but the Bible said it first. The Bible declares that the first animal life was in the water, then came birds, then came dry land animals and then the human being (Gen. 1:2). So does geology, but the Bible said it first. This proves that the Bible is of supernatural origin, that it was not invented by men, for it was written in advance of such knowledge among men. It is therefore of divine origin.

The Bible, being of divine origin, declares there is a God. This statement reason cannot contradict and the statement is supported by reason by the very good reason that all the facts, even the very order of existence, is mentioned in the Bible in perfect harmony with the known facts discovered in science.

The only contradiction existing between the Bible and what we know as science is where science goes to guessing. When science speaks with knowledge, there is always perfect harmony between science and the Bible. Then it must be the reasonable thing to believe the Bible. There is a God, this the Bible declares and reason corroborates it and we should inquire as to who He is and what He is.

At best men only worship a concept. No man has seen God at any time. We have evidence that there is a God both from the Bible and from nature, for the God of the Bible is the God of nature. But we have not seen Him. We must therefore arrive at some conclusion as to what God is and our conception of what God is will be our God. If you have a false conception of what God is you will be worshipping a false God. If you have a true conception of God, you will be worshipping the true God. Look well to your conception of God.

God is not like a physical man. Man was made in the image of God but that image was not a physical image, the image was spiritual, for my text announces God is a Spirit. Those who worship Him must worship Him in Spirit. Hence, all efforts to make an image of God will fail for a spirit is not a physical being. After Jesus arose from the dead He met His disciples suddenly and they thought they saw a spirit, but Jesus said, "Behold my hands and my feet, that it is I myself: handle me and see; for a spirit hath not flesh and bones as ye see me have." So, to make a physical image of God is the ignorance of idolatry. But if you have such an image in your mind when you worship, how much better is it than to have it in stone? When I was a boy I thought of God as an old man, a perfect giant in stature, and very tall, with long, white whiskers. In my childish prayers, I prayed to the old man. The older people about me had impressed this idea by calling God "the good man" and the devil "the bad man." When I prayed to such a man, I was worshipping an idol and did not know it. It was an idol created by my own brain. Do you worship an idol, or do you worship the Spirit God? God is a Spirit. You must get a spiritual conception of Him.

The spiritual conception of God is when we find what He has revealed Himself to be and we combine the attributes of God into one being and worship that. God is GOOD, God is PERFECT, God is LOVE, God is MERCIFUL, God is ALL POWERFUL, God is OMNISCIENT—that is, He has perfect knowledge, God is JUST, God is RIGHTEOUS, God is SU-PREME. Combine all these elements in God's character and worship that and you are a true worshipper of God.

The careful thinker will see that if this position is correct, and it undoubtedly is, then there are many who think they are worshippers of God who are really worshippers of idols of their own mental creation, having never really worshipped God a minute in their lives. They have been worshipping what they conceived to be God—worshipping their false conception of God, not God Himself. There are others, possibly, who never thought that they were worshipping God at all, yet, they held in reverence the character of God I have just described. If there are such people they, indeed, are true worshippers of the God. God is a Spirit.

Knowing that men could not get a correct conception of God, by their own reasoning, God not only stated His attributes plainly in the Bible, but He revealed Himself in Jesus Christ. Jesus was God manifested and those who want to get a correct understanding of the character of God can get it by observing the character of Jesus as He revealed it in His wonderful life and death on the cross. Jesus was LOVE, Jesus was POWERFUL, Jesus was KIND. Jesus was JUST, Jesus was RIGHTEOUS, Jesus was perfect in KNOWLEDGE, and in fact He displayed in actual bodily life all the character of God. As Paul puts it: "God was manifest in the flesh, justified in the spirit, seen of angels, preached unto the Gentiles, believed on in the world, received up into glory" (I Timothy 3).

"He that loveth is born of God" (I John 4:7). "If ye love me keep my commandments," said Jesus. Is the Bible conception of God, as revealed in words and in the life of Jesus what you love? If so, you are a child of God. If you are not in love with righteousness, mercifulness, justness, perfectness, omnipotence and goodness, then you are a stranger to God. If you love these things, it will make a good man of you for you have been born of God and thus partake of the divine nature.

(Orthodox Baptist Searchlight, March 25, 1943).

HEAVEN
(Sermon Outline)

"I go to prepare a place for you," John 14:2.

1. Heaven a place as well as a state of existence.

"I go to prepare a place for you." All of the descriptions of Heaven show that it is a place. We read of trees, river, city, mansions, a throne, of angels, etc. However, our knowledge concerning Heaven is very limited. We know little of earthly countries unless we have visited them and seen for ourselves. All our study of geography and books of travel will give us but an indefinite idea. When we get to Heaven we shall know something of its real nature, but not before.

2. A great many curious and hard questions are asked about Heaven.

John Bunyan was asked a question about Heaven about which nothing was revealed in the Bible and Bunyan simply answered by advising the enquirer to go and see for himself.

3. Whatever else there may be in Heaven, the chief object of attraction will be Jesus Christ.

When Cyrus took the King of Armenia and his son and their families prisoners, and upon complete submission, set them all free, they began to talk of the great man Cyrus, some commenting in one way and some in another. The King's son asked his wife what she thought of Cyrus and she answered that she had never seen him. "Where were thine eyes?" asked her astonished husband.

"They were fixed on thee, the one who offered his life a ransom for mine." So it will be in Heaven. The One who gave His life a ransom for my life will be the chief attraction to me.

4. The delights of Heaven will be inexhaustible.

Some imagine they shall see Heaven the first day they get there. You cannot see New York or London in a day, nor a week, when both these cities have put together but a few millions of inhabitants. You cannot see Yellowstone Park in a day nor a week; and you cannot see the United States in a year. Heaven is larger than the whole world. There will be a great many more people to live there than ever lived on earth at any one time. Revelation 7:9, "After this I beheld, and, lo, a great multitude, which no man could number, of all nations, and kindreds, and people, and tongues, stood before the throne, and before the Lamb, clothed with white robes, and palms in their hands." It will take a large place for the accommodation of all these.

5. Heaven is a place of rest.

Hebrews 4:9-11: "There remaineth therefore a rest to the people of God . . . let us labor therefore to enter into that rest." Some Indians were running for their lives before a prairie fire, and coming to a river, they plunged in and swam across, and looking back at the terrible fire, exclaimed: "Alabama—here we rest." But they knew not what they said. There were other hostile tribes in there and they were soon set upon and destroyed. So it is with all. There is no "Alabama" for the soul in this world. We seek one to come. "Come unto me all ye that labor and are heavy laden and I will give you rest."

6. The necessity of preparing for Heaven is evident.

The jailor exclaimed: "What must I do to be saved?"

The answer came from the apostle without hesitation, "Believe on the Lord Jesus Christ and thou shalt be saved." No sort of polish or culture will take the place of Christ. Sin in the soul must be killed by faith before we can reach Heaven. A family discovered that a serpent had taken up its abode in a hole in the wall of the house. The neighbors advised that the house be whitewashed, others said it should be painted, others that bouquets should be kept in all the rooms and no one suggested killing the serpent. One night it crawled from its abode and bit several of the family to death. So is the man who thinks to reform or become cultivated in the hope of being saved. The only sensible thing to do is to kill the serpent of sin by faith in Christ.

7. There will be degrees of glory in Heaven.

I Corinthians 15:41, 42, "There is one glory of the sun, and another glory of the moon, and another glory of the stars: for one star differeth from another star in glory. So also is the resurrection of the dead." The fullness of Heaven will not be realized until the resurrection of the body.

8. It should be the chief aim of our life to make sure of Heaven.

In this way we can but glorify God. This is not inconsistent with the duties of this life for the best way to serve God is to do our best in our earthly lives to live honestly, do justly with all men. We see men working for an estate. What estate can equal Heaven?

9. It should be a subject for frequent meditation.

In our hustling, busy age it has come to pass that men take but little time for Christian meditation. Often God commands His children to "be still." He told His disciples to come aside, on one occasion, and "rest awhile."

Notwithstanding the joys we anticipate and the glories we are certain to experience, we are saddened at the thought that many will fail to reach Heaven. Our meat and drink should be to seek and to save the lost.

"Must I go and empty handed,
Must I meet my Savior so?"
(Orthodox Baptist Searchlight, April 26, 1943.)

OUR WONDERFUL SAVIOR
(Sermon Outline)

"His name shall be called Wonderful," Isaiah 9:6.

The word wonderful means FULL OF WONDER. Everything about our Savior is full of wonder. He is wonderful in the contrasts found in his character.

1. He is the GREATEST and the LOWLIEST. I Timothy 6:15, "Who is the blessed and only Potentate, the King of kings and Lord of lords." Yet, in Philippians 2:7, we read, "But made himself of no reputation, and took upon him the form of a servant, and was made in the likeness of men."

That wonderful self-abasement was for us. By coming down to the level of the lowest He could suffer with them and sympathize with them. Hence He was tempted in all points as we are.

2. He was the RICHEST and yet was the POOREST. II Corinthians 8:9, "For ye know the grace of our Lord Jesus Christ, that, though he was rich, yet for your sakes he became poor, that ye through his poverty, might be rich." He created all things and all things belonged to Him, yet He did not have a shelter nor a bed He called His own. When a man said to Him that He would follow Him no matter where He went, Jesus plainly told him that there would be no earthly gain for him in so doing but that he could expect hardships for He said: "Foxes have holes, and the birds of the air have nests; but the Son of man hath not where to lay His head" (Luke 9:58). The prospect of continued poverty has kept many an unworthy man out of the ministry and nobody but a fool would enter the ministry to make money. Only a few preachers have more than a bare living and most of them have not even received a

living for their preaching. If Jesus had lived in luxury while on earth it would have made an impression that He had riches of this world to offer His followers but He had nothing but poverty to offer them, thus shutting out self seekers.

3. He was OMNIPOTENT, all powerful, yet the weakest. He commanded the waves of the sea and they obeyed Him (Mark 4:36-40). He healed the sick (Mark 5:21-41). He raised the dead (John 11). But He was hungry and tired and in John 4:6 we read of "Jacob's well." Weary from His journey He sat on the curbing of the well. While He was resting there the woman of Sychar came to draw water and though tired, He was so intent on leading that woman to repentance that He cared not for the food they brought, for when His disciples came back from town with food and asked Him to eat, He said, "I have meat to eat that ye know not of" (John 4:32). We shall have the spirit that Jesus showed here when we get so deeply interested in the salvation of souls that we care not to eat. Such as that is true fasting.

4. He was SINLESS, yet for us, He became the GREAT-EST SINNER IN THE WORLD. Jesus never sinned. His life was perfect but He took our sins on Him and stood in our stead before a sin-avenging God. II Corinthians 5:21, "For he hath made him to be sin for us, who knew no sin; that we might be made the righteousness of God in him." In Isaiah 53:6, "The Lord hath laid on Him the iniquity of us all." The weight of the world's sins sank His soul into the torments of hell. But for that we should all be compelled to go to hell for ourselves. Jesus paid the entire debt and set us free.

5. He was most GLORIOUS and yet became the most IN-FAMOUS. In John 17:5, we read where Jesus prayed the Father, "Glorify thou me with the glory I had with Thee before the world was." But He exchanged that glory for the death on the cross the most infamous death one could die. He was hanged on the cross between heaven and earth as unworthy of either and was hanged between two robbers, a more

shameful death could not have been inflicted on anyone. How we should praise Him for this voluntary humiliation for by His humiliation we shall be exalted.

6. He was the CREATOR yet became a helpless INFANT. As an infant He was helpless and had to be cared for as any other babe is cared for. He had to learn as other children did and He "grew in stature and wisdom" (Luke 2:52). Those who looked upon that Babe could not realize that He was the Creator of the universe.

7. Jesus was WONDERFUL also as a Teacher. "Never man spake like this man" (John 7:46) said those who heard Him. He was WONDERFUL as an EXAMPLE. He could calmly say to His opponents, "Which of you convinceth me of sin?" He being perfect had no sins of His own to account for, hence He could offer Himself as our WONDERFUL SUB-STITUTE.

THE ESTABLISHMENT OF THE CHURCH

INTRODUCTION: The establishment of Christ's kingdom was not the work of a day, or even one year. It was not the work of one day. Like the building of Solomon's Temple, in its complete establishment, the kingdom of Christ was progressive. The building of the temple began with the preparation of the first material and ended with the shedding of the blood of the first sacrifices, so the establishment of the church, or kingdom, of Christ, commenced with the preparation of the material by John the Baptist, who was sent to make ready a people prepared for the Lord, and closed with the shedding of the blood of the Son of God.

Baptists, universally, believe and teach that Christ in person established His own church or kingdom. If you are on a railway train, your falling asleep will not hinder you from reaching your journey's end. If you are in Christ, you will pass into glory, even though you may do so in a state of insensibility.

I. Christ was to have the glory of building the temple of the Lord, Daniel 2:44-45, Zechariah 6:12, 13, Acts 7:48, Acts 17:24, 19:26, II Corinthians 5:1, Ephesians 2:11, Colossians 2:11, John 3:29, Isaiah 54:5, Matthew 9:15.

A. John's Mission, Luke 1:17.

B. Christ's work, Luke 6:12, 13, I Corinthians 12:28.

II. The kingdom or church of Christ was established before Pentecost, Mark 12:10-11, (Compare I Kings 8:3, 4).

A. Church business, Matthew 18:15, 16, Matthew 18:17, Matthew 11:12, 23:13, Luke 16:16.

B. The Commission, Matthew 28:18-20.

III. Christ was a King here on earth, Zechariah 9:9, Luke 19:38, John 18:36-37.

IV. Christ was exalted a Prince and a Savior, Psalm 24:7-10.

V. The Church spoke of a fold, John 10:16.

VI. The kingdom was taken away from the Jews and given to the Gentiles, Matthew 21:43.

VII. Those in the kingdom were expected to understand the mysteries of the kingdom while those without were not, Mark 4:11.

VIII. Christ sang praises to God in the church; this they could not have done, had not the church been established before Pentecost, Psalm 22:18-20, Hebrews 2:11, 12, Mark 14:25, 26.

IX. The Lord's Supper is a church ordinance, Luke 22:29, 30 (See Christian System, p. 165).

X. The church transacted business before the days of Pentecost.

A. One elected to take Judas' place among the apostles, Acts 1:14-16, 24-26.

XI. The Holy Spirit before Pentecost.

A. If Christians did not possess and enjoy the Holy

Spirit before Pentecost then there were none saved before Pentecost.

The fact that Christ warned the people against the danger of blaspheming the Holy Ghost proves that the Holy Spirit was present prior to the day of Pentecost, Luke 12:10-12, Matthew 12:31, Mark 3:29.

2. The disciples spake as the Holy Spirit gave them utterance, Mark 13:11.

3. John the Baptist was filled with the Holy Ghost from his mother's womb.

4. The Holy Ghost taught the disciples.

5. Christ cast out devils by the Holy Spirit, Matthew 12:28.

6. Christ breathed on the disciples and said, "Perceive ye the Holy Spirit."

THE RELIGION OF CHRIST IS A RELIGION OF SACRIFICES

REASONABLE CHURCH SERVICE

TEXT: Romans 12:1, "I beseech you therefore, brethren, by the mercies of God, that ye present your bodies a living sacrifice, holy, acceptable unto God, which is your reasonable service."

I. The religion of Christ was first taught through patriarchal and Jewish sacrifices.
II. The religion of Christ was instituted through sacrifices.
III. The religion of Christ demands sacrifices of all.
IV. The religion of Christ has been handed down and transmitted to us through the sacrifices of the followers of Christ.
V. The religion of Christ rewards sacrifice.

THE CHURCH

TEXT: Matthew 16:18, "And I say also unto thee, That thou art Peter, and upon this rock I will build my church: and the gates of hell shall not prevail against it."

I. The Builder
    A. Who He was
    B. His qualifications
    C. The object He had in view
II. The Foundation
    A. Not Peter
    B. Not Peter's confession
    He is talking about Himself, "I the Son of man am ..."
    C. But, upon the Rock, Petra—Christ, not petros, Peter
III. The Material
    A. Not unbelievers
    B. Not unbelievers and believers mixed
    C. But baptized believers
IV. The stability of this church, "the gates of hades shall not prevail against it."

Sermon
GOD'S COVENANTS WITH MEN

A covenant is a contract or agreement between two or more parties. God has made a number of covenants with men and a misunderstanding concerning them causes confusion about other things. The purpose of this sermon is to make clear what the different covenants are and what they have to do with the people who live at this present time.

The Edenic Covenant, Gen. 1st and 2nd chapters, was made in the garden of Eden between God and the first human pair. That covenant consisted of the following items:

    1. Adam and Eve were to increase and multiply and *re-*

plenish the earth. This shows that the earth was once made empty *before* Adam and Eve were created. The earth because of sin was brought to ruin and chaos. The sin of pre-Adamic angels—spirits. How long it remained in ruin we do not know. But Adam and Eve were a new start, a new beginning—they were to *replenish the earth. Re-plenish* means to fill again. It is the same word used when God told Noah after the flood, to replenish the earth. There are in the Bible several hints at the earth being occupied by some sort of beings before Adam and Eve were created, but we know very little about it. When geologists find fossil remains that seem to indicate that the earth is millions of years old, it only adds evidence of the fact that there was a pre-Adamic age.

2. Adam and Eve were to dress the garden and keep it. They were limited to a vegetable diet for they were instructed to eat of the things that grew in the garden of Eden with only one restriction, they being forbidden to eat of the tree of knowledge of good and evil. Adam and Eve broke this covenant by their disobedience to the one restriction and the penalty was *immediate spiritual death.* Physical death, which finally came, was no part of the penalty, but only *a result of the penalty* which was spiritual death—separation from God. There was no grace in this covenant for there was no mercy offered for disobedience. Adam and Eve stood on their merits; so long as they were obedient they would continue to enjoy the wonderful garden. When they disobeyed they would be put out. Adam and Eve were created in the *spiritual or character image of God,* truly so because God is not a physical being. God is a Spirit and a "spirit does not have flesh and bones." (Luke 24:39). Since a "spirit does not have flesh and bones" and Jesus said that "God is a Spirit" (John 4:24) it follows that Adam and Eve were in the image of God in their spirits and character. This proves that man has a spirit distinct from his body else he could not be in the image of God. Adam and Eve did not fall from grace for the very good reason that they

were not under a covenant of grace, but a covenant of *good conduct,* a covenant of *strict obedience* with the penalty of spiritual death for disobedience.

The Covenant of Promise (Gen. 3rd chapter). After the *death* of Adam and Eve (spiritual death) God pronounced a curse on the serpent that was used by Satan to cause their downfall and then cursed the earth so that it would bring forth weeds and thorns and poisonous vegetation, with disease and other evils, and pronounced a curse on Eve because she led in the disobedience. The special penalty put on her was that she should have *multiplied conception,* and pain in childbirth. This multiplied conception no doubt means that several children should be born at one time such as twins, triplets and even more. This accounts for the multiplied millions who were soon inhabiting the earth. Only so many were mentioned in the Bible as were necessary to the revelation God made to us, such as Cain and Abel, and Seth and a few others. But it does not follow that just because only a few were mentioned that many others were not born. When we come to understand that possibly Eve was the mother of several hundred children, for she lived to be over nine hundred years old, and during that long period she could have been the mother of a thousand or more children; when we come to understand this simple fact, such silly questions as where Cain got his wife would never be asked. Cain married his sister of course. Such marriages were a common practice many years after Cain had passed away.

But along with these curses placed on the first pair came *a promise.* It was *"the seed of the woman shall bruise the serpent's head."* There is the promise of the Savior. If Adam and Eve were ever saved (and I think there can be no reasonable doubt that they were) they were *saved by grace through faith in the promised Savior.* There has never been any other way of salvation. Those who were saved before Christ came into the world *looked forward to Him* and we who are saved since

Christ came *look back to Him*. But salvation has been by Jesus' blood in all ages.

The fact that salvation was by grace back there in the morning of the world is seen when Cain's offering of the works of his own hands was rejected and Abel's offering of the lamb, symbolic of the Lamb of God, was accepted. There was nothing in Cain's offering that would picture the sacrifice of Christ on the cross. But the dying and bleeding lamb offered by Abel made a wonderful picture of the suffering, bleeding and dying of our Savior. Cain showed he had no faith in the promised Savior but Abel showed he was trusting that promised Lamb of God. Salvation by works was pictured by Cain's offering and salvation by grace was pictured by Abel's offering.

The Noahic Covenant is found in Genesis, 8th chapter. The world went to ruin under the *Covenant of Promise* and things became worse and worse until God destroyed the world by the great flood. Noah and his family, all eight persons, were saved from the wreck. After the waters dried on the earth God made a covenant with Noah that He would not again destroy the earth by a flood. He did not change any part of the *Covenant of Promise* and Noah lived under that covenant the same as did the people before the flood. But the covenant with Noah was that he should increase and multiply and again *replenish* the earth, which was once more empty only now there were eight persons to start over again when in the first place there were but two. The *rainbow* was given as a token that a flood would never again destroy the earth. If some one who knows why rainbows exist should say that the rainbow was no new thing because a rainbow is made by the sun shining through the falling rain, it will be enough to call their attention to the fact that the rain in connection with the flood was the first rain that ever fell. In Gen. 2:-6 we read: "God had not caused it to rain upon the earth—but there went up a mist from the earth, and watered the face of the earth." This passage tells us that at first there was no rain and since the rainbow was *a new thing* at the time of the flood, it follows that the first rain was the rain that came with the flood.

The Lord promised that while the earth should last "seed time and harvest, cold and heat, and summer and winter, and day and night shall not cease." Noah worshipped God by building an altar and offering up burnt offerings to the Lord showing he was trusting in the *Promised Savior.*

The Abrahamic Covenant is misunderstood more than any other covenant. (Genesis, Chapter 12). This covenant was *un-conditional.* God promised to make Abraham (Abram at first) great. He promised him a large posterity. He promised to make him a blessing to the world in that all the nations of earth should be blessed because of him. He further promised him the land that is now known as Palestine. The Jewish Nation (Hebrews) sprang from Abraham as a result of this covenant. It never was given to anybody except Abraham and his natural descendants. The sign of that covenant was circumcision. In a spiritual and figurative sense all children of God by faith in Jesus are children of Abraham but that has no reference to the *covenant.* The Abrahamic Covenant was a *Land* covenant and a promise of a great posterity through whom all the world should be blessed. The fulfillment of that was the fact that Jesus Christ was born from the Jewish race. Abraham was under the *Covenant of Promise* the same as were Adam, Abel, Noah and others. Abraham was saved by grace through faith in the Promised Savior, Gal. 3:14: "That the blessing of Abraham might come on the Gentiles through Jesus Christ. There never has been any other way to be saved. The different covenants, including the Abrahamic Covenant, did not alter the *Covenant of Promise,* of salvation by faith in a crucified Redeemer.

Abraham was justified by faith when he believed God. He showed his faith when he "built an altar unto the Lord who appeared unto him." (Gen. 12:17). Abraham *proved* his faith in God and showed he was a saved man when he offered up Isaac in sacrifice on the altar. Thus Romans and James are harmonized, one saying Abraham was justified by faith and the other that he was justified by works when he offered up Isaac. He was seventy-five years old when he built the altar and was justified by faith (Gen. 12:4, 7, 8). He might have been saved before that but we have evidence of it when he was seventy-five. He was a hundred years old when Isaac was born (Gen. 21:5). So it was twenty-five years after we know he was saved before Isaac was born. How old Isaac was when Abraham was about to sacrifice him we do not know but he was old enough to *carry the wood* that Abraham laid on him for the burnt offering, not less than fifteen years old which would make it *forty years* after Abraham was saved by faith in the *promised Savior* before he was *justified by works* in offering up Isaac. We are all *saved by grace through faith* and then afterwards we are justified by works, every time we do any sort of good works.

The Mosaic Covenant consists of the Law which is found in Exodus and Deuteronomy. It was the *first* covenant to the Jewish nation. It consists of the moral precepts found in the Ten Commandments and other parts of the law, and of the *ceremonials* which were symbolic of the work that Jesus did when He suffered and died on the cross. Some people ignorantly speak of the *moral* law and the *ceremonial* law. There are no such laws. The law is *one law* with moral precepts in it and ceremonials in it, not two separate laws, one moral and the other ceremonial. The law was never intended to be a Savior. The moral precepts show our need of a Savior since we so far fail to keep them. The ceremonies of the law symbolized the work Jesus did for our salvation. But men and women were never saved by obedience to the law for the law *taught them the need of a Savior*. Paul asks, "Is the law then against the promises of God? God forbid; for if there had been a law giver which could have given life, verily righteousness would have been by the law. But the scripture hath concluded all under sin, that the *promise of faith of Jesus Christ* might be given to them that believe.'' Those who were under the Mosaic Covenant, or Law Covenant, consisting of moral precepts and ceremonials, which were never intended to save any body, these Jews (for no one else was under the Mosaic Covenant) were all the time under the *covenant of promise* the same as Adam, Abel, Abraham and others. We are told in Heb. 10:4, that ''It was not possible that the blood of bulls and goats should take away sins.'' Thus we see that salvation has been by grace through faith under all covenants, for the *covenant of promise* has never been changed nor abrogated. We now have the *promise* in actual fulfillment in our Lord Jesus Christ. This *law covenant* (the Mosaic Covenant) is called by contrast the ''first'' covenant in Hebrews 8:7. It was to the Jews to whom Paul wrote. The New Covenant is only the *covenant of promise fulfilled.* The Mosaic Covenant was the first one made to the Jews as a nation and that is why it is called the *first* covenant in Hebrews. We know that the Edenic and Adamic or Promise Covenant, and the Noahic, and the Abrahamic covenants all came *before* the Mosaic covenant did. But with reference to the Jews the Mosaic was the *first*. Paul in writing to the Jews in the book of Hebrews, for that reason called it *first* . . . the first to the Jewish nation. It was imperfect and hence done away. Now what have we? We have the New Covenant which is the *covenant of promise fulfilled;* we have the *Noahic Covenant still in force;* we have the *Abrahamic Land Covenant still in force* for Palestine still belongs to the Jews and will be finally occupied by them, and circumcision for them is still the sign of that covenant. The *Mosaic Covenant, the law, has been done away* (Col. 2:14-17). We now live under the *new covenant,* which means we are under the *law of love.* We are not bound by laws and precepts, we are not under ceremonies, but we *rely upon the blood of Jesus,* by which sacrifice He hath *''perfected forever them that are sanctified"* (Hebrews 10:14) and have the *"love of God shed abroad in our hearts by the Holy Ghost"* (Rom. 5:5). How happy we should be. "The law of the spirit of life in Christ Jesus hath made me free from the law of sin and death" (Rom. 8:2). We are free and safe and happy and after awhile we shall be glorified. (*The Baptist and Commoner,* November 14, 1935).

BOGARD — THE RADIO PREACHER

In the early days of radio preaching Bogard realized the possibility long before most preachers.

IN THE EARLY DAYS OF RADIO

Radio broadcasting had just begun in Arkansas when Antioch Church presented to Mr. and Mrs. Bogard an Atwater Kent radio for Christmas in 1927. To say they were pleased with the gift is to put it mildly.

That the younger people may understand the nature of some of these radios of the "roaring twenties," we will explain that they were far different from the transistor sets of today. On most of the old time sets, the speaker was separate from the receiver, so there were, at least, two large pieces, often three, the box containing the receiver and amplifier, and the speaker. Most of them were operated by batteries which may have been wet cell, dry cell (just like a car battery today), or a combination of both. A high antennae was desirable and these were strung up on tall poles out in the yard with a lead wire coming into the house. Each set had a number of dials that had to be tuned individually and co-ordinated, then there were levers to pull or push and other dials for volume.

Extra gadgets were sold to eliminate static. When the weather was stormy it was practically impossible to tune in the set. The constant crackling and chatter was referred to as static. Terrible squeals were often times emitted which gave rise to an old joke of those days, that the slaughter and packing houses were utilizing every part of the pig—they processed the hams, sausages, pickled its feet and even sold the squeal to the broadcasting station.

When one listens to a radio today, he cannot begin to imagine the difficulty of reception thirty five and forty years ago. Very often the operator would don a set of headphones and tune in the station to his own satisfaction while those who sat about the room waited patiently. When the station was tuned in, then the headphone jack was pulled out and the

283

"loud-speaker" was plugged in. None of us would so much as walk across the room for such as that today, yet in those days, neighbors would go in droves and sit up until midnight listening to the radio of the man who owned one.

The radio was presented to the Bogards in appreciation for seven and a half years of service given the membership. It was installed a week ahead of time so they could enjoy the Yuletide programs. On Thursday evening of December 15th a number of the members gathered and presented the gift to the pastor. He was so pleased with the gift and the manner in which it was made, he printed the presentation card in the *Baptist and Commoner*, January 18, 1928:

"Well, here I am presented to Mr. and Mrs. B. M. Bogard by the Antioch Baptist Church members and friends. My mission is to bring pleasure and enjoyment to you both; not only for a day, but years to come. Should blues or petty annoyances assail you just turn my dial and wander into a magic land. Though a small gift am I, they have placed me here in their deep appreciation of you both.

"While I am just a small box, you will be surprised at my capacity to entertain, and the immense volume that I possess. Now to you folks I am sent to bring cheer, from coast to coast. Sometimes I'll have you laughing, sometimes all but weeping (that is life).

"There will be times I will be so placid, so calm and entertaining you will feel kindly to those who sent me here. There will be other times I will be so loud, shrieking, whistling and roaring, that you will feel like returning me. Just be patient with me, turn me out until the weather changes then I will please you again.

"Hoping you both enjoy the programs I will bring you is the wish of all who sent me here. Also a Happy Christmas is the wish of those who sent me to this home."

PREACHING VIA RADIO

Ben M. Bogard was the first Baptist preacher in Little Rock to recognize and utilize the opportunities offered by radio. He was deep in the fight against evolution's being taught in the schools. He took advantage of the radio to promote his bill against evolution. In the January 11th, 1928 issue of the *Baptist and Commoner,* he announced that a special issue of this paper would be printed to furnish the people "with all of the ammunition they would need in this fight." He wrote, "The next election we will be called upon in Arkansas to vote on whether we shall have evolution to continue being taught in our public schools in Arkansas. Evolution is now being taught in all the free schools in Arkansas. Shall it be put out or not? That is the question . . ."

This was his announcement about the radio program:

"BOGARD OVER THE RADIO

"On the evening of January 22, fourth Sunday evening in this month, Ben M. Bogard, editor of the *Baptist and Commoner,* and pastor of the Antioch Baptist Church, Little Rock, will speak over the radio, beginning promptly at six o'clock. Little Rock now has a radio broadcasting station and it reaches all over Arkansas and even beyond the boundaries of the state. The subject will be 'Man or Monkey, Which?' Tune in on Little Rock, Sunday evening at six o'clock, January 22. Get your batteries charged ahead of time so that you will have no difficulty in hearing and invite your neighbors that they may also hear with you. Time is almost here . . ." He explained to them that most radios would pick up the broadcast, but warned that they should learn to tune in Little Rock ahead of time as well as to see that their batteries were in order for "run down batteries will not bring in the message. The wave length is 204 meters or 1470 kilocycles." He urged them to have radio groups. "Get

About 1948-49, he was the pastor emeritus, but still doing radio preaching. Here he makes a recording for a Mexican station.

up radio parties," he wrote, "all over the country and have every room filled where there is a radio. Bogard is the first Little Rock preacher to speak over the radio." *Baptist and Commoner,* January 18, 1928.

Learning through this experience the value of a radio in promoting his interests, Bogard began more extensive use of it. In the first six months of 1929, Antioch Baptist Church carried on a radio broadcast. Preceding these programs, he announced them in the *Baptist and Commoner,* January 16, 1929:

"ANTIOCH BAPTIST CHURCH, LITTLE ROCK, ARKANSAS TO BROADCAST SERMONS BY PASTOR BEN M. BOGARD

"The Bible says that the devil is 'prince of the power of the air' and I believe that it means what it says. The devil is controlling the air. The airships will be used by the devil in war and for liquor smuggling and rum running and for criminals to escape. But the devil is also called the 'prince of the world' and it is proved by his controlling the nations and by his creation of evil in everything in the world. The broadcasting stations all over the land are used largely to promote worldly and even wicked things. Jazz and dances and evil politics—almost everything bad is promoted by the radio broadcasting all over the land. The WORST OF IT ALL IS THE BROADCASTING OF HERESY, THE DEVIL'S DOCTRINES from such men as Cadman and Fosdick and others. Up to date they have the big hook-ups on Sunday afternoons and in addition to that the smaller fry are along the same line.

"Shall we surrender the air entirely to the devil? If so why not surrender the earth also? The devil is prince of the earth as much as he is the prince of the air. Shall we stop preaching on the earth because the devil is controlling the earth? I believe that all will answer that we should not surrender. Even so with the air. We have a few orthdox preachers on the air. Frank Norris preaches the truth over the radio. M. E. Dodd, of Shreveport, preaches salvation by grace and other sound doctrines over the radio. One or two Presbyterians are on the air who preach salvation by grace and a few Methodists, and, so far as I know, only one Nazarene preacher is on the air. Whatever else we may say of the Nazarenes they do preach old fashioned salvation by the repentance and faith route and in that we should all rejoice. Well what of it?

"Just this. There is not even one Baptist preacher of our sort that is on the air. Ben M. Bogard will be the first and he begins right away at Antioch Baptist Church, Little Rock. Here is hoping that thousands will tune in on KGJF and listen in on these services. The Antioch Baptist broadcasting will be each Friday night from eight to nine o'clock.

"A radio fund has been started and those who are benefitted by these services will have the privilege of helping to support it by sending in their contributions. It takes a lot of money to maintain the broadcasting and Antioch Baptist Church needs help to fully sustain it. If you want fellowship in this great work send in your contributions and the names of those who help will be called out over the radio and also published in the *Baptist and Commoner*. If sufficient contributions come in to justify BUYING MORE TIME OVER THE RADIO more time will be used. So the more help we get the more service we can render. Address Ben M. Bogard, Room 2, Arcade Building, Little Rock, Ark."

These lectures were on the *Inspiration, Authenticity and Authority of the Bible.*

During the year 1930, he delivered ten addresses over Radio Station KGJF and one over the Church of the Open Door in Los Angeles, California. This one in California, also preached over KGJF, was printed in the *Baptist and Commoner:*

WHY CANNOT WE PERFORM MIRACLES NOW AS WAS DONE IN THE APOSTOLIC TIMES?

The Work of the Holy Spirit, Miracles, The Baptism of the Spirit, Divine Healing, Speaking With Tongues and kindred subjects are badly misunderstood by the majority of the people. This lecture, which may be heard by many thousands over the air and then read by other thousands in the *Baptist and| Commoner,* is delivered for the purpose of helping to a better understanding of the Scriptural Questions.

Many contend that since God never changes it follows that miracles must of necessity continue because we read of miracles being performed in the Bible. If that argument amounts to any thing it would follow that circumscision, burning of incense, slaughtering animals in sacrifice, and the prohibition of eating hog meat and cat fish and rabbits, and the keeping the seventh day sabbath and all the rest would necessarily continue at this time for God not only endorsed but commanded these things in Bible times. But all Bible scholars agree that circumcision, and animal sacrifices and burning of incense and such like were used for the purpose of teaching valuable spiritual lessons and that they passed away when they were no longer needed. The vast majority also believe that the old seventh day sabbath passed away when the law was nailed to the cross (Col. 2:12-17) and that circumcision passed away when the New Testament became the rule of faith and practice, and that now we may eat hog meat and rabbit and cat fish which God forbade in the Old Testament Dispensation. Certainly God has not changed but He has made these changes in His laws. Then it would not follow that God had changed if HE CHOSE TO ALLOW MIRACLES FOR THE PURPOSE OF ESTABLISHING HIS DOCTRINE AND TO CONFIRM THE WORD SPOKEN BY HIMSELF WHILE ON EARTH AND SPOKEN BY THE APOSTLES AFTER HE ASCENDED TO HEAVEN. That miracles were for the purpose of CON-

FIRMING the word spoken by Christ and the Apostles is certain. Read Heb. 2:3-4, "How shall we escape if we neglect so great salvation; which at the first began to be spoken by our Lord, and was confirmed by them that heard him, God bearing them witness, both with signs and wonders, and with divers miracles, and gifts of the Holy Ghost, according to his will?" After the Word, the New Testament was CONFIRMED, ESTABLISHED, miracles were no longer needed and having served their purpose they passed away.

What they taught and did, and how that sinners heard and believed and became Christians, and how Christians should live, is written in the New Testament for our guidance, because we are to observe the same teaching. Therefore when we hear the teaching of the New Testament, we hear the Spirit speaking to us; and when we OBEY what it teaches, we walk after the Spirit and are led by the Spirit and are the children of God, saved and sanctified. "For as many as are led by the Spirit of God, they are the sons of God" (Rom. 8:14).

Paul says, "Now we have received, not the spirit of the world, but the Spirit which is of God; THAT WE MIGHT KNOW the things that are freely given to us of God, which things we also speak not in the words which man's wisdom teacheth, but which the HOLY SPIRIT TEACHETH" (I Cor. 2:12, 13). By those WORDS given to and through the apostles, we are taught and guided today. (See I Peter 1:12.)

God gave the apostles power to lay their hands upon certain ones and give them gifts of the Spirit. (Acts 19:6 and 8:18, and II Tim. 1:16). "For to one is given by the Spirit the word of knowledge by the same Spirit; to another faith by the same Spirit; to another the gifts of healing by the same Spirit; to another the working of miracles; to another prophecy; to another discerning of spirits; to another the interpretation of tongues; to another divers kinds of tongues" (I Cor. 12:8-10). These "gifts" were not the baptism in the Spirit.

Paul says that these gifts are to CEASE "when that

which is perfect is come." He says: "But whether there be
prophecies THEY SHALL FAIL; whether there be tongues
THEY SHALL CEASE; whether there be knowledge, IT
SHALL VANISH AWAY. For we know in part, and we
prophesy in part; but when that which is perfect is come
(which is 'the perfect law of liberty,' James 1:25, the completed New Testament), then that which is in part SHALL BE
DONE AWAY" (I Cor. 13:8-10).

Paul did not teach that anything necessary for our salvation or Christian life would be "done away." Hence these gifts
are not necessary for salvation or Christian living, or they
would not have ceased.

And, moreover, the Scriptures do not even INFER that
those who received these supernatural gifts, were made better
or holier Christians, but were only better able to teach others,
who, when they obeyed, were made better and holier.

The Corinthians, like many people today, did not understand the purpose of these Spiritual gifts and Paul makes a
very plain explanation in the 12th, 13th and 14 chapters
which all should diligently study.

These powers were given to the apostles and part of them
were given to a few others on whom the apostles laid their
hands. See Acts 2:43; 5:12; Heb. 2:4; Acts 28:3-5; 19:6, 11, 12,
Acts 8:18.

These signs were to confirm the word and NOT to cure our
physical sickness, or Paul would have cured Epaphroditus
(See Phil. 2:25-30), and Trophimus (See II Tim. 4:20). Did
not Paul care if they were sick and suffering? He did not heal
them.

"Gifts of the Spirit" were the power given by the Spirit
to do the things Paul mentions in I Cor. 12:8-10, while "the
GIFT of the SPIRIT is the Spirit Himself given to all who
believe.

The baptism of the Holy Spirit, and the gifts of the Spirit,
as Jesus has explained, were to TEACH and GUIDE the re-

cipients thereof, which they did. What the Spirit guided them
to say and to write, we have now as the New Testament, which
is a "perfect law of liberty" in Christ Jesus. See James 1:25;
II Tim. 3:16, 17; I Peter 4:11.

And Paul says, "But when that which is perfect is come,
then that which is in part shall be done away" (I Cor. 13:10).

To not believe they were "DONE AWAY," would be to
disbelieve God, because Paul was taught this by the Spirit of
God.

The Bible records but three instances of persons being
baptized in the Holy Spirit: The apostles (Acts 2nd), Paul
(Acts 9th), and the household of Cornelius (Acts 10th).

Although the apostles were baptized in Holy Spirit, they
baptized their converts in water. See Acts 2:41; 10:48; 16:15,
33; Acts 18:8; 19;5; 8:36-39; 22:16. And this is what Jesus
commanded them to do. See Matt. 28:19; and that is what the
church is now commanded to do.

For awhile there were two baptisms—one in the Spirit,
and one in the water. But when Paul wrote Eph. 4:5, about A.
D. 64, he said there is "one baptism," showing us that Spirit
baptism had been "done away" before that time, leaving only
water baptism when Paul wrote Ephesians.

The Holy Spirit baptism was always seen and heard by
those present. Acts 2:2, 3. See also Mark 1:10, 11; John 1:33.
If such heavenly proofs could be seen and heard today few
would doubt Holy Spirit baptism now. Therefore "Let no man
deceive you by any means," for no living person is now baptized in the Holy Spirit, but many have been deceived because
they have believed false teachers instead of the Bible.

Neither Jesus nor His apostles ever taught that sinners or
Christians need a baptism of the Holy Spirit nor any spiritual
gifts of I Cor. 12:8-10, to be saved. Paul says, "Follow after
charity (love), and desire spiritual gifts, but rather that ye
may prophesy" or teach. Paul did not consider spiritual gifts
of great importance. He said, "Yet in the church I had rather

speak FIVE words with my understanding that by my voice I might teach others also, than TEN THOUSAND words in an unknown tongue" (I Cor. 14:1, 19).

We all need the Holy Spirit, for "if any man have not the Spirit of Christ, he is none of us" (Rom. 8:9). And God gives him to those only who believe. See Acts 5:32.

The new birth, being born of the Spirit, is not restricted to the New Testament. Jesus said to Nicodemus: "Art thou a master (teacher) in Israel and knowest not these things?" (John 3:1-16). Why should Jesus make such a statement if Nicodemus could not have learned of the birth of the Spirit in the Old Testament? The regenerating work of the Holy Spirit has gone on all through the history of the world. The abiding presence, and being filled with the Holy Spirit were experienced by men and women before Christ came into the world. Luke 1:67, "Zacharias was filled with the Holy Ghost." Simeon was led by the Spirit and received revelations from the Spirit before Christ was born (Luke 1:15). The Holy Spirit came upon Mary, the mother of Jesus, when the birth of Jesus was announced to her (Luke 1:35). Elizabeth was filled with the Holy Spirit (Luke 1:41). The Holy Spirit had worked with and in men all through the history of the world. But HIS ADMINISTRATION OVER THE KINGDOM and his miraculous BAPTISM did not exist until the Pentecost after the resurrection of Jesus Christ from the dead. The confusion that exists in the minds of many on this subject is deplorable. So many think the BAPTISM of the Spirit is the same thing as the BIRTH of the Spirit and the leadership of the Spirit. The birth of the Spirit, the indwelling of the Spirit, and the leadership of the Spirit have all been enjoyed by the Lord's people from the time of creation until now. But the ADMINISTRATION of the Spirit and the baptism of the Spirit began at Pentecost.

The baptism of the Spirit and the miraculous gifts of the Spirit were done away when the "Perfect thing" came (I Cor. 13:8-10) and as expressed in different words by James, "The perfect law of liberty'' came (James 1:25) when the church came into ''The knowledge of the Son of God'' (Eph. 4:11-14) which means the revelation of Jesus Christ was complete by the finishing of the perfect rule of faith and practice which we know as the New Testament. Since this perfect thing, this ''perfect law of liberty'' came, this ''knowledge of the Son of God'' came, since that blessed day no one has had the baptism of the Holy Spirit and no one has been able to work a miracle. Why? Because the ''gifts'' which enabled men to do that ''ceased,'' and now we have the indwelling of the Spirit, the comfort of the Spirit and sinners are born of the Spirit but nobody is baptized in the Spirit and nobody has the MIRACU-LOUS gifts of the Spirit.

Are any miracles worked now? Can anbody heal the sick, or speak in unknown tongues now? You may be surprised when I tell you that possibly some are able to work miracles even now. But such miracles are not of God. They are of the devil. When Moses worked miracles in Egypt the ''Magicians did so with their enchantments'' (Ex. 7:11). This was done over and over again. The devil has counterfeited God's work in all ages. The devil is still counterfeiting God's work by working mira-cles. THE DEVIL ENABLES HIS SUBJECTS TO WORK MIRACLES. See Rev. 13:13-14: ''He does great wonders, so that he maketh fire to come down from heaven on the earth in the sight of men. And he deceiveth them that dwell on the earth by means of those miracles which he had power to do,'' etc.

Thus we plainly see that the devil is still working miracles and if I were to see a miracle, and know it to be a miracle; if I were to see a man heal the sick or do any other wonderful thing I would not be convicted that he was of God because of that. Instead of the miracle causing me to believe that the miracle worker was of God I would be convinced of the exact opposite for the good reason that the miraculous gifts have been with-drawn from the church and all miracles are now of the devil.

Will apparently good men, who praise God, and shout and

preach and pray and seemingly good be under the power of the devil? Most assuredly. Read II Cor. 11:13-15. "For such are false apostles, deceitful workers, transforming themselves into an angel of light. Therefore it is no great thing if his ministers also be transformed as ministers of righteousness."

So we see that the devil has ministers, the devil has miracle workers, and since we know by the Scriptures that God's ministers do not now have the gift of healing, and the gift of tongues and such like because they have been done away, done away when the "PERFECT THING," the "PERFECT LAW OF LIBERTY," came, when the church came "INTO THE KNOWLEDGE OF THE SON OF GOD"; since we know that miracle workers is a thing of the past in the church of Jesus Christ, then we can as certainly know that any miracle working we now see is of the devil, no matter how wonderful and no matter how religious they may seem to be. The more prayer, and shouting, and praising God there is attached to it the more danger there is of deceiving the unsuspecting.

These plain words are necessary now because so many are claiming these miraculous gifts. The Holy Rollers, the Christian Scientists, the Mormons, the McPhersonites and others are making loud claims. We had better prepare to meet them for they are only different varieties of the same vicious species.

There is a hue and cry going up all over the land for "more SPIRITUALITY." That is well and good provided it is sure enough SPIRITUALITY that is wanted. But what is MEANT in many cases is EMOTION, DEMONSTRATION, the SO-CALLED BAPTISM OF THE SPIRIT, and a goody, goody, sort of feeling. The devil is back of all such demands. Spirituality of a Bible sort is to be in HARMONY WITH THE HOLY SPIRIT. To be in harmony with the Spirit is to respect His written word, to obey His written commandments, to be submissive to His written will. To be governed by DREAMS, EMOTIONS, FEELINGS, and then not be willing to hear what the Holy Spirit says in his word is positive proof that the individuals so governed are not spiritual. A spiritual man LOVES THE BIBLE and does not get angry when the preacher preaches the words of the Spirit on baptism, the Lord's Supper, church government, LAYING BY IN STORE OF THE MONEY GOD HAS PLACED IN HIS HANDS, and thus be a liberal contributor to His cause. To get angry at a sermon preached on contributing money and then cry for SPIRITUAL preaching is a certain indication that the one so exercising is anything but spiritual. The man or woman who can not sit and listen with pleasure at a doctrinal sermon, a sermon that plainly shows our duty and yet weeps over death bed stories and rejoices over emotional illustrations shows a lack of spirituality.

If we are led by the Spirit we shall do what the Spirit teaches us to do. If we are filled with the Spirit we shall rejoice in what the Bible teaches. If we think of Jesus and want to honor and obey Jesus we are spiritual. The Holy Spirit testifies NOT OF HIMSELF but of Jesus and if he is our GUEST he will fill us with the LOVE OF JESUS and we shall not think of the Spirit himself, and we shall feel unworthy of the Lord's service instead of boasting of our SPIRITUALITY. Spirituality produces humility and never the Pharisaical feeling that we are so very good.

Let us hear what Jesus said this baptism in the Holy Spirit was to do. "But the Comforter, which is the Holy Spirit, whom the Father will send in My name, He shall TEACH YOU ALL THINGS, and bring all things to your REMEMBRANCE, whatsoever I have said unto you" (John 14:26).

"He shall TESTIFY of Me" (John 15:26). "And when he (the Spirit) is come, he will REPROVE the world of sin, and of righteousness, and of judgment . . . I have yet many things to say unto you, but ye cannot bear them now. Howbeit when he, the Spirit of Truth is come, he will GUIDE YOU into ALL TRUTH: for he shall not speak of himself; but whatsoever he shall hear, that shall he speak; and he will SHOW you things to come. He shall glorify me for he shall receive of mine and SHALL SHOW IT UNTO YOU'' (John 16:8-14).

Note the fact that the Holy Spirit was NOT TO SPEAK OF HIMSELF but was to testify of Christ. Those who have the Holy Spirit will show that fact by thinking of Jesus and SPEAKING of Jesus. If a man is constantly talking about the wonderful things the Spirit has done for him and is always boasting of being filled with the Spirit and of being baptized by the Spirit it is positive proof that he does not have the Holy Spirit because the Spirit does not talk about Himself but He testifies of Christ.

Thus Jesus leaves no uncertainty for us to guess at, about the baptism in the Holy Spirit, but tells us in plain words the exact purpose of this baptism. It was "to TEACH" His apostles, "to SHOW" them, "to GUIDE" them, to bring to their "REMEMBRANCE, whatsoever I have said unto you," and "to TESTIFY" to the world of Jesus through them.

At that time there was no New Testament to tell people how to be saved, and how to live, hence Jesus sent the Holy Spirit to guide His apostles into what to teach men and women. And the Spirit guided them so perfectly that they spake only "AS THE SPIRIT GAVE THEM UTTERANCE" (Acts 3:4).

Thus guided and controlled by the Spirit, they could teach and testify exactly what Jesus wanted taught to the people, and could prove their words were given them from heaven, by confirming them "with signs and wonders and divers miracles" (Heb. 2:4).

What they taught and did, and how sinners heard and believed and became Christians, and how Christians should live, is written in the New Testament for our guidance, because we are to observe the same teaching. Therefore, when we hear the teaching of the New Testament, we hear the Spirit speaking to us; and when we OBEY what it teaches, we walk after the Spirit and are led by the Spirit and are the children of God, saved and sanctified. "For as many as are led by the Spirit of God, they are the sons of God" (Rom. 8:14).

Paul says, "Now we have received, not the spirit of the world, but the Spirit which is of God; THAT WE MIGHT KNOW the things that are freely given to us of God, which things we also speak not in the words which man's wisdom teacheth, but which the HOLY SPIRIT TEACHETH" (I Cor. 2:12, 13). By those WORDS given to and through the apostles, we are taught and guided today. (See I Peter 1:12).

This idea does not deny the LEADERSHIP of the Holy Spirit. The Holy Spirit leads in two ways. He instructs in WRITING, the writings of the New Testament, as to every doctrine and practice, he tells us plainly what to do under all circumstances in HIS WRITTEN WORD. The other way the Spirit leads is by HIS PROVIDENCE. He, by His providence hedges up our way at times and opens up new ways by His providence but ALL HIS INSTRUCTIONS are in the New Testament. When a man takes a dream or an IMPRESSION for the leadership of the Spirit he becomes an easy victim for the frauds and imposters who come along with plenty of such dreams and impressions. But if we give all these imposters to understand that we are UNDER WRITTEN INSTRUC-TIONS from the Holy Spirit as to our duty and that we can TRUST THE HOLY SPIRIT TO OPEN UP WAYS FOR SERVICE and to PROVIDENTIALLY PREVENT US FROM ENTERING WHERE WE SHOULD NOT, then we are safely on Bible ground and at the same time immune to at-tack from the hundred and one religious cults who prey upon the ignorant and establish their heretical cults. To hold, as some do, that we still have the "GIFTS" of the Spirit, such as will enable us to speak with tongues and heal the sick, LOG-ICALLY TURNS US OVER TO THE MORMONS, HOLY ROLLERS and others who think that these things continue till this day.

This position does not discourage prayer for the sick. We

should take every thing to God in prayer. We should pray for daily bread (Matt. 6:11) but we should do what we can to get bread, use the means God has ordained to get bread and YET HE GIVES US OUR BREAD. We should pray for the sick. But when one has malaria, for instance, when we pray for the Lord to heal the malaria we should give the patient quinine because the malaria germ is killed by quinine. We should pray the Lord to protect us from small pox and when we pray, go to a doctor and be vaccinated, thus using the means God has put in our reach to prevent small pox. How foolish it would be to pray for bread and then expect the Lord to rain it down from heaven. Pray for the salvation of souls and then, as we pray, we should preach to these same souls and use the means God ordained for their salvation. But to depend on miracles is to be depending on what has been done away.

From *Baptist and Commoner,* April 15, 1931.

SALVATION OF SOULS BY RADIO MESSAGE

In 1931, Bogard gave eleven lectures over KLRA in Little Rock, Arkansas, and in 1932, he spoke twenty four times in broadcasts. By 1933, he was preaching fairly regularly each week and from that time on carried on a radio work—for a long time from KGHI, then KLRA.

Antioch Church was still carrying on the program over KLRA with Pastor L. D. Foreman preaching each Sunday morning when Dr. Bogard died. On every opportunity in his travels, he spoke to a radio audience. Many people testified of their salvation due to a radio message and, at least, one preacher resulted from his radio ministry. Harold Johnson, well known pastor in the American Baptist Association, was an unsaved boy living in Balch, Arkansas, when he heard Bogard preaching one of his radio sermons. Saved as a result of the gospel preached by radio, he then came to the Missionary Baptist Seminary for study for he experienced more than sal-

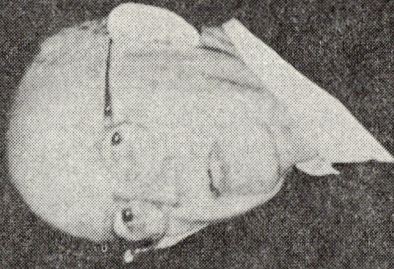

Pictured here is Dr. Bogard as he preached his last sermon to the messengers of the American Baptist Association in 1950. The marks of a heart attack and age were quite evident.

vation. He answerd the call to preach.

At the peak of the radio ministry Foreman made a survey to estimate the listening audience. The answers to his appeal for letters from the listeners giving their names and addresses pleasantly surprised the men at the radio station. They told him that, based on the response, there must be an audience of from one hundred to one hundred fifty thousand listeners.

People sent offerings in to pay for the broadcasts most of the time during Bogard's radio ministry. This was true several years after Foreman took over. Antioch Church then underwrote the expenses.

Finally three things happened. First, a number of local stations were started in smaller cities. Local pastors bought time and went on the air. More and more of the stations and local broadcasts began—each one drew a part of the vast audience. Many of them were at the exact time or near that of the Antioch broadcast.

Money needed to pay for these local broadcasts was naturally used at home rather than sent in to Little Rock. Then the price of broadcasting kept increasing. At the time this broadcast was dropped Antioch Church was paying between $1600 and $1800 per year for it.

Then, television swept the country. As these sets were bought, radios were put in the attic or thrown away. Fewer and fewer people listened. Though radio made a partial comeback after the television craze settled down, by that time, Antioch decided to cease the regular broadcast.

At the suggestion of the pastor, that this money would benefit the church more if it was used to help employ a man for visitation and/or youth director work, the church voted to drop the radio ministry.

Bogard was on the air with Dan Gilbert and Hoyt Chastain from a powerful station at Tampico, Mexico, for about one year. This, in the last years of his life, seemed to thrill him immensely. The station had powerful coverage, especially up the western coast and into Canada.

There is no way to know how many millions of people this man preached to using the agency of the radio.

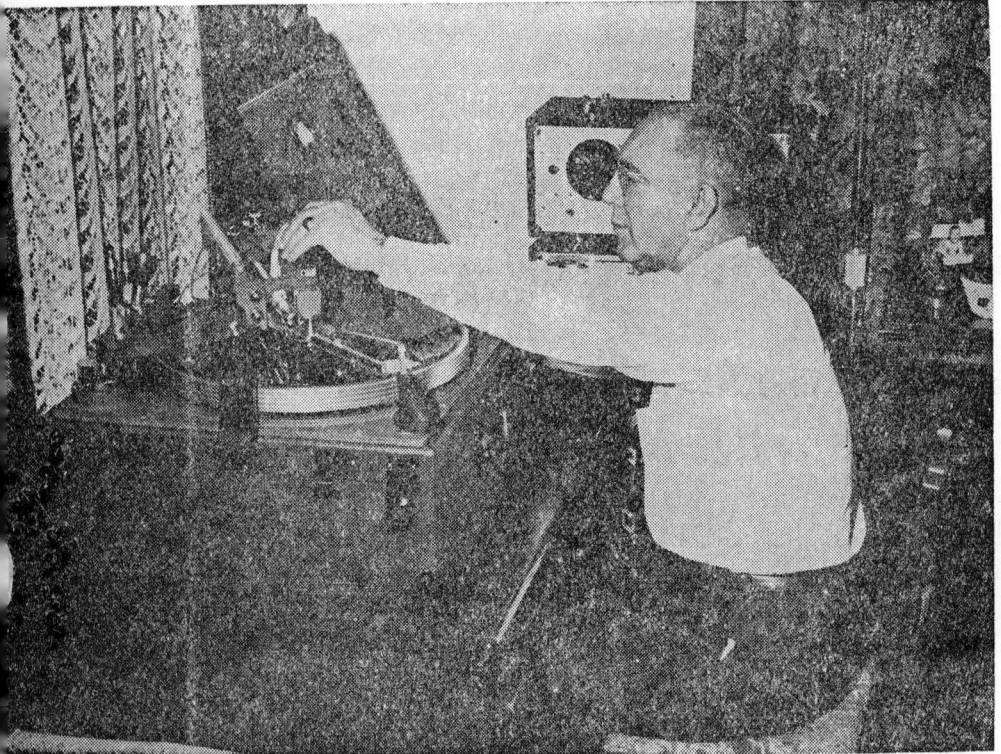

S. J. (Steve) Jaggars, a deacon in Antioch Baptist Church, at the controls of his recording studio. Brother Jaggars understood the great worth of the radio ministry of Dr. Bogard and spent many hours in recording and providing tapes and "platters" for the radio broadcasts.

BOGARD - THE WRITER

I

WHAT HE READ

One might say that Bogard began his writing career by reading. For the larger part of his ministry, he kept a journal. In the very beginning—book one, page one of his diary, he listed the books he had read "after being saved." Could he have known the value of books even then? Uncannily, he seemed to know from the very beginning of his Christian life the lasting value of books. "We become a part of what we read. Lives are molded by what we read," he said. "I was anxious to go to school and I read every good book I could get my hands on."

Good books don't necessarily have to be religious books. Some religious books are good, but our libraries are also filled with good novels, histories, biographies, reference books, subject matter and others that teach good character, philosophy, morality. From them we learn how to think. We get ideas from other people and if good, part of them are put into use for ourselves. We learn how to improve our lives by learning how other people have progressed. We learn what dangers are and how to avoid them—and it's down right fun to read!

These are the books read by Ben M. Bogard listed in the order he read them from the year 1884 and while he was in college:

1. **Chain of Sacred Wonders by S. A. Lotta**, D. D.
2. **The Household of David** by J. H. Ingraham
3: **Golden Gems of Life** by Ferguson and Allen
4. **The Protestant** (two volumes) by Wm. McGavin
5. **Catholic Mission Book**
6. **Life of Lorenzo Dow** by Lorenzo Dow
7. **Lights of Temperance** by Reverend James Young
8. **Platform Echoes** by John B. Gough
9. **The Crusader** by Michank
10. **The History of Greece**

11. **The College of Colleges** (Lectures)
12. **Preparation of Sermons** by John A. Broadus
13. **Sermons and Addresses** by H. M. Wharton
14. **Bunyan's Pilgrim's Progress** by John Bunyan
15. **Crisis of Missouri** by A. T. Pierson
16. **Pure Religion**
17. **Grace Truman** by Mrs. S. R. Ford
18. **What Baptists Baptize For** by S. H. Ford
19. **Intercommunion Inconsistent** by J. R. Graves
20. **Life and Labors of C. H. Spurgeon** by Needman
21. **Our Country** by Dr. Strong
22. **Mrs. Geolfrey** (A novel by "The Duchess")
23. **Don Quixote** (Knight Errantry) Cervantes
24. **John Halifax** by Miss Mulock (Mrs. Craik)
25. **Peck's Bad Boy** by George H. Peck
26. **Graves-Ditzler Debate**—J. R. Graves, Jacob Ditzler
27. **American Baptist Yearbook, 1889,** by L. Burrows
28. **Perfect in Christ** by William Mason, D. D.
29. **Church Manual** by J. M. Pendleton, D. D.
30. **Missiles of Truth** by W. W. Gardner, D. D.
31. **Lectures to Students** by C. H. Spurgeon
32. **The Priest, The Woman and Confessional,** Chings
33. **The Nashville Debate** by J. B. Moody and J. A. Harding
34. **The Bible in the Nineteenth Century** by L. T. Townsend
35. **Looking Backward** by Edward Bellamy
36. **Exposition of the Parables** by J. R. Graves
37. **Henry Esmond** by W. M. Thackery
38. **Ben Hur or Tale of the Christ** by Lew Wallace
39. **Brief Notes on New Testament** by Clark and Pendleton
40. **Three Reasons** by J. M. Pendleton
41. **Universalism Exposed** by J. D. Williamson
42. **Campbellism Exposed** by A. P. Williams
43. **The Devil and I** (A novel) Anonymous
44. **The True and the False** by A. C. Dixon
45. **St. Elmo** by Augusta J. Evans
46. **The Child of the Ganges** by Robert N. Barrett
47. **The Last Days of Pompeii** by E. Bulmer Lythan
48. **Natural Law in Spiritual World** by Henry Drummond
49. **Autobiography of Peter Cartwright**
50. **Uncle John Vasser or The Fight of Faith** by T. E. Vasser
51. **The Deaconship** by R. B. C. Howell
52. **Sanctification** by B. Carradine
53. **John's Baptism** by J. R. Graves
54. **The Seven Dispensations** by J. R. Graves
55. **Thoughts on Daniel and the Revelation** by U. Smith
56. **Baptist Doctrines or Lectures** by Different Authors
57. **The Book and Its Theme,** L. L. Pickett
58. **Prevailing Prayer** by D. L. Moody
59. **Paradise** by John Milton
60. **Character Sketches** by George A. Lofton
61. **Life of C. H. Spurgeon** by Russell H. Cornwell
62. **Church Communion** by W. W. Gardner

63. **Story of Baptists in All Ages** by R. B. Cook
64. **A Baptist Abroad** by W. A. Whittle
65. **Consoling Works** by John Bunyan
66. **Biography of Alfred Taylor** by W. C. Taylor
67. **Who are the Primitive Baptists?** Throgmorton-Potter Debate
68. **The Word and Works of God** by Gilbert S. Bailey
69. **What I Know About Books** by Geo. C. Lorimer
70. **Origin of Campbellism** by J. H. Milburn
71. **Baptist History** by G. H. Orchard
72. **Cooks Voyages Around the World** by A. Kippir
73. **Life of Christ** by James Stalker, M. A.
74. **Bible Introduction** by Thomas H. Horne
75. **English Harmony of the Gospels,** George W. Clark
76. **Land of the Bible** by G. W. McGarvey
77. **Christ Our Life** by Joseph Angus
78. **Immersion** by J. T. Christian
79. **The Great Redemption** by D. L. Moody
80. **History of the Christian Church** by Smith
81. **Millennial Dawn (Three Volumes)** by C. T. Russell
82. **Life and Labors of George E. Flowers** by Isaac Errett
83. **Yale Lectures on Preaching** by Henry Ward Beecher
84. **History of Preaching** by John A. Broadus
85. **Life of T. J. Fisher** by J. H. Spencer
86. **The New Era of The Coming Kingdom** by J. Strong
87. **A Converted Jew** by Carlos Martin
88. **History of the Apostolic Church** by Philip Schaff, D. D.
89. **Sartar Resartus** by Thomas Carlyle
90. **Wendell Phillips, the Agitator** by Carlos Martin
91. **The Second Advent** by David Brown
92. **Annals of Methodism in Missouri** by W. S. Woodard
93. **Close Communion or Open Communion** by C. Kennedy
94. **Mosheim's Church History** (four volumes)
95. **Dante's Inferno**
96. **Jefferson Davis** (two volumes) by his wife
97. **The Gates Ajar** by Elizabeth Stuart Phelps
98. **Baptist Church Perpetuity or History** by W. A. Jarrel
99. **Messiahship of Jesus** by Joseph S. C. G. Grey
100. **Merrie England or Socialism Explained** by R. Blatchford
101. **Manual of Theology** by J. L. Dagg
102. **Ministry of the Spirit** by A. J. Gordon
103. **The Pastor** by H. Harvey
104. **How to be a Pastor** by T. L. Cuyler
105. **Short History of the Baptists** by H. C. Vedder
106. **David Copperfield** by Charles Dickens
107. **Pickwick Papers** by Charles Dickens
108. **Ernest Maltravers** by E. Bulwer Lythan
109. **Go-ology** by J. A. Scarboro
110. **Coin's Financial School** by W. H. Harvey
111. **The Scarlet Letter** by Nathaniel Hawthorne
112. **Americanism or Romanism, Which?** by J. T. Christian
113. **At the Mercy of Tiberius** by August Evans Wilson
114. **Life and Epistles of Paul** by Coneybeare and Hawson

115. **Old Testament History** by William Smith
116. **The Mother Church** by Henry M. King
117. **Saxenhurst** by D. C. Eddy, D. D.
118. **New England's Struggles for Liberty** by David B. Ford
119. **Popular Amusements** by B. W. Sinks
120. **Imago Christo** by James A. Stalker
121. **The Old Man** by B. Carradine
123. **Lady of the Lake** by Sir Walter Scott
124. **Sesame and Lillius** by John Ruskin
125. **Snowbound Among the Hills and Songs of Labor** by J. G. Whittier
126. **Vision of Sir Launfal and Other Poems** by James Russell Lowell
127. **History of Baptists** by David Benedict
128. **The Law and the Lady** by Wilkie Collins
129. **Directory for Baptist Churches** by E. T. Hiscox
130. **History of the English Bible** by T. H. Pattison
131. **Confessions of Harry Lorregner**
132. **The Papal Controversy,** D. B. Ray and C. B. Pallen
133. **Doctrinal Works** by John Bunyan
134. **Consoling Works** by John Bunyan
135. **Quiz** by Augusta J. Evans
136. **Experimental Works** by John Bunyan
137. **Kennilworth** by Sir Walter Scott
138. **The Woman in White** by Wilkie Collins
139. **The Queen of the Air** by John Ruskin
140. **Practical Works** by John Bunyan
141. **Natural Theology** by William Paley
142. **Christ Acted Parables—Miracles** by N. S. Burton
143. **Systematic Theology and Ecclesiology** by A. H. Strong
144. **Westminister Abbey** by Ron G. Kingsley
145. **Hall-Williams Debate on the Kingdom** (State of the Dead, Resurrection, Future Punishment)
146. **Inspiration of the Scriptures** by A. Carson
147. **Life and Labors of A. Carson** by Brown
148. **Providence Unfolded in the Book of Esther,** A. Carson
149. **Autobiography of Major W. E. Penn**
150. **Sermons and Life Sketch of Richard Fuller**
151. **Memoirs of James P. Boyce** by John A. Broadus
152. **The Doctrine of the Atonement** by Alexander Carson
153. **General Membership of Ralston Health Club**
154. **Reminiscences of a Long Life** by J. M. Pendleton
155. **History of China** by Demetrius Charles Boulger

He concluded that books will have a good or bad effect on lives, that it depended on the book. Early in his preaching life he began to write what he preached. Preaching was good for the people who heard it. He sensed the need of booklets, sermons, study courses and other printed materials in the hands of the people so they could study. He wanted them to have something to read in their homes and which they could pass on to their children, so they, too, might preserve the heritage of the father's faith.

II

WHAT HE WROTE

Even as a boy, Ben M. Bogard was interested in the publication business. The *Caseyville Enterprise* was a small paper published in the town of that name where he spent a part of his boyhood. This little establishment made a lasting impression on him, for to his young eyes, it seemed a very "big operation" though in reality it was only a mere handful of type and an old Washington hand press. Just one page was printed at a time, but as far as he knew then, all print shops were like this one and he was completely fascinated with it, slipping away many times to watch the printers at work.

When the Bogard family moved to Spring Grove, Kentucky, Ben took upon himself the office of community reporter and began to send in the neighborhood news. He decided to sign his name backwards, writing Neb instead of Ben. A typographical error gave him the pen name of Nib, which designation stayed with him through several years of correspondence as he wrote a column called "Nib's Nibblings." This gave him valuable practice in writing, as well as, instructions from the kind editor on preparing and sending in manuscripts. The experience helped him to get over his "stage fright" period in writing and taught him not to get angry when all his material was not printed. He said, "It enabled me to try my wings so to speak and I actually learned I could fly, figuratively speaking."

He always loved newspaper work, as well as other types of writing. Ink was "in his blood." During the year 1889, he spent two weeks in western Tennessee working for the *Western Recorder* and on this tour preached three times and secured subscriptions for this paper. He had begun reading it when he was a boy. An agent had come to Woodland Church and sold subscriptions to it. Bogard never missed it from that time. Through this paper, he became acquainted with T. T. Eaton who, he said, "was one of the brainiest men who ever lived." Though much older than Ben, Eaton became a personal friend and did much to shape the future of the young preacher. Bogard's pastor also influenced him to subscribe for the *Christian Repository,* edited by S. H. Ford and his wife Sallie Rochester Ford, both of whom became his personal friends and helped to influence his life. Then, he came in contact with J. N. Hall, the famous preacher and debater and though he, too, was much older than Bogard, they became the closest of friends and as Ben said, "I shall never be able to tell how he influenced me and helped to shape my future. These men are all gone. They did their work and have entered into glory. But if they helped others as they did me they still live on in others as they live in me. A man becomes a part of all with which he comes in contact and that being true I thank God for contact with such men as I have just mentioned. I read their papers and their books and later I went to college."

An old friend gave Bogard a copy of the *Tennessee Baptist,* edited by J. R. Graves. He read it through and through and learned much of this great preacher. In September 1888, he went to Boardly to hear him deliver his series of lectures on salvation and one on church communion. This gave him an opportunity to become acquainted with him and ask him some simple questions. That great man patiently answered them. Bogard wrote of this incident: "It was a wonderful thing to me. I never shall forget that wonderful preacher and the impression he made on me largely shaped my future. I became a student of Graves and have read all of his books and how I do wish I could prevail on all young preachers to read Graves' books."

Bogard not only spent time reading books and papers himself, but realizing the power of the printed word, sold books and Bibles as he preached, urging his hearers to read and study for themselves.

Books

He wrote his first book in 1892, which was only a small booklet named *Four Reasons Why I Am A Baptist.* The first year of its publication saw fifteen hundred copies sold and still in great demand. Three thousand copies had been printed and by 1894, the edition was exhausted. Another small booklet called *Christian Union or the Problem Solved,* printed in July, 1894, by the Baptist Book Concern in Louisville, Kentucky, became quite popular. By 1899, thirteen thousand copies had been sold. It had been read in almost every state in the union. Plans were made to get out a new edition the next year. New editions were brought out in 1904 and 1907 bringing the distribution to 18,000.

In 1897, Bogard wrote *Church Government* of which six thousand copies were published. By 1898, only one thousand copies had been sold and he commented, "The sale of this book is slow." However by 1907 all copies had been sold.

In 1898 he engaged in a written discussion with W. P. Throgmorton on the subject of the mission question. This discussion was published in book form in 1899 and two thousand copies sold. His comment concerning the sale of the *Throgmorton-Bogard Debate* was, "Considering the nature of this book, it has sold well."

III

PILLARS OF ORTHODOXY

He began writing what was to be his first really large book in 1899 when he was only thirty years old. *Pillars of Orthodoxy or Defenders of the Faith,* a 500 page volume, was published in 1900. He said at the end of that year, "Eight hundred copies have been sold and the prospect for the book is good. The book contains biographies of seventeen 'pillars' with the pictures and a specimen sermon or essay from each. It is history, theology and an album. Price $2.00 each." By the end of 1901, two thousand copies of this book had already been sold.

Bogard's introduction to this great work reads: "This book is a history, an album and a collection of the choicest sermons and essays. It is a history of our great leaders who have fought hard and long for Bible principles and doctrines, and by their consecrated, and, in some instances, heroic lives, have shown themselves to be worthy of the title: PILLARS OF ORTHODOXY.

"The arrangement of the book is such that the reader can study separately the lives of each of these great men and read the specimen sermon or essay without reference to any of the others. Each life sketch is complete in itself, and no one chapter is dependent on another. The life sketch of Richard Fuller, and his great sermon on the 'Desire of All Nations,' for instance, is a complete chapter to itself, without reference to anything else in the book. This feature enables the busy reader to read a chapter at a time, and there is nothing lost by the long intervals between his opportunities to read. In a book where one chapter is directly connected with another, much is lost by failing to read straight through. The last chapter can be read first in this book and nothing will be lost by it.

"It is always a pleasure to look into the face of a great man. There is something elevating about it. The pictures of these men, who seem to be pillars, (Galatians 2:9) are the very best that can be obtained. The reader, therefore, while he studies the life, may look into the faces of these men who have made so much glorious history. By that means, these pillars of orthodoxy will seem to be old friends, and it will make their life work seem more real.

"It can be safely assumed that the sermons and essays, published as specimens in this book, are the best that have ever been published. Some of them are published here for the first time, while others have been published and have become famous. It is a pleasure to present to the public the volume containing the very cream of the best thought from the strongest men in the Baptist denomination.

"There is J. B. Moody's great essay on 'Conditions of Receiving the Holy Spirit for Service,' which is published here for the first time. It alone is worth the price of the book. There is J. P. Christian's strong essay on 'What Baptists Have Done for the World,' which is published for the first time. Then there are other sermons and essays of great value that can be found only in this volume.

"The published sermons and essays that are here reissued are, without exception, such as should be preserved and will be valuable additions to anyone's library. Besides the aforementioned merits, may be mentioned the fact that the discussion of Scripture doctrines are such that the book, as a whole, becomes almost a complete embodiment of the theology of the New Testament.

"It begins with Dr. Dayton's sermon on 'The Existence of God,' and 'Christ the Savior,' by Fuller; then there is discussed, by William Vaughan, the 'Relation of the Law and the Gospel'; then 'Regeneration,' by A. P. Williams; 'Baptism,' by T. T. Eaton; 'The Holy Spirit,' by J. B. Moody; 'The Divinity of Christ,' by W. E. Penn, and so on to the practical subjects, such as 'Glad Giving,' by J. A. Broadus; 'The Work of Baptists An Urgent Work,' by the prince of preachers, J. S. Coleman; and the book closes with J. N. Hall's discussion of the 'State of the Dead.'

"Other great articles by S. H. Ford, J. M. Pendleton, J. R. Graves and others might have special mention. In fact, it is hard to decide which one is best, because all are the very best and they will have to be rated by the individual taste of the reader.

"If, by sending out this book, I may be the instrument of doing good, of preserving the names and deeds of these noble men, and of helping in establishing my brethren in the faith, and of leading some wandering soul from darkness to light, I shall be well paid for the unusual labor put into its preparation."

"Very truly yours,

"Ben M. Bogard."

One can easily grasp the magnitude of this work by the forthright introduction. It is clear, concise and expresses Bogard's Christian spirit and his charitableness toward all.

A REVIEW OF PILLARS OF ORTHODOXY BY BOGARD

Amos Cooper Dayton

A footnote on page 13 introduces the first "pillar," the great Dr. A. C. Dayton: "No picture of Dr. Dayton can be secured." Amos Cooper Dayton was the author of *Theodosia Ernest and The Infidel's Daughter* which had wide publication and reading many years ago.

Dayton, the second son of Jonathan and Phebe Dayton, was born in Plainfield, New Jersey, September 4, 1813. The first sixteen years of his life was spent on his father's farm in what Dayton later explained as "plain living and high thinking." By the time he was seven years old, he showed a passionate love for books and the first money he ever earned by hauling a load of nuts to the village market was at once invested in a grammar and arithmetic book. At twelve years of age he joined the Presbyterian Church where his parents were members. When he was sixteen he was forced to leave school because of an accident that nearly destroyed his eyesight. Later, he worked his way through medical college in New York, receiving his diploma in the twenty second year of his life.

Traveling in the southern states for his health, Dayton met and, after a brief courtship, married Lucy Harrison of Shelbyville, Tennessee. They left at once for Florida where the young physician meant to practice his profession and, if possible, regain his own health. It was feared he had what was known then as "consumption." Today, it is called Tuberculosis.

In 1852 Dayton became a Baptist. How he was led to make this change is told in full in his last diary kept from 1852 to 1864. The painful struggles through which the character in his book *Theodosia* passed were not creations of his imagination but a recital of his own experiences. During this long period of illness he decided to preach the gospel. His journal has this entry: "It was the fondly cherished hope of my parents that my life should be devoted to the great work of the ministry. They intended, on account of this, to give me the benefit of a liberal education and failed to carry out their design only because I lost health and eyesight at such an early age.

"When I was under such deep conviction in 1842, this was one of the great wrongs which I felt I had done. I had not employed my time and talents in spreading the truth of God's word, but had wasted my life in other and comparatively useless labors."

Dayton and his wife had moved back to Tennessee. At Nashville, he was connected with the *Tennessee Baptist* and later published *Theodosia Ernest,* then *The Infidel's Daughter.* In 1861, the horrors of the Civil War drove him from home and in 1863, he was offered the presidency of Houston Female

College in Perry, Georgia. He spent his last days here teaching and preaching. He died June 11, 1865.''

Entire sermons by these great ''Pillars of Orthodoxy'' cannot possibly be quoted, but the reader who does not have access to a library containing this volume is given some idea of the distinguished scholarship and sermonizing by these few paragraphs from Dayton's sermon, ''The Existence of God.''

''THE EXISTENCE OF GOD

''Some years ago a lawyer who professed to be an infidel came one day into the office of a professional man, and seeing a tract lying upon his table, he picked it up and read aloud its title, 'The Life of a Christian,' and laying it down again immediately, added, 'Otherwise the life of a *fool.'*

''Some young gentlemen who were present laughed at this and thought it very witty. *Witty* perhaps it was, but was it *true?*

''Who is the fool?

''Even supposing Christianity is false and the Bible an imposture, that there *is no God* and death is an eternal sleep, it would by no means follow that all who hold the contrary are fools, for it has sometimes happened that the wisest men have been deceived, and besides, one may be allowed to think that the evidence that was sufficient to enlist the faith of such men as Locke and Newton, Milton and Bacon and others of their stamp, men who, in power of reasoning intellect, in rigid, clear analysis and logical deduction, stand among our modern would-be philosophers like giants among pigmies—the evidence, I say, which was sufficient to convince such men might reasonably be thought sufficient to justify a *common* mind in giving its assent without incurring the charge of either silliness or insanity.

''No one can *prove* there is no God. No one can *prove* that Christianity is *not* true. It is impossible in the very nature of things to prove such a negative. All that can by possibility be truly said is that we have not *evidence enough* to prove its truth. Let us grant this. Its truth is still *possible*. It may be even *probable*. Who then is the fool? Let us examine.''

Richard Fuller

Richard Fuller, D. D. 1805-1874, was born in Beaufort, South Carolina. He was first taught by a minister, Elder Brantley, of Beaufort, afterwards studied at Harvard and was first in his studies in a class of eighty students. He entered the practice of law when he returned from Harvard and became one of the most successful lawyers in the state. Bogard observed: ''His success along that line is another answer to the slander that men go to preaching when they can't successfully do anything else.''

Fuller's religious experience was unusual. First, uniting with the Episcopal Church, his keen eye discovered that only immersion was baptism. He, therefore, demanded immersion at the hands of the Episcopal clergyman. Then, under the preaching of Elder Daniel Barker, the famous evangelist, he realized that he had never been regenerated. He was converted, united with a Baptist Church in Beaufort, South Carolina, and was baptized by the authority of that church. He wrote in his Bible: ''Richard Fuller, born April 1805; born again August 27, 1832.'' Almost immediately after his conversion, he entered the ministry and became one of the greatest pulpit orators who ever lived. He was, also, a debater and a writer. His sermon in the book, *Pillars of Orthodoxy, is titled the ''Desire* of All Nations,'' taken from Haggai 2:7. It is a masterpiece.

William Vaughan

The third pillar Dr. Bogard introduced in his book was William Vaughan, born February 22, 1785 in Westmoreland

County, Pennsylvania. The family moved to Kentucky when he was only three years old. In his almost wilderness home, he had very few educational advantages and what he learned was a result of his ability more than any outside encouragement. He became a proficient scholar before he reached middle life and used his acquirement to good advantage in his long ministerial career.

Perhaps one of the wittiest things in the life of William Vaughan happened when he was a small boy only eight years old. Even at that time he had an inclination to preach. His sermon, preached to a number of playmates, was in this vein: "Boys, if you break the Sabbath, or tell stories, or swear, or don't mind your mammy and daddy, or don't mind your books and be good boys, you will die and go to hell—a lake of blue blazes, burning with fire and brimstone. And when you ask for water the devil will melt lead in a ladle and pour it down your throat." He was not converted to Christ at that time, but it was an indication of the pre-disposition of the child, and his developing into a great preacher is not to be wondered at. For the sermon, however, the brutal teacher gave him a whipping and the whipping was so severe that he carried the marks twelve months. Dr. Bogard said of this teacher, "Let us thank God that we have a more humane class of school teachers in this generation."

Vaughan was a tailor in early life. When he was saved and became a Baptist, he was licensed to preach by Friendship Church in Kentucky in February 1811. His first attempts were failures but he did not quit and later became one of the great preachers of all time. Vaughan's sermon chosen by Bogard is "The Law and the Gospel."

A. P. Williams

The fourth pillar discussed was A. P. Williams, March 13, 1813-November 9, 1868. He died just eight months after Bogard was born. His sermon chosen for publication was "Regeneration."

James P. Boyce

James P. Boyce, D. D. was the fifth pillar mentioned. James Pettigru Boyce was born in Charleston, South Carolina, January 11, 1827. His father was a wealthy banker and planter, said to be the richest man in South Carolina. Boyce was an exception to the saying that rich men's sons never amount to much. There have been very few sons of poor men who have equaled James P. Boyce. He graduated at Brown University, September 1847. He was a great theologian and his *Systematic Theology* is one of the best books of its kind. The sermon given was "The Doctrine of Divine Decrees," an excerpt from his *Theology*. This is a dissertation on what is frequently called predestination" and is, he stated, "justly considered one of the most difficult of all the doctrines in which Christians believe." He stated and explained the doctrine, giving Scriptures for his beliefs and stating objections to the teaching.

W. E. Penn

Major W. E. Penn, evangelist, was the next minister included in the "pillars" of faith. He was born in Rutherford County, Tennessee, August 11, 1832, where he spent his early life on a farm, working in the fields with the slaves until he was nearly grown. His conversion at the age of fifteen in Milan, Tennessee, 1847, came at 2 o'clock in the morning. During the preacher's sermon he had been deeply convicted of sin. The sermons, prayers, tears and entreaties of friends and parents, with the realization of God's patience and long suffering,

seemed to weight him down. He reached the place of despera-
tion when he knew he could do nothing but turn himself over
to the Lord, "bad as he was," and he was saved. As the great
change came, he said, "The light of the few tallow candles was
all we had, but the place was as bright to me as the noonday
sun." Only a few older members had stayed with him through
the night and "their faces were lighted up as with the light of
heaven." Though he had before often laughed at them, this
time when they rejoiced over his salvation and sang, he
thought it the sweetest music he had ever heard. In October of
that year, he was baptized into the fellowship of Beachgrove
Baptist Church.

James Hurt ("Uncle Jimmie") preached the sermon that
brought conviction to Penn's heart, and as Bogard said, "He
was an obscure backwoods preacher. What encouragement is
this to brethren in the out-of-the-way places, working for
nearly nothing, yet preaching the glorious gospel of the Son
of God. We owe a debt of gratitude to that class of men which
we shall never pay, but like Paul, they 'have fought a good
fight . . .' Many of them will receive a greater reward and
stand higher in heaven than any of these great men whose history is given in this book."

Major Penn began reading law with the firm of William
and Wright, Lexington, Tennessee. He began his own practice
in his twentieth year. It was very successful. He was married
to Miss Carrilla Sayle.

Mr. Penn became interested in politics, identifying himself
with the Whig Party. He opposed the secession of Tennessee
from the Union, but when secession came, he went with his
State. He raised a company for the Confederacy and became
its captain. After suffering imprisonment he was exchanged
and raised to the rank of Major which title he bore until his
death.

After the war, he practiced law in Jefferson, Texas.
Though ruined financially by the conflict between the States,

he soon again had a lucrative practice. Within two weeks from the time he opened his office with a borrowed law book, one case brought him $400.00 in gold.

Jefferson's Baptists were very weak. They had a preaching service only once a month. When Major and Mrs. Penn joined the church, he was soon made superintendent of the small Sunday School. The thirty five students in attendance on his first Sunday reached seventy five in a week and in two months, four hundred students made this the largest school in the town of ten thousand people. Bogard pointed out the lesson: "Professional and business men may learn a lesson here. To join a little, weak, unpopular church and to engage actively in its work will not hurt their business. Major Penn succeeded grandly and yet he identified himself with the smallest and most unpopular church in town."

Major Penn became an evangelist almost by accident, but God's Providence can be clearly seen now. While he lived in Jefferson, Dr. J. H. Stribbling, pastor of the church in Tyler, Texas, asked him to conduct a prayer meeting one morning. Such concern was manifested that he was prevailed on to remain for another service at night. Interest mounted to the extent that he conducted a revival meeting and many converts were made. Within two weeks he was invited to Bryan, then Calvert, Navasota, Anderson and Waco. This continued for as long as he lived for he was never idle. He held meetings in the country, in the towns and the cities of almost every southern state, as well as in England and Scotland with the result that twenty thousand people publicly professed their faith in Christ under his ministry. He strengthened the churches, helped the pastors, denounced sin and warned the sinner. The sermon selected for the *Pillars of Orthodoxy*, "Divinity of Christ" gives an example of the major's style of preaching. He died April 27, 1895 and a thousand people attended his funeral conducted by W. P. Throgmorton in Eureka Springs where he had moved some years before.

Joseph P. Moody

Joseph P. Moody, who was sixty one at the time of its publication was included in the *Pillars of Orthodoxy*. He was born June 24, 1838, in Clarksville, Virginia, and entered the ministry September 17, 1876, when he was thirty eight years old. His early life was spent in Virginia and Kentucky. He was educated at Bethel College, Russellville, Kentucky, receiving the degree of Doctor of Divinity there in June 1892.

Moody was a successful pastor and evangelist in Kentucky, Tennessee, Arkansas, Texas and Florida. At the time the book was published he was pastor in Hot Springs, Arkansas. His preaching was direct, doctrinal, pointed and practical. His evangelistic work was known for its thoroughness since the immediate results were never spectacular. Though there were numerous conversions in the meetings, the immediate results were less than those witnessed in the months and years following the meeting.

Moody had few equals as a debater, having met at that time, Guilford Jones, Methodist; Bedinger, Presbyterian; Drs. Brents, Briney, J. A. Harding, D. Lipscomb, J. S. Sweeney, S. Lucas and Morgan Morgans, Campbellites. His last debate with Mr. Harding was published in a book of about six hundred pages. His logic was invincible and he knew the Scriptures.

His books received a large circulation and at various times he was co-editor with J. N. Hall, J. R. Graves and E. E. Polk in Baptist papers.

T. T. Eaton

Dr. T. T. Eaton was born in Murfressboro, Tennessee, November 16, 1845. His father, Joseph H. Eaton, preacher and educator, was president of Union University which he had the honor of founding.

T. T. Eaton, educated in Union University, Madison University in New York and Washington College in Lexington, Virginia, was one of the very few men to whom John A. Broadus went for advice. He received the degree of D. D. from Washington and Lee University in 1878 and the title of LL.D. from Southwestern University in 1880. Mr. Eaton was pastor at Lebanon, Chattanooga and Murfreesboro, Tennessee, Petersburg, Virginia and for nineteen years at Walnut Street Church, Louisville, Kentucky, where he was at the time of the writing of Bogard's book. His success there was extraordinary and Bogard said, ''The great work accomplished in this church is another proof of the value of long pastorates. No man, who is capable of efficient service, can accomplish much in two or three years.''

Dr. Eaton taught in Union University for five years (1867-1872). Though fitted for teaching, it would have been a pity for such a life to have been spent in a school room; however, it helped him to become a scholar which benefitted him greatly in meeting the polite heresies he had to fight. He was a ready, rapid speaker driving straight to the point. He could, in five minutes, make a speech it would take another man thirty minutes to make. ''He has been known to arise in the associations and conventions which he frequently attends, and make a telling speech before the moderator could declare him out of order. Having said what he wanted to say it didn't matter if he did have to sit down,'' Bogard wrote of him.

Eaton wrote several books and was editor of the *Western Recorder* many years. He was a popular lecturer. He traveled extensively in America, Europe, Asia and Africa. The sermon chosen for this book was ''What is Baptism?'' and an editorial on ''The Defense of the Philadelphia Confession of Faith,' a paragraph of which reads: ''There is also in this Confession not the slightest suggestion that there has been a day since the Apostles when there were no Baptists in the world. On the contrary, all that is said on the subject assumes their continued existence. But since that was not then a matter of dispute, the document is not very full on that point. Thomas Crosby had just issued his great history in which he distinctly claimed, and argued at length to maintain the claim, that Baptists in Philadelphia took for granted that this was generally admitted among their brethren, and needed not to be specially declared.''

J. R. Graves

Bogard believed J. R. Graves to be the greatest preacher of his day. He said, ''Such was J. R. Graves, the greatest preacher, the most forcible writer, the ablest debater and strongest editor of his day. His equal has not yet arisen. When God has need of another like him he will raise him up. One man of that kind each century is as much as the world deserves. Yet, after all that has been said, together with much more that might be said, there is something felt by all who knew Dr. Graves that cannot be put into writing.'' Bogard, when only nineteen years old, drove twenty miles in a road cart to hear him preach. He listened for five days, bought and read his books and was proud to confess himself to be a disciple of J. R. Graves and that he ''strives to follow Graves as Graves followed Paul and the Christ.''

J. R. Graves was born in Chester, Vermont, April 10, 1820 and died June 26, 1893. When he was only three weeks old, he was left fatherless. He was forced to a greater degree of self reliance than is usual for boys. He was converted when fifteen years old and joined the church in North Springfield, Vermont.

After teaching two years in Kingsville Academy he went to Kentucky to take charge of Clear Creek Academy and while here, his church licensed him to preach without his knowledge. He at first refused to enter the ministry feeling his unworthiness, but after prayer, he determined to prepare himself for this work. He spent four years giving six hours a day to the school room and eight to study, going through a college course without a teacher. He mastered a modern language every year giving attention also to science, philosophy and literature.

Graves was editor of the *Tennessee Baptist* for about forty six years. As an editor he set the pace for other Baptist papers and his disciples became their editors. Great men like Dr. Bright of the *New York Examiner* were so influenced by him they gave up cherished opinions and adopted his ideas. The *Tennessee Baptist* at one time had the largest circulation of any Baptist paper in the world which position it held for years. To read through its files was an education within itself.

Dates and figures could not estimate such a character as Graves. His indirect influence, that is, what he influenced other men to do, was much greater than all he did directly. One sermon or editorial would start a hundred influences to work in as many different parts of the country. No other man ever had such a powerful influence over Baptists of America and in that respect he lives on.

As a writer, Graves stood in the forefront. In addition to all of his other books, he wrote *Seven Dispensations,* one of the greatest books on Systematic Theology ever written.

He was pre-eminently doctrinal, believing men should be controlled by principle. He placed the greatest emphasis on the great doctrines. The teaching of salvation by grace was his great theme, "Blood before water, Christ before the church" his motto.

As a devotional preacher, Graves had few equals. His audiences would be bathed in tears in the midst of one of his great doctrinal sermons. His power over an audience was magnetic. He has caused audiences to burst into uproarious laughter, then the next moment have them weeping and that, too, with one sentence. Bogard watched him wield this matchless power.

At one of the Southern Baptist Convention meetings in

Waco, Texas, the crowd was so uncomfortably large that it was announced a preacher would speak in the Methodist church house across the street. A few left but soon came back. Another speaker was announced but still only a few left the convention hall. When Dr. B. H. Carroll, pastor at that time in Waco, announced that Dr. J. R. Graves would preach there in ten minutes, there was such a rush for the doors, the convention hall was nearly emptied. The president urged them to return, but no one wanted to miss Graves' message which was pronounced as the greatest sermon those present had ever heard.

He had few equals as evangelist. Thousands were converted under his preaching. Before he was thirty years old, more than 1300 people had professed faith in Christ as a result of his ministry. In a meeting he conducted for J. M. Pendleton more than seventy five were baptized.

His ability as a debater was recognized as decidedly superior to any man in his day, but he was never a ready speaker in conventions or associations, hence seldom spoke and, sometimes when he did, made a failure. It was in a situation for a planned speech or sermon or in the heat of debate that he rose to the greatness that made him famous.

His sermon recorded in this book was "Extract from Sermon on the Effect of Baptism."

J. B. Jeter

Jeremiah B. Jeter was born in Bedford County, Virginia, July 18, 1802. When he was nineteen, he joined the church and as he came from the baptismal water, delivered a speech to the congregation and so began to preach. His first announced sermon was about twenty days later.

Dr. Jeter was very active throughout his life. Uniform success attended his ministry. During the first ten years of his ministry, he baptized over a thousand converts. For the next fourteen years, as pastor of First Baptist Church, Richmond,

Virginia, he baptized nearly a thousand, then became pastor of Second Baptist Church in St. Louis, Missouri. After three years he returned to Richmond to Grace Street Church.

In 1866 he became editor of the *Religious Herald,* which position he held until his death in 1880 at the age of seventy eight. He was appointed the first missionary by the General Association and, perhaps, no man had such influence in that body as he had. His sermon printed in the book was "Distinctive Baptist Principles."

S. H. Ford

S. H. Ford was born in Brostol, England, February 19, 1819, but came to America when a child. He was converted and called into the ministry early in life. He graduated with distinction from Bonne Femme College, then studied at the State University at Columbia. When only twenty five years old and in his senior year, he was called to pastor the church at Jefferson City, Missouri, being even then a great preacher. He also held pastorates in Memphis, Louisville and St. Louis.

For several years, Ford was editor of the *Western Recorder,* Louisville, and for nearly forty six years editor of *Ford's Christian Repository.* He enjoyed a longer editorial career than any other editor in America.

Dr. Ford had a part in founding William Jewel College and was the first man to sound a note of warning against representation in associations and conventions on a financial basis.

Ford wrote two valuable histories, *Ecclesiastical History* and *Brief Baptist History.* Perhaps his greatest work was *The Great Pyramids.* His best writings, according to Bogard, were not in book form but strong editorials on current topics. No other man so thoroughly exposed and answered the "Invisible, Universal, Spiritual Church" theory as he did. His discussion of that question was the work chosen for *Pillars of*

Orthodoxy.

Ford was a member of the Confederate Congress during the period of the Civil War.

At the time of the writing of Bogard's book, he was eighty one years old.

J. M. Pendleton

James Madison Pendleton was born at Twyman's Store, Spottsylvania County, Virginia, November 20, 1811. When he was only a year old, the family moved to Christian County. His educational advantage in youth were limited, but this did not prevent his becoming an exceptional scholar, learning accurate Latin and Greek and how to write and speak pure English.

He first attended a little log school house where his father was his teacher. Parts of the logs were cut to let in the light and the slab benches were made of the outside of logs. These set on a dirt floor. The children warmed by a large fireplace as they sat on benches with no backs and the feet of the small ones not touching the floor. Though not meant to be, these seats were torture instruments to children who sat there six hours a day studying Noah Webster's *Spelling Book,* Murray's *Introduction to the English Reader* and Arithmetic. Pendleton's education was often interrupted as he had to help out with the work on the farm.

The first money he received was for the sale of a lamb he had raised when the ewe died. This was used to purchase a Bible. From his earliest childhood, Pendleton was taught that the Bible was true. He could not remember a time when he did not plan to become a Christian someday. When he realized his sinfulness, he wanted to make amends. He saw he must have help so asked the Lord to supply his deficiency when he had done his best. Still, the sense of sin grew, and by reading the Bible, he knew it would be just for God to let him perish in

hell. He couldn't understand how God could justly save him
and he did not want salvation at the expense of justice. He
then read a sermon by Samuel Davies from I Corinthians 1:
22-24 and realized, "I was specially impressed with his remarks on the union of mercy and justice in the salvation of
sinners through Christ crucified. This was shown to be hap-
pily possible through the atoning death of Christ whose obedience and blood magnified the law and made it honorable."

After reading the sermon, Pendleton went into the woods
to pray. He understood that "mercy could be exercised consistently with justice through Jesus Christ." He was saved
through the reading of a sermon. Bogard commented on this,
"What a power is the consecrated page! Let writers of religious books take courage and let the colporters and book agents
magnify their office. J. M. Pendleton was converted by the
reading of a sermon! If a soul is converted by the reading of
one of the sermons in this book the author will be well paid
for his work, for 'there is joy in the presence of the angels over
one sinner that repenteth.' "

Pendleton united with Bethel Church in Christian County
when he was eighteen and the next year, 1830, he was licensed
to preach. His first attempts at preaching were miserable failures. Some brethren who heard him urged him to give up
preaching and many times, uncomplimentary remarks were
made to him about his preaching. As he said, "Those good
men, now in heaven, did not know how depressing the effect
of their words was, and how my spirit was crushed."

In 1831, he began his education in a private school at Russellville, then became a student in the academy at Hopkinsville. While there he was pastor at Bethel Church and so was
able to pay his board, buy books, tuition and clothes. He had
more work than any man ought to do but, as Bogard said,
"Out of such conditions come great men." After completing
school, he took the care of the church in Bowling Green, Ken-

tucky, where he stayed for twenty years with the exception of a few months.

Pendleton was in the organization of the first General Association of Kentucky in 1837. He was well known as a "Landmark" Baptist—some even charge him with being the father of Landmarkism, but, "That is not true, since Landmarkism is as old as the Baptists although it was not named so until Pendleton wrote his book *An Old Landmark Reset."*

Pendleton became a well known writer. An *Old Landmark Reset* reached a circulation of about sixty thousand, *Three Reasons Why I Am a Baptist,* fifty thousand. His *Church Manual* became a standard Baptist work. Other books were *Distinctive Baptist Doctrines, Christian Doctrines or a Compendium of Theology, Brief Notes on the New Testament, The Atonement of Christ* and *Notes on Sermons.* He also wrote his experiences in *Reminiscences of a Long Life.*

Preceding the Civil War, he was professor of Theology in Union University then at Murfreesboro, Tennessee. The War drove him North for he was "a strong Union man." Though not an abolitionist, he was an emancipationist, believing in a system that would gradually free the Negroes rather than immediate freedom. He believed this would avoid revolution and give the people time to adjust to the change. His views were hated by the southern people. No longer safe in Tennessee, he made his way North which led him to pastorates in Ohio and Upland, Pennsylvania.

Pendleton was not noted as an evangelist. He was a teacher—a seed sower—and other men reaped where he had sown, though he had hundreds of souls to his credit. His most notable revival was in Upland where he preached a two months' revival and two hundred were added to the church.

Pendleton's death bed testimony was, "I just expect to go into eternity, saying, Lord, here I am, a poor, weak, sinful creature, having no claim, and the only hope of being saved is that Jesus died in the place of sinners."

He died March 1891, at the age of eighty one, as he had lived—a Landmark Baptist. He stated in his *Reminiscenses* that he did not think his position had ever been answered and that he was of the same opinion in 1891 as in 1855 when he wrote it. T. T. Eaton conducted his funeral services in Bowling Green, Kentucky. *An Old Landmark Reset* was published in Bogard's book.

J. A. Broadus

John Albert Broadus was born in Culpepper County, Virginia, January 24, 1827, of Welch descent. His father was a member of the Virginia Legislature a number of years. John was educated at the University of Virginia where he received his Master of Arts Degree in 1850. He was one of the best scholars in the South. In 1851 he was elected assistant professor of Latin and Greek in the university which position he held for two years, while he was pastor at the same time of the church in Charlottesville, Virginia.

In 1855 Broadus was elected chaplain at the University, a position he held for two years, then returned to the pastorate of the Charlottesville Church. In 1859, Broadus was elected professor of Homiletics and New Testament Interpretation in the Southern Baptist Theological Seminary which position he held until his death, except for two years during the Civil War when he preached with great success as a missionary in General Robert E. Lee's Army.

Dr. Broadus was a true and a safe preacher, his judgment mature and his advice eagerly sought. The people's confidence in Broadus and Boyce gave the Southern Baptist Theological Seminary its standing and influence. This reliance on him was because he was orthodox, safe and sensible. He was a Baptist in the true sense, being opposed to alien immersion as he expressed in a widely published letter written to one who had asked advice. In an oft quoted class lecture, he announced that he was not in favor of pulpit affiliation. He was not offensive in his advocacy of Baptist views. He never engaged in a debate but did teach sound Baptist doctrines to his students.

When Broadus preached, the house was packed, frequently hundreds being turned away. The only other man in his day who could draw such crowds was Graves. Broadus' language was so simple a child could easily understand; his thought so deep the wise had to think—a strange and rare combination.

He took as great delight in preaching to the simple country people as to a great audience in Louisville, New York or Boston. At one time when the Southern Baptist Convention met near his boyhood home, he was asked to preach to a large city church and declined in order to preach to the people with whom he had grown up in the country. The hearers declared it to be the greatest sermon he ever preached.

Broadus wrote a number of books including, *Commentary on Matthew and Preparation and Delivery of Sermons* which was, in Bogard's day, used in nearly all Baptist theological schools, also adopted by the Methodists, as well as the Camplites. His book *Glad Tidings* was published in the *Pillars of Orthodoxy* because, as Bogard wrote, "Giving is a Baptist doctrine and it is announced as a Baptist doctrine in our Confession of Faith and church covenants and no other man has made so plain a statement of that Baptist doctrine as Dr. Broadus. For the reason we publish it . . ."

Broadus died of pneumonia in Louisville, Kentucky, March 16, 1895. "His mantle did not seem to fall on any other man. There was only one of him and until we shall see him in heaven we do not expect to look upon his like again," wrote Bogard. "He was gentle unto all men, apt to teach, patient, in meekness instructing those that oppose themselves; if God peradventure will give them repentance to the acknowledging of the truth."

J. S. Coleman

James Smith Coleman was born at Beaver Dam, Kentucky, February 23, 1827. He was affectionately spoken of as the "Old War Horse." In 1838 he was convicted of sin when he read Watts' old hymn, "That awful day will surely come ..." He was so deeply impressed with his sin that after two or three days, he "proposed to God that if he would let him serve God in hell that he would give up all hope of heaven and cheerfully go there." He was baptized into the fellowship of Beaver Dam Church, March 10, 1838.

Coleman's great great grandmother had been the instrument of the organization of the Beaver Dam Church. She and her husband and their young son, Henry, came from Germany. She had been given Luther's translation of the Bible into German and by reading it was brought to Christ. Wanting to obey all of His commandments, she dipped herself in the name of the Father, Son and Holy Ghost, there being no preacher nearby. The news of this strange act spread to other settlements until it came to Elder Benjamin Talbott, who saddled his horse and went in search of the woman who had baptized herself. When he found her, she was so happy she sent little Henry throughout the settlement with the announcement that a preacher would preach there. Almost everyone in the community came and the meeting resulted in a number of baptisms, one of whom was the woman who had baptized herself. This was the beginning of the Beaver Dam Church which was the mother of all the other churches in that part of Kentucky.

Coleman felt he was called to preach but attempted to evade the call. He left off prayer and Bible reading and plunged into a worldly career of politics. He prospered amazingly. Everything he touched seemed to turn to gold. He was elected sheriff of the county and served two years making money and gaining popularity. He was elected Brigadier General of the Second Congressional district and offered a nomination for a seat in Congress, when his whole life was suddenly changed. Being in a community on business he happened to attend a church service. Again, the impression to preach was stirred in him. He left the business he had come to transact and went home completely submitted to the Lord's will. He preached his first sermon in the Beaver Dam Church, then continued to preach from church to church and house to house. From the first there were conversions. Within four years he had baptized a thousand people.

Dr. Coleman was one of the first orators in the ministry. His style was peculiar, but so powerful it was unequaled by any other man of the day. Some excelled him in grace, culture, diction and resonance, but in that mysterious quality called *power,* he was unequalled.

Coleman went to J. M. Pendleton for instruction and advice. As Bogard said, "Would to God that all our preachers had such a counsellor. The chairs of theology in our seminaries are largely filled with boys whose theological setting is somewhat uncertain and it is to be feared that few such men as J. S. Coleman will be turned out by those schools."

Coleman's superior ability would have secured almost any pastorate in the country for him, but he preferred to stay in the Green River area and work with small country churches. He held a meeting in the Walnut Street Church which resulted in three hundred and fifty professions of faith. In a revival in Whitesville, he held one meeting in which there were one hundred and thirty two additions and another, one hundred and five, with still another where seventy five additions resulted. No other pastor in Kentucky had such a successful evangelistic work.

Dr. Coleman was a doctrinal preacher, constantly emphasizing the peculiarities of the Baptist faith and as a result baptized one thousand from other denominations. "Those who are opposed to doctrinal preaching may learn a lesson here. He hardly ever preached a set sermon on Baptist pecularities but he has woven it into almost every sermon. A fair sample of his preaching may be seen in the sermon at the close of this sketch on 'The Work of Baptists an Urgent Work.' ''

Coleman preached fourteen thousand sermons, witnessed ten thousand professions and baptized five thousand and twelve converts, the majority of the others being baptized by other pastors. He assisted in organizing fifty churches. He was a debater. He was for thirty seven years moderator of Davies County Association and nineteen years moderator of the General Association in Kentucky. He received the title of D. D. from Bethel College and Ph.D. from Hartford.

J. T. Christian

John T. Christian was born December 14, 1854 near Lexington, Kentucky. He professed faith in Christ and joined the Cambellsburg Church when he was sixteen. He received the D. D. degree from Bethel College, Russellville, in 1888 and his LL. D. from Keachie College, Louisiana, in 1898. He was licensed to preach in July 1876 and was eagerly sought by the churches.

At the time of this writing, Christian was forty five years old. Included in *Pillars of Orthodoxy* was his work, "What Baptists Have Done for the World."

Some excerpts: "1. Baptists have stood for the supreme authority of the Word of God. 2. Baptists have done a great thing for the world in preserving pure the ordinances of the gospel . . . 3. Baptists have done a great work for the world in emphasizing the personal element in religions." In discussing this point he quoted the New York Tribune, "The Baptists have solved the great problem. They combine the most resolute conviction, the most stubborn belief in their own special doctrines with the most admirable tolerance of the faith of other Christians . . ." 4. Baptists have done a great work in giving to the world soul liberty . . . We can trace the Baptists all through the liberties of England . . . We cannot stop to show that religious liberty in almost every State was won by Baptists . . . It is claimed that Thomas Jefferson modeled the Constitution of the United States according to the Baptist plan of church government. He was in the habit of attending the meetings of a small Baptist Church not far from his residence. It is said that the pastor, Reverend Andrew Tribble, asked Mr. Jefferson one day how he was pleased with their church government. Mr. Jefferson replied that it had struck him with great force, and had interested him much; that he considered it the only form of democracy that then existed in the world and had concluded that it would be the best form of government for the American colonies. This was several years before the Declaration of Independence.''

W. P. Harvey

William P. Harvey, born March 15, 1843, in Ireland, came to America in 1851. He was reared in the Roman Catholic faith but was led to Christ by George Hunt and baptized into the fellowship of the Baptist Church at Maysville, Kentucky. He spent two years at Maysville Seminary, three years at Georgetown College and two years at Kentucky University. He was ordained at Harrodsburg in 1872 and his labors were greatly blessed. He was secretary of the Sunday School and Colportage Board of the General Association of Kentucky Baptists and one year superintendent of missions in the Eastern District of Kentucky. One year he was vice president of Georgetown College. His sermon in the *Pillars of Orthodoxy* is ''Baptists in History.''

J. N. Hall

J. N. Hall was born at Pleasureville, Kentucky, February 5, 1849, but moved to Ballard County where he grew to manhood, he was reared in the country and never received a college education; however, like Spurgeon and D. L. Moody, he rose above many college men with his oratory, keen logic and personal magnetism. He was saved when fourteen under the ministry of C. L. Cate and baptized by Cane Run Church.

Hall confined his work to small towns and the country, having held only a few meetings in the larger centers. Though he never sought a pastorate or a place to preach, he was not able to accept half of his invitations for meetings and debates. He averaged, perhaps, a sermon a day, making not less than ten thousand during his ministry of thirty years and as he grew older his work accumulated.

Hall was a newspaper man. His first venture in this field was in helping H. L. DuPont publish the *Baptist Gleaner* at Fulton, Kentucky. The *Gleaner* consolidated with the *Baptist Banner* and for a year he worked with W. P. Throgmorton in this paper. He became connected with the *Baptist Reaper* and changed its name to *Baptist Gleaner,* then overwork compelled him to sell it to the *Western Recorder.* In 1898 he bought the *American Baptist Flag* of St. Louis, Missouri. At the time of the writing of the *Pillars of Orthodoxy,* when he was fifty years old, he was still editor of this paper and it had a circulation of fourteen thousand. It was an independent, fearless defender of the faith. He died at the age of fifty six.

"As a debater, Hall has no equal. His self-possession, keen logic, personal magnetism, oratorical power, ready repartee, broad reading, rapid speaking, clean enunciation, correct pronounciation, distinct articulation and thorough knowledge of all theological questions make him invincible in debate." He held ninety seven debates before his untimely death.

Hall's sermon "The State of the Dead" was printed in Bogard's book.

OTHER BOOKS

The *Baptist Way Book* was first published in 1908 by the Baptist Publishing Company of Little Rock and in its first

year had a sale of three thousand copies. The book was written as the result of a lecture given in Wicherville, Arkansas.
C. R. Powell, then editor of the *Arkansas Baptist,* heard the
lecture and said it ought to be in book form. Bogard told him
he was afraid he could not sell enough of them to pay for it.
Powell was willing to risk it if Bogard would prepare the
manuscript for printing. It was published and, as Bogard said,
"It went like the proverbial hot cakes. Thousands of them
were sold and the publication of the book kept the paper from
going into bankruptcy that year. Powell told me this himself.
He said the income from the book was so great that he was enabled to pay all the bills of the Baptist Publishing Company.
But none of the money came to me. My 'cold feet' saved the
Baptist Publishing Company from bankruptcy and lost a thousand dollars for me, or rather I missed the making that much
out of the book. The *Baptist Way Book* is now the property of
the American Baptist Sunday School Committee, Texarkana.
I gave the book to that concern when it was weak and struggling and it has been a good seller all along. Thirty-six thousand (1929) have been sold. They are still selling every day."
This book is now a best seller at the Baptist Book Store in
Texarkana and widely used as study course material, as well
as a text book in the theological schools.

In 1909, two books, *Fifty Two Bible Lessons* and the
Child's Question and Answer Book were written and published, as well as, his debate with E. M. Borden (Campbellite).
The Child's Question and Answer Book is still published by
the Sunday School Committee in Texarkana.

In 1910 *Fifty Two Doctrinal Lessons,* a book designed for
use in Sunday Schools, was published and in 1911, *Fifty Two
Expository Lessons* came out. These two books are still being
published by the Baptist Sunday School Committee.

Socialism Exposed was published in 1912. Two pamphlets,
Old Landmarkism Made Plain and *Campbellism Exposed*
(still in print) made their appearance in 1914 and in 1915, *A*

Manual for Sunday School Workers was published. This manual was a course of study for Bible students and teachers. It is out of print now and is being reproduced here.

MANUAL FOR SUNDAY SCHOOL WORKERS

A Course of Study for Bible Students and Teachers

INTRODUCTORY

There are several courses of study for the benefit of Bible students and teachers, but all of them are entwined with systems of doctrine and practice that sound Baptists cannot afford to endorse, and they are so arranged as to leave a favorable impression of the evil systems. The General Association of Baptist Churches is composed of sound Baptists, and their Sunday school teachers and others engaged in the study and teaching of God's Word need some help that is not mixed with error, and it is the purpose of this book to furnish that help.

The author cares nothing for red tape of modern ideas of teaching. Some books intended to help are filled more with dry nothings than with the things a teacher or student really needs to know. If the reader is really helped to study and to teach God's Word the author will have accomplished his purpose.

He has read the courses of study published by others, and knows what they are, and he has engaged in teaching both secular and sacred subjects, having special experience in Sunday school work, and has been a Bible student from boyhood, and out of his longfelt want and experience has come this book. He believes it will meet the wants of that large class of Bible students and teachers who are known as Association Baptists. To them it is offered as a help in their great work.

THE AUTHOR

THE SACRED SCRIPTURES

SECTION I

Inspiration and Credibility of the Scriptures

I

By inspiration is meant that the minds of the writers of the Bible were restrained from writing any error. Peter wrote in Peter's style and manner, and Paul wrote in his own peculiar style and manner and chose his own words, and so did all the writers of both the Old and the New New Testaments, but the writers were so controlled by the Spirit that they were infallibly prevented from expressing any error.

By credibility is meant that the Bible should be believed without question. What it says is the end of all controversy. Where philosophy or science contradicts the Bible, it is all the worse for philosophy or science, and where the Bible speaks we should speak and when it is silent we should be silent. This does not mean that the King James version or the Revised version or any other version of the Bible is entirely clear of error. The men who translated the Bible from the Hebrew and the Greek languages, the languages in which the Bible was written, made some mistakes and that is the reason we need to revise them. The Bible itself is without error, but the Bible itself is in Hebrew and Greek, and not in English. To call attention to any error of translation is very different from declaring the Bible to be in error. Every Sunday school teacher should know the fact that the English translations of the Bible may contain error. It is a comfort to know, however, that the small errors of translation do not destroy a single doctrine of vital importance. All of the versions sufficiently bring out the meaning of the original scriptures as to show the way of salvation and to mark out the clear course of Christian conduct. To illustrate: While the word baptize has not been translated at all, but is left in the Bible a Greek word, which English speaking people cannot understand without consulting a Greek dictionary (Lexicon), yet it is a fact that the Greek word baptize is used in such connections and such descriptions of the things that took place in New Testament baptisms that the ordinary English reader can really understand what baptism means. So with the other errors in translation or failure to translate, as in the word baptize, the connection generally prevents any serious damage being done by the error.

The writers of the Bible claimed to be guided in their writing and claimed to speak as they were moved by the Holy Ghost. If they were liars and frauds, we shall have a hard time to account for such liars and frauds writing the best book the world ever saw. Would liars and frauds write their own condemnation by condemning liars and frauds, as the Bible writers did? Would men of such hypocrisy write a book that has been the means of producing more good men than all other books combined?

The Bible has been kept as it was originally written by the antagonism of contending sects and partisans. If the Jews should undersake to change any part of the Old Testament to justify their refusal to accept Christ, they would be exposed by all the rest of the religious sects. If the Christian sects should undertake to add anything to the Old Testament to make the Christian claim stronger the Jews would expose the fraud. If one sect should undertake to make its claim stronger by changing any part of the scriptures, the other opposing sects would expose the fraud. Thus the evil of clashing and contending sects—an evil undoubtedly—has been overruled for good, as God always overrules evil for good. The Catholics could not have changed the Bible during the dark ages, for the good reason that the Baptists preserved the entire Bible in French in the Piedmont Valley during all of that terrible thousand years. The Masons also have preserved the Bible complete all through the ages of darkness and superstition. The fact stands out clear that we have the Bible as it was originally written. The different books of the Bible were all brought together in the year A. D. 397 at the council of Carthage.

The King James version of the Bible, the one in most common use, was made by order of King James, of England, by Episcopalian scholars in the years 1606-1611, a space of over five years being used to complete it. It was for several hundred years the best translation in existence. The Revised version was completed in 1885, and it is the work of scholars of all the leading denominations, and is the best translation ever made. It brings out the meaning of the original Hebrew and Greek scriptures better than any previous translation. No translation is perfect, for the reason that one language cannot be translated into another without losing something of the original ideas, as words in one language do not always have exact equivalents in another. This is especially true in translating from the Greek into English. But no vital doctrine is obscured because of this, and the way of salvation and all the practical doctrines are made plain enough in both the translations mentioned.

The Bible was not written in chapters and verses as we have it in the King James version. It was Hugo who divided the Bible into chapters in the year 1240. Modrecai Nathan divided the Old Testament into verses in 1445, and Robert Steven divided the New Testament into verses in 1551. Bear in mind, reading the Bible, that the chapters and verses are not the work of God, but of man, and the Bible should be read straight along, as if there were no verses. The verses are convenient as a matter of reference, but for nothing else. Frequently a thought is cut in two by a verse ending abruptly. This must be borne in mind, or a failure to understand much of the Bible will result.

QUESTIONS

What is meant by inspiration?

What is meant by credibility?

Rightly Dividing the Word

II

"Study to show thyself approved unto God, a workman that needeth not to be ashamed, rightly dividing the word of truth." (II Tim. 2:15).

A preacher or Sunday school teacher should know the Bible. The Bible is really a library of sixty six books, and these books are not all on one subject, yet they are in perfect agreement—there is no discord nor contradiction.

There are two grand divisions of the Bible—the Old Testament and the New Testament. These testaments are themselves divided. The Old Testament is divided into the Law, the Prophets and the Psalms (Luke 24:44). Our Lord Himself made this division. The Law and the Prophets have been set aside, repealed (Luke 16:16), but we nowhere have it intimated that the Psalms have been set aside. The Psalms is an inspired song book, and is for use in all dispensations. But the Law and the Prophets were set aside when Christ came.

Not only was the authority of the Law set aside by the Savior, as we see in the Sermon on the Mount (Matt. 5, 6, 7), when He said over and over again: "Moses said so and so, but I SAY unto you;" but the Law was actually "taken out of the way" when Christ died on the cross. (Col. 2:14).

If we are still under the law of Moses the following facts stare us in the face:

1. We must still keep the great feasts: Passover, Pentecost, Tabernacles (Ex. 23:14-17).

2. We are still under the death penalty for the following offenses: (a) Idolatry (Deut. 13:9-10); (c) for picking up sticks on the Sabbath day (Num. 15:32-36); and, of course, no one is so foolish as to advocate such an absurdity.

The Ten Commandments are called by Paul "The Ministration of Death" (II Cor. 3:7-11) and well it may be, for death was the penalty for its violation.

But Paul also tells us that the "ministration of death" was

"done away." (II Cor. 3:11). So we learn that the Ten Commandments were "done away" and we are, therefore, not under the Ten Commandments.

We are now under the New Testament (Heb. 7:12). "The priesthood being changed, there is made of necessity a change of the law." The New Testament, we are now under, is called by Paul "the Ministration of Righteousness" (II Cor. 3:9). Under this "Ministration of Righteousness" we are controlled by the teaching of Christ and the apostles, which embraces every principle of righteousness. (John 14:23-24; John 16:12-14).

All of the righteous principles found in the Law of Moses are restated in a different form in the New Testament—"the Ministration of Righteousness"—but the ceremonies, forms, days, feasts, etc., have been left out of the New Testament, Instead of the Old Testament ceremonies we now have baptism and the Lord's Supper. Instead of the days, such as the Sabbath day, for instance, we now have the Lord's day, or Sunday.

In the study of the Bible we must note these divisions of the word, or we shall find ourselves in hopeless confusion.

After noting these divisions we must then look for the special topic under discussion when we are reading any part of the Bible. For instance:

I Cor. 12:1 gives the topic or subject for the next three chapters, viz: "Spiritual Gifts." The "Resurrection" is the topic of the fifteenth chapter. We cannot rightly understand the individual passages in these chapters unless we understand the subject or topic of the fifteenth chapter. We cannot rightly understand the individual passages in these chapters unless we understand the subject or topic. It will pay to take time to find the special topic being discussed. The topic discovered will make the rest easy.

The New Testament is divided into History, Doctrine, Prophecy. The history should be learned, the doctrine (teaching) understood, the prophecy studied. Unless the word is rightly divided we shall fail to understand it and fail to teach it.

QUESTIONS

What did Paul tell Timothy to do?

What should a teacher in the Sunday school know?

Into what grand divisions is the Bible divided?

What are the divisions of the Old Testament?

What are the divisions of the New Testament?

Are we now under the Old Testament law?

What is now the rule of our faith and practice?

What does Paul call the Ten Commandments?

What is the rule of faith and practice in the New Testament called?

Have we lost any principle of right living in the repeal of the old law and the establishment of the new?

What should we always first find in the study of any part of the Scriptures?

The Books of the Bible
III

The sixty-six books of the Bible are divided into three general divisions, viz.: The Historical Books, the Prophetical Books and the Doctrinal Books. This does not mean that there is no prophecy and history in the Doctrinal Books, neither does it mean that there is no doctrine in the Historical and Prophetical Books. The fact is that history, doctrine and prophecy are in nearly all of the books of the Bible. It is a fact, however, that some of the books are in the main historical, and some are in the main doctrinal and some in the main prophetical. Hence the three general divisions mentioned. Some of the history is strongly suggestive of doctrine, and some of the doctrine is suggestive of history, and some the prophecies are suggestive of both doctrine and history. To illustrate: The doctrine of baptism is suggestive of the burial and resurrection of

Christ; the Lord's Supper suggests the Lord's suffering, and the prophecies of Daniel and the Revelation are based on historical beginnings.

The historical books are: Genesis, which means the book of beginning; Exodus, which means the going out, referring to the going out of the Israelites from Egypt; Leviticus, which means the book of the priesthood, the tribe of Levi being the tribe of priests; Numbers, which means the census of the Israelites or numbering of the people; Deuteronomy, which means the repeated law; Joshua, which means the leadership of Joshua in bringing the Israelites into Canaan; Judges, which means Israel under the rule of the judges before a king was given them; Ruth is a biography of a pious woman, and one of the most beautiful stories in print; First and Second Samuel is the history of the Israelites under Samuel; First and Second Kings is the history of the reign of Solomon up to the division of the Jewish nation; First and Second Chronicles is the history of the reign of Solomon and the captivity of Judah; Ezra is the history of the return from the captivity and the rebuilding of the temple; Nehemiah is the history of the building of the wall about Jerusalem; Esther is a charming story of a noble woman and shows God's providential care of His people in times of adversity; Job is a history of a man under affliction. The historical books in the New Testament are Matthew, Mark, Luke and John which give the history of our Lord from birth up to His ascension; Acts, which is an account of the administration of the Holy Spirit over the church which Christ had established during His personal ministry, Ezekiel, Daniel, Jonah in the Old and First Corinthians in the New Testaments may be considered as semi-historical, as much history is in them.

The First Book in the Bible

Genesis: The word Genesis means beginning. The following beginnings are found in the book of Genesis, hence the name:

1. The beginning of creation. Gen. 1:1.
2. The beginning of mankind. Gen. 2:26.
3. The beginning of the Sabbath day. Gen. 2:2-3.
4. The beginning of sin. Gen. 3:1-7.
5. The beginning of murder. Gen. 4:1-12.
6. The beginning of calamities. Gen. 6th and 7th chapters.
7. The beginning of the different races of men. Gen. 10:1.
8. The beginning of the different languages. Gen. 11:1-9.
9. The beginning of the Jewish race. Gen. 12:15.
10. The beginning of capital punishment. Gen. 9:5-6.
11. The beginning of promises. Gen. 3:15.
12. The beginning of covenants with God. Gen. 13:14-15.
14. The beginning of ceremonies. Gen. 23:1-20.
15. The beginning of slavery. Gen. 47:1-11.
16. The beginning of tombstones. Gen. 35:19-20.
17. The beginning of mob violence. Gen. 34:1-31.
18. The beginning of families. Gen. 41st and 42nd chapters.
19. The beginning of prophecy. Gen. 49:1-27.
20. The beginning of work in metals. Gen. 4:22.

A careful reading of Genesis may discover to the reader other beginnings. It is indeed a book of beginnings—Genesis.

QUESTIONS

How many books are in the Bible?

What are the general divisions of the books?

What are the meanings of the names of the books? Genesis?

Exodus? Leviticus? Numbers? Deuteronomy? Etc.

What are some of the beginnings in Genesis?

Doctrinal and Prophetical Books of the Bible

IV

Romans, so called because Paul wrote the letter to the church at Rome. It deals in the deep things, such as predestination, election, foreknowledge of God. It also deals in the more practical doctrines of sin and salvation.

I Corinthians, written by Paul to the church at Corinth. It discusses in the main the evils in the Corinthian church and in it we have proof of the imperfection of the saints. He rebukes these sanctified Corinthians for their sins.

II Corinthians, written by Paul, and in it he expresses his pleasure in the proof of repentance on the part of the imperfect saints at Corinth. He also gives instructions concerning many practical matters.

Galatians, written by Paul, and in it he contrasts Judaism and Christianity and that salvation is wholly by grace.

Ephesians, written by Paul. Its central thought is salvation, followed by good works.

Philippians, written by Paul to the church at Philippi, and is a receipt for a contribution sent to him by that missionary church. He incidentally discusses some practical doctrines.

Colossians, written by Paul, and he shows how the law of Moses was set aside and the new covenant established.

I and II Thessalonians, written by Paul, and the burden of the first letter is the second coming of Christ, and his teaching being misunderstood, he wrote the second letter to correct their misunderstanding and in doing it foretold the rise of the papacy as it is now seen in the Roman Catholic church.

I and II Timothy, written by Paul to Timothy, a young preacher, and thus we learn the duties of a preacher and also of the deacons. He also predicts the papacy and warns against false doctrine.

Titus, written by Paul to Titus, a Gentile convert. It gives the duties of an evangelist.

Philemon, written by Paul in behalf of a runaway slave and sent by the hand of the slave to his master.

Hebrews, supposed to have been written by Paul, and it is an expansion of the types and shadows of the Old Testament.

James, written by James, and it is a letter dealing in practical Christianity.

First and Second Peter tell of practical duties and foretell the second coming of Christ and the end of the world.

The three epistles of John have one central thought, LOVE.

Jude, written by Jude and it is a denunciation of false teachers.

Psalms and Proverbs are both doctrinal and practical.

Prophetical Books of the Bible

The prophetical books of the Bible are:

Isaiah, called the gospel prophet because he writes so much of the coming Savior and writes as if it was already a reality. See especially the 53rd chapter.

Jeremiah, called the weeping prophet because he predicted so much evil to befall the Jews.

Lamentations, written by Jeremiah, and so called because he laments so much.

Ezekiel, the prophet who foretold the destruction of Jerusalem and the ruin of the temple also bemoaned the fate of Jerusalem, gave the origin and defeat of the devil. (See 28th chapter.)

Daniel, the prophet who describes the rise and fall of the four universal empires and the establishing of Christ's kingdom and the final triumph of that kingdom.

Hosea, who denounces Israel and foretells their captivity and suffering.

Joel, the prophet who foretells the administration of the Holy Spirit.

Amos, the prophet who predicts evil for the Jews and also the surrounding nations.

Obadiah, who assures the Jews that after suffering from their enemies they would be blessed.

Jonah, the prophet who shirked duty and had to be driven to his work, but who had success beyond any expectation as a result of his preaching.

Micah, the prophet who foretold the time and the place of the Savior's birth.

Nahum foretells the destruction of Nineveh, and he also declares the goodness of God.

Habbakuk, a description of the fearful wickedness of the Jews and a promise of God's glory in the earth.

Zephaniah, a denunciation of wickedness and a call to repentance.

Haggai, the prophet who encouraged the rebuilding of the temple, and promises a priest and king, even Christ, to come.

Malachi rebukes the Jews for sin and pronounces punishment if they do not repent.

Revelation, the New Testament book of prophecy, written by John, foretelling in symbolic language the future history of the world.

QUESTIONS

Name the doctrinal books of the Bible.
Name the prophetical books of the Bible.
What special doctrines are in Romans?
What is the special doctrine in First Corinthians?
What great doctrine is in Galatians?
What is the central thought in Ephesians?
What is the Philippian letter?
What does Colossians teach?
What is the great thought in First and Second Thessalonians?
What duties do we learn in First and Second Timothy?
Whose duty is given in Titus?
Why was Philemon written?
What does Hebrews explain?
What does James discuss?
What does First and Second Peter foretell?
What is the central thought in John's epistles?
What is denounced in Jude?
Who was called the gospel prophet?
What book tells of the origin of the devil?

The Mosaic Ceremonials

V

The ceremonials of the Mosaic Law were typical of the work of Christ and the New Testament dispensation. A right understanding of these ceremonials is necessary if we get the real meaning of much of the New Testament. Those ceremonials were as follows:

1. The Sin Offering. This was an animal killed and offered symbolically for the sin of the sacrificer. This sacrifice did not take away sin, but it symbolized the taking away of sin by Jesus, our sacrifice. (See Lev. 4:3-35).

2. The Trespass Offering. This was a slain animal offered symbolically for the forgiveness of the sins of the people who had already been saved—the imperfections of the saints. This sacrifice did not in reality take away the transgressions of the saved person, but it did symbolize how that Christ, by His sacrifice, not only saves from damnation, as is typified by the sin offering, but that he also forgives the transgressions of those who are saved by faith in Jesus Christ (See Lev. 5:6-19).

3. The Burnt Offering. This symbolized the complete work of Christ in dying for the people. He was completely consumed by the sacrifice. It was not a mere death of the body—a partial sacrifice on his part—but it was soul suffering as well. He poured out his soul unto death. He suffered in both soul and body, and in doing so wrought a perfect salvation for us (See Lev. 1:3-17).

4. The Peace Offering. This was a slain animal, partly burnt to God and partly eaten by the priest and the people. It symbolized the nation and communion of God with his people. We have peace with God through our Lord Jesus Christ. (See Lev. 3:1-17.)

5. The Meat Offering. More properly this should be called the meal or bread offering, because it consisted of meal mixed with oil—the symbolism being the Lord our bread from heaven, on which we feed spiritually, and the oil representing the

Holy Spirit. (See Lev. 2).

6. The Red Heifer Offering. This is not found in Exodus, but is found in the book of Numbers. It consisted in killing a red heifer without spot or blemish and then burning the body to ashes. The ashes thus burned is red and when mixed with water has almost the same color as blood, and fitly represents blood. The red ashes were carried by the Jews on their journeys so that when it was impossible for a sacrifice to be made in the regular way, the worshipper could mix the ashes with water and pour it out before the Lord, and thus worship was maintained wherever the person might be. It symbolizes the fact that a true child of God does not have to worship at any set place. If he has accepted Christ he may worship God in spirit and in truth anywhere he may be. Jesus said as much to the woman at the well, when he said that it was not necessary to worship God at Jerusalem nor in that mountain, but anywhere the worshipper might be he could worship in spirit and in truth (See Num. 19:1-10).

Some of the Jews got the idea that the sacrifices really took away sin and they looked to the sacrifice instead of that which the sacrifice symbolized. It was never intended that the blood of bulls and goats should take away sin, but that did not prevent the misconception on the part of the people. It is even so today. There are too many people who look at the sign instead of the thing signified; they depend on the symbol instead of the thing symbolized. Baptism and the Lord's Supper symbolize the sacrifice of Christ, His broken body and shed blood, His death, burial and resurrection, and while they are nothing but symbols, there are many who look to the symbols instead of the Savior, whose work is symbolized. Men are too prone to walk by sight instead of by faith.

The ceremonies of the Old Testament all point to the Lamb of God that taketh away the sin of the world and to His power to cleanse and keep the saved. A proper understanding of them will make clear many of the New Testament passages which otherwise cannot be understood.

QUESTIONS

Of what were the ceremonials typical?
Repeat the names of the six ceremonials?
Explain the meaning of each one?
What incorrect idea did the Jews get concerning these cere-
monies?
What ceremonies have we in the New Testament?

Places and Things Mentioned in the Bible
VI

1. The River Jordan. This river is about ninety feet wide
on an average, and about an average of eight or nine feet deep
in the channel. It is a rapid flowing stream, and was the place
of John's baptism. There are some who contend that the water
is too rapid and too shallow for immersion, but those who
make this suggestion forget that Naaman was able to dip
seven times in the Jordan at the command of the prophet, and
if he could dip seven times in the shallow stream and it was
not too rapid for him, there would be nothing to hinder John
from baptizing in the river as the Bible says he did. (See II
Kings 5:10-14).

2. The Brook Kedron. This stream was water supply for
the city of Jerusalem, and it flowed between the Temple and
the Garden of Gethsemane. For most of the year it furnished
enough water for bathing purposes for the entire city. By
means of dams it could have furnished all the water needed
for immersion of the three thousand on the day of Pentecost.

3. The Pool of Siloam. This was on the south side of Jerusalem and was a favorite bathing place, big enough for baptizing,
and that pool alone could have furnished water for the baptizing of the three thousand on the day of Pentecost.

4. The Pool of Bethesda. The pool was a bathing place. It
means the pool located at a house on the east side of Jerusalem.

This reservoir was big enough for the baptism of the three thousand on the day of Pentecost.

5. The Great Sea. The Great Sea, referred to so often in the Scriptures, means the Mediterranean Sea. It bounded Palestine in the west. It was on the bank of this sea that Peter slept on the house top when the vision came for him to go to the house of Cornelius. The house of Simon, the tanner, in Joppa, was the sea side—the Mediterranean Sea. (See Acts 10).

6. The Dead Sea. The Dead Sea is twenty miles south of Jerusalem and into it the Jordan empties. It is lower than the level of the ocean, and is one of the strongest salt beds in the world. The salt is too strong for fish, and there is no living thing in it, hence it is called the Dead Sea.

7. The Sea of Gennesaret. This really is only a big lake and is not properly a sea. It was a great fishery—its waters teemed with fish, and it was subject to terrific wind storms.

8. Bethlehem was a town six miles south of Jerusalem, and it was the birthplace of Jesus.

9. Nazareth was the city where Jesus spent his boyhood, and it was situated seventy miles north of Jerusalem.

10. Capernaum, at the northern end of the Sea of Galilee, was a town frequently mentioned in the Bible. It was very wicked and the Lord threatened it with hell.

11. Bethany was two or three miles southeast of Jerusalem, beyond Mt. Olivet. It was one of the favorite stopping places of the Lord; his special friends, Lazarus, Mary and Martha, lived there. It was there He raised Lazarus from the dead.

12. Babylon was the center of the country in which the Jews were scattered, from which they longed to be delivered. It has become, for that reason, a figure of the religious ruin of the Lord's people, and those who drift away into the unscriptural organizations of the world are commanded to come out of Babylon. Babylon, figuratively, means the enslavement of the

Lord's people by the world, by means of worldly methods and organizations.

13. Samaria is thirty-six miles north of Jerusalem and the Samaritans dwelt there. They had a rival religion and a rival temple, but they adhered to the Law of Moses. Jesus was in Samaria when He talked with the woman at the well, which led to her conversion and also the conversion of the men who believed the report of the woman and came and heard for themselves. It was in Samaria that the ten tribes that rebelled against the Jewish king established their capital, and descendants of the ten tribes, mixed with other blood, made the race called the Samaritans.

QUESTIONS

How wide and how deep is Jordan?

What was the Brook Kedron used for?

What can you tell of the pools of Siloam and Bethesda?

What is meant by the Great Sea?

What and where is the Dead Sea?

What is the "Sea" of Gennesaret?

Where was Bethlehem?

Where was Nazareth?

Where was Capernaum?

Where was Bethany?

Of what is Babylon a figure?

What and where is Samaria?

Political and Religious Sects Among the Jews

VII

Bible readers need to know something of the religious and political sects or parties among the Jews if they are to really understand the Bible. Just as we have among us Democrats, Republicans, Socialists, Methodists, Presbyterians, Baptists, Catholics, etc., so the Jews had their political and religious parties or sects among them and frequent references are made to them in the Bible. Not to know what they stood for is to misunderstand many of the passages of the Scriptures.

1. Galileans. This was a party organized by Judas, of Galilee, and they were sometimes called Zealots. They advocated Jewish independence, and were bitter enemies of the Roman government that held Palestine in subjection. They taught that to pay taxes was wrong, because in so doing they would be upholding a bad government.

2. The Herodians. This party were advocates of the Herodian kings and stood firmly for the Roman government, and were, therefore, the special opponents of the Zealots, or Galileans. When the question was asked the Lord whether it was right to pay tribute to Caesar, it was for the purpose of bringing him into antagonism with one or the other of these parties. If he said it was right to pay taxes, the Zealots would be against him. He evaded the question by telling them to give Caesar what was his due and give God what belonged to Him. It was an answer that no one could countradict. This illustrates the necessity of understanding the character of the Jewish sects or parties in order to understand the Scriptures.

3. The Samaritans. The Samaritans had no dealings with the Jews, yet there was Jewish blood in the Samaritans. They were so called because they lived in Samaria. They had a rival temple at Mt. Gerizim, and they accepted the law of Moses as their scriptures, but rejected all of the prophets and the Psalms.

4. The Nazarites. The Nazarites were a strict and punctilious sect who made much of vows, and abstained from wine, let their hair grow long, and avoided all ceremonial polutions or any uncleanness of any sort. John the Baptist belonged to the Nazarites.

5. The Essenes. The Essenes were communists, held all their property in common, and lived an abstemious life. They were much like the modern Quaker fraternity. They never married; did not use meat, oil or wine; dressed in white, and devoted their energies to agriculture. They honored the spirit

of the Mosaic law, but refused to offer sacrifices, which they regarded as mere forms. They were weak and harmless and had but little influence.

6. The Pharisees. The Pharisees was the largest and most influential religious sect among the Jews. They were sticklers for the rites and ceremonies of the Mosaic law and, too often, forgot the spirit. They persistently observed the forms of godliness, but did not enjoy the power. They paid a tenth of their income to the service of God and observed all the sacrificial ceremonies, but their hearts were far from the love of God. Their outward morals were good, and their lives exemplary, but they knew not the power of God. The modern ritualist comes nearer being what ancient Pharisees were than any others.

7. The Sadducees. They were materialists. They denied that there were angels or spirits, and they denied the resurrection from the dead. They lived for material good only, believing that we get all that we shall ever get in this life and had no hope beyond this earthly life.

8. The Publicans. These were tax collectors. They oppressed the people and were hated because of it. The vicious Roman law gave them the legal right to collect more than was due and thus they enriched themselves by oppression.

9. The Scribes. These were official transcribers of the Old Testament scriptures. They made copies of the scriptures for the people. There were no printing presses then and books had to be made by hand writing. They were the publishers for the Jews. The Scribes were also members of the Pharisee sect.

QUESTIONS

With what among us do the political and religious sects among the Jews correspond?

Name these sects.

What was the chief difference between the Pharisees and Sadducees?

What was a Nazarite?
Who were the Herodians?
Who were the Galileans?
Who were the Samaritans?
Who were the Scribes?
Who were the Publicans?

Old Testament Institutions

VIII

1. The Tabernacle. The Tabernacle was a temporary place of worship built by God's direction for the worship in the wilderness. It was a big tent divided into departments. It faced the east and it had an outer court, and the Holy Place, and then the Holy of Holies. Anybody could go into the outer court and one who had properly prepared for it could go into the Holy Place. This is typical of the church of Jesus Christ. The sacrifice of Christ is first accepted by a sinner and then the blood of that sacrifice is taken into the Holy of Holies by our High Priest, who is both the sacrifice and the priest, and after that the worshiper approaches the laver or baptism and is then admitted into the Holy Place, or church. The symbolism teaches salvation without baptism and church membership, yet nobody is admitted into the church without baptism.

2. The Temple. The Temple was the permanent building for worship and it was a great building, but was built after the pattern of the Tabernacle. The only difference was in its size and value. It had the same departments, the outer court, the Holy Place and the Holy of Holies. There is no symbolic lesson that can be learned from the Temple that cannot be learned from the Tabernacle.

3. The Levites. The Levites were an order of priests. The tribe of Levi was the priestly tribe and they were maintained by the payment of tithes by the people. The priesthood descended from father to son from generation to generation. When we read of Melchisedec, who had neither father nor

mother, and who had no descendants, it does not mean that he was not a natural man. It only means that he was an isolated priest, not after the order of the Levitical priests. He did not come into the priesthood on account of his father or mother, and he left no successor to him in the priesthood. This illustration enables us to see the importance of understanding the Jewish institutions in order to understand much of the New Testament.

4. The Synagogue was a local meeting house of the Jews, and they were found in all of the principal towns. No sacrifices were offered there, and it was a place for nothing more than worship and the reading of the law and the prophets. It was a free and easy sort of service, as anybody could speak who wished to do so. That accounts for the easy access the apostles had to the Synagogues. The New Testament reader will notice that they spoke freely, whenever they wished, in the Synagogues.

5. The Passover. The Passover was a memorial of the coming out of Egypt. On the night before the Israelites departed from Egypt they were commanded each family to kill a lamb and eat its flesh and to sprinkle blood upon the door posts of their houses, for a destroying angel would pass through the land that night and kill the oldest child in each family where the blood was not found. The Israelites killed the lambs—one for each family—and sprinkled its blood upon the door posts of their houses. The angel came and where he saw the blood he passed over the house and did not molest any within. But where the blood was not found the angel entered and killed the oldest child. It was called the Passover because the angel passed over the houses of the Israelites. It was kept up as a memorial of their deliverance from Egyptian bondage. But it symbolized the sacrifice of Christ, our Passover, who has, by His death, delivered us from the bondage of the devil.

6. Pentecost. Fifty days after the Passover came Pentecost. Pentecost means fifty, and on that day the first fruits of

the harvest were offered to the Lord. The seed had been sown and the crop had been grown and the first fruits were offered to the Lord. So after the church had been established and developed, on Pentecost, fifty days after the ascension of Christ, came a great revival and three thousand souls, first fruits, were offered, as it were, to the Lord. Instead of Pentecost being the beginning of the church, it was the offering of the first fruits of a developed church, and the proof that the work was a success. Thus all of the institutions and ceremonies of the Jews help us to understand them.

QUESTIONS

What was the Tabernacle?

What was the Temple?

Who were the Levites?

What was a Synagogue?

What was the Passover?

What does the symbolism of the tabernacle teach us?

What does the Passover symbolize?

How many days between Passover and Pentecost?

IN THE SUNDAY SCHOOL
SECTION II

Some Necessities in Sunday School Work
I

A Good Superintendent is a necessity. He ought to be the best man in the church. If possible he should be a man of business and of affairs. It is too often that the young get the impression that the Sunday school is for "kids" and old women and young boys and girls and that strong men are not supposed to be Sunday school pupils. A mighty man is needed in the office of superintendent, so that the boys may see that there is in the Sunday school a place for strong manhood. The superintendent should be a man in whom the people all have confidence. A superintendent that drinks liquor, that dances, plays cards, and is otherwise worldly, has no business in the Sunday school as a leader of any sort—certainly not as a superintendent.

Good Teachers are a necessity. Too often it is thought that just anybody will do to teach a Sunday school class. There is just as much necessity for well qualified teachers in the Sunday school as there is for such teachers in any other school. In fact, there should be men and women who not only know how to teach, but they should be spiritually qualified as well, for they need to enforce the lessons taught by their godly example.

A teacher should never be disturbed during the sitting of the class. The habit of the pastor or the superintendent or a visitor dropping in on a class is bad practice. The habit of the secretary taking the class book or anything else to a class after the class begins work is a bad thing. It is serious business and nothing should distrub the teacher. Let the distribution of literature be either before the class work starts or after it is over—never during the work of the class.

Perfect order is a necessity. Order must be manifested, even if it is necessary to lead a bad boy out and not allow him to return unless he promises to obey. Obedience must be insisted upon, just the same as in any other school. The impression must not be made on the pupil that religious work is a goody, goody thing. Let them know that it is of importance and that it means business. Anything short of that makes a bad impression. It is better to get the temporary ill-will of a boy and of his parents, if they are silly enough to uphold the boy, than to make a lasting impression on him that a Christian worker does not mean real business in the Lord's work.

The use of the Bible in the Sunday School is a necessity. The way some schools are conducted half of the pupils do not know the Bible is being taught. They see the quarterlies and the cards, but they do not know the lessons are taken from the

Bible. The teacher should never read any part of the lesson from the quarterly—always read it from the Bible. Emphasize all the time the fact that the Bible is being taught. The superintendent should read the lesson from the Bible and not from the quarterly. Insist on each pupil having a Bible of his own.

Reading in concert is an abomination, and reading verse about is equally bad. Such reading is never profitable. Let somebody do all the reading while the others look on and read silently with him. Some sense can be gotten out of it that way, but not by concert reading or reading verse about. Responsive reading is bad. It is a cheap imitation of episcopal methods and never does any good.

Avoid Sunday School fads. Some want to make everything run into and for the Sunday school, when the fact is the Sunday school should be made a helper of the church service and every other good work, but its special work is to study the Bible. That is the one thing the Sunday school exists for. The modern fad of decision day is an abomination. It means that on a certain day all the children are to be prevailed upon to "decide for Jesus," and thus the Holy Spirit is ignored and the impression is made that to become a Christian is a mere matter of deciding, when the fact is the children need to be born again. The better way is to teach the need of salvation at every session of the Sunday school and extort often to accept Christ and leave the Holy Spirit to do the work. To try to help the chicken to get out of the egg nearly always kills the chicken. May God deliver us from machine-made Christians.

QUESTIONS

What sort of man should be superintendent?
What sort of teachers should be elected?
How should the teacher be treated?
What sort of discipline must be maintained?
What use should be made of the Bible in the school?
How should the reading be done?

What about Sunday school fads?

What about decision day?

How To Teach Children

II

A few suggestions as to the way to impress truth on the child mind is for the benefit of the inexperienced teacher in the Sunday school.

A teacher of children must like children. The children soon discover the feeling of the teacher, and it cannot long be hid from them. If the affection for the children is genuine it is a power over them. This is the first and most important qualification for teaching children.

The teacher must know the lesson himself. It is wonderful how well you can teach if you really know what you are talking about. Thorough preparation is important for any teacher, but most important for a primary teacher.

No doubt must be expressed at any time about the matter taught. If the teacher is in doubt the pupil cannot be certain. Really learn what you intend to teach or don't teach it.

Let there be an orderly development of the lesson. The child mind should be trained to thinking in an orderly manner. Do not get the idea that the child is incapable of thought. They do think and they can see the reason for things and the teacher must be able to give good reason for all that is taught.

A child teacher should use simple words. "Jaw-breakers" are out of place in teaching children. If you will tell what you know in plain words, the child will understand. Just tell the children exactly what and how it is and they will understand.

Object lessons are good. But object lessons can be run into the ground and harm done. Pictures are good, but be careful not to make the impression that the picture is the thing you are talking about, but the picture is only a representation of what you are talking about. A lady teacher brought a crucifix into the class and told them that this was Christ, and a little boy went home and told his mother that he did not think much of Christ, for he could put him in his pocket. Such teaching as that is an abomination. Object lessons are good if it is made plain what the objects are intended to represent.

Figures of speech are not good for children. To tell a child that Christ is like a lamb might make altogether a bad and false impression on him. Plain speech is better.

Children like stories and that is one of the best ways to teach them. To illustrate conversion, a story about the conversion of some one is better than a book full of theories. Children like to see or hear the theory as it has worked out in some individual case.

Memory work is very important. But nothing should be memorized except such things as ought to be remembered all through life. Memory work just for memory work's sake is evil. Fill the child's mind full of Bible truth and have him recite over and over again the fundamental truths you teach, and especially have him memorize scripture verses and even long passages. What he thus memorizes in youth will stay with him all through life.

Object teaching is the most effective with small pupils. To illustrate the growth of a bad habit or a secret sin, let the teacher take an apple with a small rotten speck in it. Take that to the class and ask all the pupils to look at the small rotten speck. Tell them that this is like a bad habit or secret sin. Keep the apple and the next Sunday take it to the class again and show them how the speck has become larger. Then again and again take the apple back until it has become entirely rotten. Each time you take the apple it will be a lesson of the growth of a bad habit—a lesson that children will never forget. To illustrate the power and slavery of sin, take a piece of fly paper and let a fly light upon it and show the children how it struggles to get away and all the time gets more and more entangled. It will be a lesson that they will never forget. Tell them this is like the drunkard or any other form of sin.

QUESTIONS

What is an important qualification for a teacher of children?
What must the teacher know?
What kinds of words should he use?
What use should be made of the object lessons—illustrations?
What precaution must be taken in using illustrations?
What use should be made of the memory?
How much place should be given to "stories?"

The Primary Classes
III

The most important class in the Sunday school is the primary class and the most thoroughly equipped teacher in the school should have charge of the little ones.

If possible, there should be separate rooms for the primary classes, because the little ones are easily confused and their attention can be so easily diverted from the thing in hand.

The teacher should try to hold the attention of a little child only for a few moments at a time—their young minds can't remain long on any one thing. Drive one idea into the little head, then have a change in something else. Use pictures, cards, blocks, and tell stories. But let the stories be short and easily comprehended.

This is the habit-forming period and the teacher should endeavor to drill the little ones into the habit of doing right things. This calls for doing the same thing over and over and, lest they forget, do the same thing again next Sunday. Say the same thing over and over, and then repeat next Sunday. Be sure what you do and say shall be that which will benefit the child and which will aid in the habit formation.

The child at this age has a strong imagination and he can be taught of heaven and hell and the correct idea can be forever fixed on his mind. It is therefore of vast importance that the teacher have correct ideas, so that in telling of the future estate, wrong ideas may not be fastened on the child mind.

The child is an imitator and this makes it necessary that the teacher set a good example. The teacher should use the best language, and should have only correct habits, be clean and tidy, and be gracious and gentle—as nearly as possible a perfect man or woman—for the children are watching and are indelibly impressed by the words and actions of the teacher.

A little child is very curious, and this curiosity should be used by the teacher. Make suggestions so as to arouse the curiosity, and then lead the little one to a discovery and he will never forget it. Above all, when you promise a child anything, be sure to fulfill the promise. He expects it and will never forget a broken promise.

Cultivate the memory by teaching Scripture verses and little verses of good poetry and the child will never forget it. Things present should be emphasized, for the little one is too young to take in abstract ideas. Remember you are molding character for eternity.

QUESTIONS

What is the most important class in the Sunday school?

What special arrangement should be made for the primary classes?

What should be used in teaching the little ones?

How can the teacher aid in forming good habits in children?

The Intermediate Classes
IV

Next to the primary class, the intermediate classes are the most important and the most difficult. By intermediate is meant the boys and girls of from ten to thirteen years of age—the age when habits are rapidly forming and character crystallizing. Intelligent activity is the chief characteristic of this class of students.

Along with activity there is a demand in children of this

age for variety and play. This is true of their physical and mental natures. Activity and play are predominant and the wise teacher will always recognize these peculiarities. It is an old saying, but as true as it is old, that "you can't put an old head on young shoulders." The teacher, to be successful with this class of pupils, must be in sympathy with the active and playful natures of the children and try to direct the activities in a way to form good character. Suppression will not bring good results.

At this age the children can really study and, if interest is aroused, any amount of study can be got out of the child. A child of this age can be interested in striking at the sort of things his active and playful nature calls for. To interest him in the Bible, call his attention to the Bible stories of heroism. Tell him of Gideon, of Moses and of Joshua and the fall of Jericho. A boy wants to hear about fights and war and deeds of daring. Why not read to him, or rather, have him read the story of Gideon, and Joshua taking Jericho, of Daniel in the lion's den and of the three Hebrew children, If you can get the student to read for you and pass it around from one pupil to another, it will be better, for one characteristic of a boy at the age of from ten to thirteen is to want to put forward and be permitted to help. Make each one of the pupils feel hat you are expecting him to help. Boys of that age feel that they can do things and they want the opportunity of doing it. A wise teacher will see that they are kept busy doing things.

Memory work should be emphasized. Boys and girls of that age can remember anything, and the memory should be stored with the riches of God's word. Scriptures committed to memory at this impressionable age will never be forgotten. Offer rewards (cards are best) for the one repeating the most verses from the Bible. The passages should be selected for the pupils, such as the 23rd Psalm and the Beatitudes, etc. A good teacher will be able to select many rich passages for the pupils to memorize.

Make most of two things: Memory work and Bible characters. The pupils should learn of Moses, Abraham, Elijah, Daniel, Joseph, and above all, of Jesus Christ. It is not necessary to try to fasten abstract ideas on a child of that age. Fill his mind with facts. Students at this age should have the boys in one class and the girls in another; never in mixed classes until they get older.

QUESTIONS

What is the chief characteristic of intermediate pupils?
What demand is in the nature of such children?
How should the teacher direct the activities of the intermediate pupils?
Should children be suppressed?
What kind of stories interest intermediate pupils?
What should each pupil be made to feel?
Should pupils of this age be in mixed classes?

Advanced Classes
V

This is that class of pupils from fourteen to seventeen years of age. At this age there are great physical and mental changes, as the boys and girls are turning to maturity and want to be treated as young ladies and gentlemen.

The whole range of material may be used in such classes, as pupils of that age can reason like grown people. History, poetry, philosophy are in place with them. Memory is good and should be made much of in training young people of this age. Let the memory work be of such things as are worthwhile. There is nothing so good to memorize as the words of inspiration.

This is the age when all of the pupils may be led to Christ if they have not already become children of God. The teacher should make special effort to lead them to Christ, as this is a period when they shall either accept Christ or turn away probably never to be saved. It is a fearful responsibility and a teacher should be much in prayer for the salvation of every member of the class.

Boys and girls should be in separate classes as this is the bashful age and children of that age like to be in separate classes and it has been demonstrated over and over again that they do better in separate classes. Men should be the teachers for the boys and women for the girls.

Classes should be small—not over fifteen in a class, as large classes hinder the individual work the teachers of such pupils should do. Each pupil should be dealt with individually and each one should be made to feel that he is especially noticed. Separate rooms should be had for advanced classes, if possible. Where rooms cannot be had, curtains should be used to give the seclusion necessary for the best work.

The advanced classes need some social attention and it is well for the teacher to visit them and entertain them, sometimes giving parties for them to attend. Pupils of this age are awkward, and they should be encouraged to do their best.

The advanced pupil is self-conscious. He thinks everybody is looking at him. This gives fine opportunity to impress upon him the necessity of correct behavior and, above all, impress him that God looks on.

Students of this age are changeable. You need not look for consistency in them. Their ideals change. One day it is this notion and the next day it is another. Do not censure them for this, for it is their nature. Instead of censure, sympathize with them and help them to form final and right conceptions of their future life.

This is the age of strong friendships. Make a friend of a boy or girl of this age and he is your friend forever. He will always believe in you, hence the imporance of using your personality in teaching them. It is not so much what you say, as what you are, in the estimation of these pupils.

What ever you do, never express a doubt as to the truth of anything you teach. It is the doubting age with the pupils and to encourage this in them would be criminal. Call their attention to the fact that it is manly to be a believer in God's word, and that the greatest men and women who have ever lived have been believers. They are hero worshipers and religious heroes should be held up before them.

QUESTIONS

What material may be used in teaching advanced classes?
What special effort should be made for advanced pupils?
Should advanced pupils be in mixed classes?
How large should advanced classes be?
Who should teach advanced classes?
What of friendships formed at this age?

Senior Classes
VI

The age of the senior department is from 17 to 21 years, and it embraces young men and young women of the school. They should be dealt with as young men and women and not as children.

The classes of the seniors should be mixed classes, as this is the age when the company of the opposite sex will stimulate to the very best work. Young men and women in mixed classes try to appear to the best advantage and they do not like to be left in the race.

This is the age of independent thinking, and the teacher should endeavor to give the pupil something to think about. The pupil can now deal in abstract thought and he should have plenty of it to do. This is the age of great temptations and the teacher should remember that he was young once and that these temptations, if overcome, will be the making of a student. Do all in your power to help the young man and young woman in these temptations. Character is crystallized now and what is put into character at this age will stay there for life. This is the age of comradeship and strong friendships. Make a friend of a person at that age and he will be your friend forever. The teacher should make much of this. Social meetings are well for classes at this period. Let the class be a sort of social affair—not during recitations, but during the week between the recitations. The class can have meetings at the teacher's home or at some of the homes of the pupils and have a good social time. It binds them together as nothing else can.

This is an age of doubt. The young man and woman need to be shown the facts and the results of the facts, not bare assertions. The pupil of this age is exacting and the girls especially are exacting and tyrannical. They must be dealt with kindly and firmly and in friendship. Good use of the lives of Bible characters should be made, for they are hero worshipers. The wise teacher will consult the pupils as though he thought the advice of the pupil was the best in the world. This stimulates individuality and strength of character. You need not take the advice. After advising with the pupil you can discover something that is better than what the pupil suggested and then frankly tell him so and it will be all right. The object of the consultation is for the good of the pupil, not your good. In fact, everything done must be for the good of the pupil—that is what you are teaching for.

The chance for conversions is growing less every day with pupils of this age, and for that reason special effort should be made to bring all of the class to Christ, for if they pass this age there is small hope to ever bring them to salvation.

Bible history, doctrine and practical duties should be impressed every time you meet the senior class. This is the time to fill them full of Bible truth and equip them for service. Discover the gifted ones and encourage them to do their best. You are training some who will be preachers and Sunday school teachers in the near future, and what you now do will tell in eternity. The work is difficult, but the reward is great, and the time will come when you shall be proud of the men and women who were once in your class. Teach in deep earnestness, as nothing has a better influence on pupils of this age than genuine earnestness.

QUESTIONS

Should seniors be mixed classes?
What of temptations overcome?
Should social meetings be held?
What should be shown pupils of this age?
Should teachers consult the pupils?
Must the teacher take the pupil's advice?
What chance is there for conversion at this age?
What social features should be used?

Adult Classes

VII

The adult classes are those who have reached full grown manhood and womanhood. The ages will range from twenty-one years up to ninety—for none are too old to be in Sunday school.

It is very important to get the older people into the Sunday school, because they not only need to learn God's word, but their example is very much needed for the benefit of the younger people. If there were some way to get the old people to come to Sunday school there would be no difficulty in enlisting the young. If boys could see the older people—the merchants, the farmers, the school teachers, the doctors and the lawyers, together with their wives, in the Sunday school they would never get the idea that the Sunday school is for the "kids" as they sometimes contemptuously say. The older people may never know how much harm they do when they refuse to make students of God's word in the Sunday school.

The adults should study the doctrines of the Bible, and,

as they live more in the past than younger people, they should study the past—the history of the Lord's dealings with His people. Bible history should be made much of by the teacher of the adults.

The teacher can lecture freely to the older people in his class, for this is the period in life when the mind grasps the difficult parts of God's truth. Teach principle, reason out everything, and take nothing for granted.

Lessons that are practical are suitable to adults. They are compelled to meet the world in all its variations, and how to meet it is often a problem. If God's word can give any light on the problems of life the teacher should bring it out. Most of the adult students will be already saved and they need development as Christians. Emphasis should be put on living an active Christian life and the teacher should endeavor to train them to take public part in religious work. Teach them to talk in public by getting them to talk in the class and it will be easy to transfer the talking to the church meeting. There will be very few in the adult classes to lead to Christ, but when one is found the most prayerful effort should be made for his salvation, for old people are seldom saved. It is generally best for both men and women to be in the same classes. One of the adult classes should be used as a normal class from which supply teachers may be drawn when some of the teachers of the school are absent. A good normal class will solve the teacher problem.

QUESTIONS

Why is it important that older people attend Sunday school?
What should the adults study?
What may the teacher of adults do?
Should practical matters be considered in adult classes?
What should the teacher endeavor to train adults to do?
Is there any probability that adults may be led to Christ?
Is a teacher training class advisable?

THE SUNDAY SCHOOL AT WORK

SECTION III

The Teacher's Importance

I

With the exception of pulpit preaching there is no other work so important as that of the Sunday school teacher. The true teacher is closer to his pupil than the preacher is to his hearer and in that particular he has the advantage of usefulness over the preacher. Teachers should magnify their office, and the best equipment is none too good for them.

The teachers' text book is the Bible. The lesson helps usually found in well ordered schools are only helps and should never displace the Bible. These helps may be used in preparing the lesson, but should seldom, or never, he used in teaching the lesson. The teacher should impress upon the pupils that they are studying the Bible, and in order to do this the teacher himself should keep the Bible, in his hand while teaching, and when a part of the lesson is read it should be read from the Bible and not from the quarterlies or other helps. The pupils should be encouraged to use their Bibles and the teachers should see to it that each pupil has a Bible of his own. The teacher will be surprised to find many young men and women who do not own a Bible and some not even a Testament.

Since the Bible is the text book, we should know what the Bible is and what it teaches before we undertake to teach it. There are too many teachers who themselves need to be taught. Some know but little or nothing about the Bible and hence are as likely to teach false doctrine as true. Eternal issues are, at stake, and what is taught is of so much importance that the teachers should know the whole Bible, in a general way, and each lesson in particular.

How to Study and Teach the Lesson

The teacher should always prepare and teach the lesson in prayer. It is the study and the teaching of God's word and it is of entirely too much importance to be done lightly. Prayer will give power, both to learn and to teach. It follows as a matter of course that no one should teach in the Sunday school who is not a Christian and a prayerful Christian.

The teacher should learn the science of literature, a science easily mastered, and use it in the study and in the teaching of the Bible lesson. This science enables the teacher to master the lesson accurately and fully, as it cannot be done in any other way. But a working knowledge of this science can be had by carefully noticing the expositions found in the senior lessons in the Senior Quarterly of the Sunday school literature. This literature is the only literaure that uses the methods of the Science of Literature, but all first-class expositors will some day use it, because it not only simplifies, but it amplifies, the lesson when it is once mastered.

Without fully mastering the science any teacher or student can observe the following principles and be greatly benefited:

The first thing to do in the study of the lesson is to ask yourself the question: What? What is the passage I am studying talking about? You cannot write without writing about something. That something you write or talk about is called, in the Science of Literature, the object. The object is the fact of the lesson. There is always an object or fact in every lesson. Every lesson also has a subject. The subject is the thought. After you have answered the question, What? and in that way have found the object or fact of the lesson, then ask another question: Why? When you learn the why you will have the thought or subject. The object and the subject, joined together, give the theme. Thus you see there are three elements in every lesson, viz.: Object (fact); Subject (thought); Theme. The theme is what the preacher sometimes improperly calls his subject. What he calls his "subject" is really the "object" and "subject" joined together.

What is meant by "analysis" is to state all the facts connected with the object—the thing talked about in the lesson—and what is meant by the argument is to give all the reasons you can find why it is as it is. Analysis is done by what the science calls induction, and the argument is what the science calls deduction. This science, once mastered, means a mastery of the Scriptures.

Having learned the "object" or central fact of the lesson, then comes the "analysis" and the way to ask questions about the "fact" or "object" is to ask one question for each phase or particular of the object or fact, and in the Baptist Sunday School Committee's Sunday school literature each of these phases or particulars is made very clear. For instance, let us take as a lesson, "The Ten Lepers Healed." That lesson is found in Luke 17:11-19. We can illustrate the method of study and of teaching. We should begin with the question: What? What is the "object" or "fact" of the lesson? In other words, what image or object is in the mind of the writer of the lesson? The answer is: The ten lepers. So the ten lepers are the "object" or "fact" of the lesson.

The next question should be: What do we know about the ten lepers? The answer to that question is the analysis. The answer would be something like the following: (1) They were afflicted with an incurable disease. (2) They had a contagious disease. (3) They had a disease that might be inherited from their parents. (4) They had a loathesome disease. (5) In their distress they cried to Jesus for help. (6) They were commanded to go to the priest and offer for their cleansing. (7) They were cleansed by the power of the Lord. (8) One returned to give thanks and the nine showed ingratitude.

Thus we have the analysis—that is, we have, item by item, all we know about the ten lepers. Thus we see that the more we learn of the fact the fuller our analysis will be. There is nothing mysterious about thus making an analysis. The trouble is when we get "thought" and "fact" mixed. So far we have not had a thing to say about the subject or thought of the lesson. If you were to ask some teachers what the "subject" of the lesson is they would say: "The Ten Lepers." That would be incorrect. The ten lepers are the object, or fact, of the lesson, and on this object, or fact, we have a great central thought and the "thought" expressed is the "subject." What is the thought, or subject, of this lesson? It is "Healed by Faith." So the thought being "healed by faith" to express that thought briefly, is the theme," and it would be "The Lepers Healed By Faith." Thus we have the theme and it embraces the object (fact) and the thought (subject). The proposition is a clear sentence expressing the object and the subject, and in this case it would be: "The Ten Lepers Were Cleansed by Faith."

In asking questions about the thought (subject) we should use the question, Why? It is what for the object and why for the subject. Why were the lepers cleansed or healed? The answer to this question gives what is called the argument or reason why. In this case the reasons why the lepers were healed are: (1) They believed Jesus could heal. (2) They asked Him to heal them. (3) They did what He told them to do. (4) Their cleansing was a type of the cleansing of the soul from sin and the Savior used it as such. (5) It gave Jesus an opportunity to illustrate salvation by faith. Thus we see that there is no great mystery about analysis and argument. One deals with the fact and the other with the reason.

QUESTIONS

How important is the Sunday school teacher?

What is the teacher's text book?

What should the teacher impress upon the pupil?

How should the teacher prepare to teach?

What science should the teacher learn?

What is the first thing to do in learning a lesson?
What is the "fact" called?
What is the "thought" called?
What is the "theme?"
What is meant by analysis?
What is the proposition?

The Country Sunday School
II

All the books, or nearly all, prepared for the training of Sunday school teachers and officers were written from the standpoint of the city school.

But a majority of our Sunday schools are in the country—at least in small towns and villages—and thousands of them in the open country. For usefulness they excel. Their methods are poor, as a rule, but in their blundering way they do a world of good. To the workers in the country school these words are especially addressed.

Every country Sunday school can at least have and observe the following things. You do not have to be in town to be up-to-date in the following particulars:

1. Have a blackboard. What for? Have written on the board the name or number of each class and the report of the number of each class and the report of the number in attendance, the number of good lessons, etc., should be put on the board so that all the school can see. Nothing stimulates the young more than public notice of what they are doing. The blackboard will accomplish that.

2. Have the livest man in the church for superintendent. His qualifications are expressed in three words: Intellectuality, spirituality, dependability. The superintendent must be a spiritual man. Better lack in other particulars than to not be a devout Christian. He must have at least good common sense—a fool has no business trying to manage a Sunday school. He must be dependable. A superintendent who is present one Sun-

day and absent the next is not fit for the office. He must be a man who can be depended upon. The membership of a church should seek such a man and put him into the leadership of the Sunday school.

3. The teachers and superintendents of the country Sunday school can at least read Sunday school books and papers. Read everything about Sunday school work. They do not have to endorse all they read, but in books and papers that have a lot of rubbish in them they can find many nuggets of pure gold. Sometimes good ideas can be found in heretical literature. We can learn by contrast, if not actual example and precept. Many officers and teachers of Sunday schools never read a line on Sunday school work and barely read the lesson in the quarterly and thus make a mess in their poor efforts in running the school.

4. Look after the music. If there is no organ or piano, get busy and buy one. It will help the music, and music should be a prominent feature in the Sunday school work. Get a singing teacher, if need be, and train the young people to sing. Then sing. Don't sing the new songs altogether. Teach the children to sing the old standard hymns as well. Many of the new songs are good, and there can be no mistake in singing them. But sing.

5. Keep a constant lookout for new scholars. In every community there are boys and girls who are not in Sunday school. Get them. If at first you don't succeed, try, try again. Then there are many older people who never think of attending Sunday school. They ought to be ashamed of themselves, but they are not. Keep after them till they get ashamed and they will, some of them, become useful where they now are mere cumberers on the ground. Dig about them, fertilize them, and perchance they may bear fruit to the glory of God.

6. Start the school on the dot. That is one of the hardest things for country people to learn. Their habit of life is not on the dot like railroad men, and they get into a way of doing it

any time during the day, and few of them are prompt. That kills interest in anything, and it accounts for the decline and death of more country schools than any other thing. Begin on time—the very minute—and it will build up the school.

7. Stop on time. Just because some slow teacher drags along and fails to get through is no good reason for prolonging the work of the school. Promptness in starting and stopping is a very important item in the success of the school.

8. Co-operation must be had. If all do not pull together there is but little chance for success. If you can't have your way about anything, let the other person have his way, but let there be co-operation by all means. The superintendent is the leader—the boss, if you please—and he should be respected. That is what you elected him for, and if this is not recognized you had as well have no superintendent. If he does not do to suit the majority of the school, let him be put out by vote and another elected. But so long as he is superintendent he must be respected as such. That is the only way to have co-operation, and lack of co-operation is the ruin of the school.

9. Don't one man try to do it all. The superintendent should not be teacher. The pastor should not be superintendent. Have a job for all, but only one job to the man.

10. Put in as many men as possible for teachers. Of course, women can teach and some of them are better teachers than most men, but other things being equal, give the work of teaching to men. Why? Because so many, boys especially, regard the Sunday school as a "sissy" affair, and the presence of strong men as teachers and officers will correct that erroneous idea. By all means get a man teacher for the boys.

11. The country school can buy literature and encourage the scholars to read. A good Sunday school library of the best books will do a world of good. This is needed in the country more than it is in the city, because in the city there are many more books in reach of the scholars. You will never know the good a book may do when read by the members of the Sunday

school.

12. Don't lie down on the job because bad weather comes. You go to town in bad weather. You go to the postoffice, or, in fact, anywhere you really want to go in bad weather. Why lie down on the Sunday school job just because the weather is bad?

Finally, don't worry, and if in your heart you are really discouraged, for the love of the cause, do not let anybody else find it out. Keep at it, and things will get better.

QUESTIONS

From what viewpoint are most books on Sunday schools written?

Where are a majority of the Sunday schools?

Why have a blackboard?

What kind of man should be the superintendent?

What kind of music should be had?

When should Sunday school start and stop?

Who should do the work in the school?

Why have men for teachers?

Should a library be secured?

What should be done in bad weather?

If we feel discouraged, should we tell it?

The Pastor in Sunday School

III

The pastor should be an important factor in the Sunday school. But it is sadly true that many pastors take only a passing interest in this teaching service of the church, for that is exactly what a Sunday school should be. The Sunday school should be nothing more nor less than the church engaged in teaching the people the word of God while the members themselves study the word. The unconverted, the non-church members and the little children should be members of the Sunday school in the same sense they are members of the congregation during the preaching service. We want them there both in the preaching service and in the Sunday school and in exactly the same sense. That school is improperly conducted when the unconverted pupils are asked to run the school by electing the officers and deciding what the school shall do. They should not be allowed to control this teaching service of the church any more than they should be allowed to control the preaching service. But just as the preacher sometimes consults his entire congregation about minor matters, such as hours of meeting, and asks any one who will to select a song and sometimes even asks for suggestions from any who are present, even so the students in the school who are not church members may be consulted. But the church must run the school as certainly as it runs the preaching service and attends to its other business. The Sunday school, being only the church engaged in teaching by means of appointed teachers, just as the preaching service is the church preaching by means of the pastor, why should not the preacher take an active interest in the work of the school?

It should be remembered that the Sunday school is not an end, but it is a means to an end. The end that is sought is the salvation of souls and the building up of the church. Just as the preaching service is not an end, but the means to an end— the salvation of souls and the building up of the church. Unless this is borne in mind very incorrect ideas will prevail. Some act and talk as if the real idea is to have a big crowd at both Sunday school and the preaching service. But, while the big crowd is to be desired, the real object is to induce those who come, whether many or few, to accept Christ and be saved and then to unite with the church. If large crowds are the end sought, it will come to pass that everything will be done to induce the crowds to come, and it will be seen too that nothing is said or done to displease anybody or that will cross anybody's doctrine, lest the crowd be diminished. But what is the use of having a big crowd if you do not teach them anything when they come? Better far to have a half dozen and teach them the whole truth and get them lined up savingly with church than to have a thousand who are coming much as they would go to a show, merely for the pleasant time they have while there. Since the Sunday school is a serious work, why should not the pastor take an active part in it?

The pastor should be a close observer of the teaching of the school and be ready to follow up the impressions made in the school in his endeavor to lead the students to Christ. Some pastors run this into the ground and have what they call a "decision day" once a year, on which day they seek to get all the unsaved ones in the school to "decide for Jesus." Alas! as if he could force the grace of God. But while some have gone to the extreme, which is to be deplored, we should not neglect the opportunity furnished by the school to lead souls to Christ.

The pastor should always thoroughly master the lesson and be ready at all times to help any class out of a tight place by his helpful expositions of the lessons when called upon. He should not intrude on a class and voluntarily offer his explanation, but if he is known to be always ready to explain there will be many opportunities for him to do so. It is pitiable when he is called on and he does not know what to say. He should be ashamed to be found unprepared and hence he should always learn the lesson so that he can answer any question that may be asked. In this way he can be a real help to the teacher and students as well.

The pastor should be a teacher and counsellor of the teachers and the superintendent. They should rely on his judgment concerning the best thing to do. No pastor on earth can really know always what should be done unless he studies the problems of the school. He should read good books on Sunday school work, and above all, read the Bible and thus be ready to give an answer every time his advice is sought. It is well for him to teach a teachers' training class, from which material can be drawn by the superintendent to teach the classes when the regular teachers may be absent, and from this training class teachers can be drawn for permanent classes as they may be needed. Then the preacher should, if possible, meet all the teachers as often as possible and teach them how to teach. Of course, he cannot do this unless he is prepared to teach himself. If he does not know how, he should learn. A pastor should feel the weight of his responsibility and measure up to it, and he will find that his labors are not in vain.

If the pastor only visits his churches once a month he should take just as much interest in the school on the day he does visit the church as he would if he were there every Sunday. He can show his interest by helping the teachers and the often discouraged superintendent, and above all, his example, in favor of the school.

If there is some special point that may be emphasized in the lesson, let the preacher, in a short talk, bring it out. But no Sunday school talk should be long. Five minutes is long enough as a rule. The children can't listen long without getting restless. Bear that in mind and be brief. It is only the man who is well prepared who can make a short talk, and it is an evidence of lack of knowledge when a pastor stands before a school and chews and chews and really says nothing worth while.

Pastors should seek for students in their pastoral visits. Ask the children where they go to Sunday school, and if they go nowhere, make an effort to get them to come to the school. Talk to their parents about it. It is an important matter, and the best of results will be seen from such pastoral efforts.

Would it really hurt your school if the pastor should move away or die? If not, he is a poor pastor. If pastors should ask themselves that question it might jar them into doing better. The fact is, the pastor should be the most important factor in the Sunday school. He should control the school without seeming to do so—control it by wise suggestions and by managing the officers and teachers, without seeming to do so. If he shows that he is trying to control, it will be resented and he will fail. By suggestion, by counselling, by working through others on whom he can depend, by clear expositions when called upon, he can soon be master of the school. And who, better than a wise pastor, should lead?

Too many pastors are tombstones instead of sign boards. They are monumental and strong and polished, but accomplish nothing and direct nobody. I had rather be a pine sign board than be a marble tombstone. Pastors should make themselves felt for good in the Sunday school.

In order to be a success in Sunday school the pastor must like children and make them like him. The best way in the world to make children like you is to really like children and take interest in them and notice them. The sad-faced, dignified pastor will never win children. They are worth winning, for when the children like you it is a direct road to the hearts of their parents. It is a foolish preacher who does not cultivate the children's love.

The pastor should come to the school on time. His example is too valuable to set the bad example of being tardy. It shows interest to be a little ahead of time, and thus have the happy privilege of meeting the people, and especially the children, as they come in. It makes everybody feel better and it is better. Let pastors wake up on Sunday school work.

The Sunday school is not understood by a great many really intelligent people. Some regard it as a thing apart from the church and therefore should not be. The Sunday school is only the church teaching the word of God. The unconverted members of the Sunday school are members in the same sense the unconverted are members of the congregation during preaching service. They are no more actually in the Sunday school than they are actually in the church when they come to preaching. We want the unconverted in both the Sunday school and the preaching service of the church. The church has the gospel preached by means of a preacher and he preaches both to the saved and the unsaved. The church also teaches the word of

God by means of selected teachers and these teachers teach both the saved and the unsaved. If we can only get the brethren everywhere to take this view of the work of the school it will be a long step in the right direction.

The Sunday school is no more for the children than it is for the old. Grey hairs should be seen in the Sunday school for two reasons. They should come to teach, if they are competent to do so, and they should come to learn if they do not already know it all. In either case they should be in the Sunday school. A pastor should no more think of being away from the Sunday school, than he would think of being away from the preaching service, and he should not think of such a thing as being absent from either unless providentially hindered.

QUESTIONS

What is a Sunday school?

In what sense are the unsaved in the Sunday school?

What should the pastor do in the Sunday school?

Should the pastor know the lesson?

What is the pastor's duty toward the superintendent and teachers?

How should the pastor work for the school during the week days?

Would it injure your school if your pastor should die?

How long should a Sunday school talk be?

Some Faults in the Sunday School

IV

The preaching of the gospel is the most important thing in the world. If the teachers and officers in the Sunday school do not emphasize the preaching of the gospel in their Sunday school work, they fail of one of their most important duties. Some common faults in Sunday school workers are pointed out in this article.

1. To leave the meeting house after Sunday school and not

remain for church service, as some teachers and officers do, should entirely disqualify such an one from holding any position in the school. A church member who does such a thing should be excluded from the church. Of course, there are exceptions. Sometimes a man can attend Sunday school and is prevented, by circumstances over which he has no control, from attending the morning service. With such exceptions noted, it is well-nigh criminal for a teacher or officer to leave the church house after Sunday school and fail to be at church service. The example of attending church services must tbe set before the children.

2. Trying to entertain the pupils instead of trying to instruct them is a great fault. The Sunday school can never compete with the show in entertainment, and if the teacher or officer undertakes to entertain the pupils, who are accustomed to much better shows than can be put on in the Sunday school, they will have a feeling of disgust and will probably quit the school. Be pleasant and cheerful, but emphasize all the time that the thing the class is there for is to study God's word and to be made wise in spiritual things.

3. The habit of encouraging the little children to leave the meeting house after Sunday school and not remain for church is a criminal habit. It is contended that the little ones get tired by having to stay so long in the church. But those same children stay for hours in the public school on other days in the week and nobody gets sorry for them. To encourage the children to leave before service is to convey to their young minds that the church service does not amount to much and the result is that the habit of non-church going is established in youth that may follow them through life.

QUESTIONS

What is the most important thing?

What faults are seen in Sunday schools?

What criminal habit is sometimes encouraged in pupils?

DOCTRINES TO BE GUARDED
SECTION IV

The Doctrine of God
I

There is a supreme being (Gen. 1:18) and He is invisible to the natural eye (Col. 1:15). We must not imagine that He is a material being such as we are (John 4:24), and being a spirit He has not flesh and bones (Luke 24:39). God is not a mere force in nature, as many vainly believe, but He is a person, the supreme person over the whole universe (Eph. 3:4, Eph. 1:9-11). God is unchangeable (Mal. 3:6, James 1:17). God's purpose and plan are immutable, unchangeable, and when He is said to repent, that is, change His mind, it is only what is called the language of accommodation that is, He is said to do that which He appears to do.

There is only one God, but He is manifested to the world in three persons. This is a great mystery, but not unreasonable (Deut. 32:48). While God is one and only one, yet there are three persons in the Godhead, the Father, Son and Holy Spirit (Matt. 28:18-20, II Cor. 13:14). There is no exact illustration of this fact in nature, but there is one that will enable us to, in a measure, comprehend the mysterious doctrine of the Trinity. Snow, ice and frost are three, yet they are one. No one can fail to see the distinct individuality of snow and of ice and of frost. Any child can see that snow is not ice and frost is not snow. Yet the fact is they are one. They are three, yet one; just frozen water. So God is one, yet three. He manifests Himself as the Father, Creator; as the Spirit, life giver; as the Son, God manifested in human form. That Jesus is God is seen in John 1:1-14, John 20:28, Col. 2:9. The Holy Spirit is called God in Acts 5:3-4, I Cor. 12:4-6, Eph. 4:30. The Lord Himself clearly distinguishes between the three persons in the Trinity in John 14:16-17, John 14:26, John 15:26. What therefore we learn that the Son does, we know it is the doing of the God of heaven, and that which the Spirit does is likewise the work of God. These three are one and never contradict one the other. What God says in His word is not contradicted nor changed by the leadership of the Spirit. If one claims to be led by the Spirit, let him know that the Spirit leads in harmony with the written word of God. Otherwise God would contradict Himself. God is omnipresent, that is, He is everywhere at the same time (Isa. 57:15; Jer. 23:23-24; Ps. 139:6). God knows all things (Ps. 147:4; Matt. 10:29; Acts 15:8; Heb. 4:13). The way to learn God is to study His word, which reveals Him in the person of Jesus Christ (John 1:18; Eph. 2:18; I Tim. 3:16). The terms Holy Spirit and Holy Ghost mean the same thing, being only variations of translation of the same original word, different terms expressing the idea of the third person in the Trinity.

QUESTIONS

What is meant when God is said to repent?

Is there one or three Gods?

What illustration would help us to understand the Trinity?

Does the Spirit of God ever lead us to something different from what is written in the Bible?

How may we learn of God?

Is the Holy Ghost and Holy Spirit the same?

Human Depravity, or Hereditary Evil

II

The doctrine of total depravity means that all that constitutes man is inclined away from God and positively bent toward evil. It does not mean that any one is as bad as he can be, but that all are bad in all their parts. Rom. 8:8 says that "they that are in the flesh cannot please God." The word "flesh" in that place does not mean "body," for if that is so, then none can please God, even after they are saved, for even the saved are in their bodies. It means the natural man, "they that are in their natural state, cannot please God.' If there is anything good in a man God certainly would be pleased with it. But God is not pleased with any who are in their natural state, hence there is no good in any for Him to be pleased with. Eccl. 8:11 says: "The hearts of the sons of men are fully set in them to do evil." "Fully" means completely, entirely, and hence it follows that all that constitutes man is set in evil.

This evil condition of the sinner makes it necessary for a personal contact of the Holy Spirit to be experienced before he can be saved. Ezra 8:22 says: "The hand of the Lord is upon all them that seek him," and in II Cor. 3:3 we are told that the Holy Spirit touches the heart of the sinner as ink touches the paper. It is entirely impossible for a sinner to save himself as it is for an Ethiopian to change his skin or a leopard his spots. (Jer. 13:11-23).

An unsaved sinner is entirely destitute of God's love (John 5:42). The mind of the natural man is against God (Rom. 8:7), and the minds and consciences of the sinner are defiled (Titus 1:15).

The work of the Spirit upon the sinner's heart produces what is called the new birth (John 1:13). This new birth is necessary in order that the man may receive the things of the Spirit, which are discerned only by the spiritual (I Cor. 2:1-4).

This glorious salvation from sin is not produced by any good works which the sinner does, such as baptism, deeds of charity, etc., but entirely by grace that the renewed man begins to manifest his salvation by good works. (Eph. 2:8-10). Christ suffered for the sinner and it is on His merits that the sinner is saved (I Pet. 3:18, I Tim. 2:5, I John 2:2). Thus being saved from sin the renewed man partakes of the Lord's nature and has eternal life. (II Cor. 1:17, II Pet.).

QUESTIONS

What is meant by total depravity?

Quote passages of scripture to prove total depravity.

What is necessary for the Spirit to do before any one can be saved?

Does good work have anything to do in obtaining salvation?
On whose merits are we saved?

Salvation by Grace, Not of Works
III

Christ suffered for our sins and paid the penalty in full (I
Pet. 3:18). He is the only mediator between God and man,
hence we do not need an earthly priest, as the Roman Catholic
church teaches (I Tim. 2:5). He made entire satisfaction for
our sins, hence we do not need to purchase any part of salvation by our good works, as so many erroneously teach (I John
2:2).

Salvation is not secured by works nor by a mixture of
grace and works, and it is a false doctrine to teach that "if we
do our part God will do His," as we often hear. There is no
part for the sinner to do to obtain salvation (Eph. 2:8-10, Rom.
4:3-5, Rom. 11:7). To repent and believe as the sinner must do
is not to save himself, but to change his mind with reference to
God, with sorrow for sin, and to trust Christ to do all the saving. True repentance causes a sinner to utterly despair of ever
saving himself or even helping the Lord to save, and to fully
trust the Lord to do all the saving.

Good works follow as a result of salvation, but good works
do not produce salvation (Eph. 2:6-7). Good works are the
fruitage of the tree already made good, for "an evil tree cannot bring forth good fruit," said our Savior.

No one can be justified or saved by keeping the law (Gal.
3:11). The law is a statement of right principles and should be
obeyed so far as it has been transferred into the New Testament, but this obedience is the result of salvation and not the
cause of it. "If ye love me ye will keep my words," said Jesus,
but since only those who love will keep His words, it follows

that only those who are born again will obey, for "He that lov-
etht is born of God and knoweth God." (I John 4:7). So the
words of our Lord are true when He said, "Except a man be
born again he cannot see the kingdom." (John 3:3-7).

We cannot understand the mystery of salvation, but we
can see its effects (John 3:8) just as we do not understand the
movements of the wind and cannot see the wind, but we can
feel it and see its effects. So is every one born of the Spirit.

The salvation enjoyed by a child of God means a vital
union with Christ (II Cor. 5:17) and it results in a good life
and a home in heaven (Eph. 2:10, John 14:2-3, Rev. 22:1-5),
but we are not saved by being good nor by going to heaven.
Being good and going to heaven are the fruits or results of
salvation, and not the cause of salvation. We go to heaven not
by being good, but the same thing, (salvation) that takes us to
heaven causes us to be good on the way.

QUESTIONS

Who paid the penalty for our sins?
Do we need an earthly priest?
Is salvation partly by grace and partly by works?
What does true repentance cause a sinner to do?
Do good works follow salvation?
Can any one be saved by keeping the law?
What is necessary before one can see the kingdom?
Can we understand the mystery of salvation?
Do we have to go to heaven before we are saved?

The Church and the Ordinances
IV

The primary meaning of the word "church" is the called
out. It means any body of God's people called out and separated from the world and associated in the faith and fellowship of
the gospel. The church is never larger than a local congrega-

tion. In Rev. 1:4 we read: "John to the seven churches of Asia." Certainly not seven denominations in Asia, for there was only one faith and order at that time. In I Cor. 1:2 we read: "Unto the church of God at Corinth." Thus we see that a church is a local body. It is only in a figurative sense that all the redeemed are considered as the church. The mind can conceive of all the saved as being a great congregation, and this conception is called the church, but such a church never had any real existence—it is only a conception of the mind. Paul uses this conception in Eph. 5:23-26, where he says: "For the husband is the head of the wife, even as Christ is the head of the church." If the idea of a great universal church is seen in this, because Paul uses the expression, "the church," then we could, by the same process of reasoning, get the idea of a great universal husband and a great universal wife, since he says, "the husband" and "the wife." That, of course, is absurd and hence the idea of a great universal church is absurd. So it is unscriptural to talk of the "universal church and its branches," as so many do. Each local congregation is a complete church in itself, and is not in any sense a branch of some big universal church.

The ceremonial ordinances of the church—each and every local congregation of the Lord—are baptism and the Lord's Supper. The Lord commanded His church to baptize those who became disciples (Matt. 28:18-20). A baptism not administered by a church is unscriptural, since the church only is commanded to baptize. Of course, the church uses agents and the pastor or evangelist is usually the agent, but the agent must always act on the authority of the church. Baptism is the submersion in water of a disciple of the Lord in the name of the Trinity. (Matt. 28:18-20, Rom. 6:3-5, Acts 8:26-40). Baptism is not for the purpose of saving people, but it is for those who are already saved. (Acts 10:43-48).

The Lord's Supper is a memorial ordinance to commemorate the shed blood and broken body of the Lord (I Cor. 11:

23-24). It must be for only a church member, and not even for him until after he has been judged qualified by the church (I Cor. 5:11-13) and even after he has been judged qualified by the church he must for himself undergo a careful self-examination. (I Cor. 11:28). Thus we see that the Lord's Supper is closed to all except to the ones who are scripturally qualified. That is what is meant by ''close communion.'

Baptism and the Lord's Supper are too sacred to be made a social affair. Let us keep them sacredly.

QUESTIONS

What does the word church mean?

When the Bible speaks of the ''churches'' does it mean different denominations?

Is there such a thing as the great universal church?

What kind of people should be baptized?

Is baptism, not administered by the authority of the church, scriptural?

What is baptism?

What is the Lord's Supper?

Who should partake of the Supper?

Has the church the right to judge as to whether an individual shall partake of the Supper?

Must the individual also examine himself?

Is the Lord's Supper closed to all except those who are scripturally qualified?

The Doctrines of Christ

V

There are some who seem to think that there might be some difference in the doctrine of Christ as taught by Him, during His personal ministry, and the doctrines of the apostles as they taugh after His ascension. But it is a fact that Christ taught all of the doctrines that are found in the epistles as written by the apostles after His ascension. The writings of the apostles only developed the doctrines already taught by the Lord.

1. The Divinity of Christ. This is taught by him in John 5:18 and John 14.

2. The Humanity of Christ. That He was a complete and perfect man, as well as the complete and perfect God, is taught in John 5:27.

3. The Membership of Christ. That He was the Messiah of the prophets is taught in Luke 24:27.

4. The Priesthood of Christ. That He was the priest who would make a sacrifice for our sins is taught in Mark 10:45.

5. Salvation by Christ. That He came to save the lost is taught in Luke 19:10.

6. The Spirit Kingdom. That His kingdom is spiritual and not temporal is taught in John 3:3-18.

7. The New Birth or Regeneration. That the new birth is necessary to salvation is taught in John 3:3-18.

8. The Christian Code of Morality. This is found in the wonderful sermon on the Mount and summarized in Mark 12: 30-31.

9. Baptism and the Lord's Supper. He submitted to baptism (Matt. 3:16) and He baptized through His disciples (John 4:13), and He instituted the Lord's Supper (Luke 22:19), and He commanded the church to observe all things He had commanded and that was equivalent to commanding them to observe baptism and the Lord's Supper, for He had commanded them and observed them. (Matt. 28:19-20).

10. General Providence. The general providential work of the Lord is taught in Matt. 5:44. He bestows blessings on the just and the unjust.

11. Special and Particular Providence. He watches over the children of God in a special and particular manner, and not a hair on their head shall escape his eye, and he is careful for their welfare. This is taught in Matt. 6:26.

12. Divine Control of Nature. The God of nature is not

subject to natural laws, but is master of them. This is taught in Mark 4:39.

13. Perfect and Infinite Knowledge of All Things. Matt. 6:32 and other passages teach the minutest knowledge of even the so-called insignificant things. A knowledge of such details necessarily implies a knowledge of all things.

14. To Rely on God For Support and Protection. To rely on the Lord under all circumstances, depending on Him to protect and support us, is taught in Matt. 6:25.

15. Sin Is in the Heart. That the Lord looks on the heart as the seat of all sin is taught in Matt. 15:19, and hence the need of a new heart.

16. Future Eternal Punishment. The doctrine of future and eternal punishment is taught in Matt. 25:46 and Luke 13:3.

17. Satan the Author of Sin. Sin is of the devil and God is not the author of sin, either directly or indirectly, is taught in John 8:44.

18. The Holy Spirit. Jesus taught that the Holy Spirit was the Comforter (John 14:16-17) and the guide (John 3:3-17), the giver of power to honor and serve the Lord (John 7:39), the reprover of sin (John 16:8).

19. Prayer. Jesus taught His disciples to pray and gave illustrations of acceptable and prevailing prayer. (See Luke 11:1, Matt. 15, and Luke 18:9-14, John 14:13).

20. The Resurrection of the Dead. The resurrection of both the wicked and the righteous is taught in John 5:28-29, and that there will be a literal resurrection of the body (John 5:28) and Christ is the author of the resurrection, and after the resurrection there will be a general judgment (Matt. 25:31-32).

QUESTIONS

Did Jesus, during His personal ministry, teach all the doctrines of the New Testament?

Were the writings of the apostles merely a development of the doctrines taught by Jesus?

Name the doctrines Jesus taught.

Does this show that no new doctrine began at Pentecost?

If the doctrines of Jesus constitute His will or testament, did He not make His will or testament complete before His death?

Since He made His will or testament by His teaching and practice, could there be any new doctrine or practice added at Pentecost?

Scriptural Associations

There is no scriptural way by which churches may combine, but they may associate as equals. This associating does not consist in meeting at a given place, but the churches associate in the work. They may elect messengers and those messengers may meet, but that meeting of the messengers is not the association. These messengers represent the churches—the churches themselves constituting the association. The association, properly speaking, never meets. Only the messengers, from the churches composing the association, meet, and while it is common it is not proper to speak of the meeting of messengers as being the association. These messengers are nothing more or less than a joint committee appointed by the churches for the purpose of consulting about the work which the Master commissioned each of them to do.

Since the commission was given to the congregation as such, it follows that the congregations as such are the units in all associate or co-operative work. They must, therefore work together on terms of perfect equality, the large church or the rich church is only a church and should have no special privileges on account of its size or wealth. Hence the numerical and financial bases of representation in associations or conventions are equally wrong. If the Lord gave the commission to individuals the numbers of individuals should, of course, determine the number of messengers sent or, if the commission was given to churches according to their wealth, then the amount of money given should determine the number of messengers. But if the Lord gave the commission to the church, as such, it follows that an equal number of messengers should be sent from all the churches associating.

To contend logically for the convention system of co-operation one must contend that the commission was given to individuals. To argue for the association system of work one must contend that the commission was given to the churches as such. The whole matter rests right here.

What is called the association is not an organization in the common acception of the term at all. It is only an intelligent working together of independent organizations. It is independent churches associating together in the work of the Lord, but working as individual churches, independent and free. Beyond this they cannot go without violating the law of the Master, who told the individual church, as such, to "go teach all nations, baptizing them," etc. (Matt. 28:19-20).

That churches did associate in the Master's work in apostolic times is seen in II Cor. 8:19-23. Here was a joint work of the churches through "messengers," a joint committee. "Whether any do enquire of Titus, he is my partner and fellow-helper concerning you; or you brethren be enquired of, they are the messengers of the churches, and the glory of Christ."

Certainly the church may elect messengers to carry on cooperative work, but they may not do it except on terms of perfect equality, and the churches as such must engage in the work.

QUESTIONS

Can churches scripturally combine?

In what does the association consist?

Was the commission given to the churches or to individuals?

On what is the convention idea based?

Is there scripture for a joint committee?

Order of Exercises in the Sunday School
VII

1. The school should open on the exact time set for it to open. The bell should be tapped by the superintendent and perfect order secured and then two songs should be sung.

2. Prayer should be offered by the superintendent or by some one selected by him. The prayer should be short. It does not require much talk to cause God to understand, and we are not heard for our much speaking.

3. After prayer another song should be sung.

4. Reading the scripture lesson. It is generally better to read the regular Sunday school lesson, but if another passage is preferred it should be short. Whoever reads should have previous notice, so he may study the passage to be read, in order that the meaning may be made clear by the reading. Long passages should never be read. Some foolishly think they must read an entire chapter. A part of the chapter is almost certain to be better.

5. Then the superintendent will make any announcement about the conduct of the school he may think best and at the close of the announcement he will say: "The classes will now take their places for the study of the lesson."

6. Twenty-five minutes should be given to the work of study in the classes. By study is meant the reading of the lesson, the asking of questions and the recitation, and discussions in the classes. All of this is to really learn the lesson. If a pupil comes to the class entirely ignorant of the lesson he should not be allowed to leave that way, for what is said and done in the class should teach the dullest pupil the lesson.

7. When the twenty-five minutes have ended the bell should ring again and the classes should come back into the main part of the building, but each class should stay together and act as a class till the exercises are entirely over.

8. The classes should all be numbered and the superintendent should call the classes by number, and when each class is

called the teacher should have the entire class to arise and stand until he gives report to the secretary. In the report he should say: Number present, 15, or whatever may be the exact number; good lesson, 6, or whatever it may be in reality; verses memorized, 50, or whatever the real number of verses may be; collection, 75 cents, or whatever the amount may be. Then the teacher should repeat a verse of scripture, and where the school is not large, each member of the class should repeat a verse. If the school is too large for each pupil to repeat a verse, then the teacher and class should repeat a verse in concert which they have previously agreed upon. When each class has been called and all have reported as indicated, then a song will be sung.

9. Secretary's report. In this report he will give what is reported by the classes in totals. Since each class has made an individual report, the secretary only needs to report the totals.

10. Another song is sung, and the pupils are then earnestly requested by the superintendent to remain for preaching, if a preaching service follows the Sunday school, and the school is dismissed.

All this will take about one hour, if there is no dragging. For instance, the first two songs will consume five minutes. The prayer and the song following will consume another five minues. The reading of the scripture lesson and the announcement of the superintendent will consume another five minutes. The recitation and study of the lesson will consume twenty-five minutes. That will be forty minutes. Then the reports of the classes and recitation of verses will take fifteen minutes in the average school. The secretary's report will take about two minutes. That will leave three minutes for the last song. If the school begins at 10 o'clock it will mean every minute must be put in to get through by the 11 o'clock service. It is generally better to begin at 9:45 a. m., so as to allow plenty of time for all the exercises and have more time for singing and for the study of the lesson.

The Sunday school should be a training school for liberality. The collection should always be taken in each class. The poor should not be embarrassed by pressure, but the student should be taught that every one should contribute. This habit, formed while young, will never leave them.

At times the lesson should be dispensed with and the Sunday school period be given over to the pastor or superintendent to make a special effort for the salvation of the pupils. This is far better than having a fixed day, as some have erroneously done. Just whenever it is thought best, turn the school into an evangelistic service. But let everything be seasoned with prayer.

CHANGING TIMES

Times have changed but truth has not. The doctrines so clearly taught in this manual written by Dr. Bogard so many years ago are still taught in the Lord's church, as they contend earnestly for that same faith "once delivered to the saints."

Methods of teaching do change, however, sometimes for the better. Most Sunday Schools today are carried on in a different manner than they were at the time of the writing of this manual when Bogard was engaged many times in organizing Sunday Schools and training their personnel. At that time, most churches were small. Both small town and rural churches were often only one room houses in which all classes met.

Bogard's Sunday School Manual represents one of the great epochs in the history of the church. It details the procedures followed by superintendents, secretaries, teachers and students. As far as we know, this is the only authentic document presenting the details of procedure, thus, it becomes a very valuable piece of history. Some are living at the time of this printing who can remember Sunday Schools following this pattern, and this bit of nostalgia will be refreshing to them—to the younger group, amazing that such schools succeeded in comparison with what they have now.

THE HARDSHELL HERESY

In 1916, the pamphlet, *The Hardshell Heresy* (first published in serial form in the *Baptist and Commoner*) was printed in booklet form. This book, long since out of print, has recently been reprinted.

In 1919, Bogard published a reply to a pamphlet published by E. P. Aldridge. Mr. Aldridge had written this work against associated work. The reply was

A STARTLING CONVENTION ONSLAUGHT
(Wilful Misrepresentation)

Shall Our People Be Misled by Falsehood and Killed With Sweetened Poison?

E. P. Alldredge Answered by Ben M. Bogard in Plain Terms

A remarkable document has just come into my hands. It is "AN OPEN LETTER TO A BROTHER," by E. P. Alldredge, and entitled, "THE BAPTIST CONVENTION OR THE STATE ASSOCIATION, WHICH?" The document is remarkable because it comes in the "sweet," goody, goody style that pretends friendship, when in fact the writer is a deadly foe. It is remarkable because the pamphlet declares that the State Association of Arkansas will surely soon die, and yet it is made the subject of an assault the like of which we have not seen for some time. Why assault a dying man? Why try to kill a dying institution? The very attack by Alldredge shows that he does not believe his own words when he declares the State Association will soon die.

Some Assurdities

1. Several times Mr. Alldredge declares that the State Association "is just like the convention" in principle and in
work. Page 10 we read: "I will show," says Alldredge, "that
there is no difference between Conventionism and Associa-
tionism—that when you condemn the State Convention you
also condemn the State Association."

Remark: If this be true, then the converse is true, that
when you condemn the State Association you condemn the
'Convention.' "Sauce that is good for the goose is good for
the gander." Alldredge does condemn the State Association
and therefore, he being witness, he condemns the Convention!

2. Mr. Alldredge declares that there is not "even any difference in methods." On page 15 he says: "There is no difference in principles, and no difference in general plans and
methods in the two bodies."

Remark: If this be true then the two bodies are EXACT-
LY ALIKE. Is Alldredge trying to kill a body of Baptists because it is like the Convention? Can you believe him to be sincere?

3. On page 7 Alldredge says: "They are adopting one by
one all the methods and machinery of the Convention."

Remark: If this be true, where has he a right to kick? If
the State Association is like the Convention in principle, methods, and machinery, as he declares, it is therefore like the Convention in every particular! Yet they do fight us for doing, if
they tell the truth, just exactly like the Conventions are doing!
Is it just because they delight in a fight, a fight on their brethren, just because they do not go in the same crowd with the
Convention people? Is Alldredge mad because the Association
Baptists work *just exactly like the Convention people do?* We
could not do more like the Conventionites, if he tells the truth.
What does he want us to do? Do you really believe he is sincere?

Some Conclusions From the Above Statements

1. If Alldredge tells the truth there is no excuse for him and others continually fighting us and trying to get us to kill the State Association. If he does not tell the truth, *it is manifestly an effort to destroy the State Association by falsehood!* Choose either horn of this dilemma you please.

2. If Alldredge tells the truth, when he says there is no difference between the two bodies, it follows that he concedes that the State Association is Scriptural, or he does not so concede. If he does concede the State Association to be Scriptural, then since it is just like the Convention, he being witness, it follows that he does not believe the Convention to be Scriptural and is trying to get us to quit one unscriptural body for another. Mark you, he says that the State Association is like the Convention in "principle," methods, and machinery and general plans of work." If that is true, it follows that when he fights the State Association he is fighting a Scriptural body. But if it is like the Convention in all these particulars and still is unscriptural, he concedes that the Convention is unscriptural. Which horn of this dilemma will he take? It makes no difference with me which horn bores him through. By the way do you believe such a man to be sincere? Is he not trying to deceive?

A Stubborn Fact

If Mr. Alldredge succeeds in making the brethren and sisters connected with the State Association believe that the State Association is just like the Convention, it will result in their either changing the methods, principles and work so as to become different from the Convention, or their quitting the State Association and going into nothing. One thing certain they are not going into the Convention for they *know that is unscriptural.* None of the sincere workers will quit the State

Association for the Convention, if it should be proved that the two bodies are just alike. If they find they have a rotten egg on hand it will be no inducement to offer them another rotten egg in exchange. We shall be obliged to Mr. Alldredge if he will show us wherein we are in any particular like the Convention for we want to quit all unscriptural practices or methods. We regard Conventionism as being *rebellion against New Testament law and we do not want to be rebels.*

A Wicked Inconsistency

After telling us that we (The State Association) are just like the Convention he turns right around and declares that the churches in the State Association are not true Baptist churches at all! On page 9 he says: "From the days of the apostles down to the year 1892, when Landmark Baptists split off from the Convention, it was never heard of that independent Baptist Churches could join anything. If they join to others, they cease that moment to be independent, separate, free, Baptist Churches. Indeed they cease to be Baptist Churches at all."

Remark: If this be true then the State Association churches are not Baptist Churches for they have joined others in the work of evangelization and missions, just as nearly all the Baptist Churches in the world have done in joining local associations. Churches are received into local associations by vote. The common form of the motion is, "Brother Moderator, I move that the church be received and the messengers seated." Alldredge knows this to be true and yet he charges that all such churches are not Baptist Churches at all! If so, nearly all the churches in the world have ceased to be Baptist Churches! Most of them are actually in local association. *They joined local associations just as the churches have joined the State Association and the General Association.*

But after telling us that the State Association is just exactly like the Convention in *principle, machinery, methods, and general plans of work, he turns right around and declares that such churches are not Baptist Churches at all!* Did he tell the truth one time or the other? If he told the truth, that we are not Baptist Churches at all, it follows that the Convention has no true Baptist Churches in it. Does he want us to understand that the Convention Churches are not Baptist Churches at all or did he tell a falsehood when he said there is no difference? Let him take either horn of this dilemma he pleases, he will be bored through either way.

Concedes That We Did Not Split Off From Convention

Does he not declare that churches can not join anything? Has he not said that if the churches are in anything at all they lose their independence and cease to be Baptist Churches at all? If so, it follows that the State Association Churches *did not split off from the Convention for the very good reason they were never in it, he being witness.* How could they split off from a thing they were never a part of? But if the churches are not really in the Convention then he tells a falsehood when he declares, page 9, "In the Southern Baptist Convention and in our State Convention the churches are all free." How can they be free in the Convention when they are not in the Convention? *Are they in it and yet not in it? Which time did he tell the truth?* There is a yarn out as sure as you live.

Detailed Statements in Alldredge's Document

1. On page 13 he compares the number of converts made by the two bodies, and makes it appear that the Convention is far ahead of the State Association. *But he neglects to tell you that the Convention method counts the converts at least three*

times! The State Association does not resort to such dishonest tactics as that and hence their reports are not so large. Here is how they count the converts three times. The Convention "missionaries (?)" are of two kinds: supplemental pastors and local associational missionaries. These supplemental pastors, misnamed missionaries, assist each other in protracted meetings. Let us suppose that in a meeting where two of these missionaries work together there are fifty converts. Each missionary reports to the State Board fifty converts. Since each reports fifty, the two fifties make one hundred. But the Home Board, Atlanta, Georgia, helps pay these missionaries through the State Board and thus the one hundred converts are reported to the Home Board. So the one hundred becomes two hundred, when in fact there were only fifty converts! In such a case the converts are multiplied by four. If all of the converts in every case were thus counted it would be counting each convert four times, but it is not always that the missionaries assist each other. But where a missionary labors alone his fifty converts would be counted by both the State Board and also by the Home Board and thus the two fifties would be one hundred. In almost every case they are counted twice and in many cases counted four times and thus we are safe in saying that the converts are counted about three times. If the State Association did that sort of business we could count many more converts than the Convention is able to show for the very good reason that most of the converts are in the country among the country churches which are overwhelmingly for the State Association.

2. Alldredge compares general work done, how many more missionaries, and everything else they have, but neglects to tell that the Home Board of Atlanta, Ga., furnishes thirty thousand dollars of the money to pay for the work. Give the State Association thirty thousand dollars from an outside source and we could make a big show too, but we would not be so dishonest as to try to palm that off as our own work, as the

State Convention does.

3. Alldredge compares institutions. He tells us the Convention has the big colleges and big everything else. But he neglects to tell you that these colleges and other institutions were built before the split by all the Baptists, and he himself concedes that the State Association churches were in a majority at the time of the split, and such men as Clark, Sims, Brown, Pasley, Box and thousands of others helped to build these colleges, and just because the deeds were in the name of the Convention the institutions were taken from those who built them. Now they brag of their big institutions. A highway robber had as well boast of his loot.

4. Alldredge judges strength by the number of messengers attending the State meetings. The reason the Convention churches are nearly all in the towns and cities and have better traveling facilities than churches in the country places where most of the State Association churches are located. The people in towns and cities have more money than country people have and hence they go in larger numbers to the general meetings. But a remarkable fact remains undisputed; almost every one of the old associations are composed of State Association churches. Saline, the oldest, is solidly for the State Association, Pine Bluff, one of the oldest, is solidly for the State Association, and one after another can be mentioned to the same end. *Not one of the old associations are solidly for the conventions.* Some new associations, which have split off from the old associations, may be counted for the Convention, but they did the splitting off. The first association to split was Benton County. The Convention men walked out of that and living witnesses will so testify. I was present. Only recently a new association has been formed by the Convention element splitting off from the old Pine Bluff, and Saline Associations. The Black River Association was formed by the Convention element splitting off from the old Spring River Association. All over the State the Convention element have split off from the

old Associations. Yet Alldredge has the affrontery to assert that State Association churches did the splitting off. But in making such an assertion as we have already seen, he contradicts himself for he said also that the churches were not in Associations and Conventions and could not be without ceasing to be Baptist churches. Of course it is common for a man who starts out to misrepresent facts to contradict himself, but sufficient has been said to prove that the State Association did not split off from anything, for they occupy the old ground both in the State body and in the local associations. But suppose the Convention is in the majority. Shall majorities control in such matters? If so we should all join the Catholics because they have a big majority over all other professed Christians. If we are to go with the majority we should all be heathen because the heathens have big majority over all claiming to be Christians.

5. Alldredge says that he will not be an accuser of his brethren for, says he, to accuse the brethren is a "work of the devil," but in the very next page (p. 4), he declares that the State Association was "organized out of a spirit of strife and division." Thus he accuses his brethren of a very bad thing, and by that confesses to be under the influence of the devil. How much influence will a man have who confesses to be under satanic influence?

Misapplication of Facts and Some Falsehoods

Mr. Alldredge declares that the State Association has gone back on five of his original contentions that were advocated in the beginning of the controversy. He specifies as follows:

1. That the churches should send out the missionaries. Everybody connected with the State Association knows that we have not abandoned this contention. Every single missionary we have was first sent out by his church and then recom-

mended to the co-operating churches for support. All the messengers do is to recommend the support of the God-called, and church-sent missionary. If Mr. Alldredge does not know this he is ignorant, and should not be writing about a matter he is ignorant of. If he does know this he willfully falsifies. Which horn of this dilemma will he take? It makes but little difference with many of us which horn gores him.

2. That the missionaries should so report as to show the destitute fields labored in. Mr. Alldredge would have you believe that we have abandoned this contention. We have not. In the first place we do not have supplemental pastors who labor as pastors and call it mission work. All of our missionaries are expected to work in destitute fields, meaning by destitution anywhere the principles held by the State Association are not believed. If a missionary goes to a self-supporting church it is with the distinct understanding that he goes there to get that church to assist in having the Gospel preached in places of real destitution. We still stand for honest reports.

3. The churches in the State Association have equal representation in the association regardless of the size of the membership or the amount of money contributed. Alldredge himself acknowledges that we still hold to this principle and practice. It is a practice, and it is a principle. If the commission was given to individuals then individuals should be represented, and that would demand the numerical basis. If the commission was given to men who contribute money, then the financial basis is right. But if the commission was given to the church as such, and to each and every church, as such, then, the church being the unit of the work the church basis necessarily follows. The whole question is as to what constitutes the unit. If money is the unit, then the financial basis results. If the church is the unit, then the church basis results. *To whom was the commission given?* if to individuals as such then the individuals should do all the commission commands, and that includes baptism and the Lord's supper, Alien immersion and

open communion would necessarily follow. This is why so many Convention men are driven to it by logic of their position. But if the commission was given to the churches as such, then follows close communion and strict baptism. That is why no Association Baptists are open communion and alien baptism advocates. There is no logical standing ground for alien immersion and open communion among association Baptists. Glad that Mr. Alldredge concedes that we differ from the Convention on this point.

4. That the office and expense of the corresponding secretary be abolished. Mr. Alldredge declares that we have in fact a corresponding secretary and that Bro. J. A. Smith is the man. There is a wide difference between the work that Bro. Smith does and that of a corresponding secretary. Let us note some of the differences. On page 8 Mr. Alldredge says that a part of the duty of the Convention secretary is "to issue membership cards to delegates on a basis of one to every $250 contributed to the work of the Convention." These membership cards admit the delegate to the Southern Baptist Convention. Such messengers are the overwhelming majority in the Southern Baptist Convention. Mark you, these delegates are appointed by the secretaries, so says Alldredge. Thus the state secretaries actually name the overwhelming majority of the delegates and that makes it absolutely impossible to reform anything in the Convention unless the secretaries decide it shall be done. Let me name the delegates to any Convention and I assure you that I can control that convention. Thus the entire Southern Baptist Convention is controlled, body and soul, by the state secretaries. Bro. Smith has no such function to perform in his work. He can't name a single messenger to the General Association. That alone is a mighty big difference. Brother Smith is a treasurer who is a missionary also, and has no authority over anybody, and the secretary of the Convention has superintendence over the Convention missionaries and thus violates the scripture where it

says: "The princes among the gentiles exercise authority over them, but it shall not be so among you." (Matt. 20:25-26). That is another big difference. Still another difference; Brother Smith has his duties plainly laid down in the Statement of Principles, but the secretary has no specified duties in the Convention constitution, and he is therefore a law unto himself. We never can know what the secretaries are doing for sure except *as it leaks out in such pamphlets as Alldredge has written.*

5. The right of churches to instruct their messengers. Mr. Alldredge says we have abandoned that idea. He does not quote any document to prove it. He simply tells that which is not true. We never have abandoned the principle that a church is capable of attending to its own business and can therefore tell its messengers what is expected of them. Why misrepresent a matter like this to deceive the people?

6. The plan of co-operating with the Home and Foreign Boards. Mr. Alldredge declares we have gone back on that. Does he mean to say that we now favor co-operating with the Home and Foreign Boards? Did he mean to be silly or did he mean to deceive? Alas! Such morals as show up here.

Some Bald Assertions

On page 5 Mr. Alldredge declares: "Every intelligent Baptist on earth knows that when a preacher is ordained by his church to the full work of the ministry, he is thereby commissioned to do any kind of work his brethren may call for and the Spirit of God prompts him to do, whether missionary, evangelistic, or pastoral work."

Remark: If so a preacher may, just because some individuals without church action, ask him to do so, become pastor of a church when the church did not call him to the pastorate. Let Mr. Alldredge try that with some Baptist church and see how he comes out. If that is true a preacher may launch an evangelistic campaign in a church where he has not been invited. Let Mr. Alldredge try that and see how he comes out. Why not apply the same principle to mission work? State Association churches do. The Bible tells us that the church at Jerusalem sent out Barnabas (Acts 11:22). If you say that was ordination, then what was Acts 13:1-6 where Barnabas was sent out again? State Association churches send out their missionaries just as is seen in Acts 11 and Acts 13. But Convention individuals go contrary to the scriptures and presume to send missionaries. Is it wrong to go by the scriptures?

On page 6 Mr. Alldredge says it is not right for a church of ten members to have as many messengers to an association as a church of several hundred members. Why not? Is it right for a man with only one child to have one vote when a man with fifteen children only has one vote? Why not make the vote in proportion to the size of a man's family? Let me hand this package back to Mr. Alldredge in another form. A church of ten members might have more money than a church of a hundred members. These ten members could give ten thousand dollars to the boards of the Convention. That would entitle them to forty delegates to the convention and they could have the secretary appoint forty delegates to represent them or rather their money. The church of one hundred members are poor and could pay only $245 to the boards and since that amount is five dollars short of the necessary two hundred and fifty the church would have no voice in the convention at all. Again the church of ten might have more genuine piety and brains than a church of a hundred. Do piety and brains count for nothing in the convention? Are numbers and money everything? Is the German idea correct that "Might," might of numbers and money, "makes right?" It seems the Convention folks think so. Why not let all the churches in on terms of perfect equality and not allow the accident of mere numbers and money allow one church to dominate another? Why not adopt God's democracy? The State Association has. The only question is to what constitutes the unit of representation. If the church is the unit then equal representation follows. The Bible makes the church the unit because the Lord gave the commission to the church and not to the individual. That settles it. Hence equality follows whether a church is large or small. Equal representation insures that no church, just because of the accident of numbers shall dominate another church that is smaller. It is God's democracy.

Another bald and false assertion is that it costs more to pay the expenses of the State and General Association than it does to pay the expenses of the Conventions. The way he figures out the cost is to take the salaries of Smith and Winters and count that as expenses. But Smith and Winters are themselves missionaries and charge for the actual time given to the work as missionaries. The secretaries of the convention are superintendents of others and not themselves missionaries. Hence it is legimate to count their salaries as a part of the expenses. But it is not legitimate to count the salaries of some of the missionaries as a part of the expenses. Thus he seeks to mislead. But suppose it costs ten times as much to run a scriptural association as it does to run an unscriptural autocracy, I would gladly foot the bills rather than submit to an evil that seeks to subvert the principles Baptists have died for. But the cost of the two bodies figures little in the real contention, for right should be upheld at any cost and evil, such as the conventions are, should not be tolerated if their services are given free.

What Is the Difference?

The above question is asked over and over again, in Alldredge's pamphlet. The reader has already seen very much difference. But the following differences will appear to every thoughtful person.

1. Difference in motive. Twice Alldredge declares that it

is the purpose of the Convention to "take the world for Christ." He said on page 16: "With your help we could put over this campaign and take the whole State for Christ in the next five or ten years." The Convention people are world-takers. The State Association churches believe with the Lord that "evil men and seducers shall wax worse and worse" and that "as it was in the days of Noah, so shall it be when the Son of man comes." When people get it into their heads that it is their duty to take the world it begets the conquest idea and the conquest idea was the foundation of Roman Catholicism. It means war in a worldly sense and not *strict obedience, leaving the results with the Lord.*

2. Difference in representation. The Convention is on a numerical and financial basis, while the State Association is on a strictly church basis. This difference is enough, all other differences being settled, to keep us apart. Difference in methods. The Conventions have superintendents of missions under the names of secretaries, while the State Association has a traveling treasurer who superintends nobody but himself.

3. The boards of the Conventions send out and control missionaries, but in the State Association the church of which the missionary is a member sends the missionary, and the messengers recommend such church-sent missionaries to the co-operating churches for support. The Convention missionaries work under the superintendence of the secretaries and the State Association missionary works under the supervision of the church that sent him out.

4. The Convention has a board of seventy-five members appointed by the Convention, no church being consulted, but in the State Association the churches are in the saddle by each church electing a member of the Missionary Committee. One has the individuals composing the Convention in the saddle and the other has the churches in the saddle.

5. The Convention access a quota on the churches, stating definitely what each church should pay. The State Association

asks all to contribute as God has prospered them, they being the judges as to how much they have been prospered. One is an imitation of the Methodist assessment system and the other the scriptural system of individual responsibility before God.

6. The Convention has "drives" for money and calls in their missionaries and evangelists to make the "drives." The State Association respects the voluntary system of the Bible and gives attention to preaching to sinners and leading souls to Christ.

7. The Convention has adopted the war methods of raising money, boldly copying after the war drives. The State Association does not believe in driving the churches nor do they believe in co-ercing the churches as men and women were co-erced during the war for money.

8. The Convention sets the number of souls they are going to save during a given period. Page 19 of Alldredge's pamphlet he says: "20,000 converts baptized every year" as a goal. State Association churches believe in preaching the gospel and not dictating to the Spirit of God how many shall be saved.

9. Convention churches "call out the called" and in doing so exhort sinners to repentance. State Association churches do not meddle with this work of the Holy Spirit in calling men into the ministry. The Convention ministry has been commercialized by their method and it will get worse as the days go by.

10. Conventions encourage unionism and the State Association and the General Association discourage it. The Southern Baptist Convention has a standing committee on unionism and they have been in actual correspondence with committees of other denominations looking to a union. A few belated Convention men in Arkansas are opposing this unionism, but the whole trend is in that direction. Nobody knows it better than does Mr. Alldredge.

Other differences could be enumerated. But these will suffice. We might mention the difference in the "spirit" of the two bodies. The Convention is domineering, come my way or not go at all. The State Association is devoutly scriptural and asks to be allowed to pursue their way in peace. The Convention people profess not to fight (see Alldredge's statements in the pamphlet) and then, hypocritically, do nothing but fight. The Convention people profess to be so very religious that sugar would not melt in their mouths, and then turn right around and make a slander sheet of their State paper and seek to ruin any man who opposes them.

Mr. Alldredge prophesies failure for the State Association. He says it will be dead in a few years. The wish is father to the thought. If he lives a few years longer he will see the proof of the fact that he is a false prophet, for a prophet who speaks falsely shall be exposed by the failure of his prophecy coming to pass.

This assault on the State Association warns us that the war is still on. We must defend ourselves and not mince words. We have the truth and, when used, the truth is invincible. But if we presume that we have the truth and do nothing, the advocates of Convention error will overrun us. They can use the seventy-five million dollars they will soon collect to fight the truth. In God we trust. So mote it be.

OTHER BOOKS

False Doctrines Answered or Modern Heresies Exposed came out in 1924 and *Modern Delusions* in 1925. This last mentioned booklet was a reprint of an issue of the *Baptist and Commoner,* the demand for it being so great that it "was thought best to give it more permanence than newspaper form." The book was designed as a help to those deluded by traditions and to combat those delusions.

Other booklets for which we have no date of publication were *President Washington a Baptist, Startling Facts Concerning Evolution, Baptist Churches in All Ages, Associations Are Scriptural, Bible Proved by Science, The Story of a Sermon* and *One Hundred Reasons for Not Being A Campbellite.* He was one of the four writers of *Conventionism Refuted.* The others were D. N. Jackson, L. S. Ballard and M. P. Matheny. In partnership with D. N. Jackson, he wrote *Evolution Unscriptural and Unscientific* in 1926.

Debates that were published in book form were *Borden-Bogard Debate, Penick-Bogard Debate, Warlick-Bogard Debate, McPherson-Bogard Debate, Porter-Bogard Debate* and *Hardeman-Bogard Debate.*

Christian Stewardship is still a popular study course Dr. Bogard gave to the Sunday School Committee. It has been used by many churches, Bible Classes, Auxiliaries and other groups for a Bible study course through the years and is still very much in demand.

One of his last books was *The Golden Key,* a text-book on Bible Analysis. It has been used in church study courses, young peoples' meetings, auxiliaries, as well as a text book in Missionary Baptist Seminaries and Institutes. This book was given to the *Seminary Press,* a printing press he established which belongs to the Missionary Baptist Seminary, the theological school he helped to found.

Ben Bogard never made any money from the books he wrote. He gave them all away. They have always sold well because churches want these valuable aids to Bible study written by the experienced old soldier of the cross.

BOOKS WRITTEN BY BEN M. BOGARD

(OP) means that this book is now out of print
The other books are available through your book stores)

1892 Four Reasons Why I Am A Baptist (OP)
1894 Christian Union or the Problem Solved (OP)
1897 Church Government (OP)
1899 Throgmorton-Bogard Debate (OP)
1900 Pillars of Orthodoxy or Defenders of the Faith (OP)
1980 Baptist Way Book
1909 Fifty Two Bible Lessons (OP)
1909 Child's Question and Answer Book
1910 Fifty Two Doctrinal Lessons
1911 Fifty Two Expository Lessons
1912 Socialism Exposed (OP)
1914 Old Landmarkism Made Plain (OP)
1914 Campbellism Exposed
1915 A Manual For Sunday School Workers (OP)
       (Reproduced on page 340 of this book)
1916 The Hardshell Heresy
1919 A Startling Convention Onslaught (OP)
       (Reproduced on page 403 of this book)
1924 False Doctrines Answered or Modern Heresies Exposed
       (OP)
1925 Modern Delusions
       President Washington A Baptist (OP)
       Startling Facts Concerning Evolution (OP)
       Baptist Churches In All Ages
       Associations Are Scriptural
       One Hundred Reasons For Not Being A Campbellite
       (OP)
       Bible Proved By Science
       Story Of A Sermon (OP)

Conventionism Refuted (Partner with three others, OP)
Evolution Unscriptural and Unscientific (Partner with
    D. N. Jackson, OP)
Christian Stewardship
Golden Key

DEBATES

Borden-Bogard
Penick-Bogard (OP)
Warlick-Bogard (OP)
McPherson-Bogard (OP)
Porter-Bogard (OP)
Hardeman-Bogard (OP)

BOGARD'S POEMS

The heart of a poet also lived in this man who often seemed stern and unyielding to those who did not know him well. He was uncompromising in his stand on matters of Baptist doctrine and defense of the faith but his gentle nature was apparent to those close to him. His love of beauty was evident in his various descriptions of the long trips which took him to many fascinating places. He delighted in all of nature's wonders.

One of his poems, "Sure as the Rainbow Spans the Sky" was set to music by Roy M. Reed and he has given us permission to print this composition.

Another of Bogard's poems was inspired when a little ten years old boy, Edwin Dando, drowned just west of the "free bridge" over the Arkansas River. Dr. Bogard was passing

SURE AS THE RAINBOW SPANS THE SKY

Ben M. Bogard

Rey M. Reed

1. Sure as the rain-bow spans the sky. The Lord has sworn
2. His oath His pro-mise and His blood, Se-cures my safe-
3. When from the gloom-y grave I rise, To claim my home

I shall not die. His blood was shed His life was giv'n;
ty and my good. A home in Heav'n He will pre--pare.
a--bove the skies, My soul in peace and joy shall be.

That I might live, with Him in Heav'n.
His joy and hon----or I shall share. Re--deem-tion O'
For my re--deem----er I shall see.

the blessed word. The price was paid by Christ the Lord; Sure

as the rainbow spans the sky; The Lord has sworn I shall not die.

422

over the bridge at the time and happened to look down into the water just as the boy went down for the last time. "I saw his hat floating off," he said. "The body lay under the water two days before it was found. Being taken with the Muses I wrote the following lines which are dedicated to the bereaved mother. Any other mother who has lost a son may be helped by the sentiment, however poorly expressed."

This is Dr. Bogard's poem:

THE DROWNING OF EDWIN DANDO

Out on the river's foaming crest,
Above the bridge, a little west,
A cry was heard, "O do your best
    To save me!"

The little darling, young and fair,
Lay cold in death for two days there;
Alas, the weeping mother fair!
    "Edwin's gone."

The cruel wind, the ruthless wave,
Have snatched the boy that fortune gave,
And put the darling in his grave,
    Edwin Dando.

A weeping mother's wail is heard,
A city's sympathy is stirred,
On lips and mind, and heart, one word,
    "Edwin."

Let pity make its earnest speech;
Let love a Christian lesson teach,

And forth a helping hand to reach
To Edwin's mother.

When from the gloomy grave he'll rise,
To claim his home above the skies,
No tears shall dim the mother's eyes,
As she greets Edwin.

At the end of this poem pasted in his scrapbook, this notation is made by Bogard's hand: "I think the best little poem I ever wrote. B. M. B."

BOGARD – THE EDUCATOR

"Bogard Court." This picture shows the Guthrie Memorial building and one of the apartment houses on the block known as Bogard Court. He gave these lots to the Seminary. There is another apartment house on the west side of the seminary building also.

BOGARD — THE EDUCATOR

Ben M. Bogard held the deepest respect for knowledge in any field, and, particularly, in the scope of Christian education. He received his own training at the cost of sacrifice and hard work but his determination kept him in school until he had completed his studies for his calling. He knew the value of preparation and knowledge. His life was spent helping young preachers to receive their ministerial training. He was connected in one way or another—by giving lectures or raising money or as publicity agent—to a number of schools.

As early as 1894 he took part in discussions in the West Kentucky and West Tennessee Baptist Institutes held in Fulton, Kentucky, in January and in Kenton, Tennessee in March. In August, 1897, he read a paper entitled *Church Government* for the Southeast Missouri Bible Institute held in Dexter, Missouri. "This was the first session of the Institute and it was agreed to hold these sessions each year." He read a paper, *Resurrection of the Dead* and preached on *Prayer and Prayer Meetings* when this school was held in Fredericktown, Missouri, in November, 1897. His paper, *Miracles,* was read when Charleston, Missouri, entertained the session in April, 1898. This same year, he wrote, "During 1898 I was instrumental in building Charleston Baptist College. A campus of four acres was bought and a brick building of four rooms was built on it and paid for. The property is worth about $5,000.00."

In 1899, his journal notes: "Attended the first session of the Arkansas Baptist Institute which met at Jonesboro, November 16. I read a paper on *The Pastor in the Highways and Hedges* which apparently was well received."

In his journal, he also noted that on the second Sunday afternoon in January, 1900, he gave an address to the Speers-Langford Military Institute and then in May, 1901, he

427

brought the Baccalureate Address at Southwest Baptist College in Bolivar, Missouri. On May 29, 1901, ''the degree of Doctor of Divinity was conferred on me by that institution, an honor which I appreciate.''

Through the years, he often brought commencement addresses to various schools, some of which were: Beavoir College at Wilmar, Arkansas in 1903, Mt. Vernon High School of Trenton, Arkansas and Buckner College in 1904, the High School in Magnolia, Arkansas, 1916, also the High School in Cotton Valley, Louisiana. At one time he brought the commencement sermon for the Searcy Presbyterian College of which this note was made in the paper: ''Searcy Presbyterian College has honored Eld. Ben M. Bogard, pastor of the Searcy Baptist Church, by selecting him to preach the commencement sermon. This is a deserved compliment to a good man . . .''

In May 1924, he brought the graduating address of the Missionary Baptist College in Sheridan and ''this college conferred the honorary degree of Doctor of Laws on me.'' In 1925 he gave the commencement sermon for ''Poughkeepsie Agricultural High School in Strawberry, Arkansas.''

Bogard worked for the Buckner College, Wicherville, Arkansas, to help them raise money on which to operate. He began this work April 8, 1907 and noted in his journal: ''I accepted work as agent for Buckner College, Wicherville, Arkansas, and began work April 8 and made a tour and preached at De-Queen, Grannis, Stamps, Waldo, McNeil in Arkansas and at Cotton Valley and Springhill, Louisiana, and two sermons at Pecan Grove, Arkansas in April. During the month of May I preached at Blue Mountain, New Prospect (near Magazine) Dayton, Argenta, Wicherville, Bald Knob, Forrest City, Marianna and LaGrange, ten sermons. At each of these places, I worked for Buckner College. May 26, I preached the commencement sermon for Buckner College. I also preached that night in the college chapel. During the month of June, I preached at Huntington, Mena, Ashdown, Buckner, Magnolia,

Prescott, Malvern, Benton, Bryant, Magnolia, as I traveled in the interest of Buckner College. Preached September 30 at Tuckerman, Arkansas, and spoke for Buckner College."

During his lifetime, Ben M. Bogard was to spend many such hours of travel, raising money for colleges so that young men could be trained. From the beginning of his ministry, he was ever busy doing all he could for the young preachers, helping them to secure a Christian education. Money was scarce and it was difficult indeed—sometimes nearly impossible—for these young men to go to school.

Bogard conducted many Bible Schools in various churches throughout the country. In 1914 he "delivered four doctrinal lectures during Argenta Bible School" and in 1913 (October 23-24) he brought two lectures before students of Jacksonville College. In 1914, he conducted a Bible Institute at Montague, Texas, for the preachers and Sunday School teachers. Fifteen students came from January 5-7. In November, 1915, he held a Bible Institute at Laurel, Mississippi and May 5-12, 1916, a Bible School and Sunday School Institute at Sharon Church near Gotebo, then in April a Bible School at Tell, Texas. In March and November, he lectured to students of Jacksonville College in Texas and in 1920, he taught a Bible School at Louin, Mississippi and one at Springdale, Arkansas in 1921. He lectured before the college in Sheridan in 1921, also in 1923, which year he taught a Bible School in Springdale, Arkansas. In 1926 he taught Bible Schools in Gurdon and Center Point. In 1931, he conducted a Bible School in Morrilton and in 1932, he taught the following Bible Schools: January—Palestine Church, near Huntington, Arkansas; February—Birdtown, near Morrilton and in Imboden; March—Sulphur Rock, Arkansas, and Calvary Church near McCrory; October—fifteen Bible lectures to the Sheridan College. In 1933, he taught a Bible School at Macedonia Church near Jonesboro. This was the year he taught the Bible School at Antioch in Little Rock. It was the last year the college in Sheridan was in existence and the year before the Missionary Baptist Seminary was started in Little Rock, Arkansas. He held Bible Schools in Jonesboro and in Corsicana, Texas, early in 1934. As he taught these schools over the country, he became more and more convinced of the need of a school designed especially for young preachers in particular, and all Christian workers.

PREPARING FOR A SCHOOL

In 1909, interest in the Buckner College was beginning to wane. According to the minutes of the State of Arkansas Missionary Baptist Association, in the report on Education, "our interest in the Buckner College is not what it should be. We have not done all we could and should for this school and others . . ." This same year, three messengers from the Big Creek Baptist Church (later named First Baptist Church) at Sheridan proposed to erect a college building on a ten acre campus at Sheridan. It was not to cost less than $10,000 and this was to be presented, both building and ground, out of debt to the Landmark Baptist Churches composing the State Association. They asked the State Association to endorse the proposition and pray for it.

Along with these resolutions was one from the trustees of the Buckner College in which churches were asked to set aside a day as Buckner College day and take offerings consisting of "the price of a day's work" for a building fund. Still another resolution was:

"Report XII.—Resolution
"WHEREAS, We all see and feel the need of a school centrally located with a sane and sound theological department, and
"WHEREAS, We are abundantly able to provide such a school, therefore
"BE IT RESOLVED, That the following brethren named

be, and they are hereby appointed, a Board of Trustees, and they are hereby empowered to do the following things:

"1st. Advertise the fact that such a school is to be founded.

"2nd. Select the location of the school and pass upon any bonuses that may be offered.

"3rd. Name the school.

"4th. Elect a president and faculty.

"5th. Erect necessary buildings.

"6th. Report their labors to the next annual meeting of this association.

"THE BOARD: M. P. Matheny, Ben M. Bogard, R. C. Walker, R. R. Adams, E. T. Sears, W. M. Webb, W. R. Cross, C. C. Winters, F. P. Davis, J. M. Langston, S. D. Sawyer, D. M. Cloud, E. R. Carswell, W. A. Crutchfield, C. R. Powell, J. A. Scarboro.

"This board is also instructed and empowered to begin their labors immediately, and to push with all possible rapidity the work committed to it." —C. R. Powell."

All of these resolutions concerning Christian Education were unanimously passed.

Though the need was recognized and the move was started, for a number of years, little was accomplished toward this goal of a Missionary Baptist School. Each year it was discussed at the annual state meeting of the messengers of the Arkansas Baptist Association. In 1914 the report on Christian Education called on the churches to give more heed to the "cause of Christian education" and said, "Therefore, since we have no Landmark school of high training, and since Jacksonville College, located at Jacksonville, Texas, stands for the principles which we advocate, we recommend it as a safe and sound institution for the training of our children and especially our young preachers." In 1915, a long report set forth the needs of a school, but once again recommended supporting Jacksonville College, though reminded the people, "We believe that the churches of this association should establish and maintain a school or college within the borders of this state."

In 1917 at Second Baptist Church in Malvern, on the afternoon of Tuesday, the first day of the messengers body meeting, M. P. Matheny offered this resolution which was adopted:

"WHEREAS, The Baptists of Arkansas are in great need of a well-equipped school in which New Testament principles may be fostered, the coming ministry trained for their high calling, and our young people trained for their life work; therefore, be it

"RESOLVED, That the Committee on Nominations be instructed to recommend for election a committee of seven well-chosen brethren to serve as a permanent committee for the establishent of a school for our people. It shall be the duty of this committee to canvass the whole situation as pertains to the school interests of our people and proceed in any way which seems best to them in securing, establishing, equipping and conducting such a school, and report at the next session of this Association."

The committee appointed was: J. A. Smith, M. P. Matheny, W. E. Sherrill, E. B. Jones, C. P. Thompson, W. R. Jones, W. A. Crutchfield. This committee met while the association was in session and organized. They began taking bids for the location of the proposed school. M. P. Matheny was the leader in the movement. It is interesting to note that in this same session in the report on Christian Education, "That the churches composing this association be urged to locate, build, equip and maintain a Baptist college of the first order at the earliest day practical. In the meantime, your committee most heartily recommends Jacksonville Baptist College . . . that a cash collection be taken to assist in paying teachers' salaries in this institution . . ."

The committee pertaining to the establishment of a school met in Little Rock March 5, 1918, to consider the bids submitted. The meeting and its purpose had been announced in the

Baptist and Commoner. After "due consideration, the committee, accepted the splendid proposition submitted by the people of Sheridan, Grant County, in Arkansas." The *Report on Christian Education* by J. L. Brown, D. N. Jackson, Ben M. Bogard and J. A. Smith, after recommending that the Jacksonville College be patronized by our people, read: "We note with pleasure the progress that has been made in building a College at Sheridan, Arkansas. The campus consisting of thirteen acres has been paid for. Plans and specifications for a commodious building have been drawn and some subscriptions have been made toward building." They recommended that a man be put on the field to raise money and the building be completed as soon as possible.

BEGINNING THE COLLEGE

More than a year passed before any definite steps were taken toward opening the school. In June, 1919, the Baptist Church at Sheridan proposed to erect an annex to their house and give the school the use of the entire building until a permanent plant could be erected for the college. The offer was accepted gladly, a faculty elected and other arrangements made for the opening session on September 23, 1919. The formal opening was September 22.

In the messenger body meeting at Big Creek Baptist Church in Sheridan, November 4-6, 1919, in the report on Christian Education, the announcement of the opening was made. The Board of Trustees made their report, noting they had accepted the First Baptist Church's offer of a building and listed the faculty: J. A. Smith, president; W. H. Hodges and E. B. Jones, teachers. Brother T. C. Rushing was treasurer of the school. The enrollment on this first opening was twenty six students "with prospects of reaching the number of forty or more by the first of next January. We have eight young ministers . . ."

Two years later in 1921, the College Trustees purchased a tract of eleven acres of land adjacent to town. The *Baptist and Commoner,* June 25, 1924, reported, "On this campus the new college administration building is being erected. This new building is a two-story brick structure with class rooms, study hall, library and large auditorium. The building is modern, well equipped and furnished."

Published as the purpose of the school was this report: "The Missionary Baptist College at Sheridan stands as a concrete expression of the desire of the Missionary Baptist Churches of the State of Arkansas. The Missionary Baptists have ever been concerned for the suitable education of their children. They are conscious of the importance of an institution where the Bible is taken as the heart of its curriculum . . . never was there greater need of a college owned, controlled and supported by the Missionary Baptist Churches of Arkansas." Hopes were high and enthusiasm warm as the work so long dreamed of got underway. However, it was soon apparent that earnestness and zeal were not enough. The school had to be financed and soon it was apparent that enough money was not being received.

On November 4-6, 1924, the messenger body met in Benton with Spring Creek Baptist Church. The report given by A. Van Der Horst, now president, sounded dismal. He said, "In view of the present conditions the educational feature of our denominational work has become significant and solemn as never before. The 'premonition of catastrophe' which has long haunted the imagination of friend and foe of our Missionary Baptist College has been actualized in an empty treasury and a gloomy prospect of the continuation of the college. We actually face a condition of the worst kind ever known. We remind ourselves that every day we are engaged in a colossal struggle . . ."

There were 76 students enrolled and others were coming in. The student body was getting stronger every year, but finances were not sufficient. Mr. Van Der Horst suggested that a College Day be set for collections to be taken, a cash collection to be taken that night and pledges made, then remember the college in prayer, and "if it must be so—let us give our college, young as it is, blessed as it was, a respectable, and honorable funeral. Let us pay its large debts first in order to prevent slanders and gossip and accusation, and then let us close its doors by the first of 1925 and attend schools and colleges which are not ours."

Ben M. Bogard was a visitor in the meeting of the Board of Trustees of the College March 23, 1920 and a proxy for C. C. Winters on August 28th of that year. On April 8th, 1924, he offered the use of the mailing list of the *Baptist and Commoner* as an aid in financing the college. By May 4, 1926, he was a member of the board and became the secretary on May 6, 1926. February 5, 1927, he became president of the board and April 7, 1927, he was on a committee to try to borrow $10,000.

In the 1927 report, J. W. Overall was president and again there was a call for increased interest in the college and the need of financial support. In 1931, the minutes reflect that this college "one of two schools of Association Baptists in America" had an enrollment of 24 in the 26-27 session, 48 in the 27-28, 186 in 28-29, 166 29-30, 129 in 30-31 and 115 in 31-32. There was still a "great need for funds for past obligations" and for improvements.

On June 21, 1932,Bogard was still chairman of the board. He had served on many committees trying to finance the college, working diligently to raise enough money to keep the school going. He wrote in January, 1933 in the *Baptist and Commoner:*

". . . Fourth, we just must not allow our college work to fail. It is gloriously succeeding so far as the good work that is being done is concerned but we are not supporting it by our contributions as we should. I have felt humiliated by reading the Campbellite papers when I see in them that the Campbellites are coming across with the thousands . . .''

Then in April, 1933:

"TWO THINGS WE MUST NOT NEGLECT

"First and most important is our Missionary Baptist College at Sheridan. The teachers are right now unable to pay their board and they are greatly embarrassed. How President Overall manages to live is more than I can tell. The teachers are in great need right now . . .''

The announcement was made in the November 4th, 1933, *Baptist and Commoner* that Missionary Baptist College in Sheridan, Arkansas, would open for the second half of the first semester Monday, October 30, 1933 and could receive credit for half a semester's work by Wednesday, December 20, that the second semester would open January 2, 1934 and close April 13. The College had been placed on the 33-34 list of first class accredited colleges, but there was still that dire need for money. "No salaries have been set for members of our faculty. We are living by faith. That living will be supplied when God causes you to send the money to the treasurer of our college. Some money must be had at once for past due obligations. A few companies have threatened to take away all we have purchased when we owe only a small percent of the cost of the materials, if we do not pay the accounts in full at once. We haven't the money to pay even small accounts . . .''

People were urged to support the college with this plea: "You are hereby called on to vote for or against our Missionary Baptist College. When you have sent one dollar or more we will know you are not in favor of the College closing. If not, we will know you are voting for our college to close. Send all votes to Mr. Guy M. Veazey . . .''

In spite of all his pleas and desperate attempts to raise the needed money to keep this college owned by the churches of Arkansas, it finally was forced to close its doors. The minutes of the 1933 session reflect a resolution that, since the public school system of Sheridan wanted to buy the property and that the indebtedness could be shifted from the State Association to the Public School District No. 37 in Grant County, an agent was appointed to represent the "said Association in closing a deal with the said public school district or any other purchaser of said properties, by means whereof the above mentioned indebtedness may be liquidated: authorizing said agent to execute deed and all other instruments necessary to the coveyance of title from the State Association to said purchaser." The resolution was signed by Guy M. Veazey, T. C. Rushing and C. N. Glover. This committee completed their work relative to the sale of Missionary Baptist College and made their last report, asking to be discharged in the 1935 State Meeting at Jonesboro.

The twelfth and last annual commencement of the Missionary Baptist College in Sheridan was held in the College Auditorium on the evening of May 19, 1933. The prayer was offered by Conrad Glover. Music was directed by Miss Lois Ferguson, music teacher, and Dr. J. W. Overall, president, presented the diplomas. The class address was delivered by Ben. M. Bogard. Even at this time when asked if the college would close, the cryptic answer was, "the college would live until it died." Dr. Bogard's comment was "Certainly we shall not arrange a funeral until there is a corpse. One reason why the college lives on is the sacrificial way the teachers go on with the work. They teach almost without salary . . . They have done without and they have actually suffered, but the school has lived . . . Of course, they can't go on this way forever." This last commencement address by Dr. Bogard is printed here:

THINGS THAT ENDURE

In a magazine called "Truth," a so-called free-thinker journal, appeared the following statement: "Bishop Manning

dodged the celebration of the bad end that came to his Savior.''
This statement had reference to a public function of some
church people in New York. The atheist who wrote the statement surely must be blind if he cannot see that everything else
that existed during the time of Christ has failed and the work
of Christ is the only thing that has endured during the near
two thousand years since the so-called ''bad end'' came to
Jesus. The Roman Empire that permitted His crucifixion has
passed away, and all the institutions of that day have passed
away, but Jesus estabished a church that exists still and He
started a movement that has revolutionized the thinking of the
world. That atheist himself was compelled to acknowledge the
work of Christ by the date he put on the top line of his magazine which was ''May, 1933.'' What is meant by May, 1933? It
means that 1933 years ago Jesus, who came to the ''bad end,''
caused a change in the calendar and all civilized nations date
their letters and legal documents from His birth. Judging
from a purely human viewpoint the work of Jesus was the
most wonderful success of any in the world.

Many of us are uncertain these days about almost everything, but we are certain about Jesus. His love fills our hearts,
His leadership directs our lives, His powers supports our efforts, His grace keeps us to the end. You may lose your life
savings deposited in the banks or laid up in lands, stocks or
bonds, but you will never lose the treasure laid up in heaven
where moth and rust doth not corrupt and where thieves do
not break through and steal. Human security fails, but God
does not fail. There is no cause for a Christian to despair so
long as God is on His throne.

It is certainly a wonderful experience when one can rest
his hope on the promises of God. We have gone through disas-
ter, through storm, floods, earthquakes, and disease. Storms
and contagion spread. The strength of man is too puny to sustain in such trials. Misfortune and calamity overcome. Therefore blessed is the man who puts his trust in Jesus, for under-

neath are his everlasting arms.

I realize that to many, such talk as this is an idle tale. A man of the world does not relish such sentiment. Men of the world build houses of brick and stone, they accumulate fortunes and put their trust in these earthly things. The cruel days through which we have been passing for the past two years prove that there is nothing permanent in such things. Fortunes have been swept away. Health has been destroyed. Homes have been ruined. Men have developed a fear complex and they are afraid to turn this way or that. Men, who have been considered rich, are on the bread line. They live in fine houses and have these houses furnished with rich furniture. Cut glass and fine silverware cover their tables. But the dishes are empty in many cases. They can't eat rugs, however fine these rugs may be. Neither can they sell these fine things to buy food. These formerly rich men have no money to buy food from the farmer and the result is the farmer cannot sell and we have the strange condition of having the world filled with good things to eat and wear and yet people are going half clad and hungry. We are traveling in a vicious circle and getting nowhere. God is showing us that we cannot depend on these material things. Highly educated men and women are out of employment and cannot find it even when they would be willing to take the humblest position.

A story was recently told that impressed me. A man was on a high bridge crossing a river. He was evidently intending to jump over the banister and drown. A man near called to him and asked him what he was doing. He replied that life was not worth living. Everything had gone against him and he wanted to die and get away from it all. The man begged him to wait and talk it over before doing so desperate a thing as that. He did wait and the two talked for an hour and then both of them jumped over and drowned. What was the matter with these men? They depended on the things of this world and did not put their trust in God. They trusted things that are temporal, uncertain, when they should have trusted God.

"The foundation of God standeth sure, having this seal, the Lord knoweth them that are his." (II Tim. 2:19). If you are building on any other foundation you are certain to fall. There will not be a government on earth that will stand—they will all go the way of Greece, Rome, Babylon. The United States is certain to go the way of all the others. We hear the expression, "The stars and stripes forever," but it is a false hope when you imagine that this government will forever endure. Our governments will go down with a crash and along with it all other world systems. The kingdom of God alone will endure. If you have been translated into that kingdom then your citizenship is safe. The bride of Christ is being made up and when she is complete then shall the end come. Such as that encourages us to labor on. Who knows but that a convert I make by my preaching may be the last convert necessary to make up the bride of Christ? A missionary in China or in Africa may be honored by leading to Christ the last one who shall make up the bride. The Lord is taking out a people for Himself and what does it matter what else we may have if we fail in becoming a citizen of God's kingdom and fail to be a part of the bride of Christ?

Many men counted great in this world have found to their dismay that the world cannot satisfy and if it seems to satisfy for a time it soon fails us and we face ruin. A short time ago the richest man in Sweden, Iva Kruegor, committed suicide; the richest man in Belgium, whose name has slipped me, jumped out of his own air plane into the English Channel and his body has not been found. Hugo, the richest man in Germany, not long ago, died of his own hand. The greatest financial wizard of the United States languishes in the penitentiary. In the commercial world we have all heard of the Armours, the Stevens, the Insuls, and the McCormicks. At one time they held in their hands the wealth of the United States, could make or break anybody they pleased. Stevens built the greatest hotel in the world and committed suicide. The Armours do not own a single share of stock in the famous Armour packing houses which they built and which bear their name. Mrs. McCormick died not long ago and her brother had to pay her funeral expenses to keep her from being buried as a pauper. The Insuls built up a two billion dollar power trust and are now hiding away in a foreign land dodging justice. And there is Mitchell, one of the greatest bankers in the world headed for the penitentiary. Yet many worry, fret and fume about this world and its fortunes. The Bible says that "things that are seen are temporal and things that are not seen are eternal." (II Cor. 4:18). We should live for the eternal things that endure.

If in your youth you could learn the lesson that God makes no mistakes and that He will make your life a real success if you put yourself under His care, and that real happiness comes from serving the Lord, and treasures in heaven are the only real success, yours will be the things that endure and when the world is on fire you will live on. If an earthquake moves the mountain into the ocean you will not be moved. Underneath you will be the everlasting arms. To you all things will work together for good. I recently read a poem written by Bob Shuler which I will pass on to you:

"Some folks live to worry and fret
And most folks have troubles to let;
But I never could see what good there could be
In making a blue day your pet;
So I just smile and take it, you know.
And just live along sorter so;
Whenever it rains, why I just let it rain
And whenever it snows, let it snow.
I don't invite trouble my way,
When it comes I don't ask it to stay;
I'm glad when it's bright and the world's running right

When it's not I have nothing to say.
For I guess the Lord knows what to do
Much better than I know or you
So when clouds hide the sky, why I just let 'em fly
And wait 'till He sweeps it off blue.
What's the use in my telling Him how,
Or raising a fuss and a row;
He runs well the machine so far as I've seen
And will ever more turn it, I low.
So I just whistle on and am gay
And let the Lord run it His way.
Whenever it's night why I say it's all right
And whenever it's day, why it's day.
And when in the grave I shall lie,
I don't think I'll murmur and sigh
But I'll peacefully stay till the great judgment day
And I hear Gabriel blowing on high;
Then I know I won't raise any fight
If the angel bands dress me in white,
And I won't fuss and pout if they usher me out
But will say that God's judgements are right."

The financial depression of the late twenties and early thirties had closed many places and the college was only one of these, but it had been the only source of training for young ministers in this area. But Dr. Bogard was not ready to give up. There must be a school where Landmark Missionary Baptist preachers could receive the kind of training they needed for preaching to Missionary Baptist Churches.

Bogard had met Dr. J. Louis Guthrie of Oklahoma and prevailed upon him to preach in Antioch Church. He wanted Antioch people to hear this educator.

". . . We jumped at the chance to get Elder J. Louis Guthrie of Oklahoma, our best scholar, to hold a series of meetings with us. He was already in Arkansas, having come to attend

the American Baptist Association, and he agreed to spend a
few days with us. So, we have been in a feast of fat things
hearing him preach. The results of the meetings will be reported later." —*Baptist and Commoner,* April 2, 1934. This was
a historic meeting because at this time, the first tangible efforts were made toward a new school.

THE MISSIONARY BAPTIST SEMINARY BEGINS

Three great men—Doctors J. Louis Guthrie, Conrad N.
Glover and Ben M. Bogard—realized that without a preacher's training school, the work of the American Baptist Association was doomed to failure. Steps were taken to fill the need
of the hour. In the following pages, the recollections of the
three men are presented to give a history of the beginning of
the school whose influence would be so far reaching that none
of the men could even dream of the magnitude of this great
work—the accomplishments for the American Baptist Association and Antioch Church.

The first entry in the records of the Antioch Church, April
1, 1934, reads: "Motion made that we engage Brother Guthrie
to carry out plans recommended by deacons to organize a
Bible School in our church and to have charge of the work."
This motion carried and so the "Bible School" was started.
Dr. Bogard's journal records this historical event in these
words: "Organized a Baptist Bible School in the Antioch
Baptist meeting house October 16. Have engaged the assistance of Elder J. Louis and Mrs. J. Louis Guthrie as teachers.
I teach one hour a day. It is a training school for preachers
and other Christian workers." His summary of the year's
work 1934 concerning the school was: "The Baptist Bible
School which I began in Antioch Church house, October 16,
has prospered and every prospect is hopeful. There is associ-

Dr. Ben M. Bogard

Dr. C. N. Glover

Dr. J. Louis Guthrie

Mrs. J. Louis Guthrie

ated with me in the school Elder J. Louis Guthrie, Ph. D. Fifty
six students enrolled the first year.''

On August 10, 1934, Dr. Guthrie wrote concerning himself :

GUTHRIE'S STATEMENT

''In the issue before this a statement was made that the
idea of the Missionary Baptist Institute was in the mind of J.
Louis Guthrie for a long time. While teaching in Oklahoma
Baptist University, he became so strongly impressed with the
idea that the uneducated preacher needed Bible training if he
never got a full literary education. Our preachers generally,
and I do not mean Missionary Baptist preachers, but I really
mean our preachers of American life generally, as I said,
preachers generally think that a high class literary education
gives a man a divine right to preach the Word of God. One
who has been in and through the routine of secular education
and taught in that role for many years should have the right
to speak on this subject. Now for 40 years I have been teaching on both sides of this question and on the middle ground,
said to be secular education called Christian Education in a
college or university. Now, I should find no objections to college and university education in true Baptist conditions. But
education is like everything else, it is built on the popular
thing at the time being. Now, for the preacher to take all this
popular training with all the traditions and even superstitions
injected into it by unscrupulous educators who seem to be organized to destroy Christianity and socialize the workers of
Christianity into a compact whole of social ideals, instead of
personal faith and belief as said, for the preacher to take all
this modern education, he will have no place for peculiar certain beliefs and training which are entirely Baptist, and without which he cannot be a Baptist. Now, if the Bible teaches
these peculiar things, like Salvation by Grace, Eternal Security, and the many other things which are the creedal beliefs of

Baptists, certainly the Baptist young called preacher needs training in exactly these things and especially he needs to be taught how to interpret his Bible in the light of Baptist beliefs.

"For this very purpose, the Missionary Baptist Institute was begun and fostered by a local Baptist Church. To go back to the very beginning of this preparatory history of the founding of this kind of school, J. Louis Guthrie went out of college and university teaching in 1923. During the summer of 1922, when he took typhoid and phlebitis, after having taught in Oklahoma Baptist University for many years, and having taught young preachers the very doctrines that Missionary Baptists now hear him teach, such as the autonomy of the local church, and anti-episcopacy, and missionary endeavor from the local church, and the other things surely believed among us, he became sure of the rights and powers of a local church as against all others, conventions, conferences, associations or boards or committees, or any other outside organizations determining to destroy the rights and powers of the local church.

"In Shawnee, Oklahoma, June 6, 1921, in Louis Guthrie's home, North Church, Shawnee, Okla., was organized. This church immediately set about arranging and working her own plans and programs for doing her own work and missions. Guthrie worked out the plan of correlated work inside a local church. This was written into a tract by W. D. Moore, who is listed as one of the seven great educators of the Southern Baptist educators of the past. This tract was adopted by the Southern Baptist Convention and then by the Missionary Baptist Churches of the South. These plans were copied by Associational Baptist Churches.

"In July, 1922, North Church began to practice these plans under the superintendency in Sunday School and training of Homer Gilmore of Heraldton, Okla. He was a young preacher in North Church. Then came H. P. Stith of Buffalo, Oklahoma. He was elected Sunday School Superintendent and Training Superintendent of North Church, Shawnee, Okla.

Under his supervision and Guthrie's plans the church began her work. When North Church was organized, during the summer and fall and winter of 1922-23, 50 preachers got right into the church and went to work. Guthrie then set about doing mission work. With his two automobiles and his eldest son, then 12 years of age, he began hauling preachers to appointments as far as 25 miles in every direction from Shawnee. The result was a young preacher was preaching out of that church to most school houses and small churches that far from the church. This aroused the jealousy of the powers that be in Oklahoma Baptist University and Oklahoma Convention. The result was Guthrie was let out of the university after having a contract to do Sabbatical Leave study in university of his choice. After this Guthrie found the university falsely advertising itself and he brought this before the Board of Trustees of the university and as a result, both the president and dean of the university resigned. Still North Church was growing and going on with her work for preachers similar to the Missionary Baptist Institute. This was very displeasing to the powers that be. As a result in five years she graduated about 365 persons and preachers in her courses. Naturally this stirred up a tremendous lot of opposition. The final outcome was a depression which closed it all out, and Guthrie resigned the church because of no support because of depressing events and financial obligations, with the Guthrie family in debt about $4,000.00. Nobody was impressed with the work then, and even Missionary Baptists were trying to build up a body of overlords. At this time, Guthrie's two daughters, Mattie and Ruth, graduated from the university and began to teach. The summer of 1926 Guthrie, Mrs. Guthrie and the two girls were offered the sum of $500.00 per month to take up Caldonia Baptist Academy, at Caldonia, Ark. They took it and worked out something similar to the Missionary Baptist Institute, but the Arkansas school system was then in reformation and this being connected with the public school system, it could not be made permanent. However, the family got out of debt and Guthrie went back to Shawnee, Okla. Then he was chosen State Missionary for Oklahoma Assembly. This was in 1932-34.

"In 1933, Guthrie went to Texarkana to the American Baptist Association and was asked to preach. He did so, and two brethren got into a tremendous argument as to whether that sermon should be printed in the papers. Both of these brethren are now out of it. In 1934, Guthrie attended the American Baptist Association at Benton. They tried to elect him to the position of mission secretary. He refused the place knowing that there must be some kind of school since Sheridan College was going out. The president invited Guthrie to go to Sheridan and lecture to the college. He did so and for 10 days lectured to the students in the building of the First Baptist Church in Sheridan. These were very depressing years and it looked like Baptist education for Missionary Baptists was about ended.

Guthrie went to Sheridan, then after 10 days came to Little Rock and lectured and preached in Antioch Church building. This was in March, 1934. He lectured and preached to Antioch people, at night mostly, the rest of the two weeks until the last Thursday. One of those nights Antioch called Guthrie to tell them how to build a Bible School for young preachers and others. He did not accept until September of that year. In the meantime the brethren asked C. A. Gilbert to save Sheridan College. The brethren did not respond. The college held its summer session and did not open for the fall. Dr. C. N. Glover, during the summer, wrote Guthrie to come and lecture to Sheridan First Baptist Church for 21 days. He came and taught Bible for 21 days and on the first Tuesday of that period Ben M. Bogard came to Sheridan and in the study of the First Baptist Church the Bible School was born. Dr. Glover said, "Why not a local Baptist Church, like Antioch, let the school have her building for teaching?" The building problem was solved, but no support for the teaching force. Guthrie asked Brother Bogard to get donations. He asked Mrs. Guthrie to teach the English. There was nothing in sight, but in faith Guthrie went back to Shawnee and with an offering from Sheridan First Baptist Church and a couple of Associations making donations the funds were accumulated for his move to Little Rock. He arrived on the 12th day of October, 1934. In two small rooms in Antioch Church building the school was begun. In the spring of that year Brother Bogard wrote Guthrie to write up what he thought ought to be taught in that kind of school. He wrote out the first curriculum, and yet, it is much like it is now. Dr. Bogard taught Bible Analysis and Defense of the Faith that year and he is still teaching that, much enlarged. Mrs. Guthrie taught English, Word Analysis, and any other necessary work for the two departments. Guthrie taught Greek, Hebrew, Bible Interpretation and everything else in the Institute.

"The school took with the folks, but support was very small. Guthrie preached to two half-time churches and made the most of his expenses. Then came the opposition. Some of the brethren began to see the possibilities of this. They formulated a plan to have an advisory committee and let it become a part of the American Baptist Association work. Brother Bogard and Guthrie knowing this would further Institutionalize the churches did not wish to do this, but still desired a local church to foster the Institute. The report got out at their refusal to let a committee or board control the school, that it belonged to Antioch and it ought to be killed off and they tried to kill it. Well, it is still going.

"That first year there were 56 students enrolled. There were college men, high school students, and many others. The students soon won the folks with their preaching and it became known that the students attending the Institute began to know the Bible and could preach it. Naturally, any new thing will get undesirables. Some students came that year, soon dropped out and spread dissatisfaction and now some of those same students wish they had had a bit more wisdom and remained, and had not spread dissatisfaction. As the year went on, the students began to ask for some one to teach music and public speaking. Guthrie brought them and paid the whole bill. The students being trained in Convention singing and music did not like the instruction and the department was dropped for the time being. For two years the teaching went on with three teachers. The school closed after seven months in 1935. The donations that year were between $600.00 and $700.00 and the school closed without debt." —*Orthodox Baptist Searchlight,* August 10, 1944.

Dr. Guthrie united with Antioch Baptist Church, October 21, 1934 on promise of a letter from a Baptist Church in Shawnee, Oklahoma. Prior to his coming here, he had been teaching in a number of schools, the latest being the Oklahoma Baptist University in Shawnee, Oklahoma. He made no apologies for running into difficulties with the Baptist Convention, both in the church and in the schools. "They threw me out on my little tin ear," he would laugh and tell us. *"The reason I accepted the call to come to Antioch Baptist Church and run a Bible School was because I was called by a local church, given the privilege of running the school myself without the interference of a Board of Trustees,"* he declared. *"I would not teach where the Board of Trustees could play 'ward heel' politics with the school,"* he often stated.

DR. C. N. GLOVER'S STATEMENT

"I knew Dr. Ben M. Bogard personally from the year 1900 until his death in 1951.

"As one of the three co-founders of the Missionary Baptist Seminary in Little Rock, Arkansas, I think it proper that I give something of my own personal background with reference to Christian education.

"I was brought under conviction for my sins and was born again September 23, 1909. From this experience I had convictions that I should become a member of Harmony Baptist Church, but I was not received into that church till 1913.

"I had convictions by the time I was seventeen years of age that my life's work was to preach the gospel. This was one year before I was baptized into the fellowship of Harmony Baptist Church. This was when the need of Christian education became a problem for me. My education in the secular field was very limited and we had no school for the training of preachers. I know I was not capable to preach the gospel. I held in my heart a longing to preach the gospel, but did not make it known till 1922. All of the excuses that I had hidden behind were removed in the year 1919, when the Baptists of Arkansas opened the Missionary Baptist College here in Sheridan, even in the church house where I held membership.

"I enrolled as a part time student in 1919 but up to this time I had not made known my call to the gospel ministry. My idea in entering this college for preachers was that someday I might try to preach and I had better avail myself of the opportunity to be trained in the work while I had an opportunity. Not being a preacher, and in this college I was associated in class with almost no one except preachers, I attended class for a few weeks and then dropped out. I knew that if I stayed with that class that I was going to be compelled by my own conscience to enter the gospel ministry. The next two years were miserable years. When the fall term in 1921 opened, I again enrolled as a student. I stayed with the preachers that year and in September, 1922, I made my call to preach the gospel known to Big Creek Baptist Church and was voted the liberty to exercise in that field. By this time, I was fully convinced that my life's work was in the gospel ministry. I stayed in this school as a student and teacher for fourteen years. I finished all the courses ever offered in the school except in music and home economics.

"I earned the degree of Bachelor in Theology in 1925. I was given a high school diploma in 1930 (I was 34 years of age when I received my High School Diploma). I also received an Associate in Arts in Bible in 1930. I received an Associate in Arts in secular education in 1931. At the end of a summer semester, I received a "licentiate in instruction" in 1931 and at the Board of Trustees meeting on May 22, 1931, I received the honorary Doctor of Divinity degree, then in October, 1937, the Missionary Baptist Seminary in Little Rock, Arkansas, conferred on me the degree of Doctor in Church History and on the same date, the Seminary conferred on me the degree of Doctor in Bible. My purpose in mentioning the above conferments is to establish the fact against any doubt that I believe in Christian education as I have shown the lack of it kept me out of the gospel ministry for ten years. Knowing there were many men who were called to preach the gospel and that my problem was their problem, it was a sad day in my life when the Missionary Baptist College in Sheridan was forced to close its doors for lack of financial support. This college met my needs but with its doors closed what was going to meet the needs of the other young men who desired to receive training as I had desired ahead of them?

"I was a member of the Board of Trustees and secretary of the board from 1926 to 1934. Most of these years, Dr. Ben M. Bogard was chairman of the board. The Missionary Baptist College was organized, owned and controlled by the 'State Association of Missionary Baptist Churches of Arkansas' but the churches of the association did not make funds available for the trustees to continue the operation of the college. It was closed in a state of bankruptcy. The sale of all of its property and assets did not bring enough money to pay its debts. Previous efforts to operate such a school had failed for the same reason. It has taken a long time for our people to learn that you have to pay for what you get.

"Enemies to Dr. Bogard and others have said that the

school was deliberately closed so as to start a school that Dr. Bogard could in a dictatorial way operate to his own personal advantage. Nothing could be further from the truth. The idea of a one church owned school and operated by one church was my idea and not Dr. Bogard's.

"Dr. Bogard was a member of the Board of Trustees of the College for many years, served as secretary from May 4, 1925 till February 3, 1927. In the meeting of the board on February 3, 1927, Dr. Bogard was elected president or chairman and served in this capacity till the closing of the college in 1934. No man in the Arkansas State Association of Missionary Baptist Churches contributed more in time, effort and means to keep the college going and to keep it from closing than did Dr. Ben M. Bogard.

"I offer a few facts to confirm my declaration that the Missionary Baptist College in Sheridan was forced to close for lack of money on which to continue operation.

"The minutes of the Board of Trustees of the Missionary Baptist College reflect there was never a time during the entire existence of the college that finances on which to operate the school was not the greatest problem confronting the trustees.

"The minutes of the Board of Trustees in its meeting February 23, 1932 is worded as follows: 'The chairman asked that C. N. Glover make statements relative to the reasons why request was made that the executive committee of the Arkansas State Association call an extra-ordinary convention of the State Association. The reasons assigned were as follows: we your Board of Trustees have reached the end of our strength and wisdom and we are asking for counsel.'

"The extra-ordinary session of the State Association met in the First Baptist Church house in Sheridan on March 31, 1932 with these results:

" '. . . A committee composed of the trustees was asked to arrange a suggestive program by which the messengers could pass upon it in the interest of the M. B. C. for which purpose

1:30 was set ... A lengthy resolution was read and adopted which is filed with the clerk. The trustees, not being able to put it into effect, other plans were adopted in the regular session in November. The session only lasted one day. Elder J. E. Cobb, Moderator. J. G. Murry, Clerk.' —From Minutes of the State Association of Missionary Baptist Church, 1933, page 7.

"Even the State Association called in extra-ordinary session for the one and only purpose of trying to solve the financial problems of the college were unable to do so. The minutes of the Board of Trustees reflect that every avenue with any promise of supplying the financial problems of the college was considered, many of which were undertaken but ended in failure.

"In despair because there seemed to be no way to get the money with which to carry on the college work and preserve the honor of our churches and people, the board appealed to the State Association to take such action as it could to meet the financial needs of the college, or order it closed, the property and assets to be sold and that the money received be applied on the debts of the college. This matter is by resolution recorded in the minutes of the annual session of the State Association held in Macedonia Baptist Church in Greenbrier, Arkansas, on November 7, 8 and 9, 1933.

" 'A resolution was read by Dr. Bogard pertaining to the Missionary Baptist College as seen below. Motion to adopt. Carried.

" 'A motion was made and seconded to authorize the board of trustees of the college to sell and deed property as set forth in said resolution and according to law. Carried.' (State Association Minutes, November 7, 8, 9, 1933).

It may be thought by some that since Dr. Bogard read the resolution, he was the author of it, but that is not so. I, Conrad N. Glover, wrote the resolution and since I was not going to attend this session of the State Association, I placed the resolution in the hands of the late J. G. Murry and requested that it be read and considered at Greenbrier.

" *The minutes of the Board of Trustees of the Missionary Baptist College at Sheridan, Arkansas, and the action of the State Association on the matter forever precludes an idea in the mind of any person that Dr. Ben M. Bogard led in a movement to close the Missionary Baptist College at Sheridan so he might start a school he could control and use for his own personal advantage.*

"The idea of the kind of schools now being operated by our people had not even been dreamed of when the State Association, by vote of the messengers, authorized the Board of Trustees to sell the property of the college and pay its debts. But everyone was conscious of the need of a school in which to train our preachers and labourers after the closing of the college at Sheridan.

"My Version of the Founding of the Missionary Baptist Seminary in Little Rock, Arkansas

"I have stated already my own personal problem as a young man. I did not want other young men to have the inner struggle I had. With the closing of our college, they would be faced with the same problem. I prayed much about the matter and entreated the Lord to open up a way that would meet the needs of our people in the field of Christian education and training. In my meditations and prayers, my attention was directed to the New Testament and the history of the churches mentioned in it.

"I learned:

"That the 'Great Commission' was delivered to a local church and not to an association of churches.

"That the local church was to be the Lord's teacher of 'the all things commanded.'

"That teachers were set in the local churches and not in associations of churches. 'And he gave some apostles; and some, prophets; and some, evangelists; and some, pastors and *teachers'* (Ephesians 4:11).

" 'And God hath set some in the *church,* first apostles, secondarily prophets, thirdly *teachers* . . .' (I Corinthians 12: 28).

"The thought came to mind that to meet our needs, a local church can be found with room to house a school and a membership willing to cooperate and promote a school according to our needs in their church property.

I believed then and I believe now that such a school would be scriptural. With these ideas fixed in mind the next problem was to find a suitable teacher, or teachers, favorable to this type of school who would be willing to teach in it.

"I believe the Lord solved this problem for us. The annual messenger meeting of the State Association convened in the First Baptist Church in Magnolia, Arkansas. Dr. J. Louis Guthrie of Shawnee, Oklahoma, was there and preached a sermon on the subject, 'The Three-fold Work of Grace in Man's Salvation.' I judged this to be an unusually great sermon and was greatly impressed by the man who preached it.

"Dr. J. W. Overall was at that time president of the College and I was pastor of First Baptist Church in Sheridan. Overall invited Guthrie to speak to the student body of the college in the daytime and I, with the congregation, invited him to speak in the church in the evenings. It was evident that this man, J. Louis Guthrie, was the man for the kind of school I had been thinking about. The question was, could he be interested and obtained?

"Dr. Guthrie was a guest at the last college banquet served at the college building in Sheridan. At this banquet I first made known my plans to try to open a school for our people in the fall of 1934 since the college was closing its doors at the end of the spring semester. I remember where he and I sat in the building when I told him of my thinking and planning. When I had given him an outline of the plan, his response was,

'Praise God for this is the kind of school that I have always wanted to teach in.' In this conversation, Dr. Guthrie left the impression on me that if such a school could be started he would take charge of it and promote it. Dr. Bogard was present at this banquet but the matter of the school was not discussed with him there.

"Bogard invited Guthrie to come to Antioch Church in Little Rock. While he was in this meeting in Antioch Church, he discussed my plan for a school and teaching faculty with Dr. Bogard. Bogard saw the possibilities for such a school; then called me by phone and inquired if I would be available to talk the plan over with them. We fixed the time and place of the meeting. The three of us met in the pastor's office in the First Baptist Church in Sheridan. We prayed, we talked and we planned the necessary procedure to initiate this kind of a school for our people. It was the opinion of Drs. Bogard and Guthrie that I would undertake to house the school in the First Baptist Church building in Sheridan, Arkansas. I made about the following statement to them: "Sheridan is a small town and has no industry. I have seen students come to Sheridan to attend college, hoping to find part time employment so as to provide for the needs of their families, but there were no jobs to be found and they, in disappointment, would be forced to leave the school and seek employment elsewhere.' Based on this condition, I proposed that the school be set up in Antioch Church in Little Rock where there was at least a better chance for the students to find part time employment. Dr. Bogard accepted this suggestion and Dr. Guthrie agreed to it. These brethren, Bogard and Guthrie, took the plan to Antioch Church in Little Rock, Arkansas, and the church adopted it.

"All of the arrangements and details were worked out and the school opened in Antioch Church in the fall of 1934. From that time until the present the school has met the needs of our people in this area. The Scriptures teach that 'a tree is known by its fruits,' and I rest the soundness and success of the Missionary Baptist Seminary in the fruits it has produced through the years.

"I do not think that I could have done for the school what Dr. Bogard did for it and I am doubtful if any other man amongst us could have measured up to his stature in the founding and operating of the school. He gave it all he could give while he lived and then willed that it should have all of his worldly goods when he died.

"I hope that before any person would smear the name 'Ben M. Bogard' that his record may be completely known and that the smearer will compare records to see who has served best and given most.

"My association with these two great men, Bogard and Guthrie, has greatly influenced my life and my ministry. May the eternal God bless their memory and let their works follow them till Jesus comes again."

The three founders agreed that the commission to teach the Bible was given to a local church—"and that's where the authority is."

In planning the ideal school for Missionary Baptists, these goals were set forth by Dr. J. L. Guthrie in the earliest paper on "The American Baptist Bible School" which was a type-written "catalog" of courses offered in those first days. They declared: "These two men saw such a need arising for preachers and Christian workers, that they decided on such an institution or school, to be made a part of a local church since that is the only kind that will fill the Baptist idea in any sense.

"Because of institutionalism, many so-called Baptists have gone on the rocks as Baptists and churches have been put under the dominion of conventions, associations and other bodies arising out of the supposed need of the churches, these men felt it a need to not burden the churches with any kind of institutionalism and by fulfilling the commission in a local

church, they felt assured that then any kind of institutionalism would not be set in the associational work of the churches.

"This School must serve a definite purpose and that purpose to be entirely for preachers and Christian workers. Anything that might be worldly in its plans and programs or that
might be seized on by any self seeking individual to further
his own interests is to be left out of consideration in the establishment of this school. And further, anything that can be
seized on by the secular school systems of state or denominations shall be left entirely out of consideration in this school.

"Credits for State recognition will not be observed, yet
there shall be sufficient records kept of the work done to establish the standing of the student in other religious schools
should he care to enter and take further study. This school
shall deal entirely with matters which pertain to the Bible,
church history, preaching, the Baptist interpretation of our
faith, public speaking, gospel singing and local church business, evangelism, defense of the Faith, English Bible, Bible
Interpretation, correct English for preachers and when the
preacher can take the subjects—Greek, dealing entirely with
the New Testament, and Hebrew. Naturally these will not all
be put in at once, but the school will not be long in having a
full course in all these branches and such others as needed
when the development requires. On the whole this school will
never be in secular education and will not teach any of the four
divisions, as such, of the colleges namely, language, science,
either natural or social, not religious.

". . . The church notified Dr. Guthrie of their call and
asked him to set the time of the beginning. The Antioch Church
offered their buildings for the work of the school to begin as
soon as Dr. Guthrie can arrange for the necessary time to begin. This arrangement will put the school entirely out of institutionalism and under the work of a single church, not putting
the churches into institutionalism nor legally tying them to
any sort of a program but the program of the New Testament.

Naturally all of the churches want their young preachers trained and taught in the Bible, the book of all the churches. They will in this way cooperate with the school and help maintain it as from it they will be reaping the fruit in their preachers, trained and educated in the Bible and Bible subjects and practice.''

In November, 1934, J. Louis Guthrie was elected as one of the messengers to the State Association which met in Magnolia. In this meeting a young man, L. D. Foreman, came in contact with him and Ben Bogard. There he surrendered to the call of the ministry and came back to Little Rock in Guthrie's car. He had the closest relationship, even as a son, to both of these men from that time. He started to school as one of the first students and has been in this work since—first as student, then student teacher, professor, dean and president—the office he now holds.

In the Magnolia meeting, the first resolution relating to the new school was passed:

"WHEREAS, We have a Bible Training school at Little Rock, therefore

"BE IT RESOLVED, That we urge and assist our young men, called of God to preach the Gospel, to take advantage of this opportunity to better fit themselves for their sacred calling; and, furthermore,

"BE IT RESOLVED, That we urge these brethren to always prayerfully depend upon the Holy Spirit as the promised Divine Helper in the preparation and delivery of their sermons." —Signed, J. T. Moore.

In 1935, the *Christian Education Report* recommended:

"Arkansas Missionary Baptists have no secular college now. However we do have a Bible school furnished them by Antioch Missionary Baptist Church of Little Rock, Arkansas. This school is under the superintendency of Dr. J. Louis Guthrie, Ph. D., and management of Dr. Ben M. Bogard, who is also secretary and financial agent; with an English department under the instruction of Mrs. J. Louis Guthrie. The Bible is taught in three languages: Hebrew, Greek and English, by Dr. Guthrie, with Bible Analysis and Defense of the Faith taught by Dr. Bogard. English Bible courses taught by Dr. Guthrie are Bible by Ages, Bible Psychology and Bible Pneumatology. We have also short courses for busy pastors, missionaries, and evangelists. You are invited to come for a thirty days course if you can do no better and return to your field of labor. We recommend that an offering be taken for this school in connection with this report." Mrs. H. D. Steele taught courses in Bible History and Literature and Public Speaking. Mr. Steele taught music. One "lecture course" was carried on throughout the year by Dr. Conrad Glover who brought lectures each Thursday afternoon. His course was on doctrines and the organization and history of the Lord's church as compared with other church history, doctrines and organizations. Additional lectures were enjoyed when such men as J. Frank Norris, John A. Walker, M. D., C. A. Gilbert and Wid Gilbert came with messages on various subjects.

Of the fifty six students enrolled that first year, forty were young preachers. Support was by offerings from the churches. Only Dr. Guthrie was paid a salary, Bogard, Mrs. Guthrie and the Steeles giving their time and energy. Many food offerings were sent to help the students stay in school.

The December 2, 1934, minute of Antioch Baptist Church reports, "Upon motion duly made and seconded Elder Ben M. Bogard was made business manager and treasurer of the Bible School." On February 3, 1935, the church agreed to accept fifty cents from each student to be applied on utility bills and janitor work.

By April 1935, it was apparent more space was needed. Attendance in church had increased and also in the Bible School. The pastor asked the people to think of this need, study over the matter and "pray over and be ready for it." In June 1935 the deacons recommended the proposed enlargement, but lack of time "prevented further discussion and the church took a recess or postponement of this matter until next Wednesday night, June 5, 1935." On this night the motion was made that the building be enlarged. There was a long discussion but the motion carried with six votes opposing it. On June 12, a motion carried that "the pastor appoint a committee of three to submit plans and specifications for the addition to the church buildings. Brethren Booher Whitley and Pritchard appointed."

On June 19, 1935, the church was called to order by the pastor. The purpose for this meeting at 9:15 P. M. was "for the hearing and determining plans for the enlargement of the building. Plans were presented by Brother Booher." So, the motion was made and carried to adopt the plan and the committee who prepared it was discharged. Brethren Booher and Whitley were employed to take charge of the building in the church enlargement and Brother Bogard "was authorized to remove tree in back of church and use for wood."

Records regarding the building of this addition to the church are in the Antioch Church minutes:

July 7, 1935: "Brother Pritchard, chairman, asked the church to grant full authority to purchase materials, employ labor and all other matters pertaining to the building to C. A. Booher. It was moved and duly seconded that this be done—carried."

August 4, 1935: "Brother C. M. Pritchard, chairman of the deacons reported that building operation would begin in a few days."

The "Baptist Bible School" as it was first called enrolled 74 students during the 35-36 year which began October 1, 1935.

It took a few years to complete this building project. Much of the work done in construction of the annex on the church was by the student body in the Seminary—"donated labor." On December 6, 1936, "Brother C. M. Pritchard asked the church to thank the Baptist Institute students for the work on church, also ask all who can to come Friday night next to help. Brother M. M. Donham asked that the men help him with flooring and other work tomorrow (Thursday).''

In August 1937 there was ''nearly enough money in the treasury'' to lay the concrete floor in the basement and the church authorized the deacons to proceed with the work.

The school opened in 1934 with an all day service, the ladies of Antioch furnishing dinner for all guests. This continued to be an annual affair on school opening day'' for visitors to attend and make it a day of fellowship and ''homecoming.'' In the *Baptist and Commoner,* September 18, 1935, Dr. Bogard made an appeal for more people to send in contributions for the school for three reasons:

''First: Because we have the Sheridan School problem out of the way. We had that on our hands last year and some were greatly embarrassed by that college debt. But that is out of the way. Thank the Lord and now all are free to help in the Baptist Bible School.

''Second: It was an experiment last year. None of us knew just how it would turn out. But the experimental stage is over now and we are dealing with certainties. The Baptist Bible School is an assured success. We now have a finishing school which will enable college graduates to come to our school and finish their education. Yet at the same time we are glad to have any student who is able to read the English Bible. Come right on no matter how little you know and we can help you. We have ten or more college graduates who say they will be here October 1.

''Third: We will be at a greater expense this year than last. It will take more of everything this year than last, hence the need for more money. We need a greater library. We need to pay Dr. Guthrie better than we did last year. This is why we are asking for more. But every contribution is to be a voluntary contribution. If you think the work is good and want to help it, don't hesitate to do so. We need your help and

Faculty: Dr. Bogard standing at the pulpit. Front row: (l[
Leo Causey, J. P. Johnson, Fred Steve[

helping will do you good. Of course, we are expecting many
boxes of things to eat for the students. In fact, we have faith
to believe that there will be a great increase along all lines
this year. But come to the opening Tuesday, October 1, and
see us start. Money should be sent to Ben M. Bogard, Treasurer.''

The experimental stage was over and even these men of
faith had little idea of the great impact the ''Baptist Bible

D. Foreman, L. D. Capell, J. P. Johnson, Edward Byrd. Second row: ...bbard, Mrs. J. L. Guthrie.

School" was to make on Missionary Baptists throughout the United States and in foreign lands. But little by little, each year, the student body increased along with financial gifts of support. Dr. Bogard never "let up" from his self imposed task of building contributors for this work. Through the paper he kept the needs of the school always before his readers. Everywhere he went he boosted the school and asked for finances.

An example of his enthusiasm for the new school is reflected in this announcement:

"BIBLE SCHOOL BEGINS OCTOBER 1

"New Class Rooms—New Library
"—J. Louis Guthrie, President—

"The Bible School will begin its second session on October 1. Students are already arriving. Letters are continually coming in and the prospect for attendance looks extremely good.

"'A large building has been rented for a boarding club for the young men who will come. Expenses will be low, if students are careful. Several of our students will board, others will do light housekeeping, and already some of our last year students have made arrangements for board and room.

"The work will not be an experiment this year. Courses have already been mapped out and several courses added. There have been no arrangements made about a teacher for Gospel Music and Public Speaking as yet on account of their being no funds to pay it. Now is the time to begin payments of pledges for the coming session. Donations on the various work of the school should begin coming in now. Send all money and food donations to Ben M. Bogard, except such as are sent personally to Dr. J. Louis Guthrie. This means that all food donations and finances of the Bible School going into salary for Dr. Guthrie should go through Dr. Bogard . . . However, everything pertaining to the Bible School please send to Dr. Bogard, for he is Secretary-Treasurer of the Bible School.

"Everywhere I have been this summer, reports are coming to me of the good work our preachers have been doing. They have showed marked increased ability as preachers from their attendance last year. This year promises much more of that kind of reports from churches, for they all say they want their pastors to attend and get the attitude of teaching.

"Students having no English training will receive instruction in these branches especially English, which will fit them for Bible Study. These courses will not be needful for students, who have already finished high school and college. The school does two things. Prepare students for the study of the Bible, and finish them in their study of the Bible. College and high school graduates will be well fitted for our courses.

"Before the year is completed, Antioch Church, which gives us free use of her building, will have about nine large class rooms, and the work will be well equipped with plenty of room. We have the theological part of the library of Sheridan College now. There are several hundred of these books for free use of the students.

"There are no problems of discipline. Students are all put on their own honor. They come and are free to receive the instruction . . ."   —*Baptist and Commoner*, Sept. 18, 1935.

During those days, Bogard did a great deal of traveling. He always gave credit to the great church he pastored for allowing him to be away so much and willing to "share" their pastor with the people of the nation who constantly demanded his services as evangelist, debater and lecturer. But, everywhere he went—whether to hold a meeting, a debate or a Bible School—he used the opportunity to get his "first love— the Baptist Bible School" before the people. He was able to be away because of Dr. Guthrie's being a resident of Little Rock and the numerous young preacher students who were willing to supply the pulpit for him. On May 5, 1937, Antioch minutes reflect this arrangement: "Dr. Bogard, our pastor, stated that he had made arrangements to be away the entire months of July and August, holding meetings in Mississippi, Alabama and Arkansas and asked that the church elect Dr. J. Louis Guthrie to supply during these months. It was moved and duly seconded and by unanimous vote of the church Dr. Guthrie was elected pastor for July and August."

School leaders have always inspired the students to be mission minded. Here, Bogard (center), John A. Walker, M. D., Shawnee, Oklahoma and J. Louis Guthrie on his left, with Seminary students, dedicate the first 1937 Ford Automobile delivered in Little Rock, Arkansas, and paid for by friends to the mission work of W. L. Randall standing on Guthrie's left. The car was taken to China on a return trip of the missionary.

In November 1937, the church "now having a surplus in the general fund" would "take over the janitor and utility bills which had been paid by the Bible School."

One of the policies of the school was that the faculty members chosen would be those trained in the Missionary Baptist Institute (by this time, it was known by this name). On the evening of May 25th, the Missionary Baptist Institute closed its fourth year with commencement exercises in the auditorium of Antioch Church. J. Louis Guthrie presided and presented diplomas to sixteen young men and women. Additions were made to the faculty to go into duty the next session. Four young men who had completed much of their work were selected as faculty members while they were "pursuing further studies." These were: Travis Hubbard, L. D. Foreman, Hoyt Chastain and Lacy Woodson. "This addition to the teaching force will enable more work to be done and at the same time release Ben M. Bogard for field work which is so much needed.

It will also enable Dr. Guthrie to occasionally get away from the school to visit churches where he may be invited. In the past the work was so heavy and exacting that neither Guthrie nor Bogard could get away without damage to the school work. But with young men thoroughly competent to handle the major part of the teaching work, both of the original teachers may get away to where they may be called.

"The Missionary Baptist Institute is educating young men to be teachers in similar schools which no doubt will be established in the future. (Note: This was a prophecy made by Bogard which came to pass as the other schools began to be formed by men trained in this original one.) Already one of the young men educated in Hebrew and Greek at the Missionary Baptist Institute, is teaching in the Columbia Bible School at Magnolia. We are delighted to furnish the principal teacher for that good institution. That school started out with the announced intention of having no Hebrew and Greek because they had no one able to teach these languages in which the Bible was written but one of their local boys learned these languages in our school and they are using him, Elder Fred Stevenson, in their school work. That is fine." —*Orthodox Baptist Searchlight,* June 10, 1938.

During these early years, only Dr. Guthrie was paid a salary. Once in a while the teachers were given a small love offering when finances permitted. By the 1939-40 term, others had been added to the faculty and some had left. James Dew, James Walker, Ernest Payne, Mrs. James Dew, Miss Mary Slack and L. D. Capell were added to faculty and Hoyt Chastain and Lacy Woodson had dropped out. In 1941, Mrs. Dew, Miss Slack and James Walker were dropped and Edward Byrd was put on the staff. In 1941-42, the faculty consisted of, besides Bogard and the Guthries, L. D. Foreman, Travis Hubbard, L. D. Capell, Ernest Payne and Edward Byrd. Leo A. Causey was added to the regular faculty in the fall of 1942. Regular lecturers who came to the Seminary at intervals

Student body, 1942-43 term. This is taken in front of the Antioch Church building. The faculty is seated before the student body. They

were C. N. Glover, John A. Walker, M. D., A. T. Powers and J. W. Kesner. The next year Dr. A. J Kirkland served on the lecture faculty. In the 1944-45 term, Fred Stevenson and Stacy Owen were added to the faculty, then in 1945-46, Paul Goodwin and J. P. Johnson became teachers. For one year, 46-47, Albert Garner served on the faculty. At Bogard's death in 1951, this group of men were on the faculty: L. D. Foreman, president, C. N. Glover, vice-president, L. D. Capell, dean, Leo A. Causey, registrar, Mrs. J. L. Guthrie, Edward Byrd, Fred Stevenson, Paul Goodwin and J. P. Johnson.

The final disposition of the Missionary Baptist College property was not completed until 1939 when Dr. C. N. Glover "made an oral report on the remaining property of the Missionary Baptist College which consisted of books and folding chairs." The messengers assembled at Central Baptist Church in Texarkana voted to appoint a new committee of three to dispose of the remaining property of the Missionary Baptist College and that the committee divide the property with Columbia Baptist Bible School and the Baptist Bible Institute in Little Rock, Arkansas.

Either oral or written reports of the progress of the school and the money received and paid out were made regularly to the church by both Guthrie and Bogard. In October, 1939, both Bogard and Guthrie made a report that Dr. Guthrie had received $204.97 from Antioch Church and from outside the membership a total of $1259.41. Then, including taxes and rent paid on the house the total offerings received for the "Bible Institute" for the associational year, 1939, was $1344.93. That same year, the 1938-39 term, the first degree of Doctor of Bible Languages was conferred on L. D. Foreman.

By the beginning of the 1939-40 term, Bogard felt the school was "here to stay." This appeared on the front page of the *Orthodox Baptist Searchlight,* Oct. 25, 1939:

"*Missionary Baptist Institute Beginning Sixth Year*

"Best opening ever. More students the first day than ever

before and the average grade of the students is higher than ever before. Others write that they are coming and the prospect is for the greatest enrollment in the history of the school. Eight regular teachers for every day in the year and five lecturers engaged to deliver lectures through the year. The experimental period has passed and the great school would now go on if both Dr. J. Louis Guthrie and Ben M. Bogard should die. Some students have spent five years in the school and are prepared to carry on even if the teachers mentioned should pass away. Don't you want to help in this great work? If so send your contribution to Ben M. Bogard, treasurer, Box 663, Little Rock, Arkansas.''

This editorial portrays, as did most of his writings, the enthusiasm with which this man worked. He always said that people would support a success. Therefore, he always publicized the good, encouraging things about a work. He did not talk of the discouraging days that come to everyone, but concentrated on putting before the public all of the good. It also shows that he was building a work for Christ—not for Bogard. Even then after only five years, he knew he had trained men to carry on the work of the Lord without him, that it would not ''fall apart'' if he were taken from it. He was accused many times by enemies of the school of building a work around himself and many of his fellow workers were dubbed *''Bogardites.''*

No work enjoying such success for the Lord could go on very long without drawing fire from the devil. The students were studying Baptist doctrines and as they learned they went out to preach. A record of a period of ten years reflects that in a decade, 67,564 sermons were preached, 10,434 conversions witnessed, 5,924 baptized, 719 revival meetings held, 135,712 tracts and Bibles distributed, 4,953,213 miles traveled in their work and 23 missions established and 46 churches organized. This impressive record shows the evangelistic fervor and the mission inclination of the faculty and students. Naturally, the arch enemy of God would not stand by and see such a work flourish without a battle against it.

The controversy that came into the ranks of the American Baptist Association work was bound to touch the Institute. The preachers who had been trained in the Seminary and those who were presently attending made a deep impact on all the work in the nation, for as they finished their training, they became pastors of churches throughout the country. They had learned the Scriptures and they taught their people, so when the battle raged over the work of the Sunday School literature in Texarkana, these young preachers made their weight felt. Some of those who were attending school were not members of the churches they pastored—some preaching to more than one church. However, often they were messengers even though not members since the practice was that the church had complete jurisdiction over the qualifications of the messengers they sent (Article 3, Section 3). This was one of the tactics of the opposition—to get a clause in the Articles of Agreement that messengers *must* be members of the churches they represented, so that these students could not wield so much influence.

By 1937, already barbs were being aimed at the school. Those fighting it claimed that Bogard had changed in his belief and was not the same in many particulars. He answered these in the *Baptist and Commoner*, January 25, 1937:

"II. 'And now he has established the Missionary Baptist Institute and did it without consulting the churches and after beginning the school without consulting other churches he is calling on them for support.'

"*Answer:* I deny that I established the Baptist Institute. The Antioch Church by unanimous vote called Dr. J. Louis Guthrie to become the church teacher and asked me to assist him in teaching in this *Church School* for the training of ministers and other church workers. It is no more an *institution* than the Sunday School is. It goes further in its teaching than the Sunday School, but the principle is the same. No individual established the school. Can't the brethren see the difference between a church and a board? The boards do what they do without church authority, but Antioch Church, as a church, established the Missionary Baptist Institute. The Lord gave the Commission to the local congregation and not to a board of individuals. I believe in Church authority and not Board authority. Anybody can see the difference if he wants to see it."

"... 'Apology'????

"I want right here to beg the pardon of certain so-called *leaders* for not consulting them when the Antioch Church established the Missionary Baptist Institute. This mean opposition to me did not develop until after the school was established, for some good brethren do not like it when they are not consulted. But if the Antioch Church had thought she needed the wise counsel of these dear brethren she would have invited them to sit in a council before the beginning of the school. But feeling perfectly competent to attend to her own business, committed to the church by the Great Commission, she did not consult them. We again beg their pardon. Those who feel that the Bible School is a good work are asked to voluntarily contribute toward its support. No demand is made on anybody."

As time went on and the controversy within the ranks of the American Baptist Association continued, the school became an important factor in the contentions because of the growing number of young men being educated and going out to pastor churches over many states. This made a great impact on the thinking of the people and the only way those opposing the school and wanting power in the associated work could fight was to oppose the Institute. The accusations were many—that the association should have control of a school, that pastors should be members of the churches whom they represented in in associations and many other indictments. These were answered in fiery editorials by Dr. Bogard and others.

"A church that has a scriptural right to elect a preacher to give the church's message to the unsaved world, to admin-

ister baptism and the Lord's Supper—to represent the church
in such important matters—certainly has a right to elect that
SAME PREACHER to represent the church at a meeting of
messengers. A man who cannot see that has something wrong
upstairs—he had better stay out of the woods or squirrels
might get him. They like nuts. —B.M.B.."

"The tale was actually started that Conrad Glover and
Ben M. Bogard killed the school (College at Sheridan) and
took the money they got out of it to start the Missionary Baptist Institute. That was the biggest kind of a lie because there
was no money left to start anything and just three of us had to
go down into our pockets and pay the debt that remained after
the trustees paid on the debt of the college as far as the money
which was received from the sale of the property would go.
The three were J. G. Murry, C. N. Glover and Ben M. Bogard.
It was five hundred dollars with interest that we three paid
out of our own pockets. The other part of the lie was that we
used the money to start the Missionary Baptist Institute. It
took no money to start the Institute. It was not started on
money, but on the Bible, which we did not have to pay for.
Yes, the Institute was founded on the Bible and faith in the
Author of the Bible. Murry, Glover and Bogard all put time,
energy and money into the college and, as for me personally, I
put three thousand dollars into it, and never got a cent out of
it. We got what we deserved because the college was not founded scripturally—there is not a word about a JOINTLY
OWNED AND JOINTLY CONTROLLED SCHOOL IN
THE BIBLE. If somebody thinks he knows of a passage of
scripture for such a school, I shall gladly publish his finding
in the *Searchlight*.

"But there is scripture for a church owned and controlled
school. Jesus placed the teaching part of the commission in the
church, just as He did the preaching and baptizing and I chal-
lenge anyone to show the contrary. Did the Missionary Bap-

tist College do good? Certainly, it did good. Good is done in
the Convention and in other unscriptural organizations. God
will bless the truth wherever taught or preached and He even
blessed the wicked work of the devil by overruling his wicked
work for God's glory, but that is no reason for us to favor unscriptural organizations and methods, and certainly, we should
not endorse the work of the devil just because God overrules
it for good. We should have scriptural organizations and
scriptural methods and then expect abundant blessings from
God. —B.M.B.''

"The Apostle Paul gave sanction to privately owned
schools by teaching in the school of one Tyrannus for a period
of two years, as a result of which, all Asia heard the story of
Jesus. Acts 19:9-10. The Apostle Paul also is credited with the
establishment of a private school of his own in his own hired
house in Rome, where, the discrimination between his preaching and his teaching is explicitly set forth in the word of God.
Here he taught the things that concerned Jesus Christ in his
own school, in his own hired house and the scriptures say 'no
man forbidding him.' —Acts 28:30-31. In view of these facts,
if the Apostle Paul lived today and belonged to the American
Baptist Association, he would have to change his attitude toward private schools or suffer persecution from a number of
the brethren and several of the papers which purpose to be
contending for the right way.

"I am accused of joining the group that obeys the commandments of Jesus Christ as set forth in Matthew 28:19-20
and follows in the example set by the Apostle Paul. I am not
ashamed of this position. I have assumed it voluntarily and
will stay on it until my convictions change. —Conrad Glover.''

"SCRIPTURAL BUT NOT WISE"

"A speaker in the recent educational meeting at Temple

Church, Little Rock, said:

" 'It is scriptural for a church to own and operate a school but it is not wise.'

"Those present seemed to sanction it . . . others present seem to think it is not wise to be scriptural. At least they did not publicly offer any objections to the statement. 'Scriptural but not wise.' What next? —Ben M. Bogard."

Such editorials as these appeared in every edition of the *Searchlight* for several years as the battle for the school and for the work of the association became hot and fierce. Right triumphed and, though the association split, the faction went out and those remaining true to associated principles went on to greater things. The work grew in every phase and the Institute continued to flourish and to nourish and train preachers for greater work.

THE SCHOOL GROWS

Dr. Bogard not only gave his heart and his time to the monumental task of establishing a school for preachers, he planned for all of his possessions to be used for this purpose. Just before the tenth session of the Missionary Baptist Institute started, this article was printed in the *Orthodox Baptist Searchlight,* which paper Bogard had already given to the Institute:

"FINE PROSPECT FOR MISSIONARY BAPTIST INSTITUTE—1943-44

"In just a few days after you read this the Missionary Baptist Institute will begin its tenth session. The exact time is Tuesday, October 5, at ten a. m. We are expecting many visitors and the reader is cordially invited. We expect to spend the day together. There will be a sermon, much singing and prayer, testimonies, getting acquainted and hearing reports

School opening day October 3, 1944, at Antioch Baptist Church.

from the students who have spent the vacation preaching as pastors, evangelists and missionaries. We are expecting wonderful reports from the great work they have been doing.

"Nine years ago we started with nothing. Dr. J. Louis Guthrie, Mrs. J. Louis Guthrie and Ben M. Bogard were the teachers. There were not many students—something over fifty enrolled for the entire year. The teaching was done in two small Sunday School rooms of Antioch Missionary Baptist Church. The financial support was meager. Dr. Guthrie did not get as much as one hundred dollars a month and he picked up most of that by going out on Sundays and preaching as supply for such churches as called him. Mrs. Guthrie and Ben M. Bogard taught free of charge. Under such cramped conditions the work was better than could be expected.

"The next year there were more students and some better financial support, but there was not enough support to really give a comfortable living to Dr. Guthrie, the one teacher who was paid for his work. There was no dormitory—not a place where the students could lay their heads to be sheltered from the weather. They had to hunt places to live and they were put to it in finding anywhere to live. But none had to leave for lack of shelter. We weathered through the second year greatly encouraged and just as our courage began to rise, opposition to the school began; it grew worse through the entire year. The demand was made that we turn the school over to the Arkansas State Association or to the American Baptist Association and have it run by a board of trustees to be elected by one or the other of these associations. We informed all comers that we had a church school under the control of a Baptist Church and meant to keep it that way. We told them of several schools under associational control that had died and we had experimented enough in that way and that we intended to stay with the Bible and have a church school. We were then informed that if Antioch Church controlled the school that Antioch Church must support it. We were given to understand that other churches would not assist in supporting the school and that it would die for want of support. Nothing daunted, we kept straight on as we started and decided we would see if the threat was carried out.

"Very soon steps were taken by the opposition to start an opposition school, one controlled by an association, and the idea was that such a school would draw all the students away from us and leave us with nothing to work on. The preliminary steps for the new school were taken but the third year of our school was better in every way. More students and still better financial support. The opposition school was finally started, but did not hinder us in the least for we kept on increasing in number and financial support. The people became more generally interested and the support came from many and unexpected sources.

"A small rooming house was secured that helped very much in solving our problem as to homes for the students. Two more small houses were rented that housed still more students and thus we got by the best we could. Now we have reached the point where we can see a glorious future. We still have the small rooming house to shelter our students, and Pastor Ben M. Bogard, who is also Dean of the Missionary Baptist Institute, bought the large house—twelve rooms—situated on a plot of ground covering seven town lots on which other buildings can be erected that will furnish all the dormitories that will ever be needed. He has given this large house and these seven town lots to the church to be used for dormitory purposes of the Missionary Baptist Institute. Pastor Bogard gave a clear title deed to this excellent property. The property as it is now, is valued at $2500. The Antioch Church by unanimous vote accepted the property from Pastor Bogard and in addition gave him a vote of thanks for the gift. (Note: This is the property known as Bogard Court, 3300 Asher Avenue on which are located the educational building, and two apartment houses. and parking area for the Seminary.)

"We are now looking for someone to give at least $20,000 to put up the other buildings and thus secure all the dormitory space that will be needed for some time to come. If you can't give $20,000 you might give $2000 or $1000. But surely there is someone among our people who could give $20,000. We have been too prone to do business for the Lord on a peanut and popcorn scale. Too long we have been giving twenty five cents or a dime. It has even been a matter of surprise when some liberal soul gave as much as one hundred dollars. This should not be. Let us do big things for God.

"Dr. Bogard having set the example by deeding this valuable property to the church for school purposes, why not others follow his example . . .

"The great school has long since passed the experimental stage and is now an assured success on all parts of the ground. Doubts having been removed as to the future, the brethren who are able to do so can afford to risk their money because the

deed is just as secure as the deed to the church house . . .''
—*Orthodox Baptist Searchlight,* Sept. 25, 1943.

Though the early years of the school were lean ones, these
hard experiences taught these first students valuable lessons.
They lived without the luxuries today's people feel they must
have. Often these young men lived in the country without
electric lights, running water or gas. Those in town many
times had one room "apartments"—a room furnished with
the barest necessities—a bed, table, perhaps a chair and a
stove—these pieces sometimes were furnished by interested,
kindly people who wanted a part in the ministry of these
young men. It was not elegant furniture but usable. Tables
doubled as places to eat and to study, or to sit about and talk.
The bed often became the divan for guests. Usually, entertainment was a communual affair for everyone brought food and
had "pot luck." The storehouse provided by the churches
from over the state kept enough food so the students did not
starve. Delicacies one might desire were not among the gifts,
but the food was nourishing. In one drafty old rooming house
rented for the purpose of providing living space for married
couples—or groups of men who "batched" together—the old
fashioned zinc wash tub doubled as a bath tub. Sometimes,
they ate cornbread and green beans and sorghum molasses for
breakfast—gifts from good people—but they did eat. One time
two young men became the proud recipients of a beef roast,
a never to be forgotten luxury. It was boiled for several
days and the stock used for soup. Finally, when they got
around to eating it, the roast was completely tasteless from
too frequent meals of soup.

Often three or four families lived in one house, sharing a
bath. Though there was very little money, these rooms were
warm with fellowship and brotherly love, for common hardships bound them together and each one wanted to help the
other. Long hours of study together passed all too swiftly and
school years were gone. These early hardship made the later

material blessings so much more enjoyable and appreciated than they would have been otherwise. Enduring friendships were formed. They were wonderful years if lean ones. These fellows found riches in things far more precious than wealth.

The Institute kept growing. It succeeded in spite of the devil and his helpers. Tragically, the devil's work has not always been done by outspoken denominational enemies, but within Association Baptist groups. This school has succeeded but it has been a fight every step of the way to keep it pure and unspoiled and out of the "institutionalizing" so repulsive to its first president. Many times, men have fought to put it under the dictatorship of a "Board of Trustees" either in an association or other would-be rulers. But, through the years and in spite of the enemies, God has blessed this Seminary and it has stayed what it was meant to be—a school for preachers —a place of training without the red tape of the public or college systems or a board of directors. The local church has sponsored it, calling a president and his staff to run it according to Bible principles and teachings. If it should ever become anything else, it will cease to be what the founding fathers established it to be.

One of the first president's expression of education for the preachers is given in this article:

WHAT IS A CREDIT SYSTEM OF EDUCATION?

"In introducing this subject, I know that I am liable to bring about a bit of discussion among our Baptist people. How did the present system of Education in America arise? Well, our colonial system during the time when the colonies were in existence as colonies of England and other countries was entirely an imitation of what the colonists had in the mother countries. The college and university systems arising in England and other countries of Europe after the Middle Age systems of the Roman Catholic Hierarchy had not advanced far enough into freedom, although these systems were largely affected by freedom, to make a distinct addition to free thought. Church ideas of the Middle Ages were largely responsible for the religious side of education as it was initiated and carried on by the nations of Europe.

The education of the colonial times of America was merely repetition of the education of the mother country. Men of the colonies did not have time or initiative to establish necessary schools for the professions in technical education, nor were they free from religious trends enough to establish genuine Christian education for the ministry. This system came to pass in all the colonies and most of our colleges and universities established in those days were set going with those things as the governing forces in their systems.

"Later, when America began to be the first to establish free state education for everyone and some schools for the professions, they assumed the older ideas of education that were given by more or less religious groups. The States had no persons trained in this peculiar kind of education, but those educated in the religious schools. But when militaristic zeal seized Germany after the Napoleonic wars of Europe, when Von Moltke said they would put the doctrine of the survival of the fittest military nation into their schools, a new cult in education arose. This coupled itself with the thing known as German higher criticism of religious matters. Both of these ideas were abetted and aided by super German educational culture. Before long Germany began to bid for the best minds out of the colleges in America and other nations. This took the form of an offer of training and degrees to those learning the German culture.

"Many men of the universities and colleges in America were sent to the German universities and were given the degrees that the German universities gave for this. Later German universities made agreements with American colleges and universities to let German professors teach in American universities. This agreement was made with English speaking people in mind. Then came Germanized Americanism. When the time was right American college and university associations were organized to standardize the educational systems of America. These self-appointed dictators of education began to set standards for every school including university, college and secondary school. This thing had worked so well that the whole system of college and high school training soon came under it. These began to actually kill off every small Christian college, and the last vestige of religious education went with the destruction of the small college regardless of the efficiency of the faculties. Most of the standardization of the associational schools and colleges was set on material subjects. Classic and religious education was discarded and the standards of material equipment was set so high that no small college could reach it.

"Take for instance, some years back, and it has not changed, since a junior college could not be standardized without a guaranteed income of at least $10,000.00 a year and have four to six heads of departments with a degree of Master of Arts from one of the accredited colleges or universities. A senior college of 500 students must have six or eight heads of departments with the degree of Doctor of Philosophy from one of the accredited universities. Besides this, all equipment in all colleges must go into even hundreds of thousands of dollars, including buildings, laboratories, campuses, and even thousands of dollars of athletic equipment. This group of self-appointed persons did not think of the possibilities of this being swept away by war, time, wear or other troubles. All these things are material and good. Yet the money spent for war, drink, and even little things of appetite would over and above thousands of times support education. The difficulty of these things is the original demands made of any school to be accredited. Religious groups would and could not meet the sudden demands, so they were compelled to gain these credits by underhand means and methods. Then they were and are always hanging by a thread to secure credits.

"Now the fact remains that credits are entirely man-made and are not made by men who are the least bit interested in Bible and Bible truth. The only reason they take any interest in this at all is they are fearful of the large constituency of the Bible believing public. As a rule, no college or university or high school can take enough Bible or Bible subjects to make it a very substantial part of education. I think it has been before stated in these articles that the educators for a long time have divided the educational field into four parts: language, social science, science, theology. Art and music naturally have place in expressing these four fields, but the educators have left off the educational list in many places languages for the theological field—Greek, Hebrew, Chaldee, Latin. This is rather a wise move for the theological field, although not generally taught as credits in colleges in the main, yet theological schools are generally prepared for this kind of teaching.

"The experiences of the theological schools in the past and for the present has not been so good and even in some cases bad, for theological schools could not generally be accredited. Here are some true stories of the past. Dr. John A. Broaddus was so filled with the ministerial education ideas for the common uneducated young preachers of the Southern Baptists that he with some others established the Southern Baptist Theological Seminary first located in the Southeast, then transferred to Louisville, Ky. Knowing the colleges and universities of the South did not give the young minister, the God-called uneducated common man, the proper education for his work, the result was the seminary now at Louisville. Dr. B. H. Carroll, before the establishment of the Southwestern Seminary of Waco and Fort Worth, while riding on a train was struck by the same idea of giving proper education to the young uneducated ministers of the Southwest. He was so impressed by this that he walked up and down in the train and forgot where he was. When he came home, he immediately began the launching of the seminary. It was first located at Waco and then moved to Fort Worth. Now the same thing came to pass a good while ago before the founding of the Missionary Baptist Institute of Little Rock. J. Louis Guthrie had for a long time this idea and then in connection with Dr. C. N. Glover and Ben M. Bogard the location of the Missionary Baptist Institute was set in Antioch Church at Little Rock. All religious schools that become worthwhile were born that way.

"One question should be continually kept in the minds of Baptist people and that is: Why go into competition with the state? Naturally, the answer to that would be: Why let the educational associations with their modernism put their interpretations on our Baptist thinking? They will do that when they make the demands for us to qualify for credits, and make demands as to what we must put up for this crediting. It seems a too large price for us to pay for their self-appointed crediting system. We have to practically dispose of our faith for their system. If any men who have been in those schools which made much of their credits can remember how faith of Christians has been ridiculed, not even to mention Baptist faith, they are a bit slow to pour their money into this system and let good Baptist money be swallowed up in that maelstrom of educational modernism.

"Baptists are at present forced to some kind of school to maintain their faith. Most of our colleges, that is, I mean Missionary Baptist colleges, have poured their graduates into other kinds of schools and thereby have lost a large majority of preachers and religious workers that way. Many years back three brethren were put on a committee to investigate all Baptist and denominational schools of the South. The purpose was to determine how they founded and how deeded and how safe for their respective religious groups. These brethren discovered that of the 325 Baptist schools in the South at that time, they were all founded by Baptists of our kind excepting a few of the late ones that dated their founding within 25 to 30 years before that time. All the older colleges and universities then of the Baptists had been founded by our kind of Baptists. Now they do not own or foster but one of them. What does this mean? This committee was about the time of the Seventy-five Million Drive. This proves several things. Baptists of our kind have no way of legally protecting their rights in such schools. Legally donations to colleges become the property of the boards of trustees of the college, and donors have no further rights over them. If the boards see fit they may give the colleges and equipment to whomsoever they choose. Now, if we need credits, will we sacrifice our rights in property to obtain those credits? It seems the boards did give the colleges away for credits. Now we have none because we did not meet the requirements for credits. This thing reaches farther than most Baptists know, and any just now in inexperience who want Baptists to have this kind of secular education must think this thing through before they wish this off on Baptists.

I have said before, we as Baptists of a peculiar kind need Bible scholarship. There is a huge field of scholarship surrounding the Bible and our kind of Baptists. I remember distinctly that James Dawson, in Waco, Texas, when this very question was up, had to admit that Baptists were unlearned and as he said were ignorant of their heritage. Now, that is putting it pretty roughly, but the question of Theistic evolution was up then and Convention Baptists were on trial by the Evolutionists of the Theistic brand. At that time I saw college and university men in Baptist colleges yield and say that God is a process of development and had not found himself or his personality. —J. Louis Guthrie.'' —*Orthodox Baptist Searchlight,* June 25, 1944.

At the close of this tenth year, the *Orthodox Baptist Searchlight* records, "The total number (preachers) has been close to seven hundred . . . More than ten thousand souls have been led to know Christ and the total sum would be twelve thousand if summed up completely. Many churches have been organized and many also revived that were dying or dead ... Up to the present we have had ninety one graduates who hold certificates for five different courses. The first course offered is that of two years in English Bible. This requires a thesis for examination of seven thousand words. A second course of two years in Bible Languages requires a thesis of twelve thousand words and two years with Hebrew and Greek as major courses. Two other courses of three years give degrees of Master in English Bible and Master in Bible Languages. The thesis of each of these is twenty-five thousand words, the major in each is for English Bible, English Courses, for Bible Languages, Hebrew and Greek. One more course is that of *Didaskolos Biblion*. This means teacher of Bible and combines English, Hebrew and Greek. Five years are required for this degree. The Greek term, 'Didaskolos,' and 'Doctor in Bible' both can be used as the name for this degree. The initial letters are D.B.'' This announcement was made in the paper May 10, 1944, by the president, J. L. Guthrie.

This report was given in addition to the announcement of the commencement in the June 10, 1944 paper: ''. . . The financial support of the Institute has been better this past year than ever before. The teachers have been paid a reasonable amount for their teaching. Ben M. Bogard is the only teacher who does not receive pay. This statement is made from time to time so that all will understand that when Bogard calls for money to support the school he is not asking money for himself.''

At this time eleven members were on the faculty and ninety eight students had graduated from the school, the degrees ranging from the *''Didaskolos Biblion''* (Doctor in Bible Languages) to the two year course.

The first printing done by the Institute was directed by Mrs. Abilene Boyd on equipment owned by the president and loaned to the Institute. Mrs. Boyd printed, during that year, three books beside the catalog and other necessary printing.

Offerings for the dormitories planned for students were beginning to come in:

"When the war is over the school will be overrun with students and there will be no place for them to stay unless the dormitories are built. The bonds (war) should be bought now while there is plenty of money and it will insure success in this great work," wrote Dr. Bogard.

The president received $1200.00 for his services and the other teachers received an average of fifty dollars a month. Eighty students were enrolled this year.

By the fall of 1944, the need of an educational building was becoming more pressing. The student body was increasing, as well as the number of classes needed. "We are thankful to God for permitting us to use the rooms in the Antioch Baptist Church for our school. But it is apparent that this is only a makeshift." And with this introduction, Bogard began an appeal for $25,000 to "erect the proposed building. It would be a fine MEMORIAL BUILDING for someone," he wrote. This was a prophecy for it became the building memorializing its first president.

(Note: The school name was changed about this time to Missionary Baptist Seminary and Institute.)

THE "MISSIONARY BAPTIST PRINTERY"

The March 10th, 1945 issue of the *Orthodox Baptist Searchlight"* was printed "by our own force and on our own machinery. The Missionary Baptist Printery is now an accomplished fact." So wrote Dr. Bogard when he announced the opening of the print shop to be operated by the Missionary Baptist Institute. Hoyt Chastain, who was editor of the *Baptist Informer* which he had been printing, brought some of his equipment to Little Rock. Dr. Bogard bought the printing machinery belonging to Mr. Alberson of Malvern, Arkansas.

Seminary Press. This is the equipment given by Dr. Bogard after it was moved into the basement of the new Seminary building. Ernest Payne, manager, is standing in the center of the picture.

This consisted of a linotype machine, a large Babcock press and other equipment needed to put out the necessary printing for the Seminary. These men gave the equipment to the Missionary Baptist Institute. It was given with the expressed aim that Missionary Baptists be able to have their own literature printed without excessively high prices. In this particular paper, Dr. Bogard wrote, regarding the work of the press: "The Missionary Baptist Institute Printery will not be a commercial shop . . . No individual will make a profit of any kind on the printing done in the shop . . ." He wrote in this same edition:

"THE BIG SURPRISE RIGHT BEFORE YOU

"We have been promising the BIG SURPRISE. Here it is. This issue of the *Orthodox Baptist Searchlight* was printed on our own press and the type set on our own linotype machines . . . We expect to keep the press hot printing this paper and the numerous books that are to be printed. It is not a commercial shop and it IS NOT A PROFIT MAKING SHOP. It is the Lord's work and nobody is making a profit on the work turned out by this printery . . . when we were getting the fine machinery installed in the Missionary Baptist Institute Print Shop a good brother said, 'I will get out and secure a lot of printing for you,' meaning that he would hunt up a lot of commercial printing for us. I thanked him for his interest and said, 'My brother, we do not need business, and we will not accept any commercial printing. Our printery will be strictly religious printing the *Orthodox Baptist Searchlight* and books written by the faculty of the Bible School and if we have time will print religious books written by our brethren whoever they may be, but no profit making work.' '' This was the dream of his heart and until this present day his desire has been carried on as he designated his gift should be used—for a completely non-profit shop, printing religious literature—missions by the printed page. He often said as he listened to the loud noise of the machinery, ''That is music to my ears!''

A GREAT LOSS

Death struck a crushing blow to the Seminary when a heart attack took the first president, J. L. Guthrie. The *Orthodox Baptist Searchlight,* April 10, 1945, records these words by Bogard: ''My right arm has been severed for I depended on him for so many things. A great scholar and theologian, a master in Greek and Hebrew, and efficient in many other things, a teacher of many years of experience and a preacher who in many ways was superior, I went to him for CORRECT INTERPRETATION that required a knowledge of the original languages to understand. It is impossible to tell how much he helped me in many ways. But I try to realize that I cannot lean on him any more. He rests from his arduous labors but his work goes on. He will live in the lives of his numerous students so long as they live.''

Dr. Guthrie had prepared a part of this very paper, helping to get it on the press and it was partially run when he met his death.

As Dr. Bogard said, ''The Baptist Institute is the crowning work of his life. It would have been impossible for me to have done this great work without him. For almost eleven years we worked together in perfect harmony.'' This great man lived until he, along with Dr. Bogard, had trained an efficient faculty. Dr. Ben often said, ''Dr. Guthrie and I could both die and the great work go on without us.'' They built a work not on themselves but an enduring one that would stand. Guthrie, like Bogard, relied on the printed page and he had his heart set on seeing a ''printery'' established and actually operating. This dream he realized.

''The workers die but the work goes on and while no man can take his place each one of us can fill our own place better in our effort to try to make up for our loss.'' Dr. Guthrie was buried April 21, 1945.

A NEW PRESIDENT

On May 3, 1945, the faculty of the Missionary Baptist Seminary met to reorganize. Hoyt Chastain was the moderator of the meeting. ''The first and most important item of business was to select a president for the school. Dr. Foreman led in the discussion, pointing out that the most logical and reasonable thing to do, was to elect Dr. Ben M. Bogard to the presidency, in as much as, he will be our main advisor and leader so long as he lives. The entire faculty spoke and all agreed to the wisdom of the first suggestion.'' —*Searchlight,* May 10, 1945.

In this meeting, L. D. Foreman was unanimously elected dean of the school and Leo Causey was elected ''secretary of the faculty'' with Conrad N. Glover given the office of vice president. The *Searchlight* reported the results of this meet-

Dr. Bogard digging the first spadeful of dirt for the first dormitory. Beside him is J. W. Kennamer with the plans.

ing: "Only God could bring a group of men together in His work, who work together as do the teachers of the Missionary Baptist Institute; no personal ambition has ever shown itself here. No jealousy has ever been detected. Every teacher is an expert in his own field, each one does his own work carefully and prayerfully, each one minding his own business and each manifesting a beautiful Christ-like spirit toward each other."

"DORMITORIES" BEGUN

Antioch Church voted by unanimous vote in May, 1945 to build a dormitory. Priorities had to be obtained for such a building, so the task was started. By July of this year a contractor had been engaged, the location chosen. It was July, 1946 before the necessary priorities were received from the government so that building could begin. One delay after another had hampered but finally July 22nd, a brief ceremony was held. Dr. Bogard dug the first spadeful of dirt and the buildings were started to house the students. These "dormitories" were actually apartment houses with eight apartments of two rooms and a bath.

On September 20, 1945, the Missionary Baptist Institute was given approval "for training ministerial students of that denomination under provisions of Public 346.''

On October 2nd, 1945, the *Searchlight* reported, ''Largest and Best Opening in History of the Missionary Baptist Institute.'' In this meeting twenty nine of the previous year's students made reports showing they had held 74 meetings, enjoyed 497 professions of faith, 208 baptisms and organized one church.

The opening message of the 1946 session was given by Dr. A. J. Kirkland and the faculty members were ''given their salaries for two months in advance.'' The large crowd for the opening and the large group of new students predicted a good year and bright future for this thirteenth opening day. By December of this year, the new ''Dormitory'' was completed and preparations begun for the second one.

In January, 1947, Ben Bogard resigned as president of the Missionary Baptist Institute and L. D. Foreman was elected as his successor. Bogard had been accused of ''building a church and school around himself that he can control at his will.'' His answer was that he was resigning both school and church and that ''If Bogard has built that great school around himself, now that Bogard has resigned as president and another has taken his place, the school will rapidly die.'' However, time proved that the school was scripturally established by the founders and built on a solid foundation. It continued to grow and train young ministers for their work in spite of the opposition and efforts of men to destroy it.

Other schools of the same kind have been started since the beginning of the Little Rock School. One of these is the Texas Baptist Institute. Dr. Bogard visited the Missionary Baptist Church in Corsicana, its founder, and the school in 1947. He wrote: ''Dr. Kirkland is a lecturer in the Missionary Baptist Institute, making trips to Little Rock for that purpose two or three times a year. His students only need to spend a brief period in Little Rock to complete the two year English Course. It is a happy arrangement because some could not come to

Little Rock, and by this arrangement they may get much of what they would receive if they had attended the Institute.'' He also wrote after visiting this work, ''There is a much better prospect in Texas for our work than ever before and much of the good situation is due to the level headed, constructive work of A. J. Kirkland.''

Other schools begun by graduates of the Little Rock Institute who began to go out into other states were: Eastern Baptist Institute, California Baptist Institute, Louisiana Baptist Institute, Oklahoma Baptist Institute and Florida Baptist Institute. Thus, the work Dr. Bogard called his greatest ''monument'' has been responsible for many schools, many churches, thousands of conversions and the work of the associations largely perpetuated by students and faculty members.

THE ALUMNI ORGANIZED

On September 30, 1947, the opening date of the 47-48 session of the Institute, the Alumni was organized. At Dr. Bogard's suggestion, C. N. Glover was elected president. Alta Payne was elected secretary. This association of students and graduates named as their purpose: ''to further the cause of the Missionary Baptist Institute, because for too long, the burden of supporting the school and of publicizing it, has been on too few people.''

In the spring meeting of the Alumni in 1948, a resolution was offered by A. J. Kirkland, one section of which was that ''we, the Alumni Association of the Missionary Baptist Institute, now in semi-annual assembly offer to the Antioch Baptist Church our fullest cooperation in every sense of the word in the raising of funds and the erection of an Administration Building adequate for the housing of the school.'' This was adopted and pledges were taken for gifts to build the new educational building. The pledges amounted to $36,350.00 and by the end of the evening meeting to $43,000.00. From this

A group of Seminary preachers. This picture shows only the pr
—some preachers' wives and others who want to prepare for better Chri

time on until the building was completed the main order of
business for this Alumni Association was the raising of funds
for an administration building.

In October of 1948, Bogard wrote: "The architect is drawing the plans for the new great educational building estimated
to cost one hundred thousand dollars and money is coming in
almost every mail to pay for this building. The supervisor is
the same man who supervised the erection of the dormitories."

led in the Seminary. Each year there are also ladies
as well as young men who are training for educational directors.

On March 8, 1949, the first spadeful of dirt was dug by L.
D. Foreman, president of the Institute. Beside him stood Ben
M. Bogard and C. N. Glover. Though there was a drizzling
rain, a large crowd was present for the happy occasion. The
building was to be known as the Guthrie Memorial building.

Much of the work done on this edifice to be dedicated to
the training of young preachers was by the student body and
professors of the Institute. Hundreds of dollars were saved as

Digging the first spadeful of dirt for the Guthrie Memorial Building. On the front row: C. N. Glover, Ben M. Bogard, L. D. Foreman. In the back row, Leo Causey, Fred Stevenson.

a result of the "labor of love" offered by those whose hearts were in their work. They dug the trenches for the forms of the foundation and, by April, the concrete was poured and soon the walls were going up. Pictures were printed in the *Searchlight* in nearly every issue showing the continuing progress.

Exactly one year from the time the first spadeful of dirt was lifted for the beginning of the new Guthrie Memorial Building, the ceremony of the laying of the cornerstone was held. March 8, 1950, the ceremony was performed by the Grand Lodge (Masonic) of Arkansas. C. N. Glover was Past Master,

Dr. Bogard offering the prayer at the cornerstone laying of Guthrie Memorial Building, March 8, 1950.

Worshipful Grand Master of the Grand Lodge, Free and Accepted Masons of Arkansas. L. D. Foreman was Grand Orator in this service. This was a happy, happy day for the old veteran preacher who had realized his dream—the establishment of a school specifically for preachers and a building to house it. He had said, "I will be eighty-two years old March 9, and I have set that day as a time to finish this task. If my friends want to please me, the best possible way to do it will be to do something for the great school right now, so I may be able to announce in the March 25th issue of the *Searchlight* that the task is finished. I am making this as my last call, for I do not

Guthrie Memorial Building. This houses the Seminary where young men are educated for their calling into the ministry.

The large crowd at the school opening for the first time in the new Guthrie Memorial Building.

intend to ever lead in another great enterprise. But I really do
want to make this a triumphant success. Unless this is accomplished, I shall not quit work, for I shall, after this, let younger
men lead and I will follow."

On the opening date of the 1950-51 school term, a huge
crowd gathered for the first term in the new building. October
3rd was a day that met the highest expectation and hope of
every member of the faculty and, especially, of Ben M. Bogard
who wrote:

"CAN'T FIND WORDS TO DESCRIBE UNDER-STANDINGLY THE GREAT OPENING OF THE SEMINARY

"How the people from twelve states did pour in to attend
the seventeenth opening of the Missionary Baptist Seminary,
October 3. A brother who had heard that the 'little toot of a
school' was dead said if this was what the enemy of God's
great work calls death, he hoped that the Seminary might die
again. This opening was decidedly the largest and best in
every way that we have ever had.

"Everybody Surprised at What They Saw

"What did they see? They saw the three large dormitories
and the great educational building standing right there side
by side covering a full city block frontage and valued at more
than two hundred thousand dollars. These dormitories were
full of students and, besides that, two other large buildings
were filled with students and, still more, a goodly number of
cottages, apartments and single rooms in different parts of
the city and even out into the country were filled with students. It was a shock that some were not prepared for. Some
said they were 'overwhelmed'—it was so far beyond their
fondest expectations. They were doubly surprised when they

heard the president, L. D. Foreman, announce that enough money was on hand, together with what was definitely promised by perfectly reliable brethren to fully pay for these four great buildings! What hath God wrought! . . .'' The greatest problem at this time was how to take care of and house the unexpectedly large number of students for this term.

The opening season was climaxed by the meeting of the messengers of the State Association of Missionary Baptist Churches of Arkansas in the new building on Thursday and Friday, November 16-17.

In spite of the continuing opposition to ''church owned'' schools, this opening proved that Bogard had indeed, with the help of the Christ he loved and served, built a work not about himself as his enemies accused, but about Scriptural principles—a work that would endure which was proved in later years. Later after his death, fire destroyed the building, but again friends of the school rebuilt and the work went on. It was built on Bible principles, the kind of work this great man did throughout his life and so it was enduring.

This opening day of school in 1950, so successful in the fulfillment of his hopes was to be his last ''opening day'' of the Seminary he so dearly loved. But during that year, he walked each day the few blocks to the building and with great joy, strolled through the classrooms, but more especially through the ''print shop.'' He loved to sit in this noisy part of the building and listen to the ''music'' of the presses. The coffee pot was usually on and he enjoyed coffee with the staff each day. Though the doctor's orders were ''no coffee'' he always found the friendly ''perking'' pot and sipped a little as he contemplated the stacks of finished printed work and listened to the sound of ink being spread across the pages. As long as he was physically able this was a routine with him.

After his death, the churches all over America raised money to buy a Miehle Letterpress in his memory. It is known as the *Bogard Press,* the most fitting monument which could

The faculty of Missionary Baptist Seminary on the day of the first opening in the new Guthrie Memorial building. This is the last time Dr. Bogard posed with the group before his death. They are: Front row: (left to right) L. D. Foreman, L. D. Capell, Leo Causey, Fred Stevenson, C. N. Glover. Second row: Ben M. Bogard, Edward Byrd, Mrs. J. Louis Guthrie, Paul Goodwin and J. P. Johnson.

be offered to this man who believed with all of his heart in the importance and value of the printed page and utilized it at every opportunity. This book is being printed on that same press.

The other memorial to him was a large window in the new Antioch Missionary Baptist Church building. Five hundred preachers gave one dollar each in order to place this beautiful window in the sanctuary as a memorial to him. Only one dollar was allowed from each so that all preachers who had benefitted from his great ministry would have the privilege of a part in this fitting memorial to the great educator.

In the center of this window is a picture of the open Bible. This was selected as it seemed that nothing else could be a more fitting tribute.

Dr. Ben M. Bogard believed, taught and practiced that everything we are and have belong to the Lord. He gave himself unstintingly to the Lord, doing the work of three men, wearing himself out in service. He gave of the material things intrusted to his stewardship while he lived, then left all he owned to the Missionary Baptist Seminary. He fervently "practiced what he preached" that "it is required in stewards, that a man be found faithful." His works do follow him in the lives of the hundreds and hundreds of preachers whose lives have been touched by his life, in the thousands of souls who have been saved under his ministry, in the Seminary faculty he helped to train and the student body who now enjoys the facilities of the buildings erected under his leadership, as well as in the lives touched by the books he wrote, the paper he established and gave to the Seminary and the press he set up which now sends out the printed word.

His will, shown here, designate only the smallest portion of what he gave to Missionary Baptists. We honor him and cherish his memory for his works' sake and because his life glorified the Lord Jesus Christ.

Missionary Baptist Institute
Ben M. Bogard, President Emeritus
Antioch Baptist Church
R. S. PETERS
County and Probate Clerk
Ben M. Bogard, PULASKI COUNTY, ARK.
Box 663
Little Rock, Arkansas

Last Will And Testament Of Ben M. Bogard.

I , Ben M. Bogard, being in my right mind and memory and desiring to make disposal, and final disposition, of my property at my death , will and bequeath same as follows:

I will and direct that all of my just debts and funeral expenses be paid.

After the payment of the foregoing matters, I will and direct, that if my beloved wife, Lynn Bogard, survives me ,.she shall hold and use all of my property of whatever kind and wherever found, so long as she shall live.

I furthermore will and direct that if my sister, Ollie B. Bogard, survives me and my wife, Lynn Bogard, that she shall hold and use all of my property so long as she shall live.

Since my son, Douglas Bogard, is well provided for and in need of nothing , I will him my good will and wish him prosperity.

I will and direct that after the death of my wife and my sister that all of my propeerty of whatever kind and wherever found,

shall go to the Missionary Baptist Institute, located in Little Rock, Ark, to be held by that institution absolutely and to be disposed of by it as it may seem best and proper.

I name as my executors and administrators, L. D. Foreman and John Paul Johnson, who may jointly or singly act as executors and administrators, for the disposition of the matters mentioned in this will.

Witness my hand and signature on this the 6th day of *July* , 1948.

Ben M. Bogard

We, the undersigned, certify that the foregoing instrument was presented to us by Ben M. Bogard and we were informed by him that said instrument was his last will and testament and he desired us to witness same; thereopon he signed his name to said will in our presence and we signrd our names as witnesses in his presence.

Witness our hands and signatures on this the 4th day of *July* 1948.

W. F. Lovelady
W. E. Regins

LECTURE OUTLINES

By Ben M. Bogard

ADMONITIONS TO STUDENTS

Dr. Bogard was not "easy" on students. He told them bluntly the practical things they needed to know along with their theology. These are some notes from one of his lectures to a new student body:

"Don't go out saying you represent the Institute.

"Cultivate saving habits. Let nothing be wasted.

"Speak OUT distinctly but don't yell. Don't mistake sound for sense.

"Don't tell BIG tales.

"Pulpit habits: do not be doing things while prayer is offered.

"Don't take God's name in vain while praying. Try writing your prayers.

"Don't lose sight of your *object* in preaching, to lead souls to Christ. You may lose sight of your *subject* but never lose sight of your *object!*"

One of his outlines for a lecture to the young preachers:

TRUE MINISTERS OF CHRIST
(I Timothy to Young Preachers)

1. Be an example in personal appearance.
2. Conduct (Conduct so loud can't hear what he says—debts, etc.)
3. Liberality.
   Give for show? Matthew 5:15, "Let your light so shine *before* men that they may *see* your good works."

4. Ask for criticism.

5. Quit talking before you wear the people out.

The following is one of his lecture outlines given before a class in *Defense of the Faith:*

THE SECURITY OF THE BELIEVER

Romans 8:1, "There is therefore now no condemnation to them which are in Christ Jesus . . ."

John 5:24, "Verily, verily, I say unto you, He that heareth my word, and believeth on him that sent me, hath everlasting life, and shall not come into condemnation; but is passed from death unto life."

I. THE OBJECTIONS TO THE TEACHING.

A. Why all these warnings, admonitions and threatenings?

B. If I just knew I was safe, I would take my fill of sin.

C. What about all of those who have made bright professions, but turned out to be desperately wicked and died so? (See John 8:31, I John 2:19)

D. Do not the scriptures say "Beware lest ye fall from your own steadfastness . . ." Psalm 37:24, Proverbs 24:16, Micah 7:8-9.

E. Did not holy angels fall? Did not Adam fall?

F. Peter sinned, David sinned, Moses sinned.

G. Judas Iscariot fell from grace and went to perdition, John 5:67-71, 13:18-19, 12:1-6.

THE DIFFERENT THEORIES AND IDEAS ENTERTAINED BY THE ADVOCATE OF FINAL APOSTASY

I. The prevailing idea is that final apostasy from God's favor is gradually and almost imperceptable; that even the apostate himself cannot tell just where nor when he lost his religion.

II. The advocates of final apostasy may be divided into the following classes:

A. One party maintains that sinners may lose their religion and be finally lost, but cannot be restored.

B. Others maintain that sinners may lose their religion and can be restored an indefinite number of times.

C. There are those who are consistent and those who are inconsistent. The former class maintains that works are necessary to bring sinners into a state of salvation, and, consequently, it takes works to keep one there. Others believe that grace brings sinners into a state of salvation, but they are kept there by works.

LOGICAL DEDUCTIONS

I. No one can consistently believe in falling from grace and believe in salvation by grace.

II. The doctrine of falling from grace reflects on the wisdom of God.

III. If final apostasy is possible then life would be the greatest curse and death the greatest blessing that could come upon a Christian.

IV. If the devil can get the children of God, but does not, then it follows that those who will finally get to heaven will be saved on account of the grace of the devil, as much as on account of the grace of God. Consequently, the finally saved ought to praise the devil forever for being gracious to them.

V. If the devil can get the children of God, but does not, and they are forced to go to heaven because the devil would not have them in hell, then it follows that those who will finally get to heaven will be just such as the devil would not have.

VI. If the devil can get one of God's children he can get all, for the same Lord and the same means which are to save the meanest sinner and the meanest Christian are to save all who will ever be saved.

ARGUMENTS

I. My first argument in defense of the security of the believer is based upon the oath of God to Christ, Psalm 89:26-35.

II. The oath of God to His people, Isaiah 54:9-19, Heb. 6:16-19.

III. The covenant of grace, Heb. 8:10-12, Jer. 32:40.

IV. God does not impute or reckon sin to His people, Rom. 4:4-8 (Compare Psa. 32:1, 2).

V. The nature of the new birth, John 3:6, I Peter 1:23.

VI. The relation God's people sustains to Him as His children, Rom. 8:16, 17, 32; John 17:22, 23.

VII. The children of God are spoken of as having eternal life, John 3:14, 15, Romans 6:23, I John 5:13, John 10:27, 28, 17:1-3.

VIII. The relation which God sustains to His people as their Shepherd, Psalm 23; John 10:11-14, Heb. 13:20, I Peter 2:2, Luke 15:3-6, I Sam. 17:32-37.

IX. The relation which Christ sustains to the children of God as their Advocate and Security, Heb. 7:22, 25, I John 2:1.

X. Christ's disciples are just as sure to appear with Him in glory as He is Himself to appear in glory, Col. 3:4.

XI. Sin shall not have dominion over the children of God, Rom. 6:14.

XII. God will be more faithful to watch over His children than the most faithful mother on earth, Isaiah 49:15.

XIII. The wicked one cannot take the hope of heaven from those who have chosen the fear of the Lord, Luke 10:41.

XIV. The analogy between the manna which fell in the wilderness for the temporal support of Israel and the gift of Christ proves the security of the children of God, Joshua 5:12, John 6:48, 51-58, Gal. 2:19-20, "Because I live ye shall live also."

XV. God seals the saved unto ultimate and final salvation, Eph. 1:13, 4:30, II Cor. 1:21, 22.

XVI. The omnipotence of God is engaged to save and protect His people, Luke 11:21, 22.

XVII. God preserves (keeps) His children forever, Psalm 37:28.

XVIII. God declares that He will in no wise cast out, John 6:37.

XIX. Should God fail to accomplish the final salvation of His people, the devil might justly mock, Luke 14:28, 29.

XX. God assures us that all things shall work together for the good of His people, Romans 8:28.

XXI. To all of those who will finally be driven from the presence of God, the Righteous Judge will say, "I never knew you." Matt. 7:23.

XXII. God affirms that no power nor creature shall be able to separate the children of God from His favor, Rom. 8:35-39.